THE MIND OF THE FOUNDER

Sources of the Political Thought of

JAMES MADISON

*The
American Heritage
Series*

THE
American Heritage
Series

UNDER THE GENERAL EDITORSHIP OF
LEONARD W. LEVY AND ALFRED F. YOUNG

THE MIND
OF THE
FOUNDER:

THE BOBBS-MERRILL COMPANY, INC.

Sources of the
Political Thought of

JAMES MADISON

Edited with Introduction and Commentary by
MARVIN MEYERS

PUBLISHERS · *INDIANAPOLIS* · *NEW YORK*

Copyright © 1973 by The Bobbs-Merrill Company, Inc.
Printed in the United States of America
Library of Congress Catalog Card Number 72-158723
ISBN 0-672-51770-1
ISBN 0-672-61183-X(pbk)
First Printing

Abel

Acknowledgments

The best scholars, I find, are often the most generous. The late Douglass Adair offered friendship, counsel, and, above all, the model of a Madisonian gentleman and scholar. I still feel rather like an intruder on his spacious domain. Professor William T. Hutchinson of the University of Chicago, the learned and meticulous editor of the Madison papers, gently corrected my first plans and thoughts for this volume as he made them seem worth correcting. Professor Ralph Lerner of the University of Chicago—as always—and my Brandeis University colleague, David Fischer, were critics of the same uncommon breed: sharp-eyed and kind-hearted. I have been talking Madison with Professor Martin Diamond of Claremont Men's College for many years. I can only hope that I have maintained some sort of boundary between his thoughts and mine. Because Irving Brant's authoritative and exhaustive biography existed, I could concentrate attention on my own distinctive subject: Madison's political thought. I thank them all and relieve them of responsibility for my failings.

Several students, particularly Barry Pomerantz, helped with the chores. My wife helped too, most skilfully, in the midst of life and work. And far more than that. My son Daniel, though not exactly a contributor, looked on my labors with filial indulgence. The general editor of the series, Professor Leonard Levy of Brandeis University, had to develop new reserves of patience as he waited for me, seemingly, until the last syllable of recorded time. I like to think that his character as well as mine profited from the Chinese torture.

Marvin Meyers
Brandeis University

vii

Foreword

Shortly before his death, Jefferson wrote an affectionate salute
to the intimate friendship he had shared for half a century with
Madison. Referring to the harmony of their political principles,
Jefferson found solace in the hope that Madison would "vindicate to posterity the course we have pursued for preserving to
them . . . the blessings of self-government, which we had assisted
too in acquiring for them." Madison replied that "pure devotion
to the public good with which we discharged the trusts committed to us" was its own reward. "And," he added, "I indulge a
confidence that sufficient evidence will find its way to another
generation, to ensure, after we are gone, whatever of justice may
be withheld whilst we are here."

Jefferson has received from posterity the justice due him, as
have Washington, Franklin, Hamilton, and Adams. Yet Madison, that other heroic figure of the time, whose name should be
a synonym for patriotic selflessness, has not fared so well—until
recently. The reputation of the shy, studious, and sober Madison
has long been obscured by the shadow cast by Long Tom as if
Madison had been merely Jefferson's disciple. Worse still, a poll
of professional historians ranked Madison as merely an "average" president, placing him in the same category as Hayes, Har-
rison, and Hoover. Lately, however, there has been a growing
recognition of Madison's accomplishments and talents—and
with the best of reasons.

In the four decades of his political life, no man did more than
he in the cause of religious liberty. In power as well as out of
it, he was a consistent civil libertarian, even as a wartime president; his record in this respect is unmatched. And no president
maintained as high a wall of separation between church and
state. Madison was not only the master architect of the Consti-

tution and the leader of the ratification forces in his home state; he was also, and this is equally important, the draftsman of the Bill of Rights which would never have gone through Congress without his persistent and eloquent support. He, even more than Jefferson, laid the political bricks on which the Democratic party was built. During Jefferson's presidency, Madison was not just his alter ego; the secretary of state was the dominant man in the cabinet in whom the president gave his utmost trust. Some political enemies, knowing Madison's talents as a politician, thought that he had "acquired a complete ascendency over him," as one of them put it. Notwithstanding Madison's political craftsmanship, he was also a political philosopher without peer in our nation's history.

Irving Brant's magisterial six volume biography, completed a little over a decade ago, finally did Madison the justice that he trusted posterity would offer. As Brant completed his work, the first publication of Madison's complete papers began, a monumental project which in seven volumes thus far has reached only the end of his career as a member of the Continental Congress. There are yet fifty-five years of his life, including the most productive, that lie ahead of the editors. They are obviously writing for posterity, and publication will probably continue until the arrival of their audience. Meanwhile there has not been in print a handy, one-volume collection of Madison's most important writings and papers for the use of students, scholars, and general readers. This book, brilliantly edited by Marvin Meyers, plugs that gap. As its title suggests, *The Mind of the Founder* focuses mainly on Madison's thought. The need for a collection of this kind, the superb introductory analysis by Meyers, and his penetrating headnotes, make *The Mind of the Founder* a model documentary anthology and one of the best books in this series.

The American Heritage series was created to provide the essential primary sources of the American experience, especially of American thought. The series constitutes a documentary library of American history, filling a need long felt among scholars, students, libraries, and general readers for authoritative collections of original materials. Some volumes illuminate the thought of significant individuals, such as James Madison or John Marshall; some deal with movements, such as the Antifederalist or the Populist; others are organized around special themes, such as Puritan political thought or American Catholic thought on social questions. Many volumes take up the large number of subjects traditionally studied in American history for which surprisingly there are no documentary anthologies; others pioneer in introducing new subjects of increasing importance to scholars and to the contemporary world. The series aspires to maintain the high standards demanded of contemporary editing, providing authentic texts, intelligently and unobtrusively edited. It also has the distinction of presenting pieces of substantial length which give the full character and flavor of the original. The series is, we believe, the most comprehensive and authoritative of its kind.

Leonard W. Levy
Alfred F. Young

Contents

Of Constitutional Construction

Of Democracy and the Union

Beyond the Sum of the Differences:
An Introduction

Lawgivers who shape the form and spirit of a new political community for generations are a special breed of men, if only by virtue of their responsibilities. Reflecting on the words and works of our ancient American demigods, the Founders, it seems both strange and sad that so many recent scholars find more to learn from given circumstance and common baggage than from choice mind and character; more to admire in the Founders' tact and craft, the little arts of ordinary management, than in their understanding and judgment, the rare gifts of political creation. The higher ranges of intellectual and moral quality that make all the difference in political life barely register on standard scales devised for measuring what most men do most of the time, and all men do some of the time. The demigods were men indeed: extraordinary men.

No small part of their special gift was the power to explain the common instincts and habits of *Homo politicus Americanus*, and thus to lead him toward the uncommon ends envisioned by the Constitution: union, justice, domestic tranquillity, safety, the general welfare, and above all liberty for "ourselves and our Posterity." The political doctor—to borrow an analogy from James Madison—should not be confused with his patient, although both are merely and fully human. Another part of their gift was the remarkable power to articulate their thoughts with rigor, clarity, and candor. Thus the curious student of the American past who wishes to recapture the original qualities of the first generation, especially the qualities of mind, does well to begin at the sources. Deeply engaged in the great events of their time, enlightened by a grasp of principle and tempered by a sense of history, the Founders are indispensable witnesses for themselves. If the volume of their writings and their care in preserving copies is fair evidence, they did not fear self-incrimination. So every man who reads, carefully and critically, can dare to be his own historian. The most helpful commentator will set the stage, turn up the lights, and get out of the way.

If there could be but a single Founder to revisit, one might well choose Washington's contriving hand at Philadelphia, Hamilton's reflective alter ego of *The Federalist,* Jefferson's long-headed partner in Republican experiment: choose James Madison because he was pre-eminently all these things to all these men. This is not to say that Madison was first among his peers. Washington, I think, was nobler, Hamilton sharper, Jefferson broader, Adams deeper. Discriminating judges might prefer Franklin's worldly wisdom, Marshall's transcendent law, even John Quincy Adams's diplomacy. The amazing point is that all were there. None—at least among the elders—could have been spared. And Madison commanded some crucial points of intersection from the Revolution to the age of Jackson.

In his twenties, Madison helped to found a free republic in Virginia. He was the life of Federalism in the eighties; at once the destroyer and the healer of Antifederalism in the Constitution and the Bill of Rights; the pen and whip of insurgent

Republicanism in the nineties. In office he served Jefferson's old cause of frugality, strict construction, and peaceable coercion so far as a harsh world (and Jefferson) could allow. Gingerly he accompanied warhawks and young Republicans into an ambitious new nationalism, Hamilton's imperial design re-woven in American homespun. If Mr. Madison's war was full of blunders and humiliations, changing nothing, it led America perhaps by grace of special providence toward a fresh pride and purpose. During forty years of public life, Madison alternately gave national principles to Virginians, Virginia principles to Americans. His was the hard side of the Jefferson coin: the side with the numbers and the motto, *E Pluribus Unum.* (In fact, Jefferson helped to devise the American decimal coinage system; and a Swiss artist first proposed that perfect motto: so much the worse for literal reality.)

At last, as the venerable keeper of the old Republican and the old Federalist heritage—Jefferson's famous bi-partisan slogan better suited his partner—Madison taught prudence to democrats, democracy to nullifiers, law to legalists, a reflective and generous patriotism to all breeds of the partisan, the provincial, the doctrinaire. Through all the political changes of his life and country Madison remained among the finest and firmest American voices of the eighteenth-century liberal tradition: the tradition of natural rights and social compact, bills of rights and constitutional government. The prime article of that faith was embodied in the final clause of the Virginia Declaration of Rights and the opening clause of the First Amendment to the U.S. Constitution, in Madison's latest as in his earliest thoughts on politics: freedom of conscience under nature's distant God. Slavery—at once the foundation of his Virginia world and the living contradiction of his republican principles—resisted his tentative reforms. If he had no effective answer to that overwhelming question, he insisted nonetheless that human bondage was a curse upon America and Virginia, a *contradiction.* Fittingly for a Founder, his last political testament bequeathed the work of 1776 and 1787 to a reckless generation with a solemn warning to cherish and perpetuate the irreplaceable gift of union.

I MASTERS AND AXIOMS

On opening the pages of Madison, or Jefferson, or Adams, one first asks where they began the discussion of politics. To many scholars, that has meant: Which masters taught them their political fundamentals? Was John Locke the great teacher of liberal axioms and empirical psychology? Did the Founders learn of property and power from Harrington, of checks and balances from Montesquieu? Did Grotius, Coke, or Blackstone form their conceptions of the law? Did their laws of nature flow from the models of Baconian or Newtonian science? Did they claim the wisdom of the ancient republics? Did their English teachers—Addison and Steele, Pope, Swift and the rest —shape more than their style? What did they borrow from a motley company of eighteenth-century Whigs: historical cicerones, political clerics, improving moralists and manual-ists, common-sense Scots and obscure "commonwealthmen"? Roughly, one can say: the Founders took something from all of these and many others; a good deal from the first and last. Their libraries, well-chosen and well-used, summed up a liberal education and a course in enlightened statesmanship. Yet the search for intellectual genealogies seems to miss the central point.

The political point of departure for Madison and the Founders was determined by who they were and what they meant to accomplish. These were American statesmen with momentous work to do. Here in the late eighteenth century they had reached a state of conviction on the immutable laws of nature and of nature's God, prescribing the rights of man, the ends of civil society, the origins and forms of commonwealth, and even

general standards of law and policy. The lights of political
philosophy from all ages, but especially from modern fathers of
the liberal tradition, could illustrate self-evident truth, arm its
advocates with ready arguments, and awaken the innocent to
the dangers inherent in human nature and in free government
itself. Custom, habit, precedent, seemingly Providence itself
confirmed belief. The urgent task of the Founding generation
was not to pierce to the roots of political truth for its own sake
but to build upon plainly good foundations—"the common
sense of the subject" (as Jefferson called his Declaration); "the
general Principles of English and American liberty" (as Adams
identified his premisses). Thus they could found a durable
Republic, surely the best for Americans, as they believed, and
ultimately the best for most men in most circumstances. Given
a set of axioms, the practical reason of politics informed by
reading and experience turned to the business of politics. And
the business of the Founders was the high enterprise of trans-
lating worthy principles into working laws and institutions with
the materials imposed by history.

If Adams and Jefferson nevertheless had a yearning for
philosophy, and touched the first principles of politics in occasional letters, notes, polemics, it was Madison (with Hamilton)
who left the most comprehensive, systematic, and enduring
exposition of their political thought, notably in The Federalist.
Not modesty but candor led Madison in retrospect to emphasize the practical character of that work "as the most authentic
exposition of the text of the federal constitution," a document
that may "be admissible as a School book [for University of
Virginia law students] if any will be that goes so much into
detail." The students would have begun their reading with
Locke and Sidney, the standard sources of Whig politics. The
Declaration of Independence, "saying everything that could
be said in the same number of words," would fix their fundamental principles. Following The Federalist, young republicans
would be prepared for the heady constitutional creed of the

Virginia Report of 1799. If that should waken old partisan resentments, Madison proposed, Washington's *Inaugural Speech*
and *Farewell Address* "may help down what might be less
readily swallowed." Locke, *The Federalist,* and all the parts of
this carefully arranged textbook of politics would be employed
to the end that "the true doctrines of liberty, as exemplified in
our Political System, should be inculcated on those who are to
sustain and may administer it."[1]

Nothing reveals so sharply what Madison and his peers
meant to accomplish by political teaching and thus what questions we can put most profitably to their own works. For example, labored enquiries into the Founders' theory of human
nature—leading to the overwhelming question, is man good
or bad?—take for their final object rough assumptions that
served the original writers as obvious points of departure.
There are disagreements among the Founders, to be sure—
most interesting ones—and elaborations and refinements; but
these are to be found not in formal theories of human nature
but rather in the flow of political analysis and judgment. Reflective statesmen are not mere mouthpieces of their postulates.
They rise to their responsibilities. Experience, necessity, in-
stinct, and the remembered lessons (orthodox or not) of a good
eighteenth-century education were improved to make formulas
sufficient to occasions.

All of this is perhaps a long way of reaching a point where
we can set down briefly some propositions that James Madison
took for granted in his political thought; not too long, however,
if the discussion has made clear why it is even more important
to put these propositions in their place than it is to put them
down. The uninitiated reader of Madison who sets his sights
for a general philosophy of man, society, and government will
find the blurred tracks of many predecessors in a well-worn

---

[1] See Document 32, p. 444 below. Jefferson first proposed the list and
Madison revised it.

trail. The living quarry, a politics of judgment and decision—learned, discerning, candid, sometimes profound, always profoundly liberal and republican—will escape.

Where, then, did Madison begin his politics? At bottom, with an understanding of man as a complex creature of reason *and* passions, of free will *and* compelling habit; as a social animal moved by self-interest. Men are capable of good, so far as public spirit, religious precept, regard for character, respect for law, and enlightened calculation of long-run interest can be made to govern conduct; and capable of evil (or harmful error) when immediate interest, blind passion, and ignorance run loose. Madison's man is an improvable being, in mind and morals, who can never transcend his limits. All men are equal in their common origin and nature, and in the resulting rights of nature; unequal in their particular virtues, talents, knowledge, experience and in their resulting capacities for ruling and bearing rule. This portrait of humanity takes little or nothing from abstract models of natural virtue or original sin. Madison draws the qualities of men from their history and interprets them in the perspective of modern liberal philosophy.

What, then, was politically decisive in Madison's view of man? The birthright of equality; the dominant motivation of self-interest; the political capacity to order society and government so that self-interested, self-governing men would be obliged to respect the rights of others and serve the permanent and aggregate interests of the community. Equality is the fundamental term: no man is so low in the order of creation that he is born to be a slave; none so elevated in wisdom and virtue that he can be trusted to be the master of others; and all alike are born to use the common advantages of nature for their preservation and happiness according to their needs and lights and gifts. Assuming this principle of equality, Madison could address himself in practical ways to the problem of making self-interest serve the ends of political reason by the means of popular government. Human nature requires government and demands self-government. He never stated this conception of man or justified it in a whole theory; yet it informs every part of his political writing.

Clearer still and more explicit—epitomized in the syllabus progression from Locke and Sidney to the Declaration—are the basic Madisonian principles of individual rights, free society, and popular government. They form another affirmation of the Revolutionary creed. The natural order, what the Creator has given and decreed in the beginning, is prior to and distinct from the social order, what man contrives for himself. God created men equal, free, and independent; obliged them by natural law to preserve themselves; and endowed them with reason and passions to realize their preservation. With reason they should recognize the equal rights of others to life, liberty and the pursuit of happiness; and again with reason, should comprehend their own nature as human beings whose happiness consists in something more, not clearly specified, than the satisfaction of the appetites. (That something more may be what we commonly put down, not very clearly, as the fulfilment of human potentialities.)

The social order is the work of men. Naturally equal, free, and independent, self-governing, men can be bound to obey human authority only by their own consent and only so far as their safety and happiness require. Thus the compact that joins men to society. Thus the convention that establishes government and subjects citizens and magistrates alike to law. Thus the constitution that defines the boundaries of legitimate power and reserves all else—belief especially—to individual choice. Thus the republican form of commonwealth that perpetuates the principle of consent in the regular workings of government. And thus finally the convenient principle of majority rule that alone can reconcile the natural equality of rights and powers shared by all with the political necessity for unitary decision.

Madison, the author of the classic American formulation of

the problem of majority tyranny, wrote so that the blind could read his purpose: majorities were to be feared in America because majorities would rule in America, according to the tradition of the country, the spirit of its people, the doctrine of its teachers, and the law of the land. His guiding question was not: What form of government is best? Rather it was: How can popular government, republican government, be made to serve its proper ends?

Recalling Madison's political syllabus, one can now say with necessary reservations understood that Locke was indeed the prime source of founding principles: Locke construed by Madison in the light of American experience and usage, i.e., with new or stricter insistence on reserved natural rights, on the secular state, and on the popular form of government. The Declaration of Independence was for Madison a fair epitome of the doctrine establishing "the right of Nations to establish their own Governments" and inspiring "a love of free ones."[2]

II THE POLITICS: X PLUS THE SUM OF THE DIFFERENCES

I have suggested some of Madison's masters and axioms in politics, insisting all the while that these can serve at best as first clues to an understanding of his thought. No ready formula will contain the substance of his political reasonings. To hit somewhere between the anarchy of detail and the tyranny of arbitrary system, one might ask broadly: Is there a distinctive Madisonian mode of reasoning about politics? But still—because the passion for simplicity overrides all cautionary counsels—*is* there a usable formula? Even a rough one could go far toward opening the politics of Madison.

To be rash for a moment: Madison's political organon can be expressed in terms of X plus the sum of the social, political,

---

[2] See Document 32, p. 444 below.

and intellectual differences in the commonwealth. In this home-
made political algebra we find unknown qualities and unknow-
able weights for every quality. As the philosopher said, "It is
the mark of an educated man to look for precision in each class
of things just so far as the nature of the subject admits." If the
problem cannot be "solved," the explication of its terms and
their relations may still prove useful.

Perhaps the most provocative modern example of political
reasoning from the sum of the differences appears in Rousseau's *Social Contract.* I know of no evidence that Madison
took lessons from that most difficult French thinker. Yet Rousseau confronted the dilemmas of modern democratic theory
with a candor and penetration that perhaps none of his predecessors and few of his successors could match. If "the sum of
the differences" turns out to be a valuable key to Madisonian
politics (as I shall argue), then a key to that key may be
sought in Rousseau's classic exposition.

Following Locke and the natural-rights philosophy, Rousseau held that each man has an "absolute and naturally independent existence." Only the voluntary compact between
each and all constitutes the "moral and collective body" of
political society. Thus the "Sovereign People," the state in its
active form, "consists exclusively of the individuals who are
its members." Rousseau's problem is plain: How can a conven-
tional order, formed of and by individual men for their own
interests, acquire the right and the capacity to act as one for
the good of each and all? His answer, at once mystifying and
enlightening to succeeding generations, was: by creating,
eliciting, and enforcing the General Will.[3]

Now, if one were to ask so many men as particular persons
what they willed society to do, each would likely reply: serve
me. The aggregate of wills derived from such partial interests

---

[3] The problem is defined broadly in Book I of *The Social Contract,* particularly Chap. VII. Among the various translations I have generally followed
the clear versions of Willmoore Kendall (Chicago: Henry Regnery, 1954).

can only be "the will of everybody," a bundle of contraries without a principle of resolution. Particular wills may run in packs, even in very large ones, but they are nonetheless partial in relation to society, only more powerful and dangerous. Society—and here we shall find a direct parallel in Madison—would do well to exclude the packs (groups, cabals, factions, partial societies) so far as possible, or else divide and thereby multiply them to the point of political impotence.[4]

Rousseau discovers the General Will—general in both origin and objects—by another mode of calculation, or rather, another figure of speech: "But take from the expression of these separate wills the pluses and minuses that cancel one another and the general will remains as the sum of the differences."[5] The distinction is subtle but crucial between an aggregate of separate, conflicting wills and the "sum of the differences," expressing in pseudo-technical language the just union of wills that emerges when the divergent desires of individuals check one another. The potentiality of such consensus for the common good is created by the very nature of the social union. In society man is still man—each naturally prefers his own concerns—but he is also an equal fellow-citizen, bound by the social compact "on the same terms as all the others" and thus "entitled to enjoy the same rights as all the others." So he identifies himself with society, and serves the happiness of all while "thinking only of himself." Just as the contract constitutes a new order derived from nature yet endowed with emergent qualities of its own, so its members acquire a second nature derived from yet capable of guiding the original. Living together on equal terms, sharing actively in the benefits and burdens of authority, men develop common customs, common feelings, common purposes: they become citizens. This is no total conversion. Self-interest narrowly conceived persists. Only

---

[4] See *The Social Contract*, Book II, Chap. III.
[5] *Ibid.* Here Kendall's translation makes little sense to me, while other editions (Everyman, Oxford, Hafner) more or less agree on the above rendering.

by canceling "the pluses and minuses' can society secure the rule of the general will for the common good.[6]

Now, with this bare outline of Rousseau's argument in view, consider the politics of Madison. He, too, began with the axioms of natural-rights philosophy, as I have proposed above. He, too, found self-interest the original, irreducible motive force of political society, grounded in human nature and so legitimized by natural law. He, too, faced the critical question: how to discover and call forth a common rule of justice among inevitably self-interested and rightfully self-governing men? Yet, as a responsible statesman, Madison could not settle for a mathematical metaphor, nor perhaps as one whose mind was trained and habituated to a politics of judgment and decision could he build a theory from the ground up. Instead we find a series of political strategies all flowing from a common rationale: loosely, "the sum of the differences."

Here all roads lead to *Federalist* 10, the heart of Madison's Great Republic. Briefly, the argument sets out to answer a theoretical question of decisive practical importance raised by Antifederalist critics of the new Constitution: Can a republican regime embrace the great distances and diversities of the American Union? Conversely, must a great nation submit to despotic rule?

Sniffing the approach of monarchy or aristocracy in every tainted national breeze, Antifederalists invoked in support of their suspicions the traditional teaching that a small homogenous society is a necessary condition of republican government. (Rousseau indeed had added strength to that position when he insisted that "only if the city is very small can the sovereign [people] possibly retain, in our day, the powers that belong to it.")[7] For Madison the history of republics ancient

---

[6] *Ibid.*, Book II, Chap. IV.
[7] See *The Social Contract*, Book III, Chap. XV, against the background of Book II, Chaps. IX–X.

and modern pronounced a devastating judgment on the thesis: in Greece, in Italy, the republican cities had drowned in their own blood with such tragic regularity that the popular form had been almost universally abandoned and the republican idea itself disgraced among men. Madison boldly turned the traditional theory (and Rousseau's) upside down. Precisely the smallness of past republics could explain their violent deaths. And the murderers lived within the walls. If every Athenian had been as wise as Socrates, and every useful invention of modern political science had been known to the ancients, still that great city must have destroyed itself by civil wars. Most older writers had recognized the advantage of size for defense against external enemies; a few had found some merits in the large commonwealth for maintaining domestic order. But until more convincing evidence appears one must give Madison the full credit he claimed for originality.[8]

A society, however small, can never remain at once free and homogeneous. Human nature yields a diversity of minds that must result in a variety and rivalry of opinions; a diversity of talents that must result in a variety and rivalry of interests. Because economic activity is a universal necessity, and because the different faculties of men, left free, necessarily result in the acquisition of different degrees and kinds of property,

---

[8] On one possible source of influence, see Douglas Adair, "That Politics May Be Reduced to a Science': David Hume, James Madison, and the *Tenth Federalist," Huntington Library Quarterly,* XX (1957), 343–360. Although Hume's essay, "Idea of a Perfect Commonwealth," might have suggested to Madison some advantages of a large republic, it does not touch the crucial Madisonian argument from the number and diversity of social-economic interests. Montesquieu's famous defense of confederate government includes an argument for controlling the violence of faction that Madison adopted; but it is not the fundamental argument of *The Federalist* No. 10. See *The Spirit of the Laws,* vol. I, Bk. IX, S1. One could even look back to Aristotle, who proposes that large political societies have a large "middle class," citizens of moderate property who sustain a moderate constitution; yet this is so, he argues, because such states are generally more *free* from factions of rich and poor, which is not exactly Madison's point. See *Politics,* Bk. IV, Chap. XI, S13.

economic interest is the most common and durable source of division and conflict. There is moreover a natural linkage between mind and passion that attaches opinion to interest, interest to opinion: the force of conflict is doubled. The necessity or the mere possibility of free public decision affecting interest and opinion, favorably or adversely, must organize warring interests, opinions, even fancies and foibles into factions contending for political power. Governments cannot be simply neutral arbiters. They are designed to secure the rights of person and property. The regulation of conflicting property interests, especially in civilized nations, is a large part of their concern. Every measure has a different mix of benefits and costs for different interests. And, finally, governments are made of interested men judging in their own cause. Neither reason and philosophy nor conscience and religion normally can be expected by their own gentle powers to tame the political agencies of interest and passion and thus to secure the rights of all and the permanent and aggregate interests of the community. Faction so understood is a natural element of free society and, if uncontrolled, the natural disease of free governments.

Under governments both popular and free the majority rules; hence the problem of faction becomes the problem of the unjust majority. In societies relatively small and simple, the factional divisions reduce to two, the majority and the minority, identified most commonly with rich and poor, few and many, aristocrats and democrats. (Later, Madison would emphasize the split into manufacturing and agricultural classes.) Their encounters are massive, direct, violent, and often fatal to the commonwealth. One dominates the other, or both seek refuge from chaos under a despot. Enlarge the sphere of the republic, Madison argues, and embrace within one community all the various conditions of a spacious country, all the finely graded, closely mingled interests of a "civilized" commercial society. In a small republic the political pursuit of economic advantage becomes a civil war of the "two nations." In the great republic, society forms one nation divided into such a vast array of factions that men can seek power only by coming to terms with many others according to the special object and occasion. The scope and intensity of political conflict are reduced to manageable proportions.

Selected representatives of large constituencies, men of some knowledge, experience, and character, look with one eye at least to the common interest that is their peculiar trust. Should they develop another roving eye for power, intra-governmental checks and balances, political decentralization, and the ultimate discipline of the ballot can keep them in line. Sheer size and distance minimize the chances for a factious majority to discover their strength and concert plans of oppression. Thus in a broad American Union the sum of many small differences is more likely to be the principles of justice and general welfare on which the majority of a great society can unite. Liberty can be reconciled with order, democracy with equity, self-interest with patriotism. The republican remedy for factional violence, injustice, and confusion was far from perfect, Madison recognized; and it would meet its real test in the future when America, like other nations, accumulated a property-less mass of citizens. In another direction, "false consciousness" might lead the people to form sectional factions corresponding almost literally to two nations: North and South. Yet the large republic under common government and a supreme law of the land would remain the best because the "least imperfect" form of political society.

Madison employs a comparable kind of reasoning to meet a wide range of political problems: of church and state, state and nation, the separation of powers, and more. Varying the terms to suit the cases, he argues from irreducible conflicts of interest, passion, and opinion to a resolution—so far as society requires one—within a common political framework by the general method of the sum of the differences. "This policy of supplying, by opposite and rival interests, the defect of better motives," Madison wrote, "might be traced through the whole system of human affairs, private as well as public." He never forgot that it was a twofold process: arresting the abuse of power and promoting the use of power for the public interest; cancellation and summation.[9]

In the case of religious rivalries (which Madison explicitly analogized to the faction problem) the resolution need only be a stand-off: the multiplicity of competing sects within the commonwealth serves to keep religion out of politics. No sect can hope to win a monopoly of power, none need strike out in fear, and so all can settle for peaceful co-existence as private, voluntary bodies. Possibly, too, a common core of useful religious truth, the moral verities, emerges from the many-sided competition, although it would seem to be enough for Madison —as for Jefferson—if the political sum of the religious differences were zero, i.e., if private conscience were left strictly free to choose the God of Nature or the God of Wrath, twenty gods or none, any moral code consistent with social order and the equal rights of all. Even absurd or pernicious opinions can be tolerated, so long as they are not armed with public power or embodied in acts of violence.[10]

Further development of this line of analysis would lead beyond the limits of an introduction. The notion of a sum of the differences will serve its modest purpose if it suggests a clue to the reading of Madison's politics. But the "X plus" of my political formula remains a mystery. Let it stand for the things needful to republican politics that the principles of natural rights, irreducible self-interest, and the sum of the differences cannot themselves provide. The sovereign reason that comprehends unreason and puts it to reasonable uses is a part of X. So is the love of country that concerns itself with the honor of ancestors,

---

[9] See *The Federalist* No. 51, Document 12, p. 173 below.
[10] See, for example, Document 2, pp. 7–16 below.

the happiness of posterity, and all such distant or intangible things. So too is the love of liberty and republican principles for their own sake that resists the tug of avarice, ambition, and the other "political passions." The values of X intrude themselves into Madison's politics at many points, typically where the greatest questions and the greatest needs are met. The reader often may detect their appearance when he sees something like the following rhetoric: Having made all the provisions for (safety) (security) against (passion) (interest) that prudent foresight can suggest, we must now give/use our (trust) (loyalty) (reason). . . .

Among the functions of X, the most fundamental is the provision of a framework within which differences can be resolved, the unity that makes divisions salutary or at least harmless. Madison's discussions of founding go to the heart of the matter. Mere partisans cannot order parties for the public good. Mere avarice or ambition cannot conceive or choose the political conditions for disarming these unlimited passions. Mere interest cannot frame a constitution to serve the country with all its varied interests and a supreme enduring interest of the whole. On the contrary, Madison pointed out in *Federalist* 38, "although this variety of interests . . . may have a salutary influence on the administration of the government when formed, yet everyone must be sensible of the contrary influence which must have been experienced in the task of forming it."

Madison, in short, faced the same dilemma that had forced Rousseau to go outside his political society to enlist a more than human legislator. It is not strange that Jefferson, no great believer in the supernatural, should have called the Constitutional Convention "an assembly of demigods,"[11] or that John Adams, no easy flatterer of his contemporaries, should have praised their work as "the greatest single effort of national de-

---

[11] Jefferson to John Adams, Aug. 30, 1787, in *Adams-Jefferson Letters* (Chapel Hill: University of North Carolina Press, 1959), I, p. 196.

liberation that the world has ever seen."[12] And Madison, the reputed Father of the Constitution and candid teacher of the facts of political procreation, concluded: "It is impossible for the man of pious reflection not to perceive [in the result of the Convention] a finger of that Almighty hand which has been so frequently and signally extended to our relief. . . ."[13] Yet Madison, like the others, judged the Constitution a second-best regime, built of guesses, hopes, concessions, by a method of framing governments—the convention—so perilous that the wise and jealous republicans of Athens dared not try it.[14]

Madison's analysis of the problems of founding is full and complex: his explanations for the great imperfect solution are short and simple.

The first is, that the convention must have enjoyed, in a very singular degree, an exemption from the pestilential influence of party animosities—the disease most incident to deliberative bodies, and most apt to contaminate their proceedings. The second conclusion is that all the deputations composing the convention were satisfactorily accommodated by the final act, or were induced to accede to it by a deep conviction of the necessity of sacrificing private opinions and partial interests to the public good, and by a despair of seeing the necessity diminished by delays or by new experiments.[15]

Nearly half a century after the event, preparing his accounts for posterity, Madison had not changed his mind:

But whatever may be the judgment pronounced on the competency of the architects of the Constitution, or whatever may be the destiny of the edifice prepared by them, I feel it a duty to express my profound and solemn conviction, derived from my inti-

---

[12] John Adams, *A Defence of the Constitutions of Government of the United States of America*, in *The Works of John Adams* (Boston: Little and Brown, 1850–1856), VI, p. 220.
[13] *The Federalist*, No. 37, Document 12, p. 144 below.
[14] *The Federalist*, No. 38.
[15] *The Federalist*, No. 37, Document 12, p. 145 below.

mate opportunity of observing and appreciating the views of the Convention, collectively and individually, that there never was an assembly of men, charged with a great and arduous trust, who were more pure in their motives, or more exclusively or anxiously devoted to the object committed to them, than were the members of the Federal Convention of 1787, to the object of devising and proposing a constitutional system which should best supply the defects of that which it was to replace, and best secure the permanent liberty and happiness of their country.[16]

When the logic of interest reaches this level, it might as well be termed X. The whole is greater than the sum of the differences.

III   THE STATESMAN: FACES AND MASKS

A statesman is judged by the laws he makes and the decisions he takes. If he is like Madison, reflective and articulate, seeking the reason of policy and teaching as he leads, then the record of his thoughts provides an invaluable guide to the understanding of his actions, indeed conveys an essential part of his statesmanship. The better part, one is tempted to say in the case of Madison.

A suggestion of Madison's axioms and a hint of his characteristic mode of reasoning about politics can barely reach the threshold of the thoughts of a lifetime on men and affairs, laws and constitutions; on diplomacy, finance, economy, and the problems of the next election. The selected texts that follow will offer their own introduction to the range and quality of his political thinking. Again, however, the editor may serve the reader by directing attention to one broad question that leads to all the rest: Was there a distinctive Madisonian spirit of statesmanship, or in riddle form, how many Madisons shall we

---

[16] "Preface to Debates in the Convention of 1787," in Farrand, *Records*, III, p. 551.

find? Madison, we observed earlier, was different things to different men. The masks changed as the plot of American politics unfolded from the eve of Revolution to the close of Jackson's administration. Beneath the masks, one face or many?

In one important sense, to maintain political consistency over the span of two generations is simply impossible. History never puts exactly the same question twice. Repeating identical words and acts twenty or sixty years later would suit a well-trained parrot (should it live so long), not a firm statesman. If justice is always and everywhere the same, the prudent course in politics—the pursuit of justice adapted to the time, the place, the men, the situation—has as many turnings as there are varieties and changes in human affairs. Only a superficial historian would believe that in itself a shift of position on a policy issue tells anything significant of the consistency of statesmanship. We ask rather: Did Madison pursue constant ends in a constant spirit, according to the circumstances? Did he accommodate ends as well as means to the evolving state of the nation?

After each stage of Madison's long career, and through the twenty years of his retirement, there were angry men to charge him with betrayal: Hamiltonians, Old Republicans, Neo-Federalists, Nullifiers. Now the leaders of the Founding generation guarded their political reputations jealously. They had a sense of history and a sense of pride. Hamilton almost eagerly confessed adultery in order to spike a rumor of corruption in office. Adams composed lengthy answers to Hamilton's charges of ineptitude and folly for the use of his descendants and could not wait: impetuously he poured out his vindication in the columns of a Boston paper. Jefferson meticulously preserved his records, added suitable explanations, and solemnly entrusted his good name to Madison: "Take care of me when dead. . . ." Madison was peculiarly vulnerable to accusations of political infidelity or at best slippery equivocation. He did shift alignments and tactics; he did so knowingly; and he carefully provided contemporaries and posterity with a defense of his course. Madison's explanations deserve our serious consideration.

On a few specific matters Madison frankly confessed a change of opinion, although never of course a casual or capricious inconsistency. For instance, he had first argued at Philadelphia for a national veto power over state legislation, but the debate apparently convinced him that his object—a uniform law of the land upheld by a common authority—could be achieved more conveniently and less offensively by the reviewing power of the federal judiciary. On the evidence of *Federalist* 39 and many later comments he was willing to learn from the wisdom of his peers. Yet Madison was anything but a humble, wide-eyed pupil to his convention colleagues, as his tough resistance on many debated issues testifies. Thus on the question of the Presidential veto he stubbornly insisted that a mixed executive-judicial council could best exercise the broad power of "revising" federal legislation on the grounds of constitutionality and policy. And this father of "a bundle of compromises" was among the last and most reluctant to concede the vital point of state equality in the Senate. Many such changes at Philadelphia reflected nothing more than Madison's final willingness to pay a price for avoiding a second convention and, as he thought, chaos.

Madison originally viewed a national Bill of Rights with a skeptical eye. No man of his generation had a broader or deeper commitment to the general principles of civil liberty and procedural justice. Yet in the situation of the new republic Madison thought that institutional checks and balances would be worth far more than "parchment barriers" to restrain arbitrary power. He disliked absolute prohibitions that would have to yield to political necessity. He relied finally on enlightened public opinion under a system of popular government. Jefferson's urgent pleas from Paris could not quite convince his friend; but the determined voices of many state ratifying

conventions (conspicuously including Virginia's) persuaded
Madison to lead the First Congress to the passage of the ten
amendments. He would follow the deep convictions of his
countrymen, ensuring their loyalty to the Constitution, in a
choice that he regarded as right in principle if doubtful in
practice. And he quickly learned to use the Bill of Rights as a
trenchant instrument of political opposition. That is, by example and argument he helped to give the Bill of Rights the practical value that he had questioned initially. Not only that: his
defense of free speech enlarged the meaning of that vital principle for succeeding generations.

In still another kind of case, Madison had approved the
Bank of North America as an unconstitutional necessity
(1781), denounced the establishment of the First Bank of the
United States as an unwarrantable usurpation of power (1791),
and then, some twenty-five years later, signed into law a bill
creating the Second Bank (1816). What had changed? The
Constitution, like the Articles of Confederation, was silent on
the specific point. During the bank's existence, national opinion, congressional policy, and informed legal judgment, all had
converged in support of congressional authority in the field.
Whatever the men of Philadelphia had intended—and Madison
never believed they meant to authorize the creation of federal
banking corporations—the nation through its appropriate organs had settled the usage of the Constitution. President Madison, bedeviled by financial disorder and distress, willingly
availed himself of the services of a new national bank with no
apologies to Hamilton's grinning ghost.

On the comparable question of federal internal improvements, Madison consistently defended the expediency of the
policy while challenging its constitutionality. He had silently
accepted national road-building during Jefferson's administration. He never could say why. As President, however, he vetoed
on constitutional grounds a measure pledging federal funds for
constructing roads and canals (1817), arguing then and later

for an amendment that would satisfy the public need and demand for such a program and still preserve the principle of strict construction. Inevitably the friends of internal improvements, commanding broad popular support, would have their way. The only choice lay between a careful, explicit grant of congressional authority or the continual assumption of new powers under the pliable "general welfare" or "necessary and proper" clauses of the Constitution, until the fundamental law lost all restrictive meaning. A prudent regard for both the principle of limited government and the requirements of national growth demanded a formal grant of additional powers.

His several reasons for change are most instructive: the lessons of rational deliberation; the necessity of political conciliation; the authority of persistent usage and of popular consent; and reinforcing all of these, the emerging necessities and even conveniences of the nation. Specific changes of this order, however, do not reach the fundamental question of Madison's constancy. Apparently, he threw his considerable weight to the side of national authority in the beginning, swung to the opposite extreme in his role of opposition leader, moved back toward the nationalist position during the years of power, and came to rest, just a little uncertainly, where he had started. The arguments of *Federalist* 10, or the *Virginia Report*, show clearly that the problem of nationalism for Madison always involved much more than drawing a jurisdictional line between two levels of government; it could determine the fate of the American Union and of popular government itself.

One would be basically correct, and a shade too tricky, in arguing the proposition that the Madison of the eighties, the creative Madison, had explained in advance all the shifts that his career might require. The success of a republican regime depended upon a firm Union to control internal and external dangers. When had Madison preached disunion? At the extreme point of opposition, 1798–1800, he argued that he was *defending* the Union by resisting the Federalist approach to tyranny. The dividers of America were those who violated the Constitution in pursuit of class, sectional, party, and private ambition. Or, as Locke taught, the true rebels are men who break the compact and throw society back into a state of war.

This in indeed one way of maintaining union. Yet it is obvious that Madison, at the height of party passion, walked a thin line between loyal opposition and subversion of national authority. In a time of external and domestic crisis, while America was still a large idea in search of a body, he drove the party debate down to the roots of political order and the nature of the Union. Later nullifiers and secessionists of the New England or South Carolina schools had more right to invoke the authority of the Virginia doctrine than a deeply troubled Madison would allow. If Madison meant to do no more than arouse and concert public opinion against Federalist measures through the medium of the states, and if the Republican electoral victory of 1800 was the sole outcome intended and logically accomplished by the Virginia protests—these were Madison's subsequent claims—nevertheless he forged a mighty, explosive weapon for the purpose.

By the very standards of Madisonian statesmanship, a leader stands responsible for all the consequences of his words and acts, including those he never intended. Madison had not been gentle, for example, with sincere proponents of a second Constitutional Convention who could only undo the work of the first without a rational hope of replacing it. It was not enough for Madison, in retrospect, to play upon grammatical niceties (he had referred to the action of "states" not "a state") or verbal ambiguities (what does "interposition" really mean?). He had helped to sharpen the knife of separatism, and only one of his public arguments, made more harshly in his private communications, would wholly justify him on Madisonian grounds: namely, that the Adams administration was hell-bent on subverting the republican order, gagging lawful opposition, and enslaving America to Britain. In the late 1790s that view was at least understandable; and some Jeffersonian histories still manage to preserve its lurid colors.

There was undoubtedly a change in Madisonian principles that could be reconciled with his earlier analysis only by straining words and switching subordinate clauses into the place of major propositions. The theory of union by state compact set forth in the *Virginia Resolutions* does not flatly contradict Madison's earlier and subsequent views. That the people acting distinctly by states gave their consent to establish the new Constitution and joined themselves to the new nation was a plain fact that Madison constantly affirmed. That "We the people of the United States" consented to form "a *more perfect* Union"; that nine states were deemed sufficient to ratify the Constitution and create a new nation within the limits of the old; and that three-fourths of the states were deemed sufficient to amend the Constitution, binding the dissenters: these were equally plain facts with a different bearing on state sovereignty, left to speak for themselves in the days of party wrath.

In the context of the Virginia argument, the peculiar role assigned to the state in construing the Constitution for itself, and maintaining such constructions within its own limits, surely departed from Madison's previous and later emphasis upon the essential need for one tribunal established under national authority to decide disputes in the final instance, as the sole alternative to wild confusion and the dissolution of the compact. Or, if Madison introduced the state compact theory into his protests only to remind men of the natural right of revolution, he waited many years to explain that such a right in the states was equivalent to the right a county might claim against a state, or an individual—if he were so rash—against the whole society. The Madison of 1787–1788 had not mixed revolutionary rights with constitutional rights so that enflamed citizens might easily confuse the two.

The jurisdictional line that looked so clear and neatly logical to Virginia-Republican eyes in the nineties had seemed a jun-

gle trail to the earlier Madison contemplating the creation of a
new nation. Then, neither experience nor reason offered sure
guides to defining the national and local spheres. The very im-
precision of the human mind, the intrinsic ambiguity of language, and the mixed qualities of political things themselves,
precluded a perfect division. Madison entered the Philadelphia
Convention gravely doubting that the boundaries of national
authority could be specified with tolerable exactness. The famous enumeration of congressional powers in the Constitution,
sacred truth to the Republican opposition, had been a product
of convention debate. Madison's own preliminary plan said
simply (and frighteningly to many): "that the National Legislature ought to be impowered to enjoy the Legislative Rights
vested in Congress by the Confederation and moreover to legislate in all cases to which the separate States are incompetent,
or in which the harmony of the United States may be interrupted by the exercise of individual legislation."[17] Correspond-
ingly, the explicit reservation of ungranted powers to the states
and people in the Tenth Amendment expressed a view of union
that Madison at first would have left to be inferred from the
general nature of the Constitution. Important ratifying conventions demanded formal guarantees and Madison acceded. At
Philadelphia, he had first proposed a very different sort of
border guard: the Congress armed with power "to negative all
laws passed by the several states, contravening in the opinion
of the National Legislature the articles of Union."[18]

Beyond the theory of state compact and the legal point of
jurisdiction, the comprehensive Madisonian analysis of the
political nature and merits of a Federal Republic required serious alterations in the nineties. The Madison of *The Federalist*,
no less than Hamilton, had seen the main threat to liberty and
union in the centrifugal tendency of power, in the ambitious

---

[17] The Virginia Plan, in Farrand, *Records*, I, p. 21.
[18] *Ibid.*

states and not the domineering nation. Neither gave states' rights an absolute, self-sufficient claim. Both accepted the rough constitutional division of authority as a prudent accommodation to historical fact and public opinion that could under skilful handling serve the ends of union. Positively, there were vital details of government that a single remote authority could not manage well; and for the sake of liberty and equity such details were best controlled by the people immediately affected. Negatively, the state units could provide useful centers for concerting popular action—lawful within the limits of endurance, revolutionary in the final case—should the central government fulfil the worst Antifederalist prophecies of usurpation and tyranny.

Again, however, the burden of the Federalist argument had been the urgent need to establish an expanded national jurisdiction against the heavy tide of anticentralist sentiment; to reverse the natural and historical tendency for the parts to overwhelm the whole. If, contrary to plausible expectation, the general government were to win the primary loyalty of Americans, and thus draw greater power to itself, the only reason could be its superior administration of public affairs, i.e., its convincing merit as a servant of the people. "Was, then, the American Revolution effected, was the American Confederacy formed, was the precious blood of thousands spilt, and the hard-earned substance of millions lavished, not that the people of America should enjoy peace, liberty, and safety, but that the government of the individual states, that particular municipal establishments, might enjoy a certain extent of power and be arrayed with certain dignities and attributes of sovereignty."[19] Thus spoke James Madison of Virginia, alias Publius, in 1788.

This argument had to be put to sleep a decade later, while Madison adopted much of the very Antifederalist case that he had taken such pains to refute. A cynical clique of insiders,

---

[19] *The Federalist*, No. 45, Document 12, p. 154 below.

wielding the powers of purse and sword, were rapidly establishing an oppressive oligarchy on the ruins of the Republic, and even squinting towards monarchy. Not merit but conniving ambition explained their successes. Popular jealousy and suspicion of central authority, provincial loyalties, divisions over foreign policy, small-minded fears of taxes and of military strength: these had been viewed a few years earlier as threats to union, sharpened by irresponsible and interested agitation. The opposition leader transformed them into republican virtues and built a party on their strength.

Most dramatically, the analysis of *Federalist* 10 disappeared for a season. The mortal disease of popular governments, the tyranny of majority faction, ceased to trouble Madison. The few lines he had given to the dangers of minority rule in a republic were expanded into the book of political evils. The great division of society now fell between republicans and antirepublicans, those who loved and trusted the people and those who hated and despised them, those who wielded national power and those who bore its burdens. Publius loved liberty and defended popular government; yet it is hard to imagine that prudent republican embracing the French Revolution after the Directory succeeded the Terror and prepared a place for Napoleon. If Madison was no Tom Paine, he did come to see reflections of the great world struggle in American party battles of the nineties. The interplay of many interests, chiefly economic, leading to majority decision in favor of the permanent and aggregate interest now meant little to Madison. No more did he invoke the law of the dispersion of power in a federal system, the principle of refining and enlarging public views through the choice of national representatives, or the fundamental proposition that impotence, instability, and confusion were the great enemies to liberty in a republic. Once again, Madison exchanged his earlier views for a modified version of Antifederalism. If he was historically justified, he must have been nevertheless theoretically embarrassed, for his previous case had rested not upon temporary circumstance but on the general nature of man and society under free government.

The case is, I think, that Madison in opposition subordinated his subtle and powerful political analytics to a simpler statesman's rule of thumb. The Union was, from day to day and year to year, a state of mind among the people of America. The Constitution was essentially what the men of the ratifying conventions, responsive to constituents, believed it should be. Henceforth that would be Madison's understanding of the Constitution on doubtful points, for that was the real basis of consent. A national policy that might be sound in principle yet alienate large sections of opinion from the Union could not serve national ends. A policy that seemed to deviate from the original intent of the Constitution, yet gathered broad support among the people and their spokesmen, could become legitimate by usage. This does not mean that anything was possible for Madison. The axioms of politics remained constant. His legal conception of the nature of the Union could never stretch so far as Calhoun's position at one limit, or, say, John Marshall's at the other. And the principles of *The Federalist*, however neglected in the nineties, always remained ready for new use. Madison seemed uncomfortable without them and argued at the peak of his powers when they could be employed again in the fine reflections and counsels of his later years.

Perhaps this is to say no more than the obvious: Madison thought as a working statesman. His concrete perceptions of clear and present danger to liberty and union directed his practical choices. When the concentration of power in the national government appeared to threaten freedom, corrupt government, or drive substantial parties or sections to despair, he would organize countervailing powers and emphasize anti-centralist, libertarian principles. When the reckless pursuit of local objects or absolute claims for minority rights appeared to threaten the national authority or undermine republican government then Madison would throw his weight to the center and emphasize the principle of majority rule. Such a notion of effective balance among the actual and shifting forces of American politics demanded flexibility. The object of balance was the perfection of a lasting American republic.

As revolutionary, as Virginia nationalist in the eighties, as Framer, as President, as elder statesman—through most of his long career—Madison found the main task to be the controlling of divisive tendencies. State leaders did not need to be told to look after their own dignities and powers. Sections all too readily pursued their local interests. Parties were by definition partisans. Men felt for themselves the painful burdens of taxes, military service, or commercial regulations imposed by a remote authority for distant ends. Americans had been individuals, neighbours, provincials before they became fellow-countrymen. Nationhood was a new and tenuous condition, the product of a very recent convention.

Madison never discounted the danger of overgrown central power. He had based an important part of his *Federalist* argument on the analysis of majority tyranny and its republican remedies. Yet his chief concern in the eighties had been the creation of sufficient power in the national government to serve the will of the nation. His pressing problem as President had been the use and even the extension of that power, over the opposition of party and sectional minorities. In his later years, his counsels were addressed sometimes to over-zealous nationalists, more often to old school Jeffersonians and new-light Nullifiers, reminding them that union was the necessary condition of safety and happiness for Americans and that an unqualified doctrine of minority and state rights would mean the death of union and of the very principle of republican government. The divisions and checks established by the Constitution were still adequate security against the oppression of official cliques and cabals. Conflicts over the meaning of the Constitution could still be resolved reasonably by case law in the federal courts, short of the ultimate appeal to revolutionary force.

Nullification and secession were bastard doctrines, and none of his.

Finally, Madison taught, persistent national majorities must have their way in America. Prudent statesmen would make all possible provisions for the enlightenment of the people, would cultivate their prosperity, make interests and sections feel their interdependence, moderate majorities, conciliate minorities— and play for time. Under wise government the experience of union would confirm its value, the habits of national citizenship make nationality real. An enduring constitution would nurture that "reverence for the laws" which binds men to their nation. And in the classic Madisonian terms—the course of economic growth in a large republic would so multiply and diversify the interests of each part of America, so intertwine the several interests of the several parts, that national majorities must embrace all sections and a broad range of classes, occupations, and opinions. Decisions by majority rule would come as close as men can approach to a rule of equity. Republican government remained "the best of all governments, because the lease imperfect."[20]

Virginians of the 1820s who built an extravagant case for minority rights within the nation upon the assumed foundation of a peculiar state economic interest would live to see their own rapidly diverging minorities attack the state majority with the same doctrinal weapon. Those who dreamed of a restoration of state sovereignty had simply forgotten the terrors of the Confederation period, when the impotence of national authority and the impending tyranny of local majorities forced Americans to try the experiment of the large republic comprehending many interests. State abuses had been far more frequent and palpable than those committed by national majorities, and would be so again under a restoration of the old conditions.

Beneath the reasonings of Madison's politics—his liberal

---

[20] [Majority Governments], Document 40, p. 530 below.

axioms, his calculation of the sum of the differences plus something more, his balancing strategy, his persistent quest for union—lay a primary commitment. If a philosopher knows no ordinary country, a statesman must have a place to take his stand. Virginia was Madison's native land, his home, the seat of property and friendship, the source of character. All that is biography. America was his chosen land: the common country consecrated by "the kindred blood which flows in the veins of American citizens, the mingled blood which they have shed in defence of their sacred rights;"[21] the model and vindication to the world of a nation founded on republican principles. His last political testament, found among his papers, gave the purpose of his life and thought: "The advice nearest to my heart and deepest in my convictions is that the Union of the States be cherished and perpetuated. Let the open enemy to it be regarded as a Pandora with her box opened; and the disguised one, as the Serpent creeping with its deadly wiles into Paradise."[22] The death mask was the face of Madison.

---

[21] *The Federalist,* No. 14, Document 12, 136 below.
[22] "Advice to My Country," Document 43, p. 576 below.

Note on Texts

This volume is for the use of the student and the general reader. It would have been both foolish and futile to attempt single-handed the editorial labors that the expert staff of the Madison Papers has been engaged in for a decade or so and will no doubt continue for many long years. Unfortunately for me (and you), *The Papers of James Madison,* edited by William T. Hutchinson and William M. E. Rachal and published by The University of Chicago Press (1962——), are still making their stately progress through the mid-1780s. Fortunately, there is a reasonably reliable and representative edition that one can find in most established college libraries: Gaillard Hunt, ed., *The Writings of James Madison.* 9 vols. New York: G. P. Putnam's Sons, 1900–1910. I have borrowed most of my texts from that edition, citing the source in the short form, *Writings.* Some additional writings come from the older and less faithful "Congressional Edition": [William C. Rives and Philip R. Fendall, eds.], *Letters and Other Writings of James Madison,* 4 vols. Philadelphia: J. B. Lippincott, 1865. (The editors do not seriously corrupt the manuscripts, but they put so many commas and semi-colons in Madison's mouth that they make him an almost pathological stutterer.) My short citation is *Letters*. A few items from other printed sources are cited by full title.

Hunt's style of presenting manuscript texts achieves, I think, a sensible blend of authenticity and convenience for the modern reader. I have generally followed his example, making only a few silent emendations for the sake of readability, understanding, or historical accuracy: spelling out abbreviations, revising punctuation when necessary to make sense, standardizing some proper names. A handful of larger changes—chiefly based on a comparison of the several editions—are indicated by square brackets or omission marks. The notes in Brant's *Madison* have aided me in ascertaining or correcting the dates of several papers.

Despite my best intentions, space limits have compelled me to abbreviate some writings and to eliminate others that deserve reprinting. Rarely have I broken into Madison's rigorous argument or fractured his lucid prose. I do regret my annihilation of the friendly aliens in the lengthy *Virginia Report* (Document 21) and, even more, my forced omission of some of Madison's exemplary *Federalist* essays (which can be found, however, in several paperback editions).

I could give many plausible reasons for my choice of writings to include in this volume, but they would all come down to this: I followed my best judgment of what was intrinsically important, with a secondary concern for representing the range of his career and interests and the dominant issues of his age.

Selected Bibliography

I. SELECTED WRITINGS OF MADISON

In addition to the printed collections cited in the Note on Texts, the following are reliable and accessible sources of important Madison papers:

Adair, Douglass. "James Madison's 'Autobiography,'" *William and Mary Quarterly*, Third Series, II (April 1945), 191–209.

Burnett, Edmund C., ed. *Letters of Members of the Continental Congress*. 8 vols. Washington: Government Printing Office, 1921–1938.

Cooke, Jacob, E., ed. *The Federalist*. Middletown, Conn.: Wesleyan University Press, 1961.

Elliott, Jonathan, ed. *The Debates in the Several State Conventions on the Adoption of the Federal Constitution*. . . . Philadelphis: J. B. Lippincott, 1836. Vol. III.

Farrand, Max, ed. *The Records of the Federal Convention of 1787*. Revised edition. 4 vols. New Haven: Yale University Press, 1937.

Richardson, James D., ed. *A Compilation of the Messages and Papers of the Presidents, 1789–1897.* Washington: Government Printing Office, 1897, Vol. I.

Madison's intimate partnership with Jefferson over fifty years makes the following a virtual extension of his writings:

Boyd, Julian P. *et al.*, eds. *The Papers of Thomas Jefferson.* 16 vols. to date. Princeton: Princeton University Press, 1950—.

Lipscomb, A. A. *et al.*, eds. *The Writings of Thomas Jefferson.* 19 vols. Washington: The Thomas Jefferson Memorial Assn., 1903–1905.

II. SELECTED WRITINGS ON MADISON AND HIS TIMES

Abernethy, Thomas P. *The South in the New Nation, 1789–1819.* Baton Rouge, La.: Louisiana State University Press, 1961.

Adair, Douglass. " 'That Politics May Be Reduced to a Science': David Hume, James Madison, and the Tenth Federalist," *Huntington Library Quarterly,* XX (August 1957), 343–360.

————. "The Tenth Federalist Revisited," *William and Mary Quarterly,* Third Series, VIII (January 1951), 48–67.

Adams, Henry. *History of the United States During the Administrations of Jefferson and Madison.* 9 vols. New York: Scribner's, 1889–1891.

Bailyn, Bernard. *The Theological Origins of the American Revolution.* Cambridge, Mass.: Harvard University Press, 1967.

Beard, Charles A. *An Economic Interpretation of the Constitution of the United States.* New York: Macmillan Co., 1913.

Boorstin, Daniel J. *The Lost World of Thomas Jefferson.* New York: Henry Holt and Co., 1948.

Brant, Irving. *James Madison.* 6 vols. Indianapolis: Bobbs, Merrill and Co., 1941–1961.

Brown, Robert E. *Charles Beard and the Constitution.* Princeton: Princeton University Press, 1956.

Burns, Edward McNall. *James Madison: Philosopher of the*

Constitution. New Brunswick, N. J.: Rutgers University Press, 1938.

Coles, Harry L. *The War of 1812*. Chicago: University of Chicago Press, 1965.

Crosskey, William W. *Politics and the Constitution*. 2 vols. Chicago: University of Chicago Press, 1953.

Cunningham, Noble E. *The Jeffersonian Republicans: The Formation of Party Organization, 1789–1801*. Chapel Hill, N. C.: University of North Carolina Press, 1957.

————. *The Jeffersonian Republicans in Power: Party Operations, 1801–1809*. Chapel Hill, N. C.: University of North Carolina Press, 1963.

Dahl, Robert A. *A Preface to Democratic Theory*. Chicago: University of Chicago Press, 1956.

Davis, Richard Beale. *Intellectual Life in Jefferson's Virginia*. Chapel Hill, N. C.: University of North Carolina Press, 1964.

Dietze, Gottfried. *The Federalist*. Baltimore: The Johns Hopkins University Press, 1960.

Diamond, Martin. "Democracy and *The Federalist:* A Reconsideration of the Framers' Intent," *American Political Science Review*, LIII (March 1959), 52–68.

————. "*The Federalist*." In Leo Strauss and Joseph Cropsey, eds. *History of Political Philosophy*. Chicago: Rand McNally and Co., 1963.

Ketcham, Ralph L. "James Madison and the Nature of Man," *Journal of the History of Ideas*, XIX (January 1958), 62–76.

Koch, Adrienne. *Jefferson and Madison: The Great Collaboration*. New York: Oxford University Press, 1964. Galaxy Book edition.

————. *Madison's "Advice to My Country."* Princeton: Princeton University Press, 1966.

————. *Power, Morals, and the Founding Fathers: Essays in the Interpretation of the American Enlightenment*. Ithaca, N. Y.: Cornell University Press, 1961.

Levy, Leonard W. *Legacy of Suppression: Freedom of Speech*

and Press in Early American History. Cambridge, Mass.: Harvard University Press, 1960.

Malone, Dumas. Jefferson the Virginian. Boston: Little, Brown, and Co., 1948.

————. Jefferson and the Rights of Man. Boston: Little, Brown and Co., 1951.

————. Jefferson and the Ordeal of Liberty. Boston: Little, Brown and Co., 1962.

Mason, Alpheus T. "The Federalist—A Split Personality," American Historical Review, LVII (April 1952), 625–643.

Miller, John C. The Federalist Era, 1789–1801. New York: Harper and Row, 1960.

Mosteller, Frederick and David L. Wallace. Inference and Disputed Authorship: The Federalist. Reading, Mass.: Addison Wesley Publishing Co., 1964.

Perkins, Bradford. Prologue to War: England and the United States, 1805–1812. Berkeley, Cal.: University of California Press, 1961.

Riemer, Neal. "The Republicanism of James Madison," Political Science Quarterly, LXIX (March 1954), 45–64.

Risjord, Norman K. The Old Republicans: Southern Conservatism in the Age of Jefferson. New York: Columbia University Press, 1965.

Rives, William C. History of the Life and Times of James Madison. 3 vols. Boston: Little, Brown, and Co., 1859–1868.

Smelser, Marshall. The Democratic Republic, 1801–1815. New York: Harper and Row, 1968.

Warren, Charles. The Making of the Constitution. Boston, Little, Brown, and Co., 1928.

White, Leonard D. The Jeffersonians: A Study in Administrative History, 1801–1829. New York: Macmillan, 1951.

Wright, Benjamin F., ed. The Federalist. Cambridge, Mass.: Harvard University Press, 1961. Introduction.

THE MIND OF THE FOUNDER

Sources of the Political Thought of

JAMES MADISON

Part One

**ANTICIPATIONS:
REVOLUTIONARY YEARS**

The Liberal Theme

1.   Young Man of the Revolution: To William Bradford

James Madison came of age in a time of revolutionary crisis. As the son of a leading planter in the Piedmont country of Virginia, young Madison heard the angry talk of the local gentry on stamps and customs duties. He would remember well the harassment of dissenting Baptists in his neighbourhood. Local schoolmasters taught him the rudiments of a standard eighteenth-century classical and English education with a strong Scottish, that is to say, austere, common-sensical, and Whiggish flavor. From 1769 to 1772, the studious Virginian absorbed the expansive ideas of religious and political liberty, and of American destiny, that filled the air in President Witherspoon's College of New Jersey (Princeton). Madison found college friends from New York, New Jersey, Pennsylvania, and colonies to the South—a fair sample of the future leadership of America—who

To William Bradford, Jr., January 24, 1774 and April 1, 1774, in *Writings,* I, pp. 18–1, 22–24.

corrected his provincialism with a broader continental focus. In this company, Madison made his mark as a scholar and a good fellow of the American Whig Society with a knack for bawdy rhyming.

After returning to the family estate in Orange County, Madison kept up an intimate correspondence from 1772 to 1775 with a fellow Princetonian, William Bradford, Jr., of the Philadelphia family distinguished for nearly a century as printers and booksellers. They traded gossip of college friends, tried out their thoughts on books and politics, and weighed the merits of the various careers open to ambitious young Americans. Here Madison first sketched his political notions, with insistent emphasis on the social value of religious liberty as practised in Bradford's Pennsylvania. To a young man who had glimpsed a wider world, Virginia with its established church seemed a backward country. In December of 1774, Madison committed himself to the protest movement by joining the Orange County Committee of Safety headed by his father. Bradford would serve as a state and continental Revolutionary officer, and go on to become U. S. Attorney General in the Washington administration.

January 24, 1774.

MY WORTHY FRIEND,—Yours of the 25th of last month came into my hands a few days past. It gave singular pleasure, not only because of the kindness expressed in it, but because I had reason to apprehend the letter you received last from me had miscarried, and I should fail in procuring the intelligence I wanted before the trip I designed in the spring.

I congratulate you on your heroic proceedings in Philadelphia with regard to the tea. I wish Boston may conduct matters with as much discretion as they seem to do with boldness. They seem to have great trials and difficulties by reason of the obduracy and ministerialism of their Governor. However, political contests are necessary sometimes, as well as military, to afford exercise and practice, and to instruct in the art of defending liberty and property. I verily believe the frequent assaults that have been made on America (Boston especially) will in the end prove of real advantage.

If the Church of England had been the established and general religion in all the northern colonies as it has been among us here, and uninterrupted tranquillity had prevailed throughout the continent, it is clear to me that slavery and subjection might and would have been gradually insinuated among us. Union of religious sentiments begets a surprising confidence, and ecclesiastical establishments tend to great ignorance and corruption; all of which facilitate the execution of mischievous projects.

But away with politics! Let me address you as a student and philosopher, and not as a patriot, now. I am pleased that you are going to converse with the Edwards and Henrys and Charleses, &c., &c., who have swayed the British sceptre, though I believe you will find some of them dirty and unprofitable companions, unless you will glean instruction from their follies, and fall more in love with liberty by beholding such detestable pictures of tyranny and cruelty.

I was afraid you would not easily have loosened your affection from the belles lettres. A delicate taste and warm imagination like yours must find it hard to give up such refined and exquisite enjoyments for the coarse and dry study of the law. It is like leaving a pleasant flourishing field for a barren desert; perhaps I should not say barren either, because the law does bear fruit, but it is sour fruit, that must be gathered and pressed and distilled before it can bring pleasure or profit. I perceive I have made a very awkward comparison; but I got the thought by the end, and had gone too far to quit it before I perceived that it was too much entangled in my brain to run it through; and so you must forgive it. I myself used to have too great a hankering after those amusing studies. Poetry, wit, and criticism, romances, plays, &c., captivated me much; but I began to discover that they deserve but a small portion of a mortal's time, and that something more substantial, more durable, and more profitable, befits a riper age. It would be exceedingly improper for a laboring man to have nothing but flowers in his garden, or to determine to eat nothing but sweet meats and confections. Equally absurd would it be for a scholar and a man of business to make up his whole library with books of fancy, and feed his mind with nothing but such luscious performances.

When you have an opportunity and write to Mr. Brackenridge, pray tell him I often think of him, and long to see him, and am resolved to do so in the spring. George Luckey was with me at Christmas, and we talked so much about old affairs and old friends, that I have a most insatiable desire to see you all. Luckey will accompany me, and we are to set off on the 10th of April, if no disaster befalls either of us.

I want again to breathe your free air. I expect it will mend my constitution and confirm my principles. I have indeed as good an atmosphere at home as the climate will allow; but have nothing to brag of as to the state and liberty of my country. Poverty and luxury prevail among all sorts; pride, ignorance, and knavery among the priesthood, and vice and wickedness among the laity. This is bad enough, but it is not the worst I have to tell you. That diabolical, hell-conceived principle of persecution rages among some; and to their eternal infamy, the clergy can furnish their quota of imps for such business. This vexes me the worst of anything whatever. There are at this time in the adjacent country not less than five or six well-meaning men in close jail for publishing their religious sentiments, which in the main are very orthodox. I have neither patience to hear, talk, or think of anything relative to this matter; for I have squabbled and scolded, abused and ridiculed, so long about it to [so] little purpose, that I am without common patience. So I must beg you to pity me, and pray for liberty of conscience to all.

I expect to hear from you once more before I see you, if time will admit; and want to know when the synod meets, and where; what the exchange is at, and as much about my friends and other matters as you can [tell,] and think worthy of notice Till I see you,

Adieu!

Virginia, Orange County, April 1, 1774.

MY WORTHY FRIEND,—I have another favor to acknowledge in the receipt of your kind letter of March the 4th. I did not intend to have written again to you before I obtained a nearer communication with you; but you have too much interest in my inclinations ever to be denied a request.

Mr. Brackenridge's illness gives me great uneasiness; I think he would be a loss to America. His merit is rated so high by me that I confess, if he were gone, I could almost say with the poet, that his country could furnish such a pomp for death no more. But I solace myself from Finley's ludicrous descriptions as you do.

Our Assembly is to meet the first of May, when it is expected something will be done in behalf of the dissenters. Petitions, I hear, are already forming among the persecuted Baptists, and I fancy it is in the thoughts of the Presbyterians also, to intercede for greater liberty in matters of religion. For my own part, I cannot help being very doubtful of their succeeding in the attempt. The affair was on the carpet during the last session; but such incredible and extravagant stories were told in the House of the monstrous effects of the enthusiasm prevalent among the sectaries, and so greedily swallowed by their enemies, that I believe they lost footing by it. And the bad name they still have with those who pretend too much contempt to examine into their principles and conduct, and are too much devoted to the ecclesiastical establishment to hear of the toleration of dissentients, I am apprehensive, will be again made a pretext for rejecting their request.

The sentiments of our people of fortune and fashion on this subject are vastly different from what you have been used to. That liberal, catholic, and equitable way of thinking, as to the rights of conscience, which is one of the characteristics of a free people, and so strongly marks the people of your province, is but little known among the zealous adherents to our hierarchy. We have, it is true, some persons in the Legislature of generous principles both in Religion and Politics; but number, not merit, you know, is necessary to carry points there. Besides, the clergy are a numerous and powerful body, have great influence at home by reason of their connection with and dependence on the Bishops and Crown, and will naturally employ all their art and interest to depress their rising adversaries; for such they must consider dissenters who rob them of the good will of the people, and may, in time, endanger their livings and security.

You are happy in dwelling in a land where those inestimable privileges are fully enjoyed; and the public has long felt the good effects of this religious as well as civil liberty. Foreigners have been encouraged to settle among you. Industry and virtue have been promoted by mutual emulation and mutual inspection; commerce and the arts have flourished; and I cannot help attributing those continual exertions of genius which appear among you to the inspiration of liberty, and that love of fame and knowledge which always accompany it. Religious bondage shackles and debilitates the mind, and unfits it for every noble enterprise, every expanded prospect. How far this is the case with Virginia will more clearly appear when the ensuing trial is made. . . .

2. Freedom of Conscience:
Memorial and Remonstrance

The crisis of the 1770s opened wide possibilities to talented young men like Madison. Wealth, family position, and local political favor were his by inheritance. A liberal education marked him for quick advancement. At twenty-five, Madison was chosen to the Virginia Convention of 1776, then to the House of Delegates, the Governor's Council (1777–1779), and the Continental Congress (1780–1783), where he won recognition as a major national leader. By contemporary standards, Madison suffered no loss of dignity when in 1784 he returned to the Virginia House of Delegates to attend to the reformation of the republican commonwealth at home.

Madison's hatred of political controls over religious belief and practice first found a public channel in the Virginia Convention of 1776. He drafted amendments to the proposed Bill of Rights that helped to place religious liberty on the founda-

Memorial and Remonstrance Against Religious Assessments, 1785, in *Writings*, II, pp. 183–191.

tion not of toleration but of natural right. During the first session of the House of Delegates, Madison and Jefferson took the lead in moving Virginia toward the disestablishment of the Episcopal Church by denying public funds to the clergy. The policy was confirmed and extended in 1779. Five years later, a stream of petitions to the legislature, complaining of the decay of public morals, encouraged Patrick Henry and other friends of tax-supported churches to seek a cautious reversal of direction. Madison, playing for time to work on public opinion, maneuvered the House into a postponement. When a new legislature met in October, 1785, the religious assessment bill died without a formal vote. Popular sentiment, aroused by liberals and religious dissenters, convinced the Assembly to enact the thoroughgoing Bill for Religious Liberty that Jefferson had first proposed in 1779. Madison's *Memorial and Remonstrance,* circulated through the state in handwritten and printed copies during the previous summer, did much to prepare Virginians for the change. This classic defense of the principle of religious freedom pointed toward the sharp separation of church and state that Madison would later write into the federal Bill of Rights.

The text printed below is based on a broadside issued by the Phenix Press of Alexandria, Virginia. Many such copies, with long lists of signatures appended, reached the General Assembly in October 1785.

To the Honorable the General Assembly
OF
the Commonwealth of Virginia.
A Memorial and Remonstrance.

We, the subscribers, citizens of the said Commonwealth, having taken into serious consideration, a Bill printed by order of the last Session of General Assembly, entitled "A Bill establishing a provision for Teachers of the Christian Religion," and conceiving that the same, if finally armed with the sanctions of a law, will be a dangerous abuse of power, are bound as faithful members of a free State, to remonstrate against it, and to declare the reasons by which we are determined. We remonstrate against the said Bill,

1. Because we hold it for a fundamental and undeniable truth, "that Religion or the duty which we owe to our Creator and the Manner of discharging it, can be directed only by reason and conviction, not by force or violence."[1] The Religion then of every man must be left to the conviction and conscience of every man; and it is the right of every man to exercise it as these may dictate. This right is in its nature an unalienable right. It is unalienable; because the opinions of men, depending only on the evidence contemplated by their own minds, cannot follow the dictates of other men: It is unalienable also, because what is here a right towards men, is a duty towards the Creator. It is the duty of every man to render to the Creator such homage, and such only, as he believes to be acceptable to him. This duty is precedent both in order of time and degree of obligation, to the claims of Civil Society. Before any man can be considered as a member of Civil Society, he must be considered as a subject of the Governor of the Universe: And if a member of Civil Society, who enters into any subordinate Association, must always do it with a reservation of his duty to the general authority; much more must every man who becomes a member of any particular Civil Society, do it with a saving of his allegiance to the Universal Soverign. We maintain therefore that in matters of Religion, no man's right is abridged by the institution of Civil Society, and that Religion is wholly exempt from its cognizance. True it is, that no other rule exists, by which any question which may divide a Society, can be ultimately deter-

---

[1] Decl. Rights, Art. 16. [Note in the original.]

mined, but the will of the majority; but it is also true, that the majority may trespass on the rights of the minority.

2. Because if religion be exempt from the authority of the Society at large, still less can it be subject to that of the Legislative Body. The latter are but the creatures and vicegerents of the former. Their jurisdiction is both derivative and limited: it is limited with regard to the co-ordinate departments, more necessarily is it limited with regard to the constituents. The preservation of a free government requires not merely, that the metes and bounds which separate each department of power may be invariably maintained; but more especially, that neither of them be suffered to overleap the great Barrier which defends the rights of the people. The Rulers who are guilty of such an encroachment, exceed the commission from which they derive their authority, and are Tyrants. The People who submit to it are governed by laws made neither by themselves, nor by an authority derived from them, and are slaves.

3. Because, it is proper to take alarm at the first experiment on our liberties. We hold this prudent jealousy to be the first duty of citizens, and one of [the] noblest characteristics of the late Revolution. The freemen of America did not wait till usurped power had strengthened itself by exercise, and entangled the question in precedents. They saw all the consequences in the principle, and they avoided the consequences by denying the principle. We revere this lesson too much, soon to forget it. Who does not see that the same authority which can establish Christianity, in exclusion of all other Religions, may establish with the same ease any particular sect of Christians, in exclusion of all other Sects? That the same authority which can force a citizen to contribute three pence only of his property for the support of any one establishment, may force him to conform to any other establishment in all cases whatsoever?

4. Because, the bill violates that equality which ought to be the basis of every law, and which is more indispensible, in pro-

portion as the validity or expediency of any law is more liable to be impeached. If "all men are by nature equally free and independent,"[2] all men are to be considered as entering into Society on equal conditions; as relinquishing no more, and therefore retaining no less, one than another, of their natural rights. Above all are they to be considered as retaining an *"equal* title to the free exercise of Religion according to the dictates of conscience."[3] Whilst we assert for ourselves a freedom to embrace, to profess and to observe the Religion which we believe to be of divine origin, we cannot deny an equal freedom to those whose minds have not yet yielded to the evidence which has convinced us. If this freedom be abused, it is an offence against God, not against man: To God, therefore, not to men, must an account of it be rendered. As the Bill violates equality by subjecting some to peculiar burdens; so it violates the same principle, by granting to others peculiar exemptions. Are the Quakers and Menonists the only sects who think a compulsive support of their religions unnecessary and unwarantable? Can their piety alone be intrusted with the care of public worship? Ought their Religions to be endowed above all others, with extraordinary privileges, by which proselytes may be enticed from all others? We think too favorably of the justice and good sense of these denominations, to believe that they either covet pre-eminencies over their fellow citizens, or that they will be seduced by them, from the common opposition to the measure.

5. Because the bill implies either that the Civil Magistrate is a competent Judge of Religious truth; or that he may employ Religion as an engine of Civil policy. The first is an arrogant pretension falsified by the contradictory opinions of Rulers in all ages, and throughout the world: The second an unhallowed perversion of the means of salvation.

---

[2] Decl. Rights, Art 1. [Note in the original.]
[3] Art: 16. [Note in the original.]

6. Because the establishment proposed by the Bill is not requisite for the support of the Christian Religion. To say that it is, is a contradiction to the Christian Religion itself; for every page of it disavows a dependence on the powers of this world: it is a contradiction to fact; for it is known that this Religion both existed and flourished, not only without the support of human laws, but in spite of every opposition from them; and not only during the period of miraculous aid, but long after it had been left to its own evidence, and the ordinary care of Providence: Nay, it is a contradiction in terms; for a Religion not invented by human policy, must have pre-existed and been supported, before it was established by human policy. It is moreover to weaken in those who profess this Religion a pious confidence in its innate excellence, and the patronage of its Author; and to foster in those who still reject it, a suspicion that its friends are too conscious of its fallacies, to trust it to its own merits.

7. Because experience witnesseth that ecclesiastical establishments, instead of maintaining the purity and efficacy of Religion, have had a contrary operation. During almost fifteen centuries, has the legal establishment of Christianity been on trial. What have been its fruits? More or less in all places, pride and indolence in the Clergy; ignorance and servility in the laity; in both, superstition, bigotry and persecution. Enquire of the Teachers of Christianity for the ages in which it appeared in its greatest lustre; those of every sect, point to the ages prior to its incorporation with Civil policy. Propose a restoration of this primitive state in which its Teachers depended on the voluntary rewards of their flocks; many of them predict its downfall. On which side ought their testimony to have greatest weight, when for or when against their interest?

8. Because the establishment in question is not necessary for the support of Civil Government. If it be urged as necessary for the support of Civil Government only as it is a means of supporting Religion, and it be not necessary for the latter pur-

pose, it cannot be necessary for the former. If Religion be not within [the] cognizance of Civil Government, how can its legal establishment be said to be necessary to civil Government? What influence in fact have ecclesiastical establishments had on Civil Society? In some instances they have been seen to erect a spiritual tyranny on the ruins of Civil authority; in many instances they have been seen upholding the thrones of political tyranny; in no instance have they been seen the guardians of the liberties of the people. Rulers who wished to subvert the public liberty, may have found an established clergy convenient auxiliaries. A just government, instituted to secure & perpetuate it, needs them not. Such a government will be best supported by protecting every citizen in the enjoyment of his Religion with the same equal hand which protects his person and his property; by neither invading the equal rights of any Sect, nor suffering any Sect to invade those of another.

9. Because the proposed establishment is a departure from that generous policy, which, offering an asylum to the persecuted and oppressed of every Nation and Religion, promised a lustre to our country, and an accession to the number of its citizens. What a melancholy mark is the Bill of sudden degeneracy? Instead of holding forth an asylum to the persecuted, it is itself a signal of persecution. It degrades from the equal rank of Citizens all those whose opinions in Religion do not bend to those of the Legislative authority. Distant as it may be, in its present form, from the Inquisition it differs from it only in degree. The one is the first step, the other the last in the career of intolerance. The magnanimous sufferer under this cruel scourge in foreign Regions, must view the Bill as a Beacon on our Coast, warning him to seek some other haven, where liberty and philanthropy in their due extent may offer a more certain repose from his troubles.

10. Because, it will have a like tendency to banish our Citizens. The allurements presented by other situations are every day thinning their number. To superadd a fresh motive to emi-

gration, by revoking the liberty which they now enjoy, would be the same species of folly which has dishonoured and de-populated flourishing kingdoms.

11. Because, it will destroy that moderation and harmony which the forbearance of our laws to intermeddle with Religion, has produced amongst its several sects. Torrents of blood have been split in the old world, by vain attempts of the secular arm to extinguish Religious discord, by proscribing all difference in Religious opinions. Time has at length revealed the true remedy. Every relaxation of narrow and rigorous policy, wherever it has been tried, has been found to assuage the disease. The American Theatre has exhibited proofs, that equal and compleat liberty, if it does not wholly eradicate it, sufficiently destroys its malignant influence on the health and prosperity of the State. If with the salutary effects of this system under our own eyes, we begin to contract the bonds of Religious freedom, we know no name that will too severely reproach our folly. At least let warning be taken at the first fruits of the threatened innovation. The very appearance of the Bill has transformed that "Christian forbearance,[4] love and charity," which of late mutually prevailed, into animosities and jealousies, which may not soon be appeased. What mischiefs may not be dreaded should this enemy to the public quiet be armed with the force of a law?

12. Because, the policy of the bill is adverse to the diffusion of the light of Christianity. The first wish of those who enjoy this precious gift, ought to be that it may be imparted to the whole race of mankind. Compare the number of those who have as yet received it with the number still remaining under the dominion of false Religions; and how small is the former! Does the policy of the Bill tend to lessen the disproportion? No; it at once discourages those who are strangers to the light

---

[4] Art. 16. [Note in the original.]

of [revelation] from coming into the Region of it; and coun-
tenances, by example the nations who continue in darkness,
in shutting out those who might convey it to them. Instead of
levelling as far as possible, every obstacle to the victorious
progress of truth, the Bill with an ignoble and unchristian
timidity would circumscribe it, with a wall of defence, against
the encroachments of error.

13. Because attempts to enforce by legal sanctions, acts obnoxious to so great a proportion of Citizens, tend to enervate
the laws in general, and to slacken the bands of Society. If it
be difficult to execute any law which is not generally deemed
necessary or salutary, what must be the case where it is
deemed invalid and dangerous? and what may be the effect
of so striking an example of impotency in the Government, on
its general authority.

14. Because a measure of such singular magnitude and delicacy ought not to be imposed, without the clearest evidence
that it is called for by a majority of citizens: and no satisfactory
method is yet proposed by which the voice of the majority in
this case may be determined, or its influence secured. "The
people of the respective countries are indeed requested to
signify their opinion respecting the adoption of the Bill to the
next Session of Assembly." But the representation must be
made equal, before the voice either of the Representatives or
of the Counties, will be that of the people. Our hope is that
neither of the former will, after due consideration, espouse the
dangerous principle of the Bill. Should the event disappoint
us, it will still leave us in full confidence, that a fair appeal to
the latter will reverse the sentence against our liberties.

15. Because, finally, "the equal right of every citizen to the
free exercise of his Religion according to the dictates of conscience" is held by the same tenure with all our other rights. If
we recur to its origin, it is equally the gift of nature; if we

weigh its importance, it cannot be less dear to us; if we consult the Declaration of those rights which pertain to the good people of Virginia, as the "basis and foundation of Government,"[5] it is enumerated with equal solemnity, or rather studied emphasis. Either then, we must say, that the will of the Legislature is the only measure of their authority; and that in the plentitude of this authority, they may sweep away all our fundamental rights; or, that they are bound to leave this particular right untouched and sacred: Either we must say, that they may controul the freedom of the press, may abolish the trial by jury, may swallow up the Executive and Judiciary Powers of the State; nay that they may despoil us of our very right of suffrage, and erect themselves into an independant and hereditary assembly: or we must say, that they have no authority to enact into law the Bill under consideration. We the subscribers say, that the General Assembly of this Commonwealth have no such authority: And that no effort may be omitted on our part against so dangerous an usurpation, we oppose to it, this remonstrance; earnestly praying, as we are in duty bound, that the Supreme Lawgiver of the Universe, by illuminating those to whom it is addressed, may on the one hand, turn their councils from every act which would affront his holy prerogative, or violate the trust committed to them: and on the other, guide them into every measure which may be worthy of his [blessing, may re]dound to their own praise, and may establish more firmly the liberties, the prosperity, and the Happiness of the Commonwealth.

---

[5] Decl. Rights-title. [Note in the original.]

The National Theme

3. Revolutionary Chaos: To Thomas Jefferson

The Revolutionary crisis awakened a new sense of nationality in Americans whose political outlook had been predominantly colonial and provincial. If positive visions of a new American Republic gave purpose to their struggle, the harsh experience of confusion and frustration in the conduct of the Revolution taught the leaders unforgettable lessons about political survival. Men like Washington, Franklin, Madison, or John Adams, who faced the urgent responsibilities of fighting, governing, and negotiating, emerged from the Revolutionary years with the deep conviction that the Union, under a strong central authority, was a necessary condition for maintaining republican liberty in America.

In December 1779 the Virginia Assembly chose Madison as one of five delegates to the Continental Congress. His willing-

---

To Thomas Jefferson, March 27, 1780 and May 6, 1780, in *Writings*, I, pp. 59–63.

ness to give almost four years of service to that decaying symbol of national authority distinguished Madison from most
Virginia notables (and state leaders generally) who preferred
familiar duties closer to home. The small size of the Congress
—thirty would have been a remarkable attendance at Philadelphia—and the relative scarcity of first-class talent and established reputation among its members left Madison, at
twenty-nine the youngest delegate, ample room to make his
mark.

It was quite natural that Madison, soon after taking his seat,
should have addressed his candid analysis of Congressional
weakness and state delinquencies to Thomas Jefferson, Governor of Virginia and since 1776 his personal friend and political
partner. For half a century the short road between Jefferson's
Monticello and Madison's Montpelier would link them when
they were not acting together at Richmond, Philadelphia, or
Washington, or exchanging thoughts and plans by mail from
separate public posts. The enduring alliance between these two
great princes of the Virginia Republic dynasty, secured by
common principles and complementary differences in political
outlook and temper, became itself a formidable factor in early
American history. (See Documents 7, 13, 15, 18, 32.)

The current of Madison's political thought runs directly from
these immediate reactions to a moribund Congress to the financial reforms of 1783 and the grand national designs of 1787.

Philadelphia, March 27, 1780

DEAR SIR,—Nothing under the title of news has occurred
since I wrote last week by express, except that the enemy on
the first of March remained in the neighbourhood of Charles-
ton, in the same posture as when the preceding account came
away. From the best intelligence from that quarter, there
seems to be great encouragement to hope that Clinton's oper-

ations will be again frustrated. Our great apprehensions at present flow from a very different quarter. Among the various conjunctures of alarm and distress which have arisen in the course of the Revolution, it is with pain I affirm to you, sir, that no one can be singled out more truly critical than the present. Our army threatened with an immediate alternative of disbanding or living on free quarter; the public treasury empty; public credit exhausted, nay the private credit of purchasing agents employed, I am told, as far as it will bear; Congress complaining of the extortion of the people; the people of the improvidence of Congress; and the army of both; our affairs requiring the most mature and systematic measures, and the urgency of occasions admitting only of temporizing expedients, and these expedients generating new difficulties; Congress [from a defect of adequate statesmen more likely to fall into wrong measures and of less weight to enforce right ones,]¹ recommending plans to the several States for execution, and the States separately rejudging the expediency of such plans, whereby the same distrust of concurrent exertions that has damped the ardor of patriotic individuals must produce the same effect among the States themselves; an old system of finance discarded as incompetent to our necessities, an untried and precarious one substituted, and a total stagnation in prospect between the end of the former and the operation of the latter. These are the outlines of the picture of our public situation. I leave it to your own imagination to fill them up. Believe me, sir, as things now stand, if the States do not vigorously proceed in collecting the old money, and establishing funds for the credit of the new, that we are undone; and let them be ever so expeditious in doing this, still the intermediate distress to our army, and hindrance to public affairs,

---

¹ The bracketed passage, deleted by Hunt no doubt for pious reasons, is found in Edmund C. Burnett, ed., *Letters of the Members of the Continental Congress* (8 vols., Washington, 1921–1936), V, p. 97. [*Ed.*]

are a subject of melancholy reflection. General Washington writes that a failure of bread has already commenced in the army; and that, for any thing he sees, it must unavoidably increase. Meat they have only for a short season; and as the whole dependence is on provisions now to be procured, without a shilling for the purpose, and without credit for a shilling, I look forward with the most pungent apprehensions. It will be attempted, I believe, to purchase a few supplies with loan-office certificates; but whether they will be received is perhaps far from being certain; and if received will certainly be a most expensive and ruinous expedient. It is not without some reluctance I trust this information to a conveyance by post, but I know of no better at present, and I conceive it to be absolutely necessary to be known to those who are most able and zealous to contribute to the public relief.

Philadelphia, May 6, 1780.

DEAR SIR,—I am sorry that I can give you no other account of our public situation, than that it continues equally perplexed and alarming as when I lately gave you a sketch of it. Our army has as yet been kept from starving, and public measures from total stagnation, by draughts on the States for the unpaid requisitions. The great amount of these you may judge of from the share that has fallen to Virginia. The discharge of debts due from the purchasing departments has absorbed a great proportion of them, and very large demands still remain. As soon as the draughts amount to the whole of the monthly requisitions up to the end of March, they must cease, according to the new scheme of finance. We must then depend wholly on the emissions to be made in pursuance of that scheme, which can only be applied as the old emissions are collected and destroyed. Should this not be done as fast as the current expenditures require, or should the new emissions fall into a course of depreciation, both of which may but too justly be feared, a most melancholy crisis must take place. A punctual compliance on the part of the States with the specific supplies will indeed render much less money necessary than would otherwise be wanted; but experience by no means affords satisfactory encouragement that due and unanimous exertions will be made for that purpose,—not to mention that our distress is so pressing that it is uncertain whether any exertions of that kind can give relief in time. It occurs besides, that as, the ability of the people to comply with the pecuniary requisitions is derived from the sale of their commodities, a requisition of the latter must make the former proportionably more difficult and defective. Congress have the satisfaction, however, to be informed that the legislature of Connecticut have taken the most vigorous steps for supplying their quota both of money and commodities; and that a body of their principal merchants have associated for supporting the credit of the new paper, for which purpose they have, in a public address, pledged their faith to the assembly to sell their merchandise on the same terms as if they were to be paid in specie. A similar vigor throughout the Union may perhaps produce effects as far exceeding our present hopes, as they have heretofore fallen short of our wishes.

It is to be observed that the situation of Congress has undergone a total change from what it originally was. Whilst they exercised the indefinite power of emitting money on the credit of their constituents, they had the whole wealth and resources of the continent within their command, and could go on with their affairs independently and as they pleased. Since the resolution passed for shutting the press, this power has been entirely given up, and they are now as dependent on the States as the King of England is on the Parliament. They can neither enlist, pay nor feed a single soldier, nor execute any other purpose, but as the means are first put into their hands. Unless the legislatures are sufficiently attentive to this change of circumstances, and act in conformity to it, every thing must necessarily go wrong, or rather must come to a total stop. All that Congress can do in future will be to administer public affairs with prudence, vigor and economy. In order to do which they have sent a committee to Head-Quarters with ample powers, in concert with the Commander-in-Chief and the heads of the Departments, to reform the various abuses which prevail, and to make such arrangements as will best guard against a relapse into them.

4. Public Credit and the Republican Cause: Address to the States

After taking his seat in Congress on March 20, 1780, Madison quickly joined the handful of leaders—including his future adversary, Hamilton—who kept the central government alive and fought persistently to remove crippling limitations on its powers. No dazzling orator or pamphleteer, Madison excelled in the quiet work of shaping policy and winning consent by rigorous, informed, and penetrating argument. If prudence warned him to conciliate state prejudices, a strong sense of necessity forced him constantly to press for enlarged congressional authority that would fill an empty treasury, support a neglected army, bring the disputed western territory under federal control, and strengthen America's hand in negotiations with the European powers.

The Confederation government in the early 1780s was on the verge of bankruptcy. The power of the purse rested finally

---

"Address to the States, by the United States in Congress Assembled," April 26, 1783, in *Writings*, I, pp. 455n–46on.

in the state legislatures that decided when and how to meet the tax requisitions of Congress. State contributions were erratic and grossly inadequate to the most urgent needs of the Union. By 1783, Congress faced severe inflation, increasingly distrustful foreign and domestic creditors, and an unpaid army seething with resentment. Repeated efforts to create an independent source of revenue through federal import duties had been blocked by one state or another, fearing the establishment of tyranny or simply pursuing its own local interests. Madison tried unsuccessfully to form a coalition around an omnibus plan carefully designed to tempt a variety of interests into conceding power to Congress. The package included federal import duties; land cessions by Virginia and other states with extensive western claims; tax requisitions on the states; federal assumption of state debts; tax abatements for states suffering enemy invasion; and a shift from land value to population (including three-fifths of the slaves) as the basis for tax quotas. The nationalist leaders could persuade Congress only to recommend a five per cent federal impost, limited to twenty-five years and administered by state officials, together with further tax requisitions on the states, proportioned to population. Under the Articles of Confederation, the revenue acts of April 18, 1783, required the unanimous consent of the several states.

Thus Congress assigned to a committee of Madison, Alexander Hamilton (former aide to General Washington), and Oliver Ellsworth (future Chief Justice of the U.S. Supreme Court), the drafting of an address to the states in support of the revenue proposal. Madison's text was approved by Congress on April 26, 1783, and printed as a pamphlet. Private editions widened the circulation. The reasoning of Madison, the authority of Congress, and the endorsement of General Washington all failed to secure reform under the fatal unanimity rule. When Hamilton presented his own plan for restoring the public credit in 1790, he might well have drawn on Madison's "Address"—and expected Madison's support.

"The prospect which has for some time existed, and which is now happily realized, of a successful termination of the war, together with the critical exigencies of public affairs have made it the duty of Congress to review and provide for the debts which the war has left upon the United States and to look forward to the means of obviating dangers, which may interrupt the harmony and tranquillity of the Confederacy. The result of their mature & solemn deliberations on these great Objects is contained in their several recommendations of the 18th instant, herewith transmitted. Although these recommendations, speak themselves the principles on which they are founded, as well as the ends which they propose, it will not be improper to enter into a few explanations and remarks in order to place in a stronger view the necessity of complying with them. The first measure recommended is effectual provision for the debts of the United States. The amount of these debts, as far as they can now be ascertained is forty-two millions three hundred and seventy-five dollars . . . To discharge the principle of this aggregate debt at once or in any short period is evidently not within the compass of our resources; and even if it could be accomplished the ease of the community would require that the debt itself should be left to a course of gradual extinguishment and certain funds be provided for paying in the meantime the annual Interest. The amount of the annual interest as will appear by the paper last referred to is computed to be two millions four hundred and fifteen thousand nine hundred and fifty-six dollars. Funds, therefore, which will certainly & punctually produce this annual sum at least, must be provided. In devising these funds Congress did not overlook the mode of supplying the common treasury provided by the Articles of

Confederation. But after the most respectful consideration of that mode, they were constrained to regard it as inadequate & inapplicable to the form into which the public debt must be thrown. The delays & uncertainties incident to a revenue to be established & collected from time to time by thirteen independent authorities is at first view irreconcilable with the punctuality essential in the discharge of the interest of a national debt. Our own experience, after making every allowance for transient impediments has been a sufficient illustration of this truth. Some departure therefore in the recommendation of Congress from the federal constitution was unavoidable; but it will be found to be as small as could be reconciled with the object in view and to be supported besides by solid considerations of interest and sound policy.

The fund which first presented itself on this as it did on a former occasion, was a tax on imports. . . . It will suffice to recapitulate that taxes on consumption are always least burdensome because they are least felt and are borne too by those who are both willing and able to pay them; that of all taxes on consumption those on foreign commerce are most compatible with the genius and policy of free states; that from the relative positions of some of the more commercial States it will be impossible to bring this essential resource into use without a concerted uniformity; that this uniformity cannot be concerted through any channel so properly as through Congress, nor for any purpose so aptly as for paying the debts of a revolution from which an unbounded freedom has accrued to Commerce.

In renewing this proposition to the states we have not been unmindful of the objections which heretofore frustrated the unanimous adoption of it. We have limited the duration of the revenue to the term of twenty five years and we have left to the States themselves the appointment of the officers who are to collect it. If the strict maxims of national credit alone were to be consulted, the revenue ought manifestly to be co-existent with the object of it; and the collection placed in every respect under that authority, which is to dispense the former and is responsible for the latter. These relaxations will, we trust, be regarded, on one hand as the effect of a disposition in Congress to attend at all times to the sentiments of those whom they serve, and on the other hand, as a proof of their anxious desire that provision may be made in some way or other for an honorable and just fulfilment of the engagements which they have formed.

To render this fund as productive as possible and at the same time to narrow the room for collusions and frauds, it has been judged an improvement of the plan to recommend a liberal duty on such articles as are most susceptible of a tax according to their quantity and are of most equal and general consumption, leaving all other articles, as heretofore proposed, to be taxed according to their value.

The amount of this fund is computed to be 915,956 dollars. . . . Accuracy in the first essay on so complex and fluctuating a subject is not to be expected. It is presumed to be as near the truth as the defect of proper materials would admit.

The residue of the computed interest is 1,500,000 dollars & is referred to the States to be provided for by such funds as they may judge most convenient. Here again the strict maxims of public credit gave way to the desire of Congress to conform to the sentiments of their constituents. It ought not to be omitted however with respect to this portion of the revenue that the mode in which it is to be supplied varies so little from that pointed out in the articles of Confederation and the variations are so conducive to the great object proposed, that a ready & unqualified compliance on the part of the States may be the more justly expected. In fixing the quotas of this sum, Congress, as may be well imagined, were guided by very imperfect lights, and some inequalities may consequently have ensued. These however can be but temporary; and as far as they may exist at all, will be redressed by a retrospective adjustment as soon as a constitutional rule can be applied.

The necessity of making the two foregoing provisions one indivisible & irrevocable act is apparent. Without the first quality, partial provision only might be made, where complete provision is essential; nay as some states might prefer and adopt one of the funds only, and the other States the other fund only, it might happen that no provision at all would be made. Without the second, a single state out of the thirteen might at any time involve the nation in bankruptcy; the mere practicability of which would be a fatal bar to the establishment of national credit. Instead of enlarging on these topics, two observations are submitted to the justice and wisdom of the legislatures. First, the present creditors or rather the domestic part of them having either made their loans for a period which has expired or having become creditors in the first instance involuntarily, are entitled on the clear principles of justice and good faith to demand the principal of their credits instead of accepting the annual interest. It is necessary therefore as the principal cannot be paid to them on demand, that the interest should be so effectually & satisfactorily secured as to enable them, if they incline to transfer the stock at its full value. Secondly if the funds be so firmly constituted as to inspire a thorough & universal confidence, may it not be hoped that the capital of the domestic debt, which bears the high interest of 6 per cent. may be cancelled by other loans obtained at a more moderate interest? The savings by such an Operation would be a clear one, and might be a considerable one. . . .

Thus much for the interest of the national debt. For the discharge of the principal, within the term limited, we rely on the natural increase of the revenue from commerce, on requisitions to be made from time to time for that purpose as circumstances may dictate, and on the prospect of vacant territory. If these resources should prove inadequate it will be necessary at the expiration of 25 years to continue the funds now recommended or to establish such others as may then be found more convenient.

With a view to the resource last mentioned, as well as to obviate disagreeable controversies and confusions, Congress have included in their present recommendations a renewal of those of the 6 day of September and of the 10 day of October 1780. In both these respects a liberal and final accommodation of all interfering claims of vacant territory is an object, which cannot be pressed with too much solicitude.

The last object recommended is a constitutional change of the rule by which a partition of the common burthens is to be made. The expediency and even necessity of such a change, has been sufficiently enforced by the local injustice and discontents which have proceeded from valuations of the soil in every state where the experiment has been made. But how infinitely must these evils be increased on a comparison of such valuations among the States themselves! On whatever side indeed this rule be surveyed the execution of it must be attended with the most serious difficulties. If the valuations be referred to the authorities of the several states, a general satisfaction is not to be hoped for. If they be executed by Officers of the United States traversing the country for that purpose, besides the inequalities against which this mode would be no security, the expense would be both enormous and obnoxious. If the mode taken in the act of the 17th day of February last, which was deemed on the whole least objectionable, be adhered to, Still the insufficiency of the data to the purpose to which they are to be applied must greatly impair, if not utterly destroy all confidence in the accuracy of the result; not to mention that as far as the result can be at all a just one, it will be indebted for the advantage to the principle on which the rule proposed to be substituted is founded. This rule, although not free from objections, is liable to fewer than any other that could be devised. The only material difficulty, which attended it in the deliberations of Congress was to fix the proper difference between the labour and industry of free inhabitants and of all other inhabitants. The ratio ultimately agreed on was the effect of mutual concessions, and if it should be supposed not to correspond precisely with the fact, no doubt ought to be entertained that an equal spirit of accommodation among the several legislatures will prevail against little inequalities which may be calculated on one side or on the other. But notwithstanding the confidence of Congress as to the success of this proposition, it is their duty to recollect that the event may possibly disappoint them, and to request that measures may still be pursued for obtaining and transmitting the information called for in the act of the 17 of February last, which in such event will be essential.

The plan thus communicated & explained by Congress must now receive its fate from their constituents. All the objects comprised in it are conceived to be of great importance to the happiness of this confederated Republic; are necessary to render the fruits of the Revolution a full reward for the blood, the toils, the cares, and the calamities which have purchased it. But the object, of which the necessity will be peculiarly felt, and which it is peculiarly the duty of Congress to inculcate, is the provision recommended for the national debt. Although this debt is greater than could have been wished, it is still less on the whole than could have been expected: and when referred to the cause in which it has been incurred and compared with the burthens which wars of ambition and of vain glory have entailed on other nations ought to be borne not only with cheerfulness but with pride. But the magnitude of the debt makes no part of the question. It is sufficient that the debt has been fairly contracted and that justice and good faith demand that it should be fully discharged. Congress had no option but between different modes of discharging it. The same option is the only one that can exist with the states. The mode which has after long and elaborate discussion been preferred is we are persuaded, the least objectionable of any that would have been equal to the purpose. Under this persuasion we call upon the justice and plighted faith of the several states to give it its proper effect, to reflect on the consequences of rejecting it; and to remember that Congress will not be answerable for them.

If other motives than that of justice could be requisite on this occasion, no nation could ever feel stronger. For to whom are the debts to be paid?

To an ally, in the first place, who, to the exertion of his arms in support of our cause has added the succours of his treasure; who to his important loans has added liberal donations, and whose loans themselves carry the impression of his magnanimity and friendship. . . .

To individuals in a foreign country, in the next place, who were the first to give so precious a token of their confidence in our justice, & of their friendship for our cause; and who are members of a republic, which was second in expousing our rank among nations. . . .

Another class of creditors is *that illustrious & patriotic band of fellow-citizens,* whose blood and whose bravery have defended the liberties of their country, who have patiently borne, among other distresses, the privation of their stipends, whilst the distresses of their country disabled it from bestowing them; and who even now ask for no more than such a portion of their dues as will enable them to retire from the field of victory and glory into the bosom of peace and private citizenship, and for such effectual security for the residue of their claims as their country is now unquestionably able to provide. . . .

The remaining class of creditors is composed partly of such of our fellow citizens as originally lent to the public the use of their funds, or have since manifested most confidence in their country by receiving transfers from the lenders; and partly of those, whose property has been either advanced or assumed for the public service. To discriminate the merits of these several descriptions of creditors would be a task equally unnecessary & invidious. If the voice of humanity plead more loudly in favour of some than of others; the voice of policy no less than of justice pleads in favour of all. A wise nation will never permit those who relieve the wants of their country, or who rely most on its faith, its firmness and its resources, when either of them is distrusted, to suffer by the event.

Let it be remembered finally that it has ever been the pride and boast of America, that the rights for which she contended were the rights of human nature. By the blessing of the Author of these rights on the means exerted for their defence they have prevailed against all opposition and form the basis of thirteen independent States. No instance has heretofore occurred, nor can any instance be expected hereafter to occur, in which the unadulterated forms of Republican government can pretend to so fair an opportunity of justifying themselves by their fruits. In this view the citizens of the United States are responsible for the greatest trust ever confided to a political society. If justice, good faith, honor, gratitude and all the other qualities which enoble the character of a nation & fulfil the ends of government, be the fruits of our establishments, the cause of liberty will acquire a dignity and lustre, which it has never yet enjoyed, and an example will be set, which cannot but have the most favourable influence on the rights of Mankind. If on the other side, our governments should be unfortunately blotted with the reverse of these cardinal and essential virtues, the great cause which we have engaged to vindicate, will be dishonored and betrayed; the last and fairest experiment in favor of the rights of human nature will be turned against them; and their patrons and friends exposed to be insulted and silenced by the votaries of tyranny and usurpation.

5.   Completion of Independence: "The North American"

The "North American" essays, originally published in *The Pennsylvania Journal* of September 17 and October 8, 1783, seem shockingly un-Madisonian in their pathos and grandiloquence. Yet Irving Brant, the leading Madison authority, argues persuasively for the Virginian's authorship. Strict evidence aside, one can well imagine that a long frustrated nationalist leader, who had recently witnessed the humiliating flight of Congress from Philadelphia to the jeers of mutinous soldiers, would have written with uncommon fervor. As peace with Great Britain seemed imminent, the men like Madison who had held together the ramshackle Union could rejoice only with trembling. Once the enemy force withdrew, what would prevent America from splitting into rival nation-states? The "North American" bore down hard on his pen to save the country from that bitter fruit

"The North American No. 1," September 17, 1783, in Irving Brant, ed., "Two Neglected Madison Letters," *William and Mary Quarterly*, 3rd series, III (October, 1946), 571–580. Footnotes have been deleted.

of victory. When these essays appeared, Madison was preparing to leave Philadelphia and take up in Virginia the work
of liberal and nationalist reform. As he clearly understood,
little could be done for the Confederation until public opinion
in the states was prepared for new departures. His anonymous
farewell message was a dramatic portrait of a young country
already "cursed with the impotence of old age."

THE NORTH AMERICAN NO. 1

The British Empire in America (prior to the late revolution)
in the progress of population, and the rapid encrease of wealth
and power, had no paralel in the annals of mankind.—These
are proofs of the influence of mild and gentle forms of government and of an happy state of civil society, which must enforce
conviction in every candid and enlightened mind, and which
however of late discoloured by British insolence and barbarity,
and veiled by necessary prejudices, may in the present stage of
the contest, meet with the unreserved acknowledgements of
the most strenuous assertors of American independence.—The
principles too of political liberty, deeply rooted in the first establishments of the colonies, had flourished with such unrestrained luxuriance, that the anticipation of distant tyranny
gave birth to opposition more firm and unanimous, than the
iron rod of despotism, weilded with unrelenting fury, had ever
roused mankind to, in other climes.

The independence of the Thirteen States, has added dignity
to our government, but if for *this* our peace and social happiness are to be exchanged; the splendor of sovereignty will only
rescue from obscurity the wretchedness of our citizens, and
transmit a melancholy lesson, to future ages, never to desert
solid systems which have yielded freedom and tranquility, to
pursue the dreams and phantoms of theory and speculation.

It is indulgence to the present civil institutions of America, when we only say that they are cursed with the impotence of old age, when they should enjoy the vigor of youth.

If the authors of the revolution, who now survive, view peace with Britain, as the completion of their object, and sink into supineness, whilst the horrors of anarchy and domestic confusion succeed a dissolution of the strict bonds of the former government, the bitter execrations of their fellow citizens, who see violence and discord purchased at the expence of their blood and treasure, will be their first reward, and that posterity, on whom they have entailed misery, when happiness was their birth-right, will perpetuate the infamy of their names.

It becomes them then, boldly to stand forth, and by one generous effort to accomplish the work they have begun.—Let them by a government adequate to the ends of society, secure those blessings to which the virtues, sacrifices and sufferings of America have an undeniable claim.—Let them do this—and then, when corroding time, shall separate pure and immortal virtues from attendant frailities, which at first obscure their lustre—when envy and jealousy shall be no more—a just and grateful fame will rank them amidst those idolized patriots of Greece and Rome, whose names antiquity has already consecrated at her venerable shrine.—The eye of posterity will hang with a fervid glow of admiration over the historic page, which paints the patriots of this infant world.—A world where reason early diffused her illuminated empire, and reflection became the parent of virtues, which in the savage and remote ages of Europe were the offspring of violence, or the ebullition of ungovernable passion.

Our governments were framed in the moment of turbulence and war—hasty productions on the spur of exigency, they can only be considered as the necessary but temporary instruments, to work out the revolution.—Their most enlightened framers viewed them at their formation, but as the foundations of permanent systems, to be reared in peace and tranquility.—

Six years experience has now unfolded their imperfections and defects, and the acknowledgment of our independence has developed prospects, which (pending the contest) were obscured by the clouded uncertainty of the event.

This then is the auspicious moment!—At an aera so awful and so critical, it is the design of this address deliberately to investigate and to expose with freedom, the real situation of these States, and in anticipating evil and misfortune, to suggest their remedy. In pursuing these objects the reasonable hopes of their preserving internal tranquility, will be the first, as it is the most important enquiry.

And here let it be observed—that the same active and predominant passion of the human breast, which prompts mankind to arrogate superiority and to the acquirement of riches, honor and power, which restricted to the selfish purposes of an individual we term *ambition,* is when extended to the disinterested object of aggrandizing a community, what we dignify with the appelation of *patriotism*—that the exertion of this principle being as advantageous to a republic, as it is useful to a man,—whoever will make the interest of his country his own, and shew a blind devotion to its views and prejudices, will find the road open to its dignities and employments, and will be honoured with the flattering distinction of *patriot*—and that the competition of interests and the desire of rulers to exalt their respective communities have laid the foundation of those wars which have desolated the world, and entailed misery on the human race.

Unhappily then for America, the separate sovereignties of our respective States, have left these principles to act with a force, but feebly restrained by the weak barrier of a nominal union. An undeviating adherence to state interests, state prejudices, state-aggrandizement, (or to comprehend the evil in a term to state politics), is the sad prognostic of that discord, confusion and never ceasing war, which has been the invariable lot of separate Sovereignties and neighbouring States.

A cause every way adequate to such pernicious effects aggravated by old and new disputes between the different States, and inflammatory reflections reciprocally cast, will not fail of receiving additional weight from a number of unhappy circumstances; each sufficient to disorder, even the best connected and organized system.

'Ere the war had yet terminated, the States betrayed the baleful effects of divided councils, and want of mutual confidence. Requisitions for men and money for general purposes, if not contemptuously neglected, were most commonly answered by heated assertions of the prior, undue and superior exertions of each State respectively:—This illusion originating in their *partial* view of Continental Affairs was supported by their unliquidated Accounts, and every attempt on the part of the general Council to dissipate the one or settle the other, have by the prejudice of ignorance or insinuations of design in the one case, or the neglect or inability to the States in the other, invariablly proved abortive.

Individuals in the commercial States, attached to the American cause, had received the currency of the union, in discharge of their private Debts, and became in most instances gradually possessed of it to the full amount of their fortunes, which generally consist in money:—They obeyed the public call, and with implicit confidence entrusted those rulers whose fidelity they relied on, with the hopes and support of themselves and families: Hence it is that those States find their citizens at the close of the war, in advance on Continental loans, in a degree that exceeds all measure of proportion; during its continuance, this class of creditors have suffered with patience and with fortitude, the total deprivation of the use of their fortunes, whilst the pressing exigencies of the times, seemed to apologize for withholding their right;—but peace terminating that excuse, when the general plan for fulfilling Continental engagements, lately proposed by that body, who were authorized; nay compelled to make them, (whose honor, with that of the nation, is to be supported by its success, or sacrificed by its failure,) proves abortive, and the regular and proper source of payment remains obstructed. Those States to which they pay allegiance, and which are bound to protect them, cannot refuse—either to pay them, and thereby burthen themselves with an unjust and unequal load, or interpose their powers and force, to extort them justice whence it is due.

On some parts of the continent the war has pressed sorely and partially—her bloody scourge has desolated the state of New York each successive year, and what has escaped the depredations of the enemy, has been wrested from her *citizens* by a rigorous military impress.—To whom shall they apply for payment?—Shall their own state pay them?—Would not unfeeling injustice herself blush to load New York, just emerging from such complicated distress, with an unequal share of the general debt.

I fear it has already become unpopular to *mention* that there *was* an American army, during the *late* war—that they have claims on the gratitude of their fellow citizens, and the justice of the continent, which are equally unpaid.—Unpleasing as the theme may be—Yet once more, oh ye Americans! ye shall listen to their tale—to shield and protect you and yours, their youths have passed away in rigorous campaigns, amidst hunger and amidst nakedness,—exposed to bleak colds of the north, without tents and without cloaths—the eye of him whose hand now writes these lines, has often traced their route, on the cold snow, with the blood of their bare feet, thence unsheltered have they marched thro' the burning sands of Carolina and each state thro'-out this long extended continent has been stained with their best blood.—They have gone home unpaid, many of them to contemplate the sad remnants, the ruined relicts of once splendid fortunes.—Shall it be to wear away their old age in poverty, until they find in the all healing grave, the only cure for wounds which ingratitude inflicts on the feeling mind?—Shall it be to rot? to perish in your jails? Or shall the different states pay their respective lines all their demands?—Some of them have acted generously, they have acted nobly, and of them there can be no apprehensions.—But are there not grounds to fear, that a very principal demand will never be paid by the northern states if referred to them? Admitting that those states who have failed in the heat and burthen of the day, are now to escape their proportion by this unequal and unfair distribution, and to be rewarded for their remissness and delinquencies.—Still to whom shall that part of the continental army apply, whom no state will now acknowledge.—They are a body of men not contemptible for their number or services, should they become so for their poverty or their wretchedness.

Here let it be remembered that there are many of the states, who have no back lands, no western wild, where they may seclude in solitude their war-worn veterans, from the fastidious eye of wealth and luxury.—These things should be considered in due time, and we should recollect, that those who have been reared by the iron hand of ruthless war, have in no age or clime, been marked for a tame passion of evil and injustice.

It is a maxim that has stood the test of time, and is now sanctified by experience that government should be founded in justice and good faith—and that the institution which shall be proven incapable of dispensing the one and preserving the other, cannot be long respected, and will never be supported. —Let the government of the United States submit to this ignominy, and be exposed to this danger, and the contracts which they have formed, depend for their execution on others, and that faith which they have plighted will be interpreted broken or preserved, according to the caprice, avarice or resentment of the ignorant, interested or designing.—Let it be admitted that each state shall in all cases pay its own citizens of all classes, and let us view the probable consequence which will result from the measure independent of those which must flow from the total departure from and violation of a confoederation, which seems to have been created only to be the derision of the people, and the embarrassment of those whom they depute to rule.—What now excites *clamour* would then produce *commotion*, the unavailing complaints of individuals, rend the hearts of the honest man, the man of feeling and sentiment—but they touch not the callous multitude, who are secured from the effects of their resentment, by their imbecility.—But when a state, by paying its citizens becomes possessed of their claims, the style will be instantly changed.— It will be then do us justice, or we will pay ourselves.—The language of Massachusetts, when she became possessed of an overproportion of the paper currency, was but a feeble throb of a pulse, which would then beat with a convulsive strength.— The northern and middle states, among whom most of the paper money, and other continental securities now rest, might be tempted by their naval superiority to pay themselves out of the rich commerce of the Southern States, who would necessarily seek the protection of foreign nations.—What a prospect does this idea present for America?

Now let us turn our eyes to the ample western territory, which Britain has acknowledged by the late treaty, to be within our limits, and we shall find it one of the most fertile sources of endless discord and war between the different States. Will those States, who by their chartered boundaries are excluded from a participation of them, ever consent, by the laborious industry and toil of their citizens, to dig out of the earth their proportion of the expences of the war and general debt? When the States, who claim this country as within their chartered limits, may by the meer act of selling lands almost boundless, not only wipe out their proportion of the general debt, but in addition accumulate an immense public property? Will they not with an united voice, and the voice of truth alledge, that these lands were wrested from the Crown of England, for whose emolument, and not for the benefit of any class of citizens of these United States would they have been sold, but

for that revolution which has been effected by their joint expence of blood & treasure. On the other hand the States, who
claim under their charters, most considerable in number, and
incomparably so in power, will most probably contend for and
defend rights, which they asserted as early as the Confederation was proposed, and which seem to be established by the
unanimous concurrence of the States in that act of union.

This train of reasoning leads to a question, which strikes
home to the feelings, and will be decisive on the most essential
interests of the different States. It must now soon receive a
most serious agitation, whether one State will submit to be
taxed at the arbitrary will of another, which will be itself
exonerated in proportion to the burthen it imposes on its
neighbour; for this is the direct operation of imposts on trade,
laid for the separate emolument of the respective States. It
is a truth which has become familiar to minds, even the most
uninformed, that the consumer ultimately pays the tax on importation: The inhabitants then of those States, who are not
favoured with the natural advantages of commodious harbours,
must pay to their neighbours in the commercial States, whatever tax, they in their mercy and discretion may choose to load
them with;—and forced to make use of their ports, they may
with equal injustice be compelled to pay a tax (from which
they are to derive no benefit,) on every ounce of produce their
industry may raise for exportation: A revolution then effected
by joint efforts, has destroyed the general government, under
which taxes were collected for common benefit, and substituted
in its place separate Sovereignities, which are to exalt one part
of the Empire, to the utter depression and impoverishment of
the other.

The refinements of sophistry cannot suggest a distinction between that principle which requires a division of unappropri-
ated western lands between the States, and that which directs
a fair and equal participation of the blessings of our unbounded commerce among those, who fitting out originally on

the same ground, have made equal exertions in the common cause, and now demand an equal reward;—and yet so enveloped in the midst of state prejudices has Rhode Island been, that whilst she contended with an heated anxiety for the one, with a determined perseverance she opposed the other.

Let any rational man with this view ask, what reasonable hopes we can have of voluntarily discharging our *foreign debt;* that is a debt which can never be divided among the different States: First, the terms on which it has been contracted, expressly stipulate against any such apportionment, and secondly the confederal rule for affixing the quota of each State has never been applied—is despaired of as impracticable, and there remains but little prospect of the defect being remedied;—under these circumstances, in vain (I fear) will national honor plead the cause of honesty and justice.

Indeed it has already become a fashionable mark of independance of sentiment to depreciate the merit of France to whom the greatest portion of our foreign debt is due.—Ingratitude and injustice have ever went hand in hand!

Let vain speculatists, in the sequestered recess of study and retirement, invent frigid maxims of policy, and lay it down as an invariable rule, that States are actuated by self-interest alone.—Let them treat with ridicule all acknowledgement of national favors; still those who are conversant with human nature and public affairs, will despise the fallacious doctrine and illiberal tenet: They well know that men, whether at the head of governments or in private stations, still are *men,* subjected too, to the dominations, and acting under the influence of human passions and prejudices; and that in Monarchies more especially, the measures of State receive their tone from the virtues or vices of the Prince. Impressed with this unalterable truth, all true Whigs—friends to the freedom, independance, and honor of America, will for ever feel a glow of gratitude to that Monarch and that nation, who first espoused our hopeless cause with an enthusiastic fervor, and then with persevering assistance and magnanimous exertion protected our infant fortunes. They will feel the blush of indignant shame if France, or even Holland, should be compelled to have recourse to our commerce (as their last resource) for repayment: A measure ever in their power—which must be the result of disappointment in a regular and pacific mode—and which (if ever adopted) will record our *infamy* as well as our *impotence*.

6. Small Republics: A Constitution for Kentucky

Madison was chairman of the committee appointed by the Virginia Assembly to review the statehood petition of the Kentucky Convention of 1785. Kentuckians found that they could gain his support only if the terms of separation from the parent state did not release them from their federal ties or their financial obligations to Virginia. Several western leaders including Caleb Wallace, an old Princeton friend who had migrated to the Kentucky District in 1783, turned to Madison for expert guidance in forming a constitution for the future state. The Virginian's broad experience in state and continental affairs, and his reputation as a learned statesman, made him a natural consultant.

Viewing the constitutions of the several states as continuing experiments in republican government, Madison sorted out the most promising forms and marked the errors that he found,

---

Madison to Caleb Wallace, August 23, 1785, in *Writings*, II, pp. 166–177.

particularly in the Virginia system. In the end, he recognized, "local circumstances and opinions" would control many of the choices, and the changing situation of a young state would require later revision of the fundamental law. His brief and businesslike remarks to Wallace offer no profound thoughts on politics. Rather, they reflect the informed opinion of a moderate republican statesman of the 1780s who was searching for the institutional arrangements that would lend "*wisdom* and *steadiness*" to popular government, and secure the rights of liberty and property under majority rule.

Orange, August 23, 1785.

Dr Sir,—Your favour of the 12th of July was safely delivered to me by Mr. Craig. I accept with pleasure your proposed exchange of Western for Eastern intelligence and though I am a stranger to parental ties can sufficiently conceive the happiness of which they are a source to congratulate you on your possession of two fine sons & a Daughter. I do not smile at the Idea of transplanting myself into your wilderness. Such a change of my abode is not indeed probable yet I have no Local partialities which can keep me from any place which promises the greatest real advantages, but if such a removal was not even possible I should nevertheless be ready to communicate as you desire my Ideas towards a constitution of Government for the State in embryo. I pass over the general policy of the measure which calls for such a provision. It has been unanimously embraced by those who being most interested in it must have best considered it, & will I dare say be with equal unanimity acceded to by the other party which is to be consulted. I will first offer some general remarks on the Subject, & then answer your several queries.

1. *The Legislative Department* ought by all means, as I think to include a Senate constituted on such principles as will give *wisdom* and *steadiness* to legislation. The want of these

qualities is the grievance complained of in all our republics. The want of *fidelity* in the administration of power having been the grievance felt under most Governments, and by the American States themselves under the British Government, it was natural for them to give too exclusive an attention to this primary attribute. The Senate of Maryland with a few amendments is a good model. Trial has I am told verified the expectations from it. A Similar one made a part of our constitution as it was originally proposed but the inexperience & jealousy of our then Councils, rejected it in favor of our present Senate; a worse could hardly have been substituted & yet, bad as it is, it is often a useful bit in the mouth of the house of Delegates. Not a single Session passes without instances of sudden resolutions by the latter of which they repent in time to intercede privately with the Senate for their Negative. For the other branch models enough may be found; care ought however to be taken against its becoming too numerous, by fixing the number which it is never to exceed. The quorum, wages, and privileges of both branches ought also to be fixed. A majority seems to be the natural quorum. The wages of the members may be made payable for —— years to come in the medium value of wheat for years preceding as the same shall from period to period be rated by a respectable Jury appointed for that purpose by the Supreme Court. The privileges of the members ought not in my opinion to extend beyond an exemption of their persons and equipage from arrests during the time of their actual service. If it were possible it would be well to define the extent of the Legislative power but the nature of it seems in many respects to be indefinite. It is very practicable however to enumerate the essential exceptions. The Constitution may expressly restrain them from medling with religion— from abolishing Juries—from taking away the Habeas corpus —from forcing a citizen to give evidence against himself—from controuling the press—from enacting retrospective laws at least in criminal cases, from abridging the right of suffrage, from taking private property for public use without paying its full Value, from licensing the importation of Slaves, from infringing the confederation, &c &c.

As a further security against fluctuating & indigested laws the Constitution of New York has provided a Council of Revision. I approve much of such an institution & believe it is considered by the most intelligent citizens of that State as a valuable safeguard both to public interests & to private rights. Another provision has been suggested for preserving System in Legislative proceedings which to some may appear still better. It is that a standing committee composed of a few select & skilful individuals should be appointed to prepare bills on all subjects which they may judge proper to be submitted to the Legislature at their meetings & to draw bills for them during their Sessions. As an antidote both to the jealousy & danger of their acquiring an improper influence they might be made incapable of holding any other Office Legislative, Executive, or Judiciary. I like this Suggestion so much that I have had thoughts of proposing it to our Assembly, who give almost as many proofs as they pass laws of their need of some such Assistance.

2. *The Executive Department.* Though it claims the 2d place is not in my estimation entitled to it by its importance, all the great powers which are properly executive being transferred to the fœderal Government. I have made up no final opinion whether the first Magistrate should be chosen by the Legislature or the people at large or whether the power should be vested in one man assisted by a council or in a council of which the President shall be only primus inter pares. There are examples of each in the U. States and probably advantages & disadvantages attending each. It is material I think that the number of members should be small & that their Salaries should be either unalterable by the Legislature or alterable only in such manner as will not affect any individual in place. Our Execu-

tive is the worst part of a bad Constitution. The Members of it are dependent on the Legislature not only for their wages but for their reputation and therefore are not likely to withstand usurpations of that branch; they are besides too numerous and expensive, their organization vague & perplexed & to crown the absurdity some of the members may without any new appointment continue in Office for life contrary to one of the Articles of the Declaration of Rights.

3d. *The Judiciary Department* merits every care Its efficacy is Demonstrated in G. Brittain where it maintains private Right against all the corruptions of the two other departments & gives a reputation to the whole Government which it is not in itself entitled to. The main points to be attended to are 1. that the Judges should hold their places during good behavior 2. that their Salaries should be either fixed like the wages of the Representatives or not be alterable so as to affect the Individuals in office. 3. that their Salaries be liberal   The first point is obvious; without the second the independence aimed at by the first will be ideal only; without the 3d. the bar will be superior to the bench which destroys all security for a Systematick administration of Justice.   after securing these essential points, I should think it unadvisable to descend so far into detail as to bar any future Modification of this department which experience may recommend   An enumeration of the Principal courts with Power to the Legislature to Institute inferior Courts may suffice. The Admiralty business can never be extensive in your situation and may be referred to one of the other Courts. With regard to a Court of Chancery as distinct from a Court of Law, the reasons of Lord Bacon on the affirmative side outweigh in my Judgment those of Lord Kaims on the other side. Yet I should think it best to leave this important question to be decided by future lights without tying the hands of the Legislature one way or the other. I consider our county courts as on a bad footing and would never myself consent to copy them into another constitution.

All the States seem to have seen the necessity of providing for Impeachments but none of them to have hit on an unexceptionable Tribunal. In some the trial is referred to the Senate, in others to the Executive, in others to the Judiciary department. It has been suggested that a tribunal composed of members from each Department would be better than either and I entirely concur in that opinion. I proceed next to your queries.

1, "Whether is a representation according to numbers, or property, or in a joint proportion to both, the most Safe? or is a representation by counties preferable to a more equitable mode that will be difficult to adjust?" Under this question may be considered 1. the right of Suffrage. 2. the mode of suffrage. 3. the Plan of representation. As to the 1. I think the extent which ought to be given to this right a matter of great delicacy and of critical importance. To restrain it to the land holders will in time exclude too great a proportion of citizens; to extend it to all citizens without regard to property, or even to all who possess a pittance may throw too much power into hands which will either abuse it themselves or sell it to the rich who will abuse it. I have thought it might be a good middle course to narrow this right in the choice of the least popular, & to enlarge it in that of the more popular branch of the Legislature. There is an example of this Distinction in N. Carolina if in none of the other States. How it operates or is relished by the people I cannot say. It would not be surprising if in the outset at least it should offend the sense of equality which reigns in a free Country. In a general view I see no reason why the rights of property which chiefly bears the burden of Government & is so much an object of Legislation should not be respected as well as personal rights in the choice of Rulers. It must be owned indeed that property will give influence to the holder though it should give him no legal privileges and will in general be safe on that as well as on other Accounts especially if the business of legislation be guarded with the provisions hinted at. 2. As to the mode of suffrage I lean strongly to that of the ballot, notwithstanding the objections which lie against it   It appears to me to be the only radical cure for those arts of Electioneering which poison the very fountain of Liberty The States in which the Ballott has been the Standing mode are the only instances in which elections are tolerably chaste and those arts in disgrace. If it should be thought improper to fix this mode by the constitution I should think it at least necessary to avoid any constitutional bar to a future adoption of it.[1] 3. By the Plan of representation I mean 1. the classing of the Electors. 2. the proportioning of the representatives to each class. The first cannot be otherwise done than by geographical description as by Counties. The second may easily be done in the first instance either by comprising within each county an equal number of electors; or by proportioning the number of representatives of each county to its number of electors. The difficulty arises from the disproportionate increase of electors in different Counties. There seem to be two methods only by which the representation can be equalized from time to time. The 1st is to change the bounds of the counties; the 2d to change the number of representatives allotted to them respectively; as the former would not only be most troublesome & expensive but would involve a variety of other adjustments the latter method is evidently the best. Examples of a Constitutional provision for it exists in several of the States. In some it is to be executed periodically, in others, pro re nata. The latter seems most accurate and very practicable. I have already intimated the propriety of fixing the number of representatives, which ought never to be exceeded; I should suppose 150 or even 100, might safely be made the ne plus ultra for Kentucky

[1] The Constitution of N. York directs an experiment on this Subject. [Note in MS.]

2. "Which is to be preferred an Annual, Triennial, or Septennial Succession to Offices or frequent elections without limitations in choice or that officers when chosen should continue quamdiu se bene gesserint?" The rule ought no doubt to be different in the different Departments of power. For one part of the Legislature Annual Elections will I suppose be held indispensable though some of the ablest Statesmen & soundest Republicans in the U. States are in favor of triennial. The great Danger in departing from annual elections in this case lies in the want of some other natural term to limit the departure. For the other branch 4 or 5 years may be the period. For neither branch does it seem necessary or proper to prohibit an indefinite re-eligibility. With regard to the Executive if the elections be frequent & particularly if made as to any member of it by the people at large a re-eligibility cannot I think be objected to; if they be unfrequent, a temporary or perpetual incapacitation according to the degree of unfrequency at least in the case of the first Magistrate may not be amiss. As to the Judiciary department enough has been said & as to the Subordinate officers civil & Military nothing need be said more than that a regulation of their appointments may under a few restrictions be safely trusted to the Legislature.

3. "How far may the same person with propriety be employed in the different departments of Government in an infant country where the counsel of every individual may be needed?" Temporary deviations from fundamental principles are always more or less dangerous. When the first pretext fails, those who become interested in prolonging the evil will rarely be at a loss for other pretexts. The first precedent too familiarises the people to the irregularity, lessens their veneration for those fundamental principles, & makes them a more easy prey to ambition & self Interest. Hence it is that abuses of every kind when once established have been so often found to perpetuate themselves. In this caution I refer chiefly to an im-

proper mixture of the three great Departments within the State. A Delegation to Congress is I conceive compatible with either.

4. "Should there be a periodical review of the Constitution?" Nothing appears more eligible in theory nor has sufficient trial perhaps been yet made to condemn it in practice. Pennsylvania has alone adopted the expedient. Her citizens are much divided on the subject of their Constitution in general & probably on this part of it in particular. I am inclined to think though am far from being certain, that it is not a favorite part even with those who are fondest of their Constitution. Another plan has been thought of which might perhaps Succeed better and would at the same time be a safeguard to the equilibrium of the constituent Departments of Government. This is that a Majority of any two of the three departments should have authority to call a plenipotentiary convention whenever they may think their constitutional powers have been Violated by the other Department or that any material part of the Constitution needs amendment. In your situation I should think it both imprudent & indecent not to leave a door open for at least one revision of your first Establishment, imprudent because you have neither the same resources for supporting nor the same lights for framing a good establishment now as you will have 15 or 20 Years hence, indecent because an handful of early settlers ought not to preclude a populous Country from a choice of the Government under which they & their posterity are to live. Should your first Constitution be made thus temporary the objections against an intermediate union of offices will be proportionably lessened. Should a revision of it not be made thus necessary & certain there will be little probability of its being ever revised. Faulty as our Constitution is as well with regard to the Authority which formed it as to the manner in which it is formed, the Issue of an experiment has taught us the difficulty of amending it: & although the issue might have pro-

ceeded from the unseasonableness of the time yet it may be questioned whether at any future time the greater depth to which it will have stricken its roots will not counterbalance any more auspicious circumstances for overturning it.

5 & 6. "Or will it be better unalterably to fix some leading Principles in Government and make it consistant for the Legislature to introduce such changes in lesser matters as may become expedient? Can censors be provided that will impartially point out deficiencies in the Constitution & the Violations that may happen?"

Answers on these points may be gathered from what has been already said.

I have been led to offer my sentiments in this loose form rather than to attempt a delineation of such a Plan of government as would please myself not only by my Ignorance of many local circumstances & opinions which must be consulted in such a work but also by the want of sufficient time for it. At the receipt of your letter I had other employment and what I now write is in the midst of preparations for a Journey of business which will carry me as far as Philadelphia at least & on which I shall set out in a day or two.

I am sorry that it is not in my power to give you some satisfactory information concerning the Mississippi. A Minister from Spain has been with Congress for some time & is authorised as I understand to treat on whatever subjects may concern the two nations. If any explanations or propositions have passed between him & the Minister of Congress, they are as yet in the list of Cabinet Secrets. As soon as any such shall be made Public & come to my knowledge, I shall take the first opportunity of transmitting them. Wishing you & your family all happiness,

I am, DEAR SIR,

Your friend & servant.

The Constitutions of the several States were printed in a small Volume a year or two ago by order of Congress; a perusal of them need not be recommended to you. Having but a single copy I cannot supply you. It is not improbable that you may be already possessed of one. The revisal of our laws by Jefferson, Wythe & Pendleton beside their Value in improving the legal code may suggest something worthy of being attended to in framing a Constitution.

7. Further Thoughts on State Constitutions: Critique of Jefferson

In 1788, Kentuckians were again weighing plans for statehood. John Brown, another old Princetonian and a political leader of the Kentucky District, wrote to Madison that summer seeking further counsel. Fresh from his triumph at the Philadelphia Convention, Madison now ranked among the great men of the new republic. Specifically, Brown wanted Madison's judgment on the draft of a constitution for Virginia that Jefferson had composed in 1783 and later published with his *Notes on the State of Virginia*. Madison responded in October, 1788, with a respectful but critical commentary on his friend's plan. Plainly, even if his silence on many provisions implies assent, he considered it a flawed model for Virginia or Kentucky. The Jefferson draft, he argued, gave too little weight to the excesses of democracy, the evils of local spirit, the domination of the legislature over the other branches. Some of Jefferson's bolder innovations, Madison gently warned, "ought to be well con-

---

"Remarks on Mr. Jefferson's Draught of a Constitution," sent to John Brown, October [12], 1788, in *Writings*, V, pp. 284–294.

sidered." His views on such key points as senatorial stability and suffrage qualifications had not changed substantially since 1785, although he did modify some significant details of his earlier recommendations to Kentucky. (See Document 6.) Altogether, Madison's remarks on the political order of the small republics—the states—present instructive parallels to his more famous and important discussions of the national constitution in 1787–1788. (See Part II.)

REMARKS ON MR. JEFFERSON'S DRAUGHT OF A CONSTITUTION

SENATE.   The term of two years is too short. Six years are not more than sufficient. A Senate is to withstand the occasional impetuosities of the more numerous branch. The members ought therefore to derive a firmness from the tenure of their places. It ought to supply the defect of knowledge and experience incident to the other branch, there ought to be time given therefore for attaining the qualifications necessary for that purpose. It ought finally to maintain that system and steadiness in public affairs without which no Government can prosper or be respectable. This cannot be done by a body undergoing a frequent change of its members. A Senate for six years will not be dangerous to liberty, on the contrary it will be one of its best guardians. By correcting the infirmities of popular Government, it will prevent that disgust against that form which may otherwise produce a sudden transition to some very different one. It is no secret to any attentive & dispassionate observer of the political situation of the U. S., that the real danger to republican liberty has lurked in that cause.

The appointment of Senators by districts seems to be objectionable. A spirit of *locality* is inseparable from that mode. The evil is fully displayed in the County representations, the members of which are everywhere observed to lose sight of the aggregate interests of the Community, and even to sacrifice

them to the interests or prejudices of their respective constituents. In general these local interests are miscalculated. But it is
not impossible for a measure to be accommodated to the par-   *rep.*
ticular interests of every County or district, when considered
by itself, and not so, when considered in relation to each other
and to the whole State; in the same manner as the interests of
individuals may be very different in a state of nature and in a
Political union. The most effectual remedy for the local bias is
to impress on the minds of the Senators an attention to the
interest of the whole Society, by making them the choice of the
whole Society, each citizen voting for every Senator. The objection here is that the fittest characters would not be suffi-*constant*
ciently known to the people at large. But in free governments,   *to*
merit and notoriety of character are rarely separated, and such   *ant bods*
a regulation would connect them more and more together.
Should this mode of election be on the whole not approved,
that established in Maryland presents a valuable alternative.
The latter affords perhaps a greater security for the selection of
merit. The inconveniences chargeable on it are two: first that
the Council of electors favors cabal. Against this the shortness
of its existence is a good antidote, secondly that in a large State
the meeting of the Electors must be expensive if they be paid,
or badly attended if the service is onerous. To this it may be
answered that in a case of such vast importance, the expense,
which could not be great, ought to be disregarded. Whichever
of these modes may be preferred, it cannot be amiss so far to
admit the plan of districts as to restrain the choice to persons
residing in different parts of the State. Such a regulation will
produce a diffusive confidence in the Body, which is not less
necessary than the other means of rendering it useful. In a
State having large towns which can easily unite their votes the
precaution would be essential to an immediate choice by the
people at large. In Maryland no regard is paid to residence.
And what is remarkable vacancies are filled by the Senate itself. This last is an obnoxious expedient and cannot in any

point of view have much effect. It was probably meant to obviate the trouble of occasional meetings of the Electors. But the
purpose might have been otherwise answered by allowing the
unsuccessful candidates to supply vacancies according to the
order of their standing on the list of votes, or by requiring pro-
visional appointments to be made along with the positive ones.
If an election by districts be unavoidable and the ideas here
suggested be sound, the evil will be diminished in proportion to
the extent given to the districts, taking two or more Senators
from each district.

ELECTORS.   The first question arising here is how far
property ought to be made a qualification. There is a middle
way to be taken which corresponds at once with the Theory of
free Government and the lessons of experience. A freehold or
equivalent of a certain value may be annexed to the right of
voting for Senators, & the right left more at large in the election of the other House. Examples of this distinction may be
found in the Constitutions of several States, particularly if I
mistake not, of North Carolina & New York. This middle mode
reconciles and secures the two cardinal objects of Government; the rights of persons, and the rights of property. The
former will be sufficiently guarded by one branch, the latter
more particularly by the other. Give all power to property, and
the indigent will be oppressed. Give it to the latter and the
effect may be transposed. Give a defensive share to each and
each will be secure. The necessity of thus guarding the rights
of property was for obvious reasons unattended to in the commencement of the Revolution. In all the Governments which
were considered as beacons to republican Patriots & lawgivers
the rights of persons were subjected to those of property. The
poor were sacrificed to the rich. In the existing state of American population & American property the two classes of rights
were so little discriminated that a provision for the rights of
persons was supposed to include of itself those of property,
and it was natural to infer from the tendency of republican

laws, that these different interests would be more and more identified. Experience and investigation have however produced more correct ideas on this subject. It is now observed that in all populous countries, the smaller part only can be interested in preserving the rights of property. It must be foreseen that America, and Kentucky itself will by degrees arrive at this stage of Society that in some parts of the Union a very great advance is already made towards it. It is well understood that interest leads to injustice as well where the opportunity is presented to bodies of men as to individuals; to an interested majority in a Republic, as to the interested minority in any other form of Government. The time to guard against this danger is at the first forming of the Constitution, and in the present state of population when the bulk of the people have a sufficient interest in possession or in prospect to be attached to the rights of property, without being insufficiently attached to the rights of persons. Liberty not less than justice pleads for the policy here recommended. If *all* power be suffered to slide into hands not interested in the rights of property which must be the case whenever a majority fall under that description, one of two things cannot fail to happen; either they will unite against the other description and become the dupes & instruments of ambition, or their poverty & dependence will render them the mercenary instruments of wealth. In either case liberty will be subverted: in the first by a despotism growing out of anarchy, in the second, by an oligarchy founded on corruption.

The second question under this head is whether the ballot be not a better mode than that of voting viva voce. The comparative experience of the States pursuing the different modes is in favor of the first. It is found less difficult to guard against fraud in that than against bribery in the other.

EXCLUSIONS.   Does not The exclusion of Ministers of the Gospel as such violate a fundamental principle of liberty by punishing a religious profession with the privation of a civil right? does it [not] violate another article of the plan itself which exempts religion from the cognizance of Civil power? does it not violate justice by at once taking away a right and prohibiting a compensation for it? does it not in fine violate impartiality by shutting the door against the Ministers of one Religion and leaving it open for those of every other.

The re-eligibility of members after accepting offices of profit is so much opposed to the present way of thinking in America that any discussion of the subject would probably be a waste of time.

LIMITS OF POWER.   It is at least questionable whether death ought to be confined to "Treason and murder." It would not therefore be prudent to tie the hands of Government in the manner here proposed. The prohibition of pardon, however specious in theory, would have practical consequences which render it inadmissible. A single instance is a sufficient proof. The crime of treason is generally shared by a number, and often a very great number. It would be politically if not morally wrong to take away the lives of all even if every individual were equally guilty. What name would be given to a severity which made no distinction between the legal & the moral offence—between the deluded multitude and their wicked leaders. A second trial would not avoid the difficulty; because the oaths of the jury would not permit them to hearken to any voice but the inexorable voice of the law.

The power of the Legislature to appoint any other than their own officers departs too far from the Theory which requires a separation of the great Departments of Government. One of the best securities against the creation of unnecessary offices or tyrannical powers is an exclusion of the authors from all share in filling the one, or influence in the execution of the other. The proper mode of appointing to offices will fall under another head.

EXECUTIVE GOVERNOUR.   An election by the Legislature is liable to insuperable objections. It not only tends to faction intrigue and corruption, but leaves the Executive under the influence of an improper obligation to that department. An election by the people at large, as in this[1] & several other States —or by Electors as in the appointment of the Senate in Maryland, or, indeed, by the people through any other channel than their legislative representatives, seems to be far preferable. The ineligibility a second time, though not perhaps without advantages, is also liable to a variety of strong objections. It takes away one powerful motive to a faithful & useful administration, the desire of acquiring that title to a reappointment. By rendering a periodical change of men necessary, it discourages beneficial undertakings which require perseverance and system, or, as frequently happened in the Roman Consulate, either precipitates or prevents the execution of them. It may inspire desperate enterprises for the attainment of what is not attainable by legitimate means. It fetters the judgment and inclination of of the Community; and in critical moments would either produce a violation of the Constitution or exclude a choice [which] might be essential to the public safety. Add to the whole, that by putting the Executive Magistrate in the situation of the tenant of an unrenewable lease, it would tempt him to neglect the constitutional rights of his department, and to connive at usurpations by the Legislative department, with which he may connect his future ambition or interest.

The clause restraining the first magistrate from the immediate command of the military force would be made better by excepting cases in which he should receive the sanction of the two branches of the Legislature.

COUNCIL OF STATE.   The following variations are suggested. 1. The election to be made by the people immediately, or through some other medium than the Legislature.   2. A distributive choice should perhaps be secured as in the case of the Senate. 3. Instead of an ineligibility a second time, a ro-

---

[1] N. York, where these remarks were penned. [Madison's note]

tation in the federal Senate, with an abridgment of the term, to be substituted.

The appointment to offices is, of all the functions of Republican & perhaps every other form of Government, the most difficult to guard against abuse. Give it to a numerous body, and you at once destroy all responsibility, and create a perpetual source of faction and corruption. Give it to the Executive wholly, and it may be made an engine of improper influence and favoritism. Suppose the power were divided thus: let the Executive alone make all the subordinate appointments, and the Government and Senate, as in the Federal Constitution, those of the superior order. It seems particularly fit that the Judges, who are to form a distinct department should owe their offices partly to each of the other departments, rather than wholly to either.

JUDICIARY.   Much detail ought to be avoided in the Constitutional regulation of this Department, that there may be room for changes which may be demanded by the progressive changes in the state of our population. It is at least doubtful whether the number of Courts, the number of Judges, or even the boundaries of Jurisdiction ought to be made unalterable but by a revisal of the Constitution. The precaution seems no otherwise necessary than as it may prevent sudden modifications of the establishment, or addition of obsequious Judges, for the purpose of evading the checks of the Constitution & giving effect to some sinister policy of the Legislature. But might not the same object be otherwise attained? by prohibiting, for example, any innovations in those particulars without the consent of that department: or without the annual sanction of two or three successive Assemblies, over & above the other pre-requisites to the passage of a law.

The model here proposed for a Court of Appeals is not recommended by experience. It is found as might well be presumed that the members are always warped in their appellate decisions by an attachment to the principles and jurisdiction of their respective Courts, & still more so by the previous decision on the case removed by appeal. The only efficient cure for the evil is to form a Court of Appeals, of distinct and select Judges. The expence ought not to be admitted as an objection. 1. because the proper administration of Justice is of too essential a nature to be sacrificed to that consideration. 2. The number of interior judges might in that case be lessened. 3. The whole department may be made to support itself by a judicious tax on law proceedings.

The excuse for non-attendance would be a more proper subject of enquiry somewhere else than in the Court to which the party belonged. Delicacy, mutual convenience &c., would soon reduce the regulation to mere form; or if not, it might become a disagreeable source of little irritations among the members. A certificate from the local Court or some other local authority where the party might reside or happen to be detained from his duty, expressing the cause of absence as well as that it was judged to be satisfactory, might be safely substituted. Few Judges would improperly claim their wages, if such a formality stood in the way. These observations are applicable to the Council of State.

A Court of Impeachments is among the most puzzling articles of a Republican Constitution; and it is far more easy to point out defects in any plan than to supply a cure for them. The diversified expedients adopted in the Constitutions of the several States prove how much the compilers were embarrassed on this subject. The plan here proposed varies from all of them, and is perhaps not less than any a proof of the difficulties which pressed the ingenuity of its author. The remarks arising on it are 1. That it seems not to square with reason that the right to impeach should be united to that of trying the impeachment, & consequently in a proportional degree, to that of sharing in the appointment of, or influence on the Tribunal to which the trial may belong. 2. As the Executive & Judiciary would form a majority of the Court, and either have a right to impeach, too much might depend on a combination of these departments. This objection would be still stronger if the members of the Assembly were capable as proposed of holding offices, and were amenable in that capacity to the Court. 3. The House of Delegates and either of those departments could appoint a majority of the Court. Here is another danger of combination, and the more to be apprehended as that branch of Legislation would also have the right to impeach, a right in their hands of itself sufficiently weighty; and as the power of the Court would extend to the head of the Executive, by whose independence the constitutional rights of that department are to be secured against Legislative usurpations. 4. The dangers in the two last cases would be still more formidable, as the power extends not only to deprivation, but to future incapacity of office. In the case of all officers of sufficient importance to be objects of factious persecution, the latter branch of power is in every view of a delicate nature. In that of the Chief Magistrate it seems inadmissible, if he be chosen by the Legislature; and much more so, if immediately by the people themselves. A temporary incapacitation is the most that could be properly authorized.

The great desiderata in a Court of Impeachments are 1. impartiality. 2. respectability—the first in order to a right, the second in order to a satisfactory decision. These characteristics are aimed at in the following modification. Let the Senate be denied the right to impeach. Let ⅓ of the members be struck out, by alternate nominations of the prosecutors & party impeached; the remaining ⅔ to be the *stamen* of the Court. When the House of Delegates impeach let the Judges, or a certain proportion of them—and the Council of State be associated in the trials; when the Governor or Council impeaches, let the Judges only be associated; when the Judges impeach let the Council only be associated. But if the party impeached by the House of Delegates be a member of the Executive or Judiciary, let that of which he is a member not be associated. If the party impeached belong to one & be impeached by the other of these branches, let neither of them be associated, the decision being in this case left with the Senate alone; or if that be thought exceptionable, a few members might be added by the House of Delegates. ⅔ of the Court should in all cases be necessary to a conviction, & the Chief Magistrate *at least* should be exempt from a sentence of perpetual if not of temporary incapacity. It is extremely probable that a critical discussion of this outline may discover objections which do not occur. Some do occur; but appear not to be greater than are incident to any different modification of the Tribunal.

The establishment of trials by Jury & viva voce testimony in *all* cases and in *all* Courts, is, to say the least, a delicate experiment; and would most probably be either violated, or be found inconvenient.

COUNCIL OF REVISION. A revisionary power is meant as a check to precipitate, to unjust, and to unconstitutional laws. These important ends would it is conceded be more effectually secured, without disarming the Legislature of its requisite authority, by requiring bills to be separately communicated to the Executive & Judiciary Departments. If either of these object, let ⅔, if both ¾ of each House be necessary to overrule the objection; and if either or both protest against a bill as violating the Constitution, let it moreover be suspended notwithstanding the overruling proportion of the Assembly, until there shall have been a subsequent election of the House of Delegates and a re-passage of the bill by ⅔ or ¾ of both Houses, as the case may be. It should not be allowed the Judges or the Executive to pronounce a law thus enacted unconstitutional & invalid.

In the State Constitutions & indeed in the Federal one also, no provision is made for the case of a disagreement in expounding them; and as the Courts are generally the last in making the decision, it results to them by refusing or not refusing to execute a law, to stamp it with its final character.

This makes the Judiciary Department paramount in fact to the Legislature, which was never intended and can never be proper.

The extension of the Habeas Corpus to the cases in which it has been usually suspended, merits consideration at least. If there be emergencies which call for such a suspension, it can have no effect to prohibit it, because the prohibition will assuredly give way to the impulse of the moment; or rather, it will have the bad effect of facilitating other violations that may be less necessary. The Exemption of the press from liability in every case for *true facts* is also an innovation and as such ought to be well considered. This essential branch of liberty is perhaps in more danger of being interrupted by local tumults, or the silent awe of a predominant party, than by any direct attacks of Power.

Part Two

FOUNDING:
THE CRITICAL PERIOD

8. Lessons of History:
Of Ancient and Modern Confederacies

Through the 1780s Madison continued in the vanguard of the movement to strengthen federal authority over commerce, revenue, and foreign relations. By 1786 he was aiming at a federal convention as the last best hope of securing necessary amendments to the Articles of Confederation. In Virginia, he sponsored the call for the Annapolis Convention of September 1786 and there joined forces with his old nationalist ally, Hamilton, in recommending that Congress summon a convention of the states at Philadelphia to render the federal constitution "adequate to the exigencies of the Union."

Despite heavy political duties, Madison began a systematic course of preparation for the task of founding a new nation. At his request, Jefferson sent from Paris almost two hundred volumes, forming a model statesman's library. During the

---

"Of Ancient and Modern Confederacies," February–July 1786(?), in *Writings*, II, pp. 369–385. Lengthy quotations from sources have been omitted.

winter of 1785–1786, he combed the sources for instruction on confederate systems. The result was a manuscript pamphlet of descriptive and analytic notes that confirmed his own hard-earned judgment of the vices of confederacies. Ancient and modern, all tended to fly apart for lack of a supreme central authority. Madison would often draw upon these notes in arguing for the new constitution. Whole passages were incorporated into Numbers 18–20 of *The Federalist*. His systematic research into the nature and history of confederacies suggests the scholar's approach to politics. Yet one must remember that he used his studies as a man of action seeking ammunition for his cause, and that the chief lesson he derived from history and philosophy was the need to create a novel design for republican union in America. As Publius the Roman-Federalist put it, the history of past confederations can furnish "no other light than that of beacons, which give warning of the course to be shunned, without pointing out that which ought to be pursued." (See *The Federalist* No. 37, Document 12.)

The most heavily used references in Madison's notes were thirty-seven volumes of the *Encyclopédie Méthodique,* the great French summa of Enlightenment thought, and the thirteen volumes of Felice's *Code de l'Humanité,* both supplied by Jefferson.

LYCIAN CONFEDERACY.

In this confederacy, the number of votes allotted to each member was proportioned to its pecuniary contributions. The Judges and town magistrates were elected by the general authority in like proportion.

See Montesquieu, who prefers this mode. [*L'Esprit des Lois,* 1748.]

The name of a federal republic may be refused to Lycia, which Montesquieu cites as an example in which the importance of the members determined the proportion of their votes in the general councils. The Grison League is a juster example. —Code de l'Humanité. Confederation. . . .

AMPHICTYONIC CONFEDERACY.

Instituted by Amphictyon, son of Deucalion, King of Athens, 1522 years Ant. Christ.—Code de l'Humanité.

Seated first at Thermopylæ, then at Delphos, afterwards at these places alternately. It met half yearly, to wit, in the Spring and Fall, besides extraordinary occasions.—Id. In the latter meetings, all such of the Greeks as happened to be at Delphos on a religious errand were admitted to deliberate, but not to vote.—Encyclopedie.

The number and names of the confederated cities differently reported. The union seems to have consisted originally of the Delphians and their neighbors only, and by degrees to have comprehended all Greece. 10, 11, 12, are the different numbers of original members mentioned by different authors.—Code de l'Humanité.

Each city sent two deputies; one to attend particularly to Religious matters, the other to civil and criminal matters affecting individuals; both to decide on matters of a general nature.—Id. Sometimes more than two were sent, but they had two votes only.—Encyclopedie.

The Amphictyons took an oath mutually to defend and protect the united cities, to inflict vengeance on those who should sacrilegiously despoil the temple of Delphos, to punish the violators of this oath, and never to divert the water-courses of any of the Amphictyonic cities, either in peace or in war.— Code de l'Humanité. Æschines orat. vs. Ctesiphontem.

The Amphictyonic Council was instituted by way of defence and terror against the Barbarians.—Dictionaire de Treviux.

Federal Authority.

The Amphictyons had full power to propose and resolve whatever they judged useful to Greece.—Encyclopedie Pol. Œcon.

1. They judged in the last resort all differences between the Amphictyonic cities.—Code de l'Humanité.

2. Mulcted the aggressors.—Id.

3. Employed whole force of Greece against such as refused to execute its decrees.—Id., and Plutarch, *Cimon*.

4. Guarded the immense Riches of the Temple at Delphos, and decided controversies between the inhabitants and those who came to consult the Oracle.—Encyclopedie.

5. Superintended the Pythian games.—Code de l'Humanité.

6. Exercised right of admitting new members.—(See decree admitting Philip, in Demosthenes on Crown.)

7. Appointed General of the federal troops, with full powers to carry their decrees into execution.—Ibid.

8. Declared and carried on war.—Code de l'Humanité.

Strabo says that the Council of the Amphictyons was dissolved in the time of Augustus; but Pausanias, who lived in the time of Antoninus Pius, says it remained entire then, and that the number of Amphictyons was thirty.—Potter's Grecian Antiquities, vol. 1, pa. 90.

The institution declined on the admission of Philip, and in the time of the Roman Emperors the functions of the council were reduced to the administration and police of the Temple. This limited authority expired only with the Pagan Religion.— Code de l'Humanité.

Vices of the Constitution.

It happened but too often that the Deputies of the strongest cities awed and corrupted those of the weaker, and that Judgment went in favor of the most powerful party.—Id. See also, Plutarch: Themistocles.

Greece was the victim of Philip. If her confederation had been stricter, and been persevered in, she would never have yielded to Macedon, and might have proved a Barrier to the vast projects of Rome.—Code de l'Humanité.

Philip had two votes in the Council.—[Raleigh] History of the World, lib. 4, c. 1, Sect. 7.

The execution of the Amphictyonic powers was very different from the Theory.—Id. It did not restrain the parties from warring against each other. Athens and Sparta were members during their conflicts. Quer.: Whether Thucydides or Xenophon, in their Histories, ever allude to the Amphictyonic authority, which ought to have kept the peace?—See Gillies' History of Greece, particularly vol. II, p. 345. . . .

BELGIC CONFEDERACY.

Established in 1679, by the Treaty called the Union of Utrecht.—Code de l'Humanité.

The provinces came into this Union slowly. Guelderland, the smallest of them, made many difficulties. Even some of the Cities and Towns pretended to annex conditions to their acceding.—Id.

When the Union was originally established, a committee, composed of deputies from each province, was appointed to regulate affairs, and to convoke the provinces according to article XIX of the Treaty. Out of this Committee grew the States General, (Id.,) who, strictly speaking, are only the Representatives of the States General, who amount to 800 members.—Temple, [*Remarks on the United Provinces*] p. 112.

The number of Deputies to the States General from each province not limited, but have only a single voice. They amount commonly, altogether, to 40 or 50. They hold their seats, some for life, some for 6, 3, and 1 years, and those of Groningen and Overyssel during pleasure. They are paid, but very moderately, by their respective constituents, and are amenable to their

Tribunals only.—Code de l'Humanité. No military man is deputable to the States General.—Id.

Ambassadors of Republic have session and deliberation, but no suffrage in States General—Id. The grand pensioner of Holland, as ordinary deputy from Holland, attends always in the States General, and makes the propositions of that province to States General.—Id.

They sit constantly at the Hague since 1593, and every day in the week except Saturday and Sunday. The States of Holland, in granting this residence, reserve, by way of protestation, the rights, the honors, and prerogatives, belonging to them as sovereigns of the province, yielding the States General only a rank in certain public ceremonies.—Id.

The eldest deputy from each province presides for a week by turns. The President receives letters, &c., from the Ministers of the Republic at foreign Courts, and of foreign Ministers residing at the Hague, as well as of all petitions presented to the Assembly; all which he causes to be read by the Secretary.—Id.

The Secretary, besides correcting and recording the Resolutions, prepares and despatches instructions to Ministers abroad, and letters to foreign powers. He assists, also, at conferences held with foreign Ministers, *and there gives his voice*. He has a deputy when there is not a second Secretary. The agent of the States General is charged with the Archives, and is also employed on occasions of receiving foreign Ministers or sending Messages to them.—Id.

Federal Authority.

The avowed objects of the Treaty of Union: 1. To fortify the Union. 2. To repel the common enemy.—Id.

The Union is to be perpetual in the same manner as if the Confederates formed one province only, without prejudice, however, to the privileges and rights of each province and City.—Id.

Differences between provinces and between cities are to be

settled by the ordinary Judges, by arbitration, by amicable agreement, without the interference of other provinces, otherwise than by way of accommodation. The Stadholder is to decide such differences in the last resort.—Id.

No change to be made in the articles of Union without unanimous consent of the parties, and everything done contrary to them to be null and void.—Id.

States General.

1. Execute, without consulting their constituents, treaties and alliances already formed.—Id.

2. Take oaths from Generals and Governors, and appoint Field Deputies.

3. The collection of duties on imports and exports, and the expedition of safe conducts, are in their name and by their officers.—Id.

4. They superintend and examine accounts of the E. India Company.—Id.

5. Inspect the Mint, appoint les Maitres de la Monnoye, fix la taille and la valeur of the coin, having always regard to the regular rights of the provinces within their own Territories.—Id.

6. Appoint a Treasurer General and Receiver General of the Quotas furnished by the provinces.—Id.

7. Elect, out of a double nomination, the fiscal and other officers within the departments of the admiralties, except that the High officers of the fleet are appointed by the Admiral General, to whom the maritime provinces have ceded this right.—Id. The Navy, supported by duties on foreign trade, appropriated thereto by the maritime provinces, for the benefit of the whole Republic.—Id.

8. They govern as sovereigns the dependent territories, according to the several capitulations.—Id.

9. They form Committees of their own body, of a member from each deputation, for foreign affairs, finances, marine, and other matters. At all these conferences the Grand Pensioner

of Holland and the secretary of the States General attend, and have a deciding voice.—Id.

10. Appoint and receive Ambassadors, negociate with foreign powers, deliberate on war, peace, alliances, the raising forces, care of fortifications, military affairs *to a certain degree,* the equipment of fleets, building of ships, directions concerning money.—Id. But they can neither make peace, nor war, nor truces, nor treaties, nor raise troops, nor impose taxes, nor do other acts requiring unanimity, without consulting and obtaining the sanction of the Provinces.—Id. Coining money also requires unanimity and express sanction of provinces.—Temple. Repealing an old law on same footing.—Burrish. Batavia illustrata. In points not enumerated in this article, plurality of voices decides.—Code de l'Humanité.

11. Composition and publication of edicts and proclamations relative both to the objects expressed in the articles of union and to the measures taken for the common good, are in the name of the States; and although they are addressed to the States of the Provinces, who announce them with their sanction, still it is in the name of the States General that obedience is required of all the inhabitants of the Provinces.—Code de l'Humanité.

The Provinces have reserved to themselves—

1. Their sovereignty within their own limits in general.—Code de l'Humanité.

2. The right of coining money, as essential to sovereignty; but agreed, at the same time, that the money which should be current throughout the Republic should have the same intrinsic value. To give effect to which regulation a mint is established at the Hague, under a chamber which has the inspection of all money struck, either in name of States General or particular provinces, as also of foreign coin.—Id. Coining money not in provinces or cities, but in the generality of union, by common agreement.—Temple.

3. Every province raises what money and by what means it pleases, and sends its quota to Receiver General.—Temple.

The quotas were not settled without great difficulty.—Id.

4. The naming to Governments of Towns within themselves; keeping keys, and giving word to Magistrates; a power over troops in all things not military; conferring Colonel's commissions and inferior posts in such Regiments as are paid by the provinces; respectively taking oath of fidelity; concerning a revocation of all which the States General are not permitted to deliberate.—Id.

The provinces are restricted—

1. From entering into any foreign treaties without consent of the rest.—Code de l'Humanité.

2. From establishing imposts prejudicial to others without general consent.—Id.

3. From charging their neighbors with higher duties than their own subjects.—Id.

Council of State composed of deputies from the provinces, in different proportions. 3 of them are for life; the rest generally for 3 years; they vote per capita.—Temple.

They are subordinate to the States General, who frequently, however, consult with them. In matters of war which require secrecy they act of themselves. Military and fiscal matters are the objects of their administration.

They execute the Resolutions of the States General, propose requisitions of men and money, and superintend the fortifications, &c., and the affairs, revenues, and Governments, of the conquered possessions.—Temple.

Chamber of Accounts was erected for the ease of the Council of State. It is subordinate to the States General; is composed of two deputies from each province, who are changed triennially. They examine and state all accounts of the several Receivers; controul and register orders of Council of State disposing of the finances.—Id.

College of Admiralty, established by the States General, 1597, is subdivided into five, of which three are in Holland, one in Zealand, one in Friezland, each composed of seven deputies, for appointed by the province where the admiralty resides, and three by the other provinces. The vice admiral presides in all of them when he is present.—Temple.

They take final cognizance of all crimes and prizes at sea; —— —— —— —— of all frauds in customs; provide quota of fleets resolved on by States General; appoint Captains and superior officers of each squadron; take final cognizance, also, of civil matters within 600 florins, an appeal lying to States General for matters beyond that sum.—Code de l'Humanité and Temple.

The authority of States General in Admiralty Department is much limited by the influence and privileges of maritime provinces, and the jurisdiction herein is full of confusion and contradiction.—Code de l'Humanité.

Stadtholder, who is now hereditary, in his *political* capacity is authorized—

1. To settle differences between provinces, provisionally, till other methods can be agreed on, which having never been, this prerogative may be deemed a permanent one.—Code de l'Humanité.

2. Assists at deliberations of States General and their particular conferences; recommends and influences appointment of Ambassadors.—Id.

3. Has seat and suffrage in Council of State.—Id.

4. Presiding in the provincial Courts of Justice, where his name is prefixed to all public acts.—Id.

5. Supreme Creator of most of the Universities.—Id.

6. As Stadtholder of the provinces, has considerable rights partaking of the sovereignty; as appointing town magistrates, on presentation made to him of a certain number. Executing provincial decrees, &c.—Id. and Mably, Etude de l'histoire.

7. Gives audiences to Ambassadors, and may have agents with their Sovereigns for his private affairs.—Mably Ibid.

8. Exercises power of pardon.—Temple.

In his *Military* capacity as Captain General—

1. Commands forces; directs marches; provides for garrisons; and, in general, regulates military affairs.—Code de l'Humanité.

2. Disposes of all appointments, from Ensigns to Colonels. The Council of State having surrendered to him the appointments within their disposal, (Id.,) and the States General appoint the higher grades on his recommendation.—Id.

3. Disposes of the Governments, &c., of the fortified towns, through the commissions issue from the States General.—Id.

In his *Marine* capacity as Admiral General—

1. Superintends and directs everything relative to naval forces and other affairs within Admiralty.—Id.

2. Presides in the admiralties in person or by proxy.—Id.

3. Appoints Lieutenant Admirals and officers under them.—Id.

4. Establishes Councils of war, whose sentences are in the name of the States General and his Highness, and are not executed till he approves.—Id.

The Stadtholder has a general and secret influence on the great machine which cannot be defined.—Id.

His revenue from appointments amounts to 300,000 florins, to which is to be added his extensive patrimonies.—Id.

The standing army of the Republic, 40,000 men.

Vices of the Constitution.

The Union of Utrecht imports an authority in the States General seemingly sufficient to secure harmony; but the jealousy in each province of its sovereignty renders the practice very different from the Theory.—Code de l'Humanité.

It is clear that the delay occasioned by recurring to seven independent provinces, including about 52 voting Cities, &c., is a vice in the Belgic Republic which exposes it to the most fatal inconveniences. Accordingly, the fathers of their country have endeavored to remedy it, in the extraordinary assemblies of the States General in 1584, in 1651, 1716, 1717, but, unhappily, without effect. This vice is, notwithstanding, deplorable.—Id. Among other evils, it gives foreign Ministers the means of arresting the most important deliberations by gaining a single Province or City. This was done by France in 1726, when the Treaty of Hanover was delayed a whole year. In 1688 the States concluded a Treaty of themselves, but at the risk of their heads.—Id. It is the practice, also, in matters of contribution or subsidy, to pass over this article of the Union; for where delay would be dangerous, the consenting provinces furnish their quotas without waiting for the others; but by such means the Union is weakened, and, if often repeated, must be dissolved.—Id.

Foreign Ministers elude matters taken ad referendum, by tampering with the Provinces and Cities.—Temple, p. 116.

Treaty of Union obliges each Province to levy certain contributions. But this article never could and probably never will be executed, because the inland provinces, who have little commerce, cannot pay an equal Quota.—Burrish. Bat. illustrat.

Deputations from agreeing to disagreeing Provinces frequent.—Temple.

It is certain that so many independent corps and interests could not be kept together without such a center of union as the Stadtholdership, as has been allowed and repeated in so many solemn acts.—Code de l'Humanité.

In the intermission of the Stadtholdership, Holland, by her riches and authority, which drew the others into a sort of dependence, supplied the place.—Temple.

With such a Government the Union never could have subsisted, if, in effect, the provinces had not within themselves a spring capable of quickening their tardiness and impelling them to the same way of thinking. This spring is the Stadtholder. His prerogatives are immense—1, &c., &c. A strange effect of human contradictions. Men too jealous to confide their liberty to their representatives, who are their equals, abandoned it to a Prince, who might the more easily abuse it, as the affairs of the Republic were important, and had not then fixed themselves.—Mably Etude D'Histoire, 205—6.

Grotius has said that the hatred of his countrymen against the House of Austria kept them from being destroyed by the vices of their Constitution.—Ibid.

The difficulty of procuring unanimity has produced a breach of fundamentals in several instances. Treaty of Westphalia was concluded without consent of Zealand, &c.—D'Albon and Temple. These tend to alter the constitution.—D'Albon.

It appears by several articles of the Union that the confederates had formed the design of establishing a General tax, [Impôt,] to be administered by the States General. But this design, so proper for bracing this happy Union, has not been executed.—Code de l'Humanité. . . .

9. Diagnosis of the American Confederacy: A Critical Case

After the Annapolis meetings of October 1786, Madison pursued the project of a constitutional convention with all his energies. In December he introduced resolutions in the Virginia Assembly calling for the appointment of delegates to Philadelphia and readily accepted a place on the list. Attending the Confederation Congress in New York, Madison used the winter and spring of 1787 to prepare himself and his political friends for the test of Philadelphia. The studies and experiences of a decade were drawn to a sharp focus in his manuscript notes, "Vices of the Political System of the United States," completed in April. His diagnosis of the ills of the Confederacy and his general prescriptions for a new regime epitomize the case that he would argue at the Convention, in the pages of *The Federalist,* and in scores of letters to American political leaders. The famous argument of *Federalist* No. 10 on factions and the large republic had already taken clear form in these

"Vices of the Political System of the United States," April, 1787, in *Writings,* II, pp. 361–369.

notes. Madison's sense of impending chaos, heightened by Shays' rebellion in Massachusetts, closed off serious consideration of any remedies short of creating "one sovereign power" under a new constitution.

VICES OF THE POLITICAL SYSTEM OF THE UNITED STATES.
APRIL 1787.

1. FAILURE OF THE STATES TO COMPLY WITH THE CONSTITUTIONAL REQUISITIONS.   This evil has been so fully experienced both during the war and since the peace, results so naturally from the number and independent authority of the States and has been so uniformly exemplified in every similar Confederacy, that it may be considered as not less radically and permanently inherent in than it is fatal to the object of the present system.

2. ENCROACHMENTS BY THE STATES ON THE FEDERAL AUTHORITY.   Examples of this are numerous and repetitions may be foreseen in almost every case where any favorite object of a State shall present a temptation. Among these examples are the wars and treaties of Georgia with the Indians. The unlicensed compacts between Virginia and Maryland, and between Pennsylvania & New Jersey—the troops raised and to be kept up by Massachusetts.

3. VIOLATIONS OF THE LAW OF NATIONS AND OF TREATIES. From the number of Legislatures, the sphere of life from which most of their members are taken, and the circumstances under which their legislative business is carried on, irregularities of this kind must frequently happen. Accordingly not a year has passed without instances of them in some one or other of the States. The Treaty of Peace—the treaty with France—the treaty with Holland have each been violated. [See the complaints to Congress on these subjects.] The causes of these irregularities must necessarily produce frequent violations of the law of nations in other respects.

As yet foreign powers have not been rigorous in animadverting on us. This moderation, however cannot be mistaken for a permanent partiality to our faults, or a permanent security against those disputes with other nations, which being among the greatest of public calamities, it ought to be least in the power of any part of the community to bring on the whole.

4. TRESPASSES OF THE STATES ON THE RIGHTS OF EACH OTHER. These are alarming symptoms, and may be daily apprehended as we are admonished by daily experience. See the law of Virginia restricting foreign vessels to certain ports—of Maryland in favor of vessels belonging to her *own citizens*—of New York in favor of the same—

Paper money, instalments of debts, occlusion of Courts, making property a legal tender, may likewise be deemed aggressions on the rights of other States. As the Citizens of every State aggregately taken stand more or less in the relation of Creditors or debtors, to the Citizens of every other State, Acts of the debtor State in favor of debtors, affect the Creditor State, in the same manner as they do its own citizens who are relatively creditors towards other citizens. This remark may be extended to foreign nations. If the exclusive regulation of the value and alloy of coin was properly delegated to the federal authority, the policy of it equally requires a controul on the States in the cases above mentioned. It must have been meant 1. to preserve uniformity in the circulating medium throughout the nation. 2. to prevent those frauds on the citizens of other States, and the subjects of foreign powers, which might disturb the tranquility at home, or involve the Union in foreign contests.

The practice of many States in restricting the commercial intercourse with other States, and putting their productions and manufacturers on the same footing with those of foreign nations, though not contrary to the federal articles, is certainly adverse to the spirit of the Union, and tends to beget retaliating regulations, not less expensive and vexatious in themselves than they are destructive of the general harmony.

5. WANT OF CONCERT IN MATTERS WHERE COMMON INTEREST REQUIRES IT. This defect is strongly illustrated in the state of our commercial affairs. How much has the national dignity, interest, and revenue, suffered from this cause? Instances of inferior moment are the want of uniformity in the laws concerning naturalization & literary property; of provision for national seminaries, for grants of incorporation for national purposes, for canals and other works of general utility, which may at present be defeated by the perverseness of particular States whose concurrence is necessary.

6. WANT OF GUARANTY TO THE STATES OF THEIR CONSTITUTIONS & LAWS AGAINST INTERNAL VIOLENCE. The confederation is silent on this point and therefore by the second article the hands of the federal authority are tied. According to Republican Theory, Right and power being both vested in the majority, are held to be synonimous. According to fact and experience a minority may in an appeal to force, be an overmatch for the majority. 1. if the minority happen to include all such as possess the skill and habits of military life, & such as possess the great pecuniary resources, one-third only may conquer the remaining two-thirds. 2. one-third of those who participate in the choice of the rulers, may be rendered a majority by the accession of those whose poverty excludes them from a right of suffrage, and who for obvious reasons will be more likely to join the standard of sedition than that of the established Government. 3. where slavery exists the republican Theory becomes still more fallacious.

7. WANT OF SANCTION TO THE LAWS, AND OF COERCION IN THE GOVERNMENT OF THE CONFEDERACY. A sanction is essential to the idea of law, as coercion is to that of Government. The federal system being destitute of both, wants the great vital principles of a Political Constitution. Under the form of

such a constitution, it is in fact nothing more than a treaty of amity of commerce and of alliance, between independent and Sovereign States. From what cause could so fatal an omission have happened in the articles of Confederation? from a mistaken confidence that the justice, the good faith, the honor, the sound policy, of the several legislative assemblies would render superfluous any appeal to the ordinary motives by which the laws secure the obedience of individuals: a confidence which does honor to the enthusiastic virtue of the compilers, as much as the inexperience of the crisis apoligizes for their errors. The time which has since elapsed has had the double effect, of increasing the light and tempering the warmth, with which the arduous work may be revised. It is no longer doubted that a unanimous and punctual obedience of 13 independent bodies, to the acts of the federal Government ought not to be calculated on. Even during the war, when external danger supplied in some degree the defect of legal & coercive sanctions, how imperfectly did the States fulfill their obligations to the Union? In time of peace, we see already what is to be expected. How indeed could it be otherwise? In the first place, Every general act of the Union must necessarily bear unequally hard on some particular member or members of it, secondly the partiality of the members to their own interests and rights, a partiality which will be fostered by the courtiers of popularity, will naturally exaggerate the inequality where it exists, and even suspect it where it has no existence, thirdly a distrust of the voluntary compliance of each other may prevent the compliance of any, although it should be the latent disposition of all. Here are causes & pretexts which will never fail to render federal measures abortive. If the laws of the States were merely recommendatory to their citizens, or if they were to be rejudged by County authorities, what security, what probability would exist, that they would be carried into execution? Is the security or probability greater in favor of the acts of Congress which depending for their execution on the will of the State legislatures, which are tho' nominally authoritative, in fact recommendatory only?

8. WANT OF RATIFICATION BY THE PEOPLE OF THE ARTICLES OF CONFEDERATION. In some of the States the Confederation is recognized by, and forms a part of the Constitution. In others however it has received no other sanction than that of the legislative authority. From this defect two evils result: 1. Whenever a law of a State happens to be repugnant to an act of Congress, particularly when the latter [former] is of posterior date to the former, [latter] it will be at least questionable whether the latter [former] must not prevail; and as the question must be decided by the Tribunals of the State, they will be most likely to lean on the side of the State.

2. As far as the union of the States is to be regarded as a league of sovereign powers, and not as a political Constitution by virtue of which they are become one sovereign power, so far it seems to follow from the doctrine of compacts, that a breach of any of the articles of the Confederation by any of the parties to it, absolves the other parties from their respective Obligations, and gives them a right if they chuse to exert it, of dissolving the Union altogether.

9. MULTIPLICITY OF LAWS IN THE SEVERAL STATES. In developing the evils which viciate the political system of the U.S., it is proper to include those which are found within the States individually, as well as those which directly affect the States collectively, since the former class have an indirect influence on the general malady and must not be overlooked in forming a compleat remedy. Among the evils then of our situation may well be ranked the multiplicity of laws from which no States is exempt. As far as laws are necessary to mark with precision the duties of those who are to obey them, and to take from those who are to administer them a discretion which might be abused, their number is the price of liberty. As far

as laws exceed this limit, they are a nuisance; a nuisance of the most pestilent kind. Try the Codes of the several States by this test, and what a luxuriancy of legislation do they present. The short period of independency has filled as many pages as the century which preceded it. Every year, almost every session, adds a new volume. This may be the effect in part, but it can only be in part, of the situation in which the revolution has placed us. A review of the several Codes will shew that every necessary and useful part of the least voluminous of them might be compressed into one tenth of the compass, and at the same time be rendered ten fold as perspicuous.

10. MUTABILITY OF THE LAWS OF THE STATES. This evil is intimately connected with the former yet deserves a distinct notice, as it emphatically denotes a vicious legislation. We daily see laws repealed or superseded, before any trial can have been made of their merits, and even before a knowledge of them can have reached the remoter districts within which they were to operate. In the regulations of trade this instability becomes a snare not only to our citizens, but to foreigners also.

11. INJUSTICE OF THE LAWS OF THE STATES. If the multiplicity and mutability of laws prove a want of wisdom, their injustice betrays a defect still more alarming: more alarming not merely because it is a greater evil in itself; but because it brings more into question the fundamental principle of republican Government, that the majority who rule in such governments are the safest Guardians both of public Good and private rights. To what causes is this evil to be ascribed?

These causes lie 1. in the Representative bodies. 2. in the people themselves.

1. Representative appointments are sought from 3 motives. 1. ambition. 2. personal interest. 3. public good. Unhappily the two first are proved by experience to be most prevalent. Hence the candidates who feel them, particularly, the second, are

most industrious, and most successful in pursuing their object: and forming often a majority in the legislative Councils, with interested views, contrary to the interest and views of their constituents, join in a perfidious sacrifice of the latter to the former. A succeeding election it might be supposed, would displace the offenders, and repair the mischief. But how easily are base and selfish measures, masked by pretexts of public good and apparent expediency? How frequently will a repetition of the same arts and industry which succeeded in the first instance, again prevail on the unwary to misplace their confidence?

How frequently too will the honest but unenlightened representative be the dupe of a favorite leader, veiling his selfish views under the professions of public good, and varnishing his sophistical arguments with the glowing colours of popular eloquence?

2. A still more fatal if not more frequent cause, lies among the people themselves. All civilized societies are divided into different interests and factions, as they happen to be creditors or debtors—rich or poor—husbandmen, merchants or manufacturers—members of different religious sects—followers of different political leaders—inhabitants of different districts—owners of different kinds of property &c &c. In republican Government the majority however composed, ultimately give the law. Whenever therefore an apparent interest or common passion unites a majority what is to restrain them from unjust violations of the rights and interests of the minority, or of individuals? Three motives only 1. a prudent regard to their own good as involved in the general and permanent good of the community. This consideration although of decisive weight in itself, is found by experience to be too often unheeded. It is often forgotten, by nations as well as by individuals, that honesty is the best policy. 2dly. respect for character. However strong this motive may be in individuals, it is considered as

very insufficient to restrain them from injustice. In a multitude its efficacy is diminished in proportion to the number which is to share the praise or the blame. Besides, as it has reference to public opinion, which within a particular Society, is the opinion of the majority, the standard is fixed by those whose conduct is to be measured by it. The public opinion without the Society will be little respected by the people at large of any Country. Individuals of extended views, and of national pride, may bring the public proceedings to this standard, but the example will never be followed by the multitude. Is it to be imagined that an ordinary citizen or even Assemblyman of Rhode Island in estimating the policy of paper money, ever considered or cared, in what light the measure would be viewed in France or Holland; or even in Massachusetts or Connecticut? It was a sufficient temptation to both that it was for their interest; it was a sufficient sanction to the latter that it was popular in the State; to the former, that it was so in the neighbourhood. 3dly. will Religion the only remaining motive be a sufficient restraint? It is not pretended to be such on men individually considered. Will its effect be greater on them considered in an aggregate view? quite the reverse. The conduct of every popular assembly acting on oath, the strongest of religious ties, proves that individuals join without remorse in acts, against which their consciences would revolt if proposed to them under the like sanction, separately in their closets. When indeed Religion is kindled into enthusiasm, its force like that of other passions, is increased by the sympathy of a multitude. But enthusiasm is only a temporary state of religion, and while it lasts will hardly be seen with pleasure at the helm of Government. Besides as religion in its coolest state is not infallible, it may become a motive to oppression as well as a restraint from injustice. Place three individuals in a situation wherein the interest of each depends on the voice of the others; and give to two of them an interest opposed to the rights of the third. Will the latter be secure? The prudence of every man would shun the danger. The rules & forms of justice suppose & guard against it. Will two thousand in a like situation be less likely to encroach on the rights of one thousand? The contrary is witnessed by the notorious factions & oppressions which take place in corporate towns limited as the opportunities are, and in little republics when uncontrouled by apprehensions of external danger. If an enlargement of the sphere is found to lessen the insecurity of private rights, it is not because the impulse of a common interest or passion is less predominant in this case with the majority; but because a common interest or passion is less apt to be felt and the requisite combinations less easy to be formed by a great than by a small number. The Society becomes broken into a greater variety of interests, of pursuits of passions, which check each other, whilst those who may feel a common sentiment have less opportunity of communication and concert. It may be inferred that the inconveniences of popular States, contrary to the prevailing Theory, are in proportion not to the extent, but to the narrowness of their limits.

The great desideratum in Government is such a modification of the sovereignty as will render it sufficiently neutral between the different interests and factions, to controul one part of the society from invading the rights of another, and at the same time sufficiently controuled itself, from setting up an interest adverse to that of the whole Society. In absolute Monarchies the prince is sufficiently nuetral towards his subjects, but frequently sacrifices their happiness to his ambition or his avarice. In small Republics, the sovereign will is sufficiently controuled from such a sacrifice of the entire Society, but is not sufficiently neutral towards the parts composing it. As a limited monarchy tempers the evils of an absolute one; so an extensive Republic meliorates the administration of a small Republic.

An auxiliary desideratum for the melioration of the Republican form is such a process of elections as will most certainly extract from the mass of the society the purest and noblest characters which it contains; such as will at once feel most strongly the proper motives to pursue the end of their appointment, and be most capable to devise the proper means of attaining it.

10. Toward a New Order: To George Washington

Madison seized every opportunity to launch the Constitutional Convention on the right course. In the Spring of 1787, he knew that he faced an uphill struggle to secure a new regime that would depart fundamentally from the design of the Confederation; and he was more than ever convinced that the attempt must be made in order to save the Union. Without Washington's full support, no strategy for a constitutional revolution could succeed. Madison helped to persuade the pre-eminent hero of the Revolution to attend the Philadelphia convention and thus, almost inevitably, to preside over its deliberations. Washington's nationalist sympathies could be taken for granted: the Commander-in-Chief of the Continental Army had spent some seven years learning the weaknesses of a loose federal system.

On the eve of the Convention, Madison carefully provided Washington and other powerful friends with specific proposals that could become the basis for debate and action. His

---

To George Washington, April 16, 1787, in *Writings*, II, pp. 344–349.

letters to Jefferson in Paris (even at a distance Jefferson's views would influence Virginians), to the popular young Virginia governor, Edmund Randolph, and his suggestions to Washington, reprinted here, sketched the main features of the plan that the Virginia delegates would present to the Convention as the agenda for discussion. Although Madison would elaborate, refine, and in some instances change his views in the course of the debates, his basic commitment to the creation of a supreme national authority would mark all his efforts through the summer of 1787. The document that emerged from Philadelphia in September was in important features—for example, in the elimination of a federal veto power over state legislation or the modification of the principle of proportional representation in Congress—more respectfful toward states' rights than Madison's original proposals and arguments had been. On the evidence of early 1787, one could not have predicted Madison's future role as a leader of the "Virginia School" of opposition to centralized power—or indeed that Virginia would lend its name to such a school.

New York, April 16th, 1787.

DEAR SIR,—I have been honored with your letter of the 31 March, and find, with much pleasure, that your views of the reform which ought to be pursued by the Convention give a sanction to those which I have entertained. Temporising applications will dishonor the Councils which propose them, and may foment the internal malignity of the disease, at the same time they produce an ostensible palliation of it. Radical attempts although unsuccessful will at least justify the authors of them.

Having been lately led to revolve the subject which is to undergo the discussion of the Convention, and formed *some* outlines of a new system, I take the liberty of submitting them without apology to your eye.

Conceiving that an individual independence of the States is utterly irreconcileable with their aggregate sovereignty, and that a consolidation of the whole into one simple republic would be as inexpedient as it is unattainable, I have sought for middle ground, which may at once support a due supremacy of the national authority, and not exclude the local authorities wherever they can be subordinately useful.

I would propose as the groundwork that a change be made in the principle of representation. According to the present form of the Union, in which the intervention of the States is in all great cases necessary to effectuate the measures of Congress, an equality of suffrage, does not destroy the inequality of importance in the several members. No one deny that Virginia and Massachusetts have more weight and influence, both within and without Congress, than Delaware or Rhode Island. Under a system which would operate in many essential points without the intervention of the State legislatures, the case would be materially altered. A vote in the national Councils from Delaware, would then have the same effect and value as one from the largest State in the Union. I am ready to believe that such a change would not be attended with much difficulty. A majority of the States, and those of greatest influence, will regard it as favorable to them. To the northern States it will be recommended by their present populousness; to the Southern, by their expected advantage in this respect. The lesser States must in every event yield to the predominant will. But the consideration which particularly urges a change in the representation is that it will obviate the principle objections of the larger States to the necessary concessions of power.

I would propose next that in addition to the present federal powers, the national Government should be armed with positive and compleat authority in all cases which require uniformity; such as the regulation of trade, including the right of taxing both exports and imports, the fixing the terms and forms of naturalization, &c., &c.

Over and above this positive power, a negative *in all cases whatsoever* on the legislative acts of the States, as heretofore exercised by the Kingly prerogative, appears to me to be absolutely necessary, and to be the least possible encroachment on the State jurisdictions. Without this defensive power, every positive power that can be given on paper will be evaded and defeated. The States will continue to invade the National jurisdiction, to violate treaties and the law of nations and to harass each other with rival and spiteful measures dictated by mistaken views of interest. Another happy effect of this prerogative would be its controul on the internal vicissitudes of State policy, and the aggressions of interested majorities on the rights of minorities and of individuals. The great desideratum, which has not yet been found for Republican Governments seems to be some disinterested and dispassionate umpire in disputes between different passions and interests in the State. The majority who alone have the right of decision, have frequently an interest, real or supposed in abusing it. In Monarchies the Sovereign is more neutral to the interests and views of different parties; but, unfortunately he too often forms interests of his own repugnant to those of the whole. Might not the national prerogative here suggested be found sufficiently disinterested for the decision of local questions of policy, whilst it would itself be sufficiently restrained from the pursuit of interests adverse to those of the whole Society? There has not been any moment since the peace at which the representatives of the Union would have given an assent to paper money or any other measure of a kindred nature.

The national supremacy ought also to be extended, as I conceive, to the Judiciary departments. If those who are to expound and apply the laws are connected by their interests and their oaths with the particular States wholly, and not with the Union, the participation of the Union in the making of the laws may be possibly rendered unavailing. It seems at least necessary that the oaths of the Judges should include a fidelity to the general as well as local constitution, and that an appeal should lie to some National tribunal in all cases to which foreigners or inhabitants of other States may be parties. The admiralty jurisdiction seems to fall entirely within the purview of the national Government.

The National supremacy in the Executive departments is liable to some difficulty, unless the officers administering them could be made appointable by the supreme Government. The Militia ought certainly to be placed in some form or other under the authority which is entrusted with the general protection and defence.

A Government composed of such extensive powers should be well organized and balanced. The legislative department might be divided into two branches; one of them chosen every years [sic] by the people at large, or by the Legislatures; the other to consist of fewer members, to hold their places for a longer term, and go out in such a rotation as always to leave in office a large majority of old members. Perhaps the negative on the laws might be most conveniently exercised by this branch. As a further check, a council of revision including the great ministerial officers might be superadded.

A National Executive must also be provided. I have scarcely ventured as yet to form my own opinion either of the manner in which it ought to be constituted or of the authorities with which it ought to be cloathed.

An article should be inserted expressly guarantying the tranquillity of the States against internal as well as external dangers.

In like manner the right of coercion should be expressly declared. With the resources of Commerce in hand, the National administration might always find means of exerting it either by sea or land. But the difficulty and awkwardness of operating by force on the collective will of a State render it particularly desirable that the necessity of it might be precluded. Perhaps the negative on the laws might create such a mutuality of dependence between the General and particular authorities, as to answer this purpose or, perhaps, some defined objects of taxation might be submitted along with commerce, to the general authority.

To give a new System its proper validity and energy, a ratification must be obtained from the people, and not merely from the ordinary authority of the Legislatures. This will be the more essential as inroads on the *existing Constitutions* of the States will be unavoidable. . . .

11. Father of the Constitution:
Speeches in the Philadelphia Convention

The honorary title of "Father of the Constitution", bestowed on Madison by later generations, is quite legitimate if one does not interpret it too literally. No one did more to build the road to Philadelphia. His Virginia plan, however modified by the debates, set the agenda of the Convention in terms that pointed directly to the radical reconstruction of the Confederation. Within the Convention, Madison's powerful arguments helped to fix the boundaries of compromise well over on the nationalist side, although Madison himself did little to assist the mediators and indeed often held out stubbornly for his own positions. Afterwards, he made invaluable contributions to the explication and defense of the Constitution in *The*

Madison, Speeches in the Constitutional Convention, June 6, 19, 21, and 28, 1787, in Max Farrand, ed., *The Records of the Federal Convention of 1787*, revised edition (New Haven: Yale University Press, 1966), I, pp. 134–136, 314–322, 356–358, 446–449, 485–487. Madison's later revisions of the manuscript are enclosed in angle brackets ⟨ ⟩.

Federalist and the debates of the divided Virginia Ratifying Convention. His title as lawgiver was strengthened by his service in the drafting and adoption of the Bill of Rights that completed the fundamental laws and won the loyalty of many who had opposed ratification.

Madison performed one further task that perhaps did more than anything else to link his name with the proceedings at Philadelphia: he made incomparably the fullest and most accurate record we have of the debates. As he later described it:

> . . . I chose a seat in front of the presiding member, with the other members, on my right and left hand. In this favorable position for hearing all that passed I noted in terms legible and in abbreviations and marks intelligible to myself what was read from the Chair or spoken by the members; and losing not a moment unnecessarily between the adjournment and the reassembling of the Convention I was enabled to write out my daily notes during the session or within a few finishing days after its close.*

More than thiry years later, Madison revised his notes, drawing on the Convention *Journal*, published in 1819, and the notes of Robert Yates of New York, published in 1821. He decided against publication of the manuscript during his lifetime, largely for political reasons. After his death in 1836, Congress bought the Madison papers and authorized their publication in 1840.

The following selections from the notes illustrate Madison's part in the Convention as a hard-line advocate of national authority, speaking his mind frankly behind closed doors. His speech of June 6, 1787, offers another early version of the classic analysis of factions that would appear in *Federalist* No. 10. His attack on the New Jersey plan of William Patterson goes well beyond his later *Federalist* arguments in its rejection of traditional federal forms of union. Note too his anticipation of an overriding North-South sectional conflict.

---

* Max Farrand, ed., *The Records of the Federal Convention of 1787,* 3, 550.

June 6, 1787.

Mr. Madison considered an election of one branch at least of
the Legislature by the people immediately, as a clear principle
of free Government and that this mode under proper regulations had the additional advantage of securing better representatives, as well as of avoiding too great an agency of the
State Governments in the General one.—He differed from the
member from Connecticut (Mr. Sherman) in thinking the objects mentioned to be all the principal ones that required a
National Government. Those were certainly important and
necessary objects; but he combined with them the necessity, of
providing more effectually for the security of private rights,
and the steady dispensation of Justice. Interferences with these
were evils which had more perhaps than any thing else, produced this convention. Was it to be supposed that republican
liberty could long exist under the abuses of it practiced in
⟨some of⟩ the States. The gentleman (Mr. Sherman) had admitted that in a very small State, faction & oppression wd.
prevail. It was to be inferred then that wherever these prevailed the State was too small. Had they not prevailed in the
largest as well as the smallest tho' less than in the smallest;
and were we not thence admonished to enlarge the sphere as
far as the nature of the Government would admit. This was the
only defence against the inconveniences of democracy consistent with the democratic form of Government. All civilized
Societies would be divided into different Sects, Factions, & interests, as they happened to consist of rich & poor, debtors &
creditors, the landed, the manufacturing, the commercial interests, the inhabitants of this district, or that district, the followers of this political leader or that political leader, the disciples
of this religious sect or that religious sect. In all cases where a
majority are united by a common interest or passion, the rights
of the minority are in danger. What motives are to restrain
them? A prudent regard to the maxim that honesty is the best

policy is found by experience to be as little regarded by bodies of men as by individuals. Respect for character is always diminished in proportion to the number among whom the blame or praise is to be divided. Conscience, the only remaining tie is known to be inadequate in individuals: In large numbers, little is to be expected from it. Besides, Religion itself may become a motive to persecution & oppression.—These observations are verified by the Histories of every Country antient & modern. In Greece & Rome the rich & poor, the creditors & debtors, as well as the patricians & plebeians alternately oppressed each other with equal unmercifulness. What a source of oppression was the relation between the parent Cities of Rome, Athens & Carthage, & their respective provinces: the former possessing the power & the latter being sufficiently distinguished to be separate objects of it? Why was America so justly apprehensive of Parliamentary injustice? Because Great Britain had a separate interest real or supposed, & if her authority had been admitted, could have pursued that interest at our expense. We have seen the mere distinction of colour made in the most enlightened period of time, a ground of the most oppressive dominion ever exercised by man over man. What has been the source of those unjust laws complained of among ourselves? Has it not been the real or supposed interest of the major number? Debtors have defrauded their creditors. The landed interest has borne hard on the mercantile interest. The Holders of one species of property have thrown a disproportion of taxes on the holders of another species. The lesson we are to draw from the whole is that where a majority are united by a common sentiment and have an opportunity, the rights of the minor party become insecure. In a Republican Government the Majority if united have always an opportunity. The only remedy is to enlarge the sphere, & thereby divide the community into so great a number of interests & parties, that in the 1st. place a majority will not be likely at the same moment to have a common interest separate from that of the whole or of the minority;

and in the 2d. place, that in case they should have such an interest, they may not be apt to unite in the pursuit of it. It was incumbent on us then to try this remedy, and with that view to frame a republican system on such a scale & in such a form as will controul all the evils which have been experienced.

June 19, 1787

Mr. M⟨adison⟩. Much stress had been laid by some gentlemen on the want of power in the Convention to propose any other than a *federal* plan. To what had been answered by others, he would only add, that neither of the characteristics attached to a *federal* plan would support this objection. One characteristic, was that in a *federal* Government, the power was exercised not on the people individually; but on the people *collectively,* on the *States.* Yet in some instances as in piracies, captures &c. the existing Confederacy, and in many instances, the amendments to it ⟨proposed by Mr. Patterson⟩ must operate immediately on individuals. The other characteristic was, that a *federal* Government derived its appointments not immediately from the people, but from the States which they respectively composed. Here too were facts on the other side. In two of the States, Connecticut and Rhode Island, the delegates to Congress were chosen, not by the Legislatures, but by the people at large; and the plan of Mr. Patterson intended no change in this particular.

It had been alledged (by Mr. Patterson) that the Confederation having been formed by unanimous consent, could be dissolved by unanimous Consent only. Does this doctrine result from the nature of compacts? does it arise from any particular stipulation in the articles of Confederation? If we consider the federal union as analogous to the fundamental compact by which individuals compose one Society, and which must in its theoretic origin at least, have been the unanimous act of the component members, it cannot be said that no dissolution of the compact can be effected without unanimous consent. A breach of the fundamental principles of the compact by a part of the Society would certainly absolve the other part from their obligations to it. If the breach of *any* article by *any* of the parties, does not set the others at liberty, it is because, the contrary is *implied* in the compact itself, and particularly by that law of it, which gives an indefinite authority to the majority to bind the whole in all cases. This latter circumstance shews that we are not to consider the federal Union as analogous to the social compact of individuals: for if it were so, a Majority would have a right to bind the rest, and even to form a new Constitution for the whole, which the Gentlemen: from New Jersey would be among the last to admit. If we consider the federal union as analogous not to the social compacts among individual men: but to the conventions among individual States. What is the doctrine resulting from these conventions? Clearly, according to the Expositors of the law of Nations, that a breach of any one article, by any one party, leaves all the other parties at liberty, to consider the whole convention as dissolved, unless they choose rather to compel the delinquent party to repair the breach. In some treaties indeed it is expressly stipulated that a violation of particular articles shall not have this consequence, and even that particular articles shall remain in force during war, which in general is understood to dissolve all susbsisting Treaties. But are there any exceptions of this sort to the Articles of confederation? So far from it that there is not even an express stipulation that force shall be used to compell an offending member of the Union to discharge its duty. He observed that the violations of the federal articles had been numerous & notorious. Among the most notorious was an Act of New Jersey herself; by which she *expressly refused* to comply with a constitutional requisition of Congress—and yielded no farther to the expostulations of their deputies, than barely to rescind her vote of refusal without passing any posi-

/

tive act of compliance. He did not wish to draw any rigid inferences from these observations. He thought it proper however
that the true nature of the existing confederacy should be investigated, and he was not anxious to strengthen the foundations on which it now stands.

Proceeding to the consideration of Mr. Patterson's plan, he
stated the object of a proper plan to be twofold. 1. to preserve
the Union. 2. to provide a Government that will remedy the
evils felt by the States both in their united and individual capacities. Examine Mr. Patterson's plan, & say whether it promises satisfaction in these respects.

1. Will it prevent those violations of the law of nations & of
Treaties which if not prevented must involve us in the calami
ties of foreign wars? The tendency of the States to these violations has been manifested in sundry instances. The files of
Congress contain complaints already, from almost every nation
with which treaties have been formed. Hitherto indulgence has
been shewn to us. This cannot be the permanent disposition of
foreign nations. A rupture with other powers is among the
greatest of national calamities. It ought therefore to be effectually provided that no part of a nation shall have it in its power
to bring them on the whole. The existing confederacy does
⟨not⟩ sufficiently provide against this evil. The proposed
amendment to it does not supply the omission. It leaves the will
of the States as uncontrouled as ever.

2. Will it prevent encroachments on the federal authority? A
tendency to such encroachments has been sufficiently exemplified among ourselves, as well in every other confederated republic antient and Modern. By the federal articles, transactions
with the Indians appertain to Congress. Yet in several instances, the States have entered into treaties & wars with them.
In like manner no two or more States can form among themselves any treaties &c without the consent of Congress yet Virginia & Maryland in one instance—Pennsylvania & New Jersey

in another, have entered into compacts, without previous application or subsequent apology. No State again can of right raise troops in time of peace without the like consent. Of all cases of the league, this seems to require the most scrupulous observance. Has not Massachusetts, notwithstanding, the most powerful member of the Union, already raised a body of troops? Is she not now augmenting them, without having even deigned to apprise Congress of Her intention? In fine Have we not seen the public land dealt out to Continue to bribe her acquiescence in the decree constitutionally awarded against her claim on the territory of Pennsylvania—? for no other possible motive can account for the policy of Congress in that measure?—if we recur to the examples of other confederacies, we shall find in all of them the same tendency of the parts to encroach on the authority of the whole. He then reviewed the Amphictyonic & Achæan confederacies among the antients, and the Helvetic, Germanic & Belgic among the moderns, tracing their analogy to the United States—in the constitution and extent of their federal authorities—in the tendency of the particular members to usurp on these authorities; and to bring confusion & ruin on the whole. —He observed that the plan of Mr. Patterson besides omitting a controul over the States as a general defence of the federal prerogatives was particularly defective in two of its provisions. 1. Its ratification was not to be by the people at large, but by the *Legislatures*. It could not therefore render the acts of Congress in pursuance of their powers even legally *paramount* to the Acts of the States. 2. It gave ‹to the federal tribunal› an appellate jurisdiction only— even in the criminal cases enumerated, The necessity of any such provision supposed a danger of undue acquittals in the State tribunals. Of what avail would an appellate tribunal be, after an acquittal? Besides in most if not all of the States, the Executives have by their respective *Constitutions* the right of pardoning. How could this be taken from them by a *legislative ratification* only?

3. Will it prevent trespasses of the States on each other? Of these enough has been already seen. He instanced Acts of Virginia & Maryland which give a preference to their own citizens in cases where the Citizens ⟨of other states⟩ are entitled to equality of privileges by the Articles of Confederation. He considered the emissions of paper money ⟨& other kindred measures⟩ as also aggressions. The States relatively to one an other being each of them either Debtor or Creditor; The Creditor States must suffer unjustly from every emission by the debtor States. We have seen retaliating acts on this subject which threatened danger not to the harmony only, but the tranquillity of the Union. The plan of Mr. Patterson, not giving even a negative on the Acts of the States, left them as much at liberty as ever to execute their unrighteous projects against each other.

4. Will it secure the internal tranquillity of the States themselves? The insurrections in Massachusetts admonished all the States of the danger to which they were exposed. Yet the plan of Mr. Patterson contained no provisions for supplying the defect of the Confederation on this point. According to the Republican theory indeed, Right & power being both vested in the majority, are held to be synonimous. According to fact & experience, a minority may in an appeal to force be an overmatch for the majority. 1. If the minority happen to include all such as possess the skill & habits of military life, with such as possess the great pecuniary resources, one third may conquer the remaining two thirds. 2. one third of those who participate in the choice of rulers may be rendered a majority by the accession of those whose poverty disqualifies them from a suffrage, & who for obvious reasons may be more ready to join the standard of sedition than that of the established Government. 3. Where slavery exists, the Republican Theory becomes still more fallacious.

5. Will it secure a good internal legislation & administration to the particular States? In developing the evils which vitiate

the political system of the U. S. it is proper to take into view those which prevail within the States individually as well as those which affect them collectively: Since the former indirectly affect the whole; and there is great reason to believe that the pressure of them had a full share in the motives which produced the present Convention. Under this head he enumerated and animadverted on 1. the multiplicity of the laws passed by the several States. 2. the mutability of their laws. 3. the injustice of them. 4. the impotence of them: observing that Mr. Patterson's plan contained no remedy for this dreadful class of evils, and could not therefore be received as an adequate provision for the exigencies of the Community.

6. Will it secure the Union against the influence of foreign powers over its members. He pretended not to say that any such influence had yet been tried: but it naturally to be expected that occasions would produce it. As lessons which claimed particular attention, he cited the intrigues practiced among the Amphictionic Confederates first by the Kings of Persia, and afterwards fatally by Philip of Macedon: Among the Achæans, first by Macedon & afterwards no less fatally by Rome: Among the Swiss by Austria, France & the lesser neighbouring Powers; among the members of the Germanic ‹Body› by France, England, Spain & Russia—: and in the Belgic Republic, by all the great neighbouring powers. The plan of Mr. Patterson, not giving to the general Councils any negative on the will of the particular States, left the door open for the like pernicious machinations among ourselves.

7. He begged the smaller States which were most attached to Mr. Pattersons plan to consider the situation in which it would leave them. In the first place they would continue to bear the whole expense of maintaining their Delegates in Congress. It ought not to be said that if they were willing to bear this burden, no others had a right to complain. As far as it led the small States to forbear keeping up a representation, by

which the public business was delayed, it was evidently a matter of common concern. An examination of the minutes of Congress would satisfy every one that the public business had been frequently delayed by this cause; and that the States most frequently unrepresented in Congress were not the larger States. He reminded the convention of another consequence of leaving on a small State the burden of Maintaining a Representation in Congress. During a considerable period of the War, one of the Representatives of Delaware, in whom alone before the signing of the Confederation the entire vote of that State and after that event one half of its vote, frequently resided, was a Citizen & Resident of Pennsylvania and held an office in his own State incompatible with an appointment from it to Congress. During another period, the same State was represented by three delegates two of whom were citizens of Pennsylvania—and the third a Citizen of New Jersey. These expedients must have been intended to avoid the burden of supporting delegates from their own State. But whatever might have been ye. cause, was not in effect the vote of one State doubled, and the influence of another increased by it? ‹ In the 2d. place › The coercion, on which the efficacy of the plan depends, can never be exerted but on themselves. The larger States will be impregnable, the smaller only can feel the vengeance of it. He illustrated the position by the history of the Amphictyonic Confederates: and the ban of the German Empire. It was the cobweb which could entangle the weak, but would be the sport of the strong.

8. He begged them to consider the situation in which they would remain in case their pertinacious adherence to an inadmissible plan, should prevent the adoption of any plan. The contemplation of such an event was painful; but it would be prudent to submit to the task of examining it at a distance, that the means of escaping it might be the more readily embraced. Let the union of the States be dissolved and one of two consequences must happen. Either the States must remain individ-

ually independent & sovereign; or two or more Confederacies must be formed among them. In the first event would the small States be more secure against the ambition & power of their larger neighbours, than they would be under a general Government pervading with equal energy every part of the Empire, and having an equal interest in protecting every part against every other part? In the second, can the smaller expect that their larger neighbours would confederate with them on the principle of the present confederacy, which gives to each member, an equal suffrage; or that they would exact less severe concessions from the smaller States, than are proposed in the scheme of Mr. Randolph?

The great difficulty lies in the affair of Representation; and if this could be adjusted, all others would be surmountable. It was admitted by both the gentlemen from New Jersey, (Mr. Brearly and Mr. Patterson) that it would not be *just to allow Virginia* which was 16 times as large as Delaware an equal vote only. Their language was that it would not be *safe for Delaware* to allow Virginia 16 times as many votes. The expedient proposed by them was that all the States should be thrown into one mass and a new partition be made into 13 equal parts. Would such a scheme be practicable? The dissimelarities existing in the rules of property, as well as in the manners, habits and prejudices of the different States, amounted to a prohibition of the attempt. It had been found impossible for the power of one of the most absolute princes in Europe (King of France) directed by the wisdom of one of the most enlightened and patriotic Ministers (Mr. Neckar) that any age has produced, to equalize in some points only the different usages & regulations of the different provinces. But admitting a general amalgamation and repartition of the States, to be practicable, and the danger apprehended by the smaller States from a proportional representation to be real; would not a particular and voluntary coalition of these with their neighbours, be less inconvenient to the whole community, and equally effectual for their own safety. If New Jersey or Delaware conceive that an advantage would accrue to them from an equalization of the States, in which case they would necessaryly form a junction with their neighbors, why might not this end be attained by leaving them at liberty by the Constitution to form such a junction whenever they pleased? and why should they wish to obtrude a like arrangement on all the States, when it was, to say the least, extremely difficult, would be obnoxious to many of the States, and when neither the inconveniency, nor the benefit of the expedient to themselves, would be lessened, by confining it to themselves.—The prospect of many new States to the Westward was another consideration of importance. If they should come into the Union at all, they would come when they contained but few inhabitants. If they should be entitled to vote according to their proportions of inhabitants, all would be right & safe. Let them have an equal vote, and a more objectionable minority than ever might give law to the whole.

June 21, 1787.

⟨Mr. Madison⟩ was of opinion that there was 1. less danger of encroachment from the General Government than from the State Governments. 2. that the mischief from encroachments would be less fatal if made by the former, than if made by the latter. 1. All the examples of other confederacies prove the greater tendency in such systems to anarchy than to tyranny; to a disobedience of the members than to usurpations of the federal head. Our own experience had fully illustrated this tendency.—But it will be said that the proposed change in the principles & form of the Union will vary the tendency, that the General Government will have real & greater powers, and will be derived in one branch at least from the people not from the Governments of the States. To give full force to this objection, let it be supposed for a moment that indefinite power should be given to the General Legislature, and the States reduced to corporations dependent on the General Legisature; why should it follow that the General Government would take from the States ⟨any⟩ branch of their power as far as its operation was beneficial, and its continuance desirable to the people? In some of the States, particularly in Connecticut, all the Townships are incorporated, and have a certain limited jurisdiction. Have the Representatives of the people of the Townships in the Legislature of the State ever endeavored to despoil the Townships of any part of their local authority? As far as this local authority is convenient to the people they are attached to it; and their representatives chosen by & amenable to them ⟨naturally⟩ respect their attachment to this, as much as their attachment to any other right or interest: The relation of a General Government to State Governments is parallel. 2. Guards were more necessary against encroachments of the State Governments—on the General Government than of the latter on the former. The great objection made against an abolition of the State Governments was that the General Government could not extend its care to all the minute objects which fall under the cognizance of the local jurisdictions. The objection as stated lay not against the probable abuse of the general power, but against the imperfect use that could be made of it throughout so great an extent of country, and over so great a variety of objects. As far as its operation would be practicable it could not in this view be improper; as far as it would be impracticable, the conveniency of the General Government itself would concur with that of the people in the maintenance of subordinate Governments. Were it practicable for the General Government to extend its care to every requisite object without the cooperation of the State Governments the people would not be less free as members of one great Republic than as members of thirteen small ones. A citizen of Delaware was not more free than a citizen of Virginia: nor would either be more free than a citizen of America. Supposing therefore a tendency in the General Government to absorb the State Governments no fatal consequence could result. Taking the reverse of the supposition, that a tendency should be left in the State Governments towards an independence on the General Government and the gloomy consequences need not be pointed out. The imagination of them, must have suggested to the States the experiment we are now making to prevent the calamity, and must have formed the chief motive with those present to undertake the arduous task.

June 28, 1787.

Mr. M⟨adison⟩ said he was much disposed to concur in any expedient not inconsistent with fundamental principles, that could remove the difficulty concerning the rule of representation. But he could neither be convinced that the rule contended for was just, nor necessary for the safety of the small States against the large States. That it was not just, had been conceded by Mr. Breerly & Mr. Patterson themselves. The expedient proposed by them was a new partition of the territory of the United States. The fallacy of the reasoning drawn from the equality of Sovereign States in the formation of compacts, lay in confounding mere Treaties, in which were specified certain duties to which the parties were to be bound, and certain rules by which their subjects were to be reciprocally governed in their intercourse, with a compact by which an authority was created paramount to the parties, & making laws for the government of them. If France, England & Spain were to enter into a Treaty for the regulation of commerce &c. with the Prince of Monacho & 4 or 5 other of the smallest sovereigns of Europe, they would not hesitate to treat as equals, and to make the regulations perfectly reciprocal. Would the case be the same if a Council were to be formed of deputies from each with authority and discretion, to raise money, levy troops, determine the value of coin &c? Would 30 or 40. million of people submit their fortunes into the hands, of a few thousands? If they did it would only prove that they expected more from the terror of their superior force, than they feared from the selfishness of their feeble ⟨associates⟩   Why are Counties of the same States represented in proportion to their numbers? Is it because the representatives are chosen by the people themselves? so will be the representatives in the National Legislature. Is it because, the larger have more at stake than the smaller? The case will be the same with the larger & smaller States. Is it because the laws are to operate immediately on their persons & properties? The same is the case in some degree as the articles of confederation stand; the same will be the case in ⟨a far greater degree⟩ under the plan proposed to be substituted. In the cases of captures, of piracies, and of offenses in a federal army, the property & persons of individuals depend on the laws of Congress. By the plan ⟨proposed⟩ a compleat power of taxation, the highest prerogative of supremacy is proposed to be vested in the National Government. Many other powers are added which assimilate it to the Government of individual States. The negative ⟨on the State laws⟩ proposed, will make it an essential branch of the State Legislatures & of course will require that it should be exercised by a body established on like principles with the other branches of those Legislatures.— That it is not necessary to secure the small States against the large ones he conceived to be equally obvious: Was a combination of the large ones dreaded? this must arise either from some interest common to Virginia, Massachusetts & Pennsylvania & distinguishing them from the other States ⟨or from the mere circumstance of similarity of size⟩. Did any such common interest exist? In point of situation they could not have been more effectually separated from each other by the most jealous citizen of the most jealous State. In point of manners, Religion and the other circumstances, which sometimes beget affection between different communities, they were not more assimilated than the other States.—In point of the staple productions they were as dissimilar as any three other States in the Union.

The Staple of Massachusetts was *fish*, of Pennsylvania, *flower*, of Virginia, *tobacco*. Was a Combination to be apprehended from the mere circumstance of equality of size? Experience suggested no such danger. The journals of Congress did not present any peculiar association of these States in the votes recorded. It had never been seen that different Counties in the same State, conformable in extent, but disagreeing in other circumstances, betrayed a propensity to such combinations. Experience rather taught a contrary lesson. Among individuals of superior eminence & weight in society, rivalships were much more frequent than coalitions. Among independent nations preeminent over their neighbours, the same remark was verified. Carthage & Rome tore one another to pieces instead of uniting their forces to devour the weaker nations of the Earth. The Houses of Austria & France were hostile as long as they remained the greatest powers of Europe. England & France have succeeded to the pre-eminence & to the enmity. To this principle we owe perhaps our liberty. A coalition between those powers would have been fatal to us. Among the principal members of antient & modern confederacies, we find the same effect from the same cause. The contentions, not the coalitions of Sparta, Athens & Thebes, proved fatal to the smaller members of the Amphictyonic Confederacy. The contentions, not the combinations of Prussia & Austria, have distracted & oppressed the Germanic empire. Were the large States formidable *singly* to their smaller neighbours? On this supposition the latter ought to wish for such a general Government as will operate with equal energy on the former as on themselves. The more lax the band, the more liberty the larger will have to avail themselves of their superior force. Here again Experience was an instructive monitor. What is ye situation of the weak compared with the strong in those stages of civilization in which the violence of individuals is least controuled by an efficient Government? The Heroic period of Antient Greece the feudal licentiousness of the middle ages of Europe, the existing condition of the American Savages, answer this question. What is the situation of the minor sovereigns in the great society of independent nations, in which the more powerful are under no controul but the nominal authority of the law of Nations? Is not the danger to the former exactly in proportion to their weakness. But there are cases still more in point. What was the condition of the weaker members of the Amphyctionic Confederacy. Plutarch (life of Themistocles) will inform us that it happened but too often that the strongest cities corrupted & awed the weaker, and that Judgment went in favor of the more powerful party. What is the condition of the lesser States in the German Confederacy? We all know that they are exceedingly trampled upon and that they owe their safety as far as they enjoy it, partly to their enlisting themselves, under the rival banners of the preeminent members, partly to alliances with neighbouring Princes which the Constitution of the Empire does not prohibit. What is the state of things in the lax system of the Dutch Confederacy? Holland contains about ½ the people, supplies about ½ of the money, and by her influence, silently & indirectly governs the whole Republic. In a word; the two extremes before us are a perfect separation & a perfect incorporation, of the 13 States. In the first case they would be independent nations subject to no law, but the law of nations. In the last, they would be mere counties of one entire republic, subject to one common law. In the first case the smaller states would have every thing to fear from the larger. In the last they would have nothing to fear. The true policy of the small States therefore lies in promoting those principles & that form of Government which will most approximate the States to the condition of Counties. Another consideration may be added. If the General Government be feeble, the large States distrusting its continuance, and foreseeing that their importance & security may depend on their own size & strength, will never submit to a partition. Give to the General Government sufficient energy & permanency, & you remove the objection. Gradual partitions of the large, & junctions of the small ⟨States⟩ will be facilitated, and time may effect that equalization, which is wished for by the small States, now, but can never be accomplished at once.

June 30, 1787.

Mr. M⟨adison. did justice to the able and close reasoning of Mr. Elseworth but must observe that it did not always accord with itself.⟩ On another occasion, the large States were described ⟨by him⟩ as the Aristocratic States, ready to oppress the small. Now the small are the House of Lords requiring a negative to defend them against the more numerous Commons. Mr. Elseworth had also erred in saying that no instance had existed in which confederated States had not retained to themselves a perfect equality of suffrage. Passing over the German system in which the Kaiser of Prussia has nine voices, he reminded Mr. Elseworth of the Lycian confederacy, in which the component members had votes proportioned to their importance, and which Montesquieu recommends as the fittest model for that form of Government. Had the fact been as stated by Mr. Elseworth it would have been of little avail to him, or rather would have strengthened the arguments against him; The History & fate of the several Confederacies modern as well as Antient, demonstrating some radical vice in their structure. In reply to the appeal of Mr. Elseworth to the faith plighted in the existing federal compact, he remarked that the party claiming from others an adherence to a common engagement ought at least to be guiltless itself of a violation. Of all the States however Connecticut was perhaps least able to urge this plea. Besides the various omissions to perform the stipulated acts from which no State was free, the Legislature of that State had by a pretty recent vote *positively refused* to pass a law for complying with the Requisitions of Congress and had transmitted a copy of the vote to Congress. It was urged, he said, continually that an equality of votes in the 2d. branch was not only necessary to secure the small, but would be perfectly safe to the large ones whose majority in the 1st. branch was an effectual bulwark. But notwithstanding this apparent defence, the Majority of States might still injure the majority of people. 1. they could *obstruct* the wishes and interests of the majority. 2. they could *extort* measures, repugnant to the wishes & interest of the majority. 3. They could *impose* measures adverse thereto; as the 2d branch will probly exercise some great powers, in which the 1st will not participate. He admitted that every peculiar interest whether in any class of citizens, or any description of States, ought to be secured as far as possible. Wherever there is danger of attack there ought be given a constitutional power of defence. But he contended that the States were divided into different interests not by their difference of size, but by other circumstances; the most material of which resulted partly from climate, but principally from ⟨the effects of⟩ their having or not having slaves. These two causes concurred in forming the great division of interests in the United States. It did not lie between the large & small States: it lay between the Northern & Southern. and if any defensive power were necessary, it ought to be mutually given to these two interests. He was so strongly impressed with this important truth that he had been casting about in his mind for some expedient that would answer the purpose. The one which had occurred was that instead of proportioning the votes of the States in both branches, to their respective numbers of inhabitants computing the slaves in the ratio of 5 to 3. they should be represented in one branch according to the number of free inhabitants only; and in the other according to the whole no. counting the slaves as ⟨if⟩ free. By this arrangement the Southern Scale would have the advantage in one House, and the Northern in the other. He had been restrained from proposing this expedient by two considerations; one was his unwillingness to urge any diversity of interests on an occasion when it is but too apt to arise of itself—the other was the inequality of powers that must be vested in the two branches, and which would destroy the equilibrium of interests.

12. Defender of the Constitution: From The Federalist

Publius Valerius Publicola was a noble Roman who, in Plutarch's classic story, helped to depose the Tarquin kings, found the ancient Republic, and defend it against its enemies with courage and prudence. Comparing Publius with the Athenian lawgiver, Solon, Plutarch gave higher rank to the Greek as the originator of republican laws. Yet he found balancing merits on the Roman side: "Solon, leaving his laws as soon as he had made them, engraven in wood, but destitute of a defender, departed from Athens; whilst Publicola, remaining both in and out of office, laboured to establish the government." The American Publius—collective pseudonym for the authors of *The Federalist*—might claim an originality as great as Solon's; but he would not leave the new republican laws of the United States "engraven in wood." The founders of the American Republic knowingly chose the Roman name.

As they knew, the achievement of the Philadelphia Convention would mean nothing until the Constitution was ratified

---

The Federalist, Numbers 10, 14, 37, 39, 45, 46, 47, 51, 57, 62, 63, in *The Federalist* (Hallowell, Maine: Glazier and Co., 1826), 50–57, 72–77, 194–216, 257–258, 289–294, 310–325, 345–358. This follows the edition of Jacob Gideon, Washington, D.C., 1818, corrected by Madison.

and established by nine states. Critics of the proposed Constitution began firing almost as soon as the Convention closed its business. George Clinton of New York, writing as "Cato," launched his attack in late September, 1787. By early October, Richard Henry Lee's persuasive anti-Federalist arguments in *Letters from the Federal Farmer* began circulating through Virginia and the country at large. Alexander Hamilton promptly recruited a Federalist writing team in New York City, including John Jay (whose ill health limited his contribution) and Madison, an old Congressional ally. Madison's presence in New York as a delegate to the dying Confederation Congress made the collaboration feasible. The first number by Hamilton appeared in *The Independent Journal* of October 27, 1787. With little time for planning and consultation, Hamilton and Madison dashed off in alternating sequences as many as four essays a week for the four New York papers that had agreed to reserve space for them. As Madison later described the hectic procedure in an autobiographical sketch, "Whilst the printer was putting into type the parts of a number, the following parts were under the pen, and to be furnished in time for the press." In March, 1788, John McLean published the first thirty-six essays as a book (*The Federalist*) and issued a second volume of the remaining papers (including the previously unpublished Numbers 78–85 on May 28, 1788. Friends of the Constitution spread the word of Publius far beyond New York. Ironically, it is doubtful that *The Federalist,* for all its surpassing merits, changed many votes in New York or any other state.

According to the custom of the time, the writers concealed the identity of Publius from all but a few friends. One unintended consequence of anonymity as well as hasty composition was a controversy over the authorship of specific numbers that scholars have resolved convincingly only within the past few years. Circumstantial evidence, textual analysis, and finally the genius of the computer have supported Madison's claims to twenty-nine of the eighty-five numbers of *The Federalist,* just as he marked them for the Washington printer, Jacob Gideon, in 1818. The following selections are taken from a reprint of the Gideon edition authorized by Madison. More interesting than the detective puzzle is the larger question: Did Publius reveal a split personality as he shifted from his Hamiltonian right hand to his Madisonian left hand? Political differences between the New Yorker and the Virginian that came to a focus in the party struggles in the 1790s lend plausibility to the schizoid hypothesis. Yet the less familiar collaboration of the two nationalist leaders during the "critical period" of the Confederation, and their joint acceptance of the new Constitution as the essential though still imperfect instrument of union argue for one Publius, whole and harmonious. In the view of the present editor, the plausibilities at least balance out, and *The Federalist* text strongly suggests the unity of Publius as explicator and defender of the Philadelphia compromise.

The selected *Federalist* essays reprinted here represent the mature political thought of Madison, writing at the peak of his powers. After almost two centuries, *The Federalist* remains the most profound commentary on the original nature of the American regime, and the best single guide to the political mind of the founders. In long retrospect, Madison agreed with Jefferson's estimate of the work: "The 'Federalist' may fairly enough be regarded as the most authentic exposition of the text of the Federal Constitution, as understood by the Body which prepared and the Authority which accepted it." (See Document 32.) Most students of American political thought consider that a very modest claim.

NO. X
THE UTILITY OF THE UNION AS A SAFEGUARD AGAINST DOMESTIC FACTION AND INSURRECTION

Among the numerous advantages promised by a well constructed union, none deserves to be more accurately developed than its tendency to break and control the violence of faction. The friend of popular governments, never finds himself so much alarmed for their character and fate, as when he contemplates their propensity to this dangerous vice. He will not fail, therefore, to set a due value on any plan which, without violating the principles to which he is attached, provides a proper cure for it. The instability, injustice, and confusion, introduced into the public councils, have, in truth, been the mortal diseases under which popular governments have everywhere perished; as they continue to be the favourite and fruitful topics from which the adversaries to liberty derive their most specious declamations. The valuable improvements made by the American constitutions on the popular models, both ancient and modern, cannot certainly be too much admired; but it would be an unwarrantable partiality, to contend that they have as effectually obviated the danger on this side, as was wished and expected. Complaints are everywhere heard from our most considerate and virtuous citizens, equally the friends of public and private faith, and of public and personal liberty, that our governments are too unstable; that the public good is disregarded in the conflicts of rival parties; and that measures are too often decided, not according to the rules of justice, and the rights of the minor party, but by the superior force of an interested and overbearing majority. However anxiously we may wish that these complaints had no foundation, the evidence of known facts will not permit us to deny that they are in some degree true. It will be found, indeed, on a candid review of our situation, that some of the distresses under which we labour, have been erroneously charged on the operation of our governments; but it will be found, at the same time, that other causes will not alone account for many of our heaviest misfortunes; and, particularly, for that prevailing and increasing distrust of public engagements, and alarm for private rights, which are echoed from one end of the continent to the other. These must be chiefly, if not wholly, effects of the unsteadiness and injustice, with which a factious spirit has tainted our public administrations.

By a faction, I understand a number of citizens, whether

amounting to majority or minority of the whole, who are united and actuated by some common impulse of passion, or of interest, adverse to the rights of other citizens, or to the permanent and aggregate interests of the community.

There are two methods of curing the mischiefs of faction: The one, by removing its causes; the other, by controling its effects.

There are again two methods of removing the causes of faction: The one, by destroying the liberty which is essential to its existence; the other, by giving to every citizen the same opinions, the same passions, and the same interests.

It could never be more truly said, than of the first remedy, that it was worse than the disease. Liberty is to faction what air is to fire, an aliment, without which it instantly expires. But it could not be a less folly to abolish liberty, which is essential to political life, because it nourishes faction, than it would be to wish the annihilation of air, which is essential to animal life, because it imparts to fire its destructive agency.

The second expedient is as impracticable, as the first would be unwise. As long as the reason of man continues fallible, and he is at liberty to exercise it, different opinions will be formed. As long as the connection subsists between his reason and his self-love, his opinions and his passions will have a reciprocal influence on each other; and the former will be objects to which the latter will attach themselves. The diversity in the faculties of men, from which the rights of property originate, is not less an insuperable obstacle to an uniformity of interests. The protection of these faculties is the first object of government. From the protection of different and unequal faculties of acquiring property, the possession of different degrees and kinds of property immediately results; and from the influence of these on the sentiments and views of the respective proprietors, ensues a division of the society into different interests and parties.

The latent causes of faction are thus sown in the nature of

man; and we see them everywhere brought into different degrees of activity, according to the different circumstances of civil society. A zeal for different opinions concerning religion, concerning government, and many other points, as well of speculation as of practice; an attachment to different leaders, ambitiously contending for preeminence and power; or to persons of other descriptions, whose fortunes have been interesting to the human passions, have, in turn, divided mankind into parties, inflamed them with mutual animosity, and rendered them much more disposed to vex and oppress each other, than to cooperate for their common good. So strong is this propensity of mankind, to fall into mutual animosities, that where no substantial occasion presents itself, the most frivolous and fanciful distinctions have been sufficient to kindle their unfriendly passions, and excite their most violent conflicts. But the most common and durable source of factions, has been the various and unequal distribution of property. Those who hold, and those who are without property, have ever formed distinct interests in society. Those who are creditors, and those who are debtors, fall under a like discrimination. A landed interest, a manufacturing interest, a mercantile interest, a moneyed interest, with many lesser interests, grow up of necessity in civilized nations, and divide them into different classes, actuated by different sentiments and views. The regulation of these various and interfering interests forms the principal task of modern legislation, and involves the spirit of party and faction in the necessary and ordinary operations of government.

No man is allowed to be a judge in his own cause; because his interest will certainly bias his judgment, and, not improbably, corrupt his integrity. With equal, nay, with greater reason, a body of men are unfit to be both judges and parties at the same time; yet what are many of the most important acts of legislation, but so many judicial determinations, not indeed concerning the rights of single persons, but concerning the rights of large bodies of citizens? and what are the different classes of legislators, but advocates and parties to the causes which they determine? Is a law proposed concerning private debts? It is a question to which the creditors are parties on one side, and the debtors on the other. Justice ought to hold the balance between them. Yet the parties are, and must be, themselves the judges; and the most numerous party, or, in other words, the most powerful faction, must be expected to prevail. Shall domestic manufactures be encouraged, and in what degree, by restrictions on foreign manufactures? are questions which would be differently decided by the landed and the manufacturing classes; and probably by neither with a sole regard to justice and the public good. The apportionment of taxes, on the various descriptions of property, is an act which seems to require the most exact impartiality; yet there is, perhaps, no legislative act, in which greater opportunity and temptation are given to a predominant party, to trample on the rules of justice. Every shilling, with which they overburden the inferior number, is a shilling saved to their own pockets.

It is in vain to say, that enlightened statesmen will be able to adjust these clashing interests, and render them all subservient to the public good. Enlightened statesmen will not always be at the helm: nor, in many cases, can such an adjustment be made at all, without taking into view indirect and remote considerations, which will rarely prevail over the immediate interest which one party may find in disregarding the rights of another, or the good of the whole.

The inference to which we are brought is, that the *causes* of faction cannot be removed; and that relief is only to be sought in the means of controling its *effects*.

If a faction consists of less than a majority, relief is supplied by the republican principle, which enables the majority to defeat its sinister views, by regular vote. It may clog the administration, it may convulse the society; but it will be unable to execute and mask its violence under the forms of the constitution. When a majority is included in a faction, the form of popular government, on the other hand, enables it to sacrifice to its ruling passion or interest, both the public good and the rights of other citizens. To secure the public good, and private rights, against the danger of such a faction, and at the same time to preserve the spirit and the form of popular government, is then the great object to which our inquiries are directed. Let me add, that it is the great desideratum, by which alone this form of government can be rescued from the opprobrium under which it has so long laboured, and be recommended to the esteem and adoption of mankind.

By what means is this object attainable? Evidently by one of two only. Either the existence of the same passion or interest in a majority, at the same time, must be prevented; or the majority, having such coexistent passion or interest, must be rendered, by their number and local situation, unable to concert and carry into effect schemes of oppression. If the impulse and the opportunity be suffered to coincide, we well know, that neither moral nor religious motives can be relied on as an adequate control. They are not found to be such on the injustice and violence of individuals, and lose their efficacy in proportion to the number combined together; that is, in proportion as their efficacy becomes needful.

From this view of the subject, it may be concluded, that a pure democracy, by which I mean a society consisting of a small number of citizens, who assemble and administer the government in person, can admit of no cure from the mischiefs of faction. A common passion or interest will, in almost every case, be felt by a majority of the whole; a communication and concert, results from the form of government itself; and there is nothing to check the inducements to sacrifice the weaker party, or an obnoxious individual. Hence it is, that such democracies have ever been spectacles of turbulence and contention; have ever been found incompatible with personal security, or the rights of property; and have, in general, been as short in their lives, as they have been violent in their deaths. Theoretic politicians, who have patronized this species of government, have erroneously supposed, that by reducing mankind to a perfect equality in their political rights, they would, at the same time, be perfectly equalized and assimilated in their possessions, their opinions, and their passions.

A republic, by which I mean a government in which the scheme of representation takes place, opens a different prospect, and promises the cure for which we are seeking. Let us examine the points in which it varies from pure democracy, and we shall comprehend both the nature of the cure and the efficacy which it must derive from the union.

The two great points of difference, between a democracy and a republic, are, first, the delegation of the government, in the latter, to a small number of citizens elected by the rest; secondly, the greater number of citizens, and greater sphere of country, over which the latter may be extended.

The effect of the first difference is, on the one hand, to refine and enlarge the public views, by passing them through the medium of a chosen body of citizens, whose wisdom may best discern the true interest of their country, and whose patriotism and love of justice, will be least likely to sacrifice it to temporary or partial considerations. Under such a regulation, it may well happen, that the public voice, pronounced by the representatives of the people, will be more consonant to the public good, than if pronounced by the people themselves, convened for the purpose. On the other hand the effect may be inverted. Men of factious tempers, of local prejudices, or of sinister designs, may by intrigue, by corruption, or by other means, first obtain the suffrages, and then betray the interests of the people. The question resulting is, whether small or extensive republics are most favourable to the election of proper guardians of the public weal; and it is clearly decided in favour of the latter by two obvious considerations.

In the first place, it is to be remarked, that however small the republic may be, the representatives must be raised to a certain number, in order to guard against the cabals of a few; and that however large it may be, they must be limited to a certain number, in order to guard against the confusion of a multitude. Hence, the number of representatives in the two cases not being in proportion to that of the constituents, and being proportionally greatest in the small republic, it follows, that if the proportion of fit characters be not less in the large than in the small republic, the former will present a greater option, and consequently a greater probability of a fit choice.

In the next place, as each representative will be chosen by a greater number of citizens in the large than in the small republic, it will be more difficult for unworthy candidates to practise with success the vicious arts, by which elections are too often carried; and the suffrages of the people being more free, will be more likely to centre in men who possess the most attractive merit, and the most diffusive and established characters.

It must be confessed, that in this, as in most cases, there is a mean, on both sides of which inconveniences will be found to lie. By enlarging too much the number of electors, you render the representative too little acquainted with all their local circumstances and lesser interests; as by reducing it too much, you render him unduly attached to these, and too little fit to comprehend and pursue great and national objects. The federal constitution forms a happy combination in this respect; the great and aggregate interests being referred to the national, the local and particular to the state legislatures.

The other point of difference is, the greater number of citizens, and extent of territory, which may be brought within the compass of republican, than of democratic government; and it is this circumstance principally which renders factious combinations less to be dreaded in the former, than in the latter. The smaller the society, the fewer probably will be the distinct parties and interests composing it; the fewer the distinct parties and interests, the more frequently will a majority be found of the same party; and the smaller the number of individuals composing a majority, and the smaller the compass within which they are placed, the more easily will they concert and execute their plans of oppression. Extend the sphere, and you take in a greater variety of parties and interests; you make it less probable that a majority of the whole will have a common motive to invade the rights of other citizens; or if such a common motive exists, it will be more difficult for all who feel it to discover their own strength, and to act in unison with each other. Besides other impediments, it may be remarked, that where there is a consciousness of unjust or dishonourable purposes, communication is always checked by distrust, in proportion to the number whose concurrence is necessary.

Hence, it clearly appears, that the same advantage, which a republic has over a democracy, in controlling the effects of faction, is enjoyed by a large over a small republic . . . is enjoyed by the union over the states composing it. Does this advantage consist in the substitution of representatives, whose enlightened views and virtuous sentiments render them superior to local prejudices, and to schemes of injustice? It will not be denied, that the representation of the union will be most likely to possess these requisite endowments. Does it consist in the greater security afforded by a greater variety of parties, against the event of any one party being able to outnumber and oppress the rest? In an equal degree does the increased variety of parties, comprised within the union, increase this security. Does it, in fine, consist in the greater obstacles opposed to the concert and accomplishment of the secret wishes of an unjust and interested majority? Here, again, the extent of the union gives it the most palpable advantage.

The influence of factious leaders may kindle a flame within their particular states, but will be unable to spread a general

conflagration through the other states: a religious sect may
degenerate into a political faction in a part of the confederacy;
but the variety of sects dispersed over the entire face of it,
must secure the national councils against any danger from that
source: a rage for paper money, for an abolition of debts, for
an equal division of property, or for any other improper or
wicked project, will be less apt to pervade the whole body of
the union, than a particular member of it; in the same proportion as such a malady is more likely to taint a particular county
or district, than an entire state.

In the extent and proper structure of the union, therefore, we
behold a republican remedy for the diseases most incident to
republican government. And according to the degree of pleasure and pride we feel in being republicans, ought to be our
zeal in cherishing the spirit, and supporting the character of
federalists.

PUBLIUS

NO. XIV

AN OBJECTION DRAWN FROM THE EXTENT
OF COUNTRY ANSWERED

We have seen the necessity of the union, as our bulwark
against foreign danger; as the conservator of peace among ourselves; as the guardian of our commerce, and other common interests; as the only substitute for those military establishments
which have subverted the liberties of the old world; and as the
proper antidote for the diseases of faction, which have proved
fatal to other popular governments, and of which alarming
symptoms have been betrayed by our own. All that remains,
within this branch of our inquiries, is to take notice of an objection, that may be drawn from the great extent of country which
the union embraces. A few observations, on this subject, will be

the more proper, as it is perceived, that the adversaries of the new constitution are availing themselves of a prevailing prejudice, with regard to the practicable sphere of republican administration, in order to supply, by imaginary difficulties, the want of those solid objections, which they endeavour in vain to find.

The error which limits republican government to a narrow district, has been unfolded and refuted in preceding papers. I remark here only, that it seems to owe its rise and prevalence chiefly to the confounding of a republic with a democracy; and applying to the former, reasonings drawn from the nature of the latter. The true distinction between these forms, was also adverted to on a former occasion. It is, that in a democracy, the people meet and exercise the government in person: in a republic, they assemble and administer it by their representatives and agents. A democracy, consequently, must be confined to a small spot. A republic may be extended over a large region.

To this accidental source of the error, may be added the artifice of some celebrated authors, whose writings have had a great share in forming the modern standard of political opinions. Being subjects, either of an absolute, or limited monarchy, they have endeavoured to heighten the advantages, or palliate the evils, of those forms, by placing in comparison with them the vices and defects of the republican, and by citing, as specimens of the latter, the turbulent democracies of ancient Greece, and modern Italy. Under the confusion of names, it has been an easy task to transfer to a republic observations applicable to a democracy only; and, among others, the observation, that it can never be established but among a small number of people, living within a small compass of territory.

Such a fallacy may have been the less perceived, as most of the popular governments of antiquity were of the democratic species; and even in modern Europe, to which we owe the great principle of representation, no example is seen of a government wholly popular, and founded, at the same time, wholly on that principle. If Europe has the merit of discovering this great mechanical power in government, by the simple agency of which, the will of the largest political body may be concentred, and its force directed to any object, which the public good requires; America can claim the merit of making the discovery the basis of unmixed and extensive republics. It is only to be lamented, that any of her citizens should wish to deprive her of the additional merit of displaying its full efficacy in the establishment of the comprehensive system now under her consideration.

As the natural limit of a democracy is that distance from the central point, which will just permit the most remote citizens to assemble as often as their public functions demand, and will include no greater number than can join in those functions: so the natural limit of a republic, is that distance from the centre, which will barely allow the representatives of the people to meet as often as may be necessary for the administration of public affairs. Can it be said, that the limits of the United States exceed this distance? It will not be said by those who recollect, that the Atlantic coast is the longest side of the union; that during the term of thirteen years, the representatives of the states have been almost continually assembled; and that the members, from the distant states, are not chargeable with greater intermissions of attendance, than those from the states in the neighbourhood of Congress.

That we may form a juster estimate with regard to this interesting subject, let us resort to the actual dimensions of the union. The limits, as fixed by the treaty of peace, are, on the east the Atlantic, on the south the latitude of thirty-one degrees, on the west the Mississippi, and on the north an irregular line running in some instances beyond the forty-fifth degree, in others falling as low as the forty-second. The southern shore of lake Erie lies below that latitude. Computing the distance between the thirty-first and forty-fifth degrees, it amounts to nine hundred and seventy-three common miles; computing it from thirty-one to forty-two degrees, to seven hundred sixty-four miles and a half. Taking the mean for the distance, the amount will be eight hundred sixty-eight miles and three fourths. The mean distance from the Atlantic to the Mississippi, does not probably exceed seven hundred and fifty miles. On a comparison of this extent, with that of several countries in Europe, the practicability of rendering our system commensurate to it, appears to be demonstrable. It is not a great deal larger than Germany, where a diet, representing the whole empire, is continually assembled; or than Poland before the late dismemberment, where another national diet was the depository of the supreme power. Passing by France and Spain, we find that in Great Britain, inferior as it may be in size, the representatives of the northern extremity of the island, have as far to travel to the national council, as will be required of those of the most remote parts of the union.

Favourable as this view of the subject may be, some observations remain, which will place it in a light still more satisfactory.

In the first place, it is to be remembered, that the general government is not to be charged with the whole power of making and administering laws: its jurisdiction is limited to certain enumerated objects, which concern all the members of the republic, but which are not to be attained by the separate provisions of any. The subordinate governments, which can extend their care to all those other objects, which can be separately provided for, will retain their due authority and activity. Were it proposed by the plan of the convention, to abolish the governments of the particular states, its adversaries would have some ground for their objection; though it would not be difficult to show, that if they were abolished, the general government would be compelled, by the principle of self-preservation, to reinstate them in their proper jurisdiction.

A second observation to be made is, that the immediate object of the federal constitution, is to secure the union of the thirteen primitive states, which we know to be practicable; and to add to them such other states, as may arise in their own bosoms, or in their neighbourhoods, which we cannot doubt to be equally practicable. The arrangements that may be necessary for those angles and fractions of our territory, which lie on our north western frontier, must be left to those whom further discoveries and experience will render more equal to the task.

Let it be remarked, in the third place, that the intercourse throughout the union will be daily facilitated by new improvements. Roads will everywhere be shortened, and kept in better order; accommodations for travellers will be multiplied and meliorated; an interior navigation on our eastern side, will be opened throughout, or nearly throughout, the whole extent of the Thirteen States. The communication between the western and Atlantic districts, and between different parts of each, will be rendered more and more easy, by those numerous canals, with which the beneficence of nature has intersected our country, and which art finds it so little difficult to connect and complete.

A fourth, and still more important consideration, is, that as almost every state will, on one side or other, be a frontier, and will thus find, in a regard to its safety, an inducement to make some sacrifices for the sake of the general protection: so the states which lie at the greatest distance from the heart of the union, and which of course may partake least of the ordinary circulation of its benefits, will be at the same time immediately contiguous to foreign nations, and will consequently stand, on particular occasions, in greatest need of its strength and resources. It may be inconvenient for Georgia, or the states forming our western or north eastern borders, to send their representatives to the seat of government; but they would find it more so to struggle alone against an invading enemy, or even to support alone the whole expense of those precautions, which may be dictated by the neighbourhood of continual danger. If they should derive less benefit therefore from the union in some respects, than the less distant states, they will derive greater benefit from it in other respects, and thus the proper equilibrium will be maintained throughout.

I submit to you, my fellow-citizens, these considerations, in full confidence that the good sense which has so often marked your decisions, will allow them their due weight and effect; and that you will never suffer difficulties, however formidable in appearance, or however fashionable the error on which they may be founded, to drive you into the gloomy and perilous scenes into which the advocates for disunion would conduct you. Hearken not to the unnatural voice, which tells you that the people of America, knit together as they are by so many chords of affection, can no longer live together as members of the same family; can no longer continue the mutual guardians of their mutual happiness; can no longer be fellow-citizens of one great, respectable, and flourishing empire. Hearken not to the voice, which petulantly tells you, that the form of government recommended for your adoption, is a novelty in the political world; that it has never yet had a place in the theories of the wildest projectors; that it rashly attempts what it is impossible to accomplish. No, my countrymen, shut your ears against this unhallowed language. Shut your hearts against the poison which it conveys. The kindred blood which flows in the veins of American citizens, the mingled blood which they have shed in defence of their sacred rights, consecrate their union, and excite horror at the idea of their becoming aliens, rivals, enemies. And if novelties are to be shunned, believe me, the most alarming of all novelties, the most wild of all projects, the most rash of all attempts, is that of rending us in pieces, in order to preserve our liberties, and promote our happiness. But why is the experiment of an extended republic to be rejected, merely because it may comprise what is new? Is it not the glory of the people of America, that whilst they have paid a decent regard to the opinions of former times and other nations, they have not suffered a blind veneration for antiquity, for custom, or for names, to overrule the suggestions of their good sense, the knowledge of their own situation, and the lessons of their own experience? To this manly spirit, posterity will be indebted for the possession, and the world for the example, of the numerous innovations displayed on the American theatre, in favour of private rights and public happiness. Had no important step been taken by the leaders of the revolution, for which a precedent could not be discovered; no government established of which an exact model did not present itself, the people of the United States might, at this moment, have been numbered among the melancholy victims of misguided councils; must at best have been labouring under the weight of some of those forms which have crushed the liberties of the rest of mankind. Happily for America, happily we trust for the whole human race, they pursued a new and more noble course. They accomplished a revolution which has no parallel in the annals of human society. They reared the fabrics of governments which have no model on the face of the globe. They formed the design of a great confederacy, which it is incumbent on their successors to improve and perpetuate. If their works betray imperfections, we wonder at the fewness of them. If they erred most in the structure of the union, this was the work most difficult to be executed; this is the work which has been new modelled by the act of your convention, and it is that act on which you are now to deliberate and to decide.

PUBLIUS

NO. XXXVII

CONCERNING THE DIFFICULTIES WHICH THE CONVENTION
MUST HAVE EXPERIENCED IN THE FORMATION
OF A PROPER PLAN

In reviewing the defects of the existing confederation, and showing that they cannot be supplied by a government of less energy than that before the public, several of the most important principles of the latter fell of course under consideration. But as the ultimate object of these papers is, to determine clearly and fully the merits of this constitution, and the expediency of adopting it, our plan cannot be completed without taking a more critical and thorough survey of the work of the convention; without examining it on all its sides; comparing it in all its parts, and calculating its probable effects.

That this remaining task may be executed under impressions conducive to a just and fair result, some reflections must in this place be indulged, which candour previously suggests.

It is a misfortune, inseparable from human affairs, that public measures are rarely investigated with that spirit of moderation, which is essential to a just estimate of their real tendency to advance, or obstruct, the public good; and that this spirit is more apt to be diminished than promoted, by those occasions which require an unusual exercise of it. To those who have been led by experience to attend to this consideration, it could not appear surprising, that the act of the convention which recommends so many important changes and innovations, which may be viewed in so many lights and relations, and which touches the springs of so many passions and interests, should find or excite dispositions unfriendly, both on one side and on the other, to a fair discussion and accurate judgment of its merits. In some, it has been too evident from their own publications, that they have scanned the proposed constitution, not only with a predisposition to censure, but with a pre-determination to condemn; as the language held by others, betrays an opposite predetermination or bias, which must render their opinions also of little moment in the question. In placing, however, these different characters on a level, with respect to the weight of their opinions, I wish not to insinuate that there may not be a material difference in the purity of their intentions. It is but just to remark in favour of the latter description, that as our situation is universally admitted to be peculiarly critical, and to require indispensably, that something should be done for our relief, the predetermined patron of what has been actually done, may have taken his bias from the weight of these considerations, as well as from considerations of a sinister nature. The predetermined adversary, on the other hand, can have been governed by no venial motive whatever. The intentions of the first may be upright, as they may on the contrary be culpable. The views of the last cannot be upright, and must be culpable. But the truth is, that these papers are not addressed to persons falling under either of these characters. They solicit the attention of those only, who add to a sincere zeal for the happiness of their country, a temper favourable to a just estimate of the means of promoting it.

Persons of this character will proceed to an examination of the plan submitted by the convention, not only without a disposition to find or to magnify faults, but will see the propriety of reflecting, that a faultless plan was not to be expected. Nor will they barely make allowances for the errors which may be chargeable on the fallibility to which the convention, as a body of men, were liable; but will keep in mind, that they themselves also are but men, and ought not to assume an infallibility in rejudging the fallible opinions of others.

With equal readiness will it be perceived, that besides these inducements to candour, many allowances ought to be made, for the difficulties inherent in the very nature of the undertaking referred to the convention.

The novelty of the undertaking immediately strikes us. It has been shown in the course of these papers, that the existing confederation is founded on principles which are fallacious; that we must consequently change this foundation, and with it the superstructure resting upon it. It has been shown, that the other confederacies which could be consulted as precedents, have been vitiated by the same erroneous principles, and can therefore furnish no other light than that of beacons, which give warning of the course to be shunned, without pointing out that which ought to be pursued. The most that the convention could do in such a situation, was to avoid the errors suggested by the past experience of other countries, as well as of our own; and to provide a convenient mode of rectifying their own errors as future experience may unfold them.

Among the difficulties encountered by the convention, a very important one must have lain, in combining the requisite stability and energy in government, with the inviolable attention due to liberty, and to the republican form. Without substantially accomplishing this part of their undertaking, they would have very imperfectly fulfilled the object of their appointment, or the expectation of the public: yet that it could not be easily accomplished, will be denied by no one who is unwilling to betray his ignorance of the subject. Energy in government is essential to that security against external and internal danger, and to that prompt and salutary execution of the laws, which enter into the very definition of good government. Stability in government is essential to national character, and to the advantages annexed to it, as well as to that repose and confidence in the minds of the people, which are among the chief blessings of civil society. An irregular and mutable legislation is not more an evil in itself, than it is odious to the people; and it may be pronounced with assurance, that the people of this country, enlightened as they are, with regard to the nature, and interested, as the great body of them are, in the effects of good government, will never be satisfied, till some remedy be applied to the vicissitudes and uncertainties, which characterize the state administrations. On comparing, however, these valuable ingredients with the vital principles of liberty, we must perceive at once the difficulty of mingling them together in their due proportions. The genius of republican liberty seems to demand on one side, not only that all power should be derived from the people: but that those entrusted with it should be kept in dependence on the people, by a short duration of their appointments; and that even during this short period, the trust should be placed not in a few, but in a number of hands. Stability, on the contrary, requires, that the hands, in which power is lodged, should continue for a length of time the same. A frequent change of men will result from a frequent return of electors; and a frequent change of measures, from a frequent change of men: whilst energy in government requires not only a certain duration of power, but the execution of it by a single hand.

How far the convention may have succeeded in this part of their work, will better appear on a more accurate view of it. From the cursory view here taken, it must clearly appear to have been an arduous part.

Not less arduous must have been the task of marking the proper line of partition, between the authority of the general, and that of the state governments. Every man will be sensible of this difficulty, in proportion as he has been accustomed to contemplate and discriminate objects, extensive and complicated in their nature. The faculties of the mind itself have never yet been distinguished and defined, with satisfactory precision, by all the efforts of the most acute and metaphysical philosophers. Sense, perception, judgment, desire, volition, memory, imagination, are found to be separated, by such delicate shades and minute gradations, that their boundaries have eluded the most subtle investigations, and remain a pregnant source of ingenious disquisition and controversy. The boundaries between the great kingdoms of nature, and, still more, between the various provinces, and lesser portions, into which they are subdivided, afford another illustration of the same important truth. The most sagacious and laborious naturalists have never yet succeeded, in tracing with certainty the line which separates the district of vegetable life, from the neighbouring region of unorganized matter, or which marks the termination of the former, and the commencement of the animal empire. A still greater obscurity lies in the distinctive characters, by which the objects in each of these great departments of nature have been arranged and assorted.

When we pass from the works of nature, in which all the delineations are perfectly accurate, and appear to be otherwise only from the imperfection of the eye which surveys them, to the institutions of man, in which the obscurity arises as well from the object itself, as from the organ by which it is contemplated; we must perceive the necessity of moderating still further our expectations and hopes from the efforts of human sagacity. Experience has instructed us, that no skill in the science of government has yet been able to discriminate and define, with sufficient certainty, its three great provinces, the legislative, executive, and judiciary; or even the privileges and powers of the different legislative branches. Questions daily occur in the course of practice, which prove the obscurity which reigns in these subjects, and which puzzle the greatest adepts in political science.

The experience of ages, with the continued and combined labours of the most enlightened legislators and jurists, have been equally unsuccessful in delineating the several objects and limits of different codes of laws, and different tribunals of justice. The precise extent of the common law, the statute law, the maritime law, the ecclesiastical law, the law of corporations, and other local laws and customs, remains still to be clearly and finally established in Great Britain, where accuracy in such subjects has been more industriously pursued than in any other part of the world. The jurisdiction of her several courts, general and local, of law, of equity, of admiralty, &c., is not less a source of frequent and intricate discussions, sufficiently denoting the indeterminate limits by which they are respectively circumscribed. All new laws, though penned with the greatest technical skill, and passed on the fullest and most mature deliberation, are considered as more or less obscure and equivocal, until their meaning be liquidated and ascertained by a series of particular discussions and adjudications. Besides the obscurity arising from the complexity of objects, and the imperfection of the human faculties, the medium through which the conceptions of men are conveyed to each other, adds a fresh embarrassment. The use of words is to express ideas. Perspicuity therefore requires, not only that the ideas should be distinctly formed, but that they should be expressed by words distinctly and exclusively appropriated to them. But no language is so copious as to supply words and phrases for every complex idea, or so correct as not to include many, equivocally denoting different ideas. Hence it must happen, that however accurately objects may be discriminated in themselves, and however accurately the discrimination may be conceived, the definition of them may be rendered inaccurate, by the inaccuracy of the terms in which it is delivered. And this unavoidable inaccuracy must be greater or less, according to the complexity and novelty of the objects defined. When the Almighty himself condescends to address mankind in their own language, his meaning, luminous as it must be, is rendered dim and doubtful, by the cloudy medium through which it is communicated.

Here, then, are three sources of vague and incorrect definitions; indistinctness of the object, imperfection of the organ of perception, inadequateness of the vehicle of ideas. Any one of these must produce a certain degree of obscurity. The convention, in delineating the boundary between the federal and state jurisdictions, must have experienced the full effect of them all.

To the difficulties already mentioned, may be added the interfering pretensions of the larger and smaller states. We cannot err, in supposing that the former would contend for a participation in the government, fully proportioned to their superior wealth and importance; and that the latter would not be less tenacious of the equality at present enjoyed by them. We may well suppose, that neither side would entirely yield to the other, and consequently that the struggle could be terminated only by compromise. It is extremely probable also, that after the ratio of representation had been adjusted, this very compromise must have produced a fresh struggle between the same parties, to give such a turn to the organization of the government, and to the distribution of its powers, as would increase the importance of the branches, in forming which they had respectively obtained the greatest share of influence. There are features in the constitution which warrant each of these suppositions; and as far as either of them is well founded, it shows that the convention must have been compelled to sacrifice theoretical propriety, to the force of extraneous considerations.

Nor could it have been the large and small states only, which would marshal themselves in opposition to each other on various points. Other combinations, resulting from a difference of local position and policy, must have created additional difficulties. As every state may be divided into different districts, and its citizens into different classes, which give birth to contending interests and local jealousies; so the different parts of the United States are distinguished from each other, by a variety of circumstances, which produce a like effect on a larger scale. And although this variety of interests, for reasons sufficiently explained in a former paper, may have a salutary influence on the administration of the government, when formed; yet every one must be sensible of the contrary influence, which must have been experienced in the task of forming it.

Would it be wonderful, if under the pressure of all these difficulties, the convention should have been forced into some deviations from that artificial structure and regular symmetry, which an abstract view of the subject might lead an ingenious theorist to bestow on a constitution planned in his closet, or in his imagination? The real wonder is, that so many difficulties should have been surmounted; and surmounted with an unanimity almost as unprecedented, as it must have been unexpected. It is impossible for any man of candour to reflect on this circumstance, without partaking of the astonishment. It is impossible, for the man of pious reflection, not to perceive in it a finger of that Almighty Hand, which has been so frequently and signally extended to our relief in the critical stages of the revolution.

We had occasion, in a former paper, to take notice of the repeated trials which have been unsuccessfully made in the United Netherlands, for reforming the baneful and notorious vices of their constitution. The history of almost all the great councils and consultations, held among mankind for reconciling their discordant opinions, assuaging their mutual jealousies, and adjusting their respective interests, is a history of factions, contentions, and disappointments; and may be classed among the most dark and degrading pictures, which display the infirmities and depravities of the human character. If, in a few scattered instances, a brighter aspect is presented, they serve only as exceptions to admonish us of the general truth; and by their lustre to darken the gloom of the adverse prospect, to which they are contrasted. In revolving the causes from which these exceptions result, and applying them to the particular instance before us, we are necessarily led to two important conclusions. The first is, that the convention must have enjoyed, in a very singular degree, an exemption from the pestilential influence of party animosities; the diseases most incident to deliberative bodies, and most apt to contaminate their proceedings. The second conclusion is, that all the deputations composing the convention were either satisfactorily accommodated by the final act; or were induced to accede to it, by a deep conviction of the necessity of sacrificing private opinions and partial interests to the public good; and by a despair of seeing this necessity diminished by delays, or by new experiments.

PUBLIUS

NO. XXXIX
THE CONFORMITY OF THE PLAN TO REPUBLICAN PRINCIPLES:
AN OBJECTION IN RESPECT TO THE POWERS
OF THE CONVENTION, EXAMINED

The last paper having concluded the observations, which were meant to introduce a candid survey of the plan of government reported by the convention, we now proceed to the execution of that part of our undertaking.

The first question that offers itself is, whether the general form and aspect of the government be strictly republican? It is evident that no other form would be reconcilable with the genius of the people of America; with the fundamental principles of the revolution; or with that honourable determination which animates every votary of freedom, to rest all our political experiments on the capacity of mankind for self-government. If the plan of the convention, therefore, be found to depart from the republican character, its advocates must abandon it as no longer defensible.

What, then, are the distinctive characters of the republican form? Were an answer to this question to be sought, not by recurring to principles, but in the application of the term by political writers, to the constitutions of different states, no satisfactory one would ever be found. Holland, in which no particle of the supreme authority is derived from the people, has passed almost universally under the denomination of a republic. The same title has been bestowed on Venice, where absolute power over the great body of the people is exercised, in the most absolute manner, by a small body of hereditary nobles. Poland, which is a mixture of aristocracy and of monarchy in their worst forms, has been dignified with the same appellation. The government of England, which has one republican branch only, combined with a hereditary aristocracy and monarchy, has, with equal impropriety, been frequently placed on the list of republics. These examples, which are nearly as dissimilar to each other as to a genuine republic, show the extreme inaccuracy with which the term has been used in political disquisitions.

If we resort, for a criterion, to the different principles on which different forms of government are established, we may define a republic to be, or at least may bestow that name on, a government which derives all its powers directly or indirectly from the great body of the people, and is administered by persons holding their offices during pleasure, for a limited period, or during good behaviour. It is *essential* to such a government, that it be derived from the great body of the society, not from an inconsiderable proportion, or a favoured class of it; otherwise a handful of tyrannical nobles, exercising their oppressions by a delegation of their powers, might aspire to the rank of republicans, and claim for their government the honourable title of republic. It is *sufficient* for such a government, that the persons administering it be appointed, either directly or indirectly, by the people; and that they hold their appointments by either of the tenures just specified; otherwise every government in the United States, as well as every other popular government that has been or can be well organized or well executed, would be degraded from the republican character. According to the constitution of every state in the union, some or other of the officers of government are appointed indirectly only by the people. According to most of them, the chief magistrate himself is so appointed. And according to one, this mode of appointment is extended to one of the coordinate branches of the legislature. According to all the constitutions also, the tenure of the highest offices is extended to a definite period, and in many instances, both within the legislative and executive departments, to a period of years. According to the provisions of most of the constitutions, again, as well as according to the most respectable and received opinions on the subject, the members of the judiciary department are to retain their offices by the firm tenure of good behaviour.

On comparing the constitution planned by the convention, with the standard here fixed, we perceive at once, that it is, in the most rigid sense, conformable to it. The house of representatives, like that of one branch at least of all the state legislatures, is elected immediately by the great body of the people. The senate, like the present congress, and the senate of Maryland, derives its appointment indirectly from the people. The president is indirectly derived from the choice of the people, according to the example in most of the states. Even the judges, with all other officers of the union, will, as in the several states, be the choice, though a remote choice, of the people themselves. The duration of the appointments is equally conformable to the republican standard, and to the model of the state constitutions. The house of representatives is periodically elective, as in all the states; and for the period of two years, as in the state of South Carolina. The senate is elective, for the period of six years; which is but one year more than the period of the senate of Maryland; and but two more than that of the senates of New York and Virginia. The president is to continue in office for the period of four years; as in New York and Delaware, the chief magistrate is elected for three years, and in South Carolina for two years. In the other states the election is annual. In several of the states, however, no explicit provision is made for the impeachment of the chief magistrate. And in Delaware and Virginia, he is not impeachable till out of office. The president of the United States is impeachable at any time during his continuance in office. The tenure by which the judges are to hold their places, is, as it unquestionably ought to be, that of good behaviour. The tenure of the ministerial offices generally, will be a subject of legal regulation, conformably to the reason of the case, and the example of the state constitutions.

Could any further proof be required of the republican complexion of this system, the most decisive one might be found in its absolute prohibition of titles of nobility, both under the federal and the state governments; and in its express guarantee of the republican form to each of the latter.

But it was not sufficient, say the adversaries of the proposed constitution, for the convention to adhere to the republican form. They ought, with equal care, to have preserved the *federal* form, which regards the union as a *confederacy* of sovereign states; instead of which, they have framed a *national* government, which regards the union as a *consolidation* of the states. And it is asked, by what authority this bold and radical innovation was undertaken? The handle which has been made of this objection requires, that it should be examined with some precision.

Without inquiring into the accuracy of the distinction on which the objection is founded, it will be necessary to a just estimate of its force, first, to ascertain the real character of the government in question; secondly, to inquire how far the convention were authorized to propose such a government; and thirdly, how far the duty they owed to their country, could supply any defect of regular authority.

First. In order to ascertain the real character of the government, it may be considered in relation to the foundation on which it is to be established; to the sources from which its ordinary powers are to be drawn; to the operation of those powers; to the extent of them; and to the authority by which future changes in the government are to be introduced.

On examining the first relation, it appears, on one hand, that the constitution is to be founded on the assent and ratification of the people of America, given by deputies elected for the special purpose; but on the other, that this assent and ratification is to be given by the people, not as individuals composing one entire nation, but as composing the distinct and independent states to which they respectively belong. It is to be the assent and ratification of the several states, derived from the supreme authority in each state . . . the authority of the people themselves. The act, therefore, establishing the constitution, will not be a *national*, but a *federal* act.

That it will be a federal, and not a national act, as these terms are understood by the objectors, the act of the people, as forming so many independent states, not as forming one aggregate nation, is obvious from this single consideration, that it is to result neither from the decision of a *majority* of the people of the union, nor from that of a *majority* of the states. It must result from the *unanimous* assent of the several states that are parties to it, differing no otherwise from their ordinary assent than in its being expressed, not by the legislative authority, but by that of the people themselves. Were the people regarded in this transaction as forming one nation, the will of the majority of the whole people of the United States would bind the minority; in the same manner as the majority in each state must bind the minority; and the will of the majority must be determined either by a comparison of the individual votes, or by considering the will of the majority of the states, as evidence of the will of a majority of the people of the United States. Neither of these rules has been adopted. Each state, in ratifying the constitution, is considered as a sovereign body, independent of all others, and only to be bound by its own voluntary act. In this relation, then, the new constitution will, if established, be a *federal*, and not a *national* constitution.

The next relation is, to the sources from which the ordinary powers of government are to be derived. The house of representatives will derive its powers from the people of America, and the people will be represented in the same proportion, and on the same principle, as they are in a legislature of a particular state. So far the government is *national*, not *federal*. The senate, on the other hand, will derive its powers from the states, as political and coequal societies; and these will be represented on the principle of equality in the senate, as they now are in the existing congress. So far the government is *federal* not *national*. The executive power will be derived from a very compound source. The immediate election of the president is to be made by the states in their political characters. The votes allotted to them are in a compound ratio, which considers them partly as distinct and coequal societies; partly as unequal members of the same society. The eventual election, again, is to be made by that branch of the legislature which consists of the national representatives; but in this particular act, they are to be thrown into the form of individual delegations, from so many distinct and coequal bodies politic. From this aspect of the government, it appears to be of a mixed character, presenting at least as many *federal* as *national* features.

The difference between a federal and national government, as it relates to the *operation of the government,* is, by the adversaries of the plan of the convention, supposed to consist in this, that in the former, the powers operate on the political bodies composing the confederacy, in their political capacities; in the latter, on the individual citizens composing the nation, in their individual capacities. On trying the constitution by this criterion, it falls under the *national,* not the *federal* character; though perhaps not so completely as has been understood. In several cases, and particularly in the trial of controversies to which states may be parties, they must be viewed and proceeded against in their collective and political capacities only. But the operation of the government on the people in their individual capacities, in its ordinary and most essential proceedings, will, on the whole, in the sense of its opponents, designate it, in this relation, a *national* government.

But if the government be national, with regard to the *operation* of its powers, it changes its aspect again, when we contemplate it in relation to the *extent* of its powers. The idea of a national government involves in it, not only an authority over the individual citizens, but an indefinite supremacy over all persons and things, so far as they are objects of lawful government. Among a people consolidated into one nation, this supremacy is completely vested in the national legislature. Among communities united for particular purposes, it is vested partly in the general, and partly in the municipal legislatures. In the former case, all local authorities are subordinate to the supreme; and may be controled, directed, or abolished by it at pleasure. In the latter, the local or municipal authorities form distinct and independent portions of the supremacy, no more subject, within their respective spheres, to the general authority, than the general authority is subject to them within its own sphere. In this relation, then, the proposed government cannot be deemed a *national* one; since its jurisdiction extends to certain enumerated objects only, and leaves to the several states a residuary and inviolable sovereignty over all other objects. It is true, that in controversies relating to the boundary between the two jurisdictions, the tribunal which is ultimately to decide, is to be established under the general government. But this does not change the principle of the case. The decision is to be impartially made, according to the rules of the constitution; and all the usual and most effectual precautions are taken to secure this impartiality. Some such tribunal is clearly essential to prevent an appeal to the sword, and a dissolution of the compact; and that it ought to be established under the general, rather than under the local governments; or, to speak more properly, that it could be safely established under the first alone, is a position not likely to be combated.

If we try the constitution by its last relation, to the authority by which amendments are to be made, we find it neither wholly *national,* nor wholly *federal.* Were it wholly national, the supreme and ultimate authority would reside in the *majority* of the people of the union; and this authority would be competent at all times, like that of a majority of every national society, to alter or abolish its established government. Were it wholly federal on the other hand, the concurrence of each state in the union would be essential to every alteration that would be binding on all. The mode provided by the plan of the convention, is not founded on either of these principles. In requiring more than a majority, and particularly, in computing the proportion by *states,* not by *citizens,* it departs from the *national,* and advances towards the *federal* character. In rendering the concurrence of less than the whole number of states sufficient, it loses again the *federal,* and partakes of the *national* character.

The proposed constitution, therefore, even when tested by

the rules laid down by its antagonists, is, in strictness, neither a national nor a federal constitution; but a composition of both. In its foundation it is federal, not national; in the sources from which the ordinary powers of the government are drawn, it is partly federal, and partly national; in the operation of these powers, it is national, not federal; in the extent of them again, it is federal, not national; and finally in the authoritative mode of introducing amendments, it is neither wholly federal, nor wholly national.

PUBLIUS

NO. XLV

A FURTHER DISCUSSION OF THE SUPPOSED DANGER FROM THE POWERS OF THE UNION, TO THE STATE GOVERNMENTS

Having shown, that no one of the powers transferred to the federal government is unnecessary or improper, the next question to be considered is, whether the whole mass of them will be dangerous to the portion of authority left in the several states.

The adversaries to the plan of the convention, instead of considering in the first place, what degree of power was absolutely necessary for the purposes of the federal government, have exhausted themselves in a secondary inquiry into the possible consequences of the proposed degree of power to the governments of the particular states. But if the union, as has been shown, be essential to the security of the people of America against foreign danger; if it be essential to their security against contentions and wars among the different states; if it be essential to guard them against those violent and oppressive factions, which imbitter the blessings of liberty, and against those military establishments which must gradually poison its very fountain; if, in a word, the union be essential to the happiness of the people of America, is it not preposterous, to urge as an objection to a government, without which the objects of the union cannot be attained, that such a government may derogate from the importance of the governments of the individual states? Was then the American revolution effected, was the American confederacy formed, was the precious blood of thousands spilt, and the hard-earned substance of millions lavished, not that the people of America should enjoy peace, liberty, and safety; but that the governments of the individual states, that particular municipal establishments, might enjoy a certain extent of power, and be arrayed with certain dignities and attributes of sovereignty? We have heard of the impious doctrine in the old world, that the people were made for kings, not kings for the people. Is the same doctrine to be revived in the new, in another shape, that the solid happiness of the people is to be sacrificed to the views of political institutions of a different form? It is too early for politicians to presume on our forgetting that the public good, the real welfare of the great body of the people, is the supreme object to be pursued; and that no form of government whatever has any other value, than as it may be fitted for the attainment of this object. Were the plan of the convention adverse to the public happiness, my voice would be, Reject the plan. Were the union itself inconsistent with the public happiness, it would be, Abolish the union. In like manner, as far as the sovereignty of the states cannot be reconciled to the happiness of the people, the voice of every good citizen must be, Let the former be sacrificed to the latter. How far the sacrifice is necessary, has been shown. How far the unsacrificed residue will be endangered, is the question before us.

Several important considerations have been touched in the course of these papers, which discountenance the supposition that the operation of the federal government will by degrees prove fatal to the state governments. The more I revolve the subject, the more fully I am persuaded, that the balance is much more likely to be disturbed by the preponderancy of the last than of the first scale.

We have seen, in all the examples of ancient and modern confederacies, the strongest tendency continually betraying itself in the members, to despoil the general government of its authorities, with a very ineffectual capacity in the latter to defend itself against the encroachments. Although in most of these examples, the system has been so dissimilar from that under consideration, as greatly to weaken any inference concerning the latter, from the fate of the former; yet as the states will retain, under the proposed constitution, a very extensive portion of active sovereignty, the inference ought not to be wholly disregarded. In the Achæan league, it is probable that the federal head had a degree and species of power, which gave it a considerable likeness to the government framed by the convention. The Lycian confederacy, as far as its principles and form are transmitted, must have borne a still greater analogy to it. Yet history does not inform us, that either of them ever degenerated, or tended to degenerate, into one consolidated government. On the contrary, we know that the ruin of one of them proceeded from the incapacity of the federal authority to prevent the dissensions, and finally the disunion of the subordinate authorities. These cases are the more worthy of our attention, as the external causes by which the component parts were pressed together, were much more numerous and powerful than in our case; and consequently, less powerful ligaments within would be sufficient to bind the members to the head, and to each other.

In the feudal system, we have a similar propensity exemplified. Notwithstanding the want of proper sympathy in every instance between the local sovereigns and the people, and the sympathy in some instances between the general sovereign and the latter; it usually happened that the local sovereigns prevailed in the rivalship for encroachments. Had no external

dangers enforced internal harmony and subordination; and
particularly, had the local sovereigns possessed the affections
of the people, the great kingdoms in Europe would at this time
consist of as many independent princes, as there were formerly
feudatory barons.

The state governments will have the advantage of the federal
government, whether we compare them in respect to the immediate dependence of the one on the other; to the weight of
personal influence which each side will possess; to the powers
respectively vested in them; to the predilection and probable
support of the people; to the disposition and faculty of resisting
and frustrating the measures of each other.

The state governments may be regarded as constituent and
essential parts of the federal government; whilst the latter is
nowise essential to the operation or organization of the former.
Without the intervention of the state legislatures, the president
of the United States cannot be elected at all. They must in all
cases have a great share in his appointment, and will, perhaps,
in most cases, of themselves determine it. The senate will be
elected absolutely and exclusively by the state legislatures.
Even the house of representatives, though drawn immediately
from the people, will be chosen very much under the influence
of that class of men, whose influence over the people obtains
for themselves an election into the state legislatures. Thus, each
of the principal branches of the federal government will owe
its existence more or less to the favour of the state governments, and must consequently feel a dependence, which is
much more likely to beget a disposition too obsequious, than
too overbearing towards them. On the other side, the component parts of the state governments will in no instance be
indebted for their appointment to the direct agency of the federal government, and very little, if at all, to the local influence
of its members.

The number of individuals employed under the constitution
of the United States, will be much smaller than the number

employed under the particular states. There will consequently
be less of personal influence on the side of the former than of
the latter. The members of the legislative, executive, and judiciary departments of thirteen and more states; the justices of
peace, officers of militia, ministerial officers of justice, with all
the county, corporation, and town officers, for three millions
and more of people, intermixed, and having particular acquaintance with every class and circle of people, must exceed beyond
all proportion, both in number and influence, those of every
description who will be employed in the administration of the
federal system. Compare the members of the three great departments, of the thirteen states, excluding from the judiciary
department the justices of peace, with the members of the corresponding departments of the single government of the union;
compare the militia officers of three millions of people, with
the military and marine officers of any establishment which is
within the compass of probability, or, I may add, of possibility;
and in this view alone, we may pronounce the advantage of
the states to be decisive. If the federal government is to have
collectors of revenue, the state governments will have theirs
also. And as those of the former will be principally on the sea-
coast, and not very numerous, whilst those of the latter will be
spread over the face of the country, and will be very numerous,
the advantage in this view also lies on the same side. It is true
that the confederacy is to possess, and may exercise the power
of collecting internal as well as external taxes throughout the
states: but it is probable that this power will not be resorted
to, except for supplemental purposes of revenue; that an option
will then be given to the states to supply their quotas by previous collections of their own; and that the eventual collection,
under the immediate authority of the union, will generally be
made by the officers, and according to the rules appointed by
the several states. Indeed, it is extremely probable, that in other
instances, particularly in the organization of the judicial power,
the officers of the states will be clothed with the correspondent

authority of the union. Should it happen, however, that separate collectors of internal revenue should be appointed under the federal government, the influence of the whole number would not bear a comparison with that of the multitude of state officers in the opposite scale. Within every district, to which a federal collector would be allotted, there would not be less than thirty or forty, or even more officers, of different descriptions, and many of them persons of character and weight, whose influence would lie on the side of the state.

The powers delegated by the proposed constitution to the federal government, are few and defined. Those which are to remain in the state governments, are numerous and indefinite. The former will be exercised principally on external objects, as war, peace, negotiation, and foreign commerce; with which last the power of taxation will, for the most part, be connected. The powers reserved to the several states will extend to all the objects, which, in the ordinary course of affairs, concern the lives, liberties, and properties of the people; and the internal order, improvement, and prosperity of the state.

The operations of the federal government will be most extensive and important in times of war and danger; those of the state governments in times of peace and security. As the former periods will probably bear a small proportion to the latter, the state governments will here enjoy another advantage over the federal government. The more adequate indeed the federal powers may be rendered to the national defence, the less frequent will be those scenes of danger which might favour their ascendancy over the governments of the particular states.

If the new constitution be examined with accuracy and candour, it will be found that the change which it proposes, consists much less in the addition of NEW POWERS to the union than in the invigoration of its ORIGINAL POWERS. The regulation of commerce, it is true, is a new power; but that seems to be an addition which few oppose, and from which no apprehensions are entertained. The powers relating to war and peace, armies

and fleets, treaties and finance, with the other more considerable powers, are all vested in the existing congress by the
articles of confederation. The proposed change does not enlarge
these powers; it only substitutes a more effectual mode of administering them. The change relating to taxation, may be regarded as the most important: and yet the present congress
have as complete authority to REQUIRE of the states indefinite
supplies of money for the common defence and general welfare,
as the future congress will have to require them of individual
citizens; and the latter will be no more bound than the states
themselves have been, to pay the quotas respectively taxed on
them. Had the states complied punctually with the articles of
confederation, or could their compliance have been enforced by
as peaceable means as may be used with success towards single
persons, our past experience is very far from countenancing an
opinion, that the state governments would have lost their constitutional powers, and have gradually undergone an entire
consolidation. To maintain that such an event would have ensued, would be to say at once, that the existence of the state
governments is incompatible with any system whatever, that
accomplishes the essential purposes of the union.

PUBLIUS

NO. XLVI

THE SUBJECT OF THE LAST PAPER RESUMED; WITH AN EXAMINATION OF THE COMPARATIVE MEANS OF INFLUENCE OF THE FEDERAL AND STATE GOVERNMENTS

Resuming the subject of the last paper, I proceed to inquire,
whether the federal government or the state governments, will
have the advantage with regard to the predilection and support
of the people.

Notwithstanding the different modes in which they are appointed, we must consider both of them as substantially de-

pendent on the great body of the citizens of the United States. I assume this position here as it respects the first, reserving the proofs for another place. The federal and state governments are in fact but different agents and trustees of the people, instituted with different powers, and designated for different purposes. The adversaries of the constitution seem to have lost sight of the people altogether, in their reasonings on this subject; and to have viewed these different establishments, not only as mutual rivals and enemies, but as uncontroled by any common superior, in their efforts to usurp the authorities of each other. These gentlemen must here be reminded of their error. They must be told, that the ultimate authority, wherever the derivative may be found, resides in the people alone; and that it will not depend merely on the comparative ambition or address of the different governments, whether either, or which of them, will be able to enlarge its sphere of jurisdiction at the expense of the other. Truth, no less than decency, requires, that the event, in every case, should be supposed to depend on the sentiments and sanction of their common constituents.

Many considerations, besides those suggested on a former occasion, seem to place it beyond doubt, that the first and most natural attachment of the people will be to the governments of their respective states. Into the administration of these, a greater number of individuals will expect to rise. From the gift of these, a greater number of offices and emoluments will flow. By the superintending care of these, all the more domestic and personal interests of the people will be regulated and provided for. With the affairs of these, the people will be more familiarly and minutely conversant: and with the members of these, will a greater proportion of the people have the ties of personal acquaintance and friendship, and of family and party attachments. On the side of these, therefore, the popular bias may well be expected most strongly to incline.

Experience speaks the same language in this case. The federal administration, though hitherto very defective, in comparison with what may be hoped under a better system, had, during the war, and particularly whilst the independent fund of paper emissions was in credit, an activity and importance as great as it can well have, in any future circumstances whatever. It was engaged, too, in a course of measures which had for their object the protection of every thing that was dear, and the acquisition of every thing that could be desirable to the people at large. It was, nevertheless, invariably found, after the transient enthusiasm for the early congresses was over, that the attention and attachment of the people were turned anew to their own particular governments; that the federal council was at no time the idol of popular favour; and that opposition to proposed enlargements of its powers and importance, was the side usually taken by the men, who wished to build their political consequence on the prepossessions of their fellow-citizens.

If, therefore, as has been elsewhere remarked, the people should in future become more partial to the federal than to the state governments, the change can only result from such manifest and irresistible proofs of a better administration, as will overcome all their antecedent propensities. And in that case, the people ought not surely to be precluded from giving most of their confidence where they may discover it to be most due: but even in that case the state governments could have little to apprehend, because it is only within a certain sphere, that the federal power can, in the nature of things, be advantageously administered.

The remaining points, on which I propose to compare the federal and state governments, are the disposition and the faculty they may respectively possess, to resist and frustrate the measures of each other.

It has been already proved, that the members of the federal will be more dependent on the members of the state governments, than the latter will be on the former. It has appeared also, that the prepossessions of the people, on whom both will depend, will be more on the side of the state governments, than of the federal government. So far as the disposition of each, towards the other, may be influenced by these causes, the state governments must clearly have the advantage. But in a distinct and very important point of view, the advantage will lie on the same side. The prepossessions, which the members themselves will carry into the federal government, will generally be favourable to the states; whilst it will rarely happen, that the members of the state governments will carry into the public councils a bias in favour of the general government. A local spirit will infallibly prevail much more in the members of the congress, than a national spirit will prevail in the legislatures of the particular states. Every one knows, that a great proportion of the errors committed by the state legislatures, proceeds from the disposition of the members to sacrifice the comprehensive and permanent interests of the state, to the particular and separate views of the counties or districts in which they reside. And if they do not sufficiently enlarge their policy, to embrace the collective welfare of their particular state, how can it be imagined, that they will make the aggregate prosperity of the union, and the dignity and respectability of its government, the objects of their affections and consultations? For the same reason, that the members of the state legislatures will be unlikely to attach themselves sufficiently to national objects, the members of the federal legislature will be likely to attach themselves too much to local objects. The states will be to the latter, what counties and towns are to the former. Measures will too often be decided according to their probable effect, not on the national prosperity and happiness, but on the prejudices, interests, and pursuits of the governments and people of the individual states. What is the spirit that has in general characterized the proceedings of congress? A perusal of their journals, as well as the candid acknowledgments of such as have had a seat in that assembly, will inform us, that the members have but too frequently displayed the character, rather of partisans of their respective states, than of impartial guardians of a common interest; that where, on one occasion, improper sacrifices have been made of local considerations to the aggrandizement of the federal government, the great interests of the nation have suffered on an hundred, from an undue attention to the local prejudices, interests, and views of the particular states. I mean not by these reflections to insinuate, that the new federal government will not embrace a more enlarged plan of policy, than the existing government may have pursued; much less, that its views will be as confined as those of the state legislatures: but only that it will partake sufficiently of the spirit of both, to be disinclined to invade the rights of individual states, or the prerogatives of their governments. The motives on the part of the state governments, to augment their prerogatives by defalcations from the federal government, will be overruled by no reciprocal predispositions in the members.

Were it admitted, however, that the federal government may feel an equal disposition with the state governments to extend its power beyond the due limits, the latter would still have the advantage in the means of defeating such encroachments. If an act of a particular state, though unfriendly to the national government, be generally popular in that state, and should not too grossly violate the oaths of the state officers, it is executed immediately, and, of course, by means on the spot, and depending on the state alone. The opposition of the federal government, or the interposition of federal officers, would but inflame the zeal of all parties on the side of the state; and the evil could not be prevented or repaired, if at all, without the employment of means which must always be resorted to with reluctance and difficulty. On the other hand, should an unwarrantable measure of the federal government be unpopular in particular states, which would seldom fail to be the case, or even a warrantable measure be so, which may sometimes be the case, the means of opposition to it are powerful and at hand. The disquietude of the people; their repugnance, and perhaps refusal, to cooperate with the officers of the union; the frowns of the executive magistracy of the state; the embarrassments created by legislative devices, which would often be added on such occasions, would oppose, in any state, difficulties not to be despised; would form, in a large state, very serious inpediments; and where the sentiments of several adjoining states happened to be in unison, would present obstructions which the federal government would hardly be willing to encounter.

But ambitious encroachments of the federal government, on the authority of the state governments, would not excite the opposition of a single state, or of a few states only. They would be signals of general alarm. Every government would espouse the common cause. A correspondence would be opened. Plans of resistance would be concerted. One spirit would animate and conduct the whole. The same combination, in short, would result from an apprehension of the federal, as was produced by the dread of a foreign yoke; and unless the projected innovations should be voluntarily renounced, the same appeal to a trial of force would be made in the one case, as was made in the other. But what degree of madness could ever drive the federal government to such an extremity? In the contest with Great Britain, one part of the empire was employed against the other. The more numerous part invaded the rights of the less numerous part. The attempt was unjust and unwise; but it was not in speculation absolutely chimerical. But what would be the contest, in the case we are supposing? Who would be the parties? A few representatives of the people would be opposed to the people themselves; or rather one set of representatives would be contending against thirteen sets of representatives, with the whole body of their common constituents on the side of the latter.

The only refuge left for those who prophesy the downfal of the state governments, is the visionary supposition, that the federal government may previously accumulate a military force for the projects of ambition. The reasonings contained in these papers must have been employed to little purpose indeed, if it could be necessary now to disprove the reality of this danger. That the people and the states should, for a sufficient period of time, elect an uninterrupted succession of men ready to betray both; that the traitors should, throughout this period, uniformly and systematically pursue some fixed plan for the extension of the military establishment; that the governments and the people of the states should silently and patiently behold the gathering storm, and continue to supply the materials, until it should be prepared to burst on their own heads, *a* must appear to every one more like the incoherent dreams *madness* of a delirious jealousy, or the misjudged exaggerations of a counterfeit zeal, than like the sober apprehensions of genuine patriotism. Extravagant as the supposition is, let it however be made. Let a regular army, fully equal to the resources of the country, be formed; and let it be entirely at the devotion of the federal government; still it would not be going too far to say, that the state governments, with the people on their side, would be able to repel the danger. The highest number to which, according to the best computation, a standing army can be carried in any country, does not exceed one hundredth part *½* of the whole number of souls; or one twenty-fifth part of the *country* number able to bear arms. This proportion would not yield, in *vs* the United States, an army of more than twenty-five or thirty *½* thousand men. To these would be opposed a militia amounting *country* to near half a million of citizens with arms in their hands, officered by men chosen from among themselves, fighting for their common liberties, and united and conducted by governments possessing their affections and confidence. It may well be doubted, whether a militia thus circumstanced, could ever be conquered by such a proportion of regular troops. Those, who are best acquainted with the late successful resistance of this country against the British arms, will be most inclined to deny the possibility of it. Besides the advantage of being armed, which the Americans possess over the people of almost every other nation, the existence of subordinate governments, to which the people are attached, and by which the militia officers are appointed, forms a barrier against the enterprises of ambition, more insurmountable than any which a simple government of any form can admit of. Notwithstanding the military establishments in the several kingdoms of Europe, which are carried as far as the public resources will bear, the governments are afraid to trust the people with arms. And it it is not certain, that with this aid alone, they would not be able to shake off their yokes. But were the people to possess the additional advantages of local governments chosen by themselves, who could collect the national will, and direct the national force, and of officers appointed out of the militia, by these governments, and attached both to them and to the militia, it may be affirmed with the greatest assurance, that the throne of every tyranny in Europe would be speedily over-turned in spite of the legions which surround it. Let us not insult the free and gallant citizens of America with the suspicion, that they would be less able to defend the rights of which they would be in actual possession, than the debased subjects of arbitrary power would be to rescue theirs from the hands of their oppressors. Let us rather no longer insult them with the supposition, that they can ever reduce themselves to the necessity of making the experiment, by a blind and tame submission to the long train of insidious measures which must precede and produce it.

The argument under the present head may be put into a very concise form, which appears altogether conclusive. Either the mode in which the federal government is to be constructed, will render it sufficiently dependent on the people, or it will not. On the first supposition, it will be restrained by that dependence from forming schemes obnoxious to their constituents. On the other supposition, it will not possess the confidence of the people, and its schemes of usurpation will be easily defeated by the state governments; which will be supported by the people.

On summing up the considerations stated in this and the last paper, they seem to amount to the most convincing evidence, that the powers proposed to be lodged in the federal government, are as little formidable to those reserved to the individual states, as they are indispensably necessary to accomplish the purposes of the union; and that all those alarms which have been sounded, of a meditated and consequential annihilation of the state governments, must, on the most favourable interpretation, be ascribed to the chimerical fears of the authors of them.   PUBLIUS.

NO. XLVII
THE MEANING OF THE MAXIM, WHICH REQUIRES A SEPARATION OF THE DEPARTMENTS OF POWER, EXAMINED AND ASCERTAINED

Having reviewed the general form of the proposed government, and the general mass of power allotted to it; I proceed to examine the particular structure of this government, and the distribution of this mass of power among its constituent parts.

One of the principal objections inculcated by the more respectable adversaries to the constitution, is its supposed violation of the political maxim, that the legislative, executive, and judiciary departments, ought to be separate and distinct. In the structure of the federal government, no regard, it is said, seems to have been paid to this essential precaution in favour of liberty. The several departments of power are distributed and blended in such a manner, as at once to destroy all symmetry and beauty of form; and to expose some of the essential parts of the edifice to the danger of being crushed by the disproportionate weight of other parts.

No political truth is certainly of greater intrinsic value, or is stamped with the authority of more enlightened patrons of liberty, than that on which the objection is founded. The accumulation of all powers, legislative, executive, and judiciary, in the same hands, whether of one, a few, or many, and whether hereditary, self-appointed, or elective, may justly be pronounced the very definition of tyranny. Were the federal constitution, therefore, really chargeable with this accumulation of power, or with a mixture of powers, having a dangerous tendency to such an accumulation, no further arguments would be necessary to inspire a universal reprobation of the system. I persuade myself, however, that it will be made apparent to everyone, that the charge cannot be supported, and that the maxim on which it relies has been totally misconceived and misapplied. In order to form correct ideas on this important subject, it will be proper to investigate the sense in which the preservation of liberty requires, that the three great departments of power should be separate and distinct.

The oracle who is always consulted and cited on this subject, is the celebrated Montesquieu. If he be not the author of this invaluable precept in the science of politics, he has the merit at least of displaying and recommending it most effectually to the attention of mankind. Let us endeavour, in the first place, to ascertain his meaning on this point.

The British constitution was to Montesquieu, what Homer has been to the didactic writers on epic poetry. As the latter have considered the work of the immortal bard, as the perfect model from which the principles and rules of the epic art were to be drawn, and by which all similar works were to be judged: so this great political critic appears to have viewed the constitution of England as the standard, or to use his own expression, as the mirror of political liberty; and to have delivered, in the form of elementary truths, the several characteristic principles of that particular system. That we may be sure then not to mistake his meaning in this case, let us recur to the source from which the maxim was drawn.

On the slightest view of the British constitution, we must perceive, that the legislative, executive, and judiciary departments, are by no means totally separate and distinct from each other. The executive magistrate forms an integral part of the legislative authority. He alone has the prerogative of making treaties with foreign sovereigns, which, when made, have, under certain limitations, the force of legislative acts. All the members of the judiciary department are appointed by him; can be removed by him on the address of the two houses of parliament, and form, when he pleases to consult them, one of his constitutional councils. One branch of the legislative department, forms also a great constitutional council to the executive chief; as, on another hand, it is the sole depository of judicial power in cases of impeachment, and is invested with the supreme appellate jurisdiction in all other cases. The judges again are so far connected with the legislative department, as often to attend and participate in its deliberations, though not admitted to a legislative vote.

From these facts, by which Montesquieu was guided, it may clearly be inferred, that in saying, "there can be no liberty, where the legislative and executive powers are united in the same person, or body of magistrates;" or, "if the power of judging, be not separated from the legislative and executive powers," he did not mean that these departments ought to have no *partial agency* in, or no *control!* over the acts of each other. His meaning, as his own words import, and still more conclusively as illustrated by the example in his eye, can amount to no more than this, that where the *whole* power of one department is exercised by the same hands which possess the *whole* power of another department, the fundamental principles of a free constitution are subverted. This would have been the case in the constitution examined by him, if the king, who is the sole executive magistrate, had possessed also the complete legislative power, or the supreme administration of justice; or if the entire legislative body had possessed the supreme judiciary, or the supreme executive authority. This, however, is not among the vices of that constitution. The magistrate, in whom the whole executive power resides, cannot of himself make a law, though he can put a negative on every law; nor administer justice in person, though he has the appointment of those who do administer it. The judges can exercise no executive prerogative, though they are shoots from the executive stock; nor any legislative function, though they may be advised with by the legislative councils. The entire legislature can perform no judiciary act; though by the joint act of two of its branches, the judges may be removed from their offices; and though one of its branches is possessed of the judicial power in the last resort. The entire legislature again can exercise no executive prerogative, though one of its branches[1] constitutes the supreme executive magistracy; and another, on the impeachment of a third, can try and condemn all the subordinate officers in the executive department.

The reasons on which Montesquieu grounds his maxim, are a further demonstration of his meaning. "When the legislative and executive powers are united in the same person or body," says he, "there can be no liberty, because apprehensions may arise lest *the same* monarch or senate should *enact* tyrannical laws, to *execute* them in a tyrannical manner." Again, "Were the power of judging joined with the legislative, the life and liberty of the subject would be exposed to arbitrary control, for *the judge* would then be *the legislator*. Were it joined to the executive power, *the judge* might behave with "all the violence of *an oppressor*." Some of these reasons are more fully explained in other passages; but briefly stated as they are here,

---

[1] The king.

they sufficiently establish the meaning which we have put on this celebrated maxim of this celebrated author. . . .

NO. LI

THE SAME SUBJECT CONTINUED, WITH A VIEW TO THE MEANS
OF GIVING EFFICACY IN PRACTICE TO THAT MAXIM
AND CONCLUDED

To what expedient, then, shall we finally resort, for maintaining in practice the necessary partition of power among the several departments as laid down in the constitution? The only answer that can be given is, that as all these exterior provisions are found to be inadequate, the defect must be supplied, by so contriving the interior structure of the government, as that its several constituent parts may, by their mutual relations, be the means of keeping each other in their proper places. Without presuming to undertake a full development of this important idea, I will hazard a few general observations, which may perhaps place it in a clearer light, and enable us to form a more correct judgment of the principles and structure of the government planned by the convention.

In order to lay a due foundation for that separate and distinct exercise of the different powers of government, which, to a certain extent, is admitted on all hands to be essential to the preservation of liberty, it is evident that each department should have a will of its own; and consequently should be so constituted, that the members of each should have as little agency as possible in the appointment of the members of the others. Were this principle rigorously adhered to, it would require that all the appointments for the supreme executive, legislative, and judiciary magistracies, should be drawn from the same fountain of authority, the people, though channels having no communication whatever with one another. Perhaps such a plan of constructing the several departments, would be less difficult in practice, than it may in contemplation appear. Some difficulties, however, and some additional expense would attend the execution of it. Some deviations, therefore, from the principle must be admitted. In the constitution of the judiciary department in particular, it might be inexpedient to insist rigorously on the principle; first, because peculiar qualifications being essential in the members, the primary consideration ought to be to select that mode of choice which best secures these qualifications; secondly, because the permanent tenure by which the appointments are held in that department, must soon destroy all sense of dependence on the authority conferring them.

It is equally evident, that the members of each department should be as little dependent as possible on those of the others, for the emoluments annexed to their offices. Were the executive magistrate, or the judges not independent of the legislature in this particular, their independence in every other would be merely nominal.

But the great security against a gradual concentration of the several powers in the same department, consists in giving to those who administer each department, the necessary constitutional means, and personal motives, to resist encroachments of the others. The provision for defence must in this, as in all other cases, be made commensurate to the danger of attack. Ambition must be made to counteract ambition. The interest of the man, must be connected with the constitutional rights of the place. It may be a reflection on human nature, that such devices should be necessary to control the abuses of government. But what is government itself, but the greatest of all reflections on human nature? If men were angels, no government would be necessary. If angels were to govern men, either external nor internal controls on government would be necessary. In framing a government which is to be administered by men over men, the great difficulty lies in this:

you must first enable the government to control the governed; and in the next place oblige it to control itself. A dependence on the people is, no doubt, the primary control on the government; but experience has taught mankind the necessity of auxiliary precautions.

This policy of supplying, by opposite and rival interests, the defect of better motives, might be traced through the whole system of human affairs, private as well as public. We see it particularly displayed in all the subordinate distributions of power; where the constant aim is, to divide and arrange the several offices in such a manner as that each may be a check on the other; that the private interest of every individual may be a sentinel over the public rights. These inventions of prudence cannot be less requisite in the distribution of the supreme powers of the state.

But it is not possible to give to each department an equal power of self-defence. In republican government, the legislative authority necessarily predominates. The remedy for this inconveniency is, to divide the legislature into different branches; and to render them, by different modes of election, and different principles of action, as little connected with each other, as the nature of their common functions, and their common dependence on the society, will admit. It may even be necessary to guard against dangerous encroachments by still further precautions. As the weight of the legislative authority requires that it should be thus divided, the weakness of the executive may require, on the other hand, that it should be fortified. An absolute negative on the legislature, appears, at first view, to be the natural defence with which the executive magistrate should be armed. But perhaps it would be neither altogether safe, nor alone sufficient. On ordinary occasions, it might not be exerted with the requisite firmness; and on extraordinary occasions, it might be perfidiously abused. May not this defect of an absolute negative be supplied by some qualified connexion between this weaker department, and the weaker branch of the stronger department, by which the latter may be led to support the constitutional rights of the former, without being too much detached from the rights of its own department?

If the principles on which these observations are founded be just, as I persuade myself they are, and they be applied as a criterion to the several state constitutions, and to the federal constitution, it will be found, that if the latter does not perfectly correspond with them, the former are infinitely less able to bear such a test.

There are moreover two considerations particularly applicable to the federal system of America, which place that system in a very interesting point of view.

First. In a single republic, all the power surrendered by the people, is submitted to the administration of a single government; and the usurpations are guarded against, by a division of the government into distinct and separate departments. In the compound republic of America, the power surrendered by the people, is first divided between two distinct governments, and then the portion allotted to each subdivided among distinct and separate departments. Hence a double security arises to the rights of the people. The different governments will control each other; at the same time that each will be controled by itself.

Second. It is of great importance in a republic, not only to guard the society against the oppression of its rulers; but to guard one part of the society against the injustice of the other part. Different interests necessarily exist in different classes of citizens. If a majority be united by a common interest, the rights of the minority will be insecure. There are but two methods of providing against this evil: the one, by creating a will in the community independent of the majority, that is, of the society itself; the other, by comprehending in the society so many separate descriptions of citizens, as will render an unjust combination of a majority of the whole very improbable, if not impracticable. The first method prevails in all governments possessing an hereditary or self-appointed authority. This, at best, is but a precarious security; because a power independent of the society may as well espouse the unjust views of the major, as the rightful interests of the minor party, and may possibly be turned against both parties. The second method will be exemplified in the federal republic of the United States. Whilst all authority in it will be derived from, and dependent on the society, the society itself will be broken into so many parts, interests, and classes of citizens, that the rights of individuals, or of the minority will be in little danger from interested combinations of the majority. In a free government, the security for civil rights must be the same as that for religious rights. It consists in the one case in the multiplicity of interests, and in the other in the multiplicity of sects.

The degree of security in both cases will depend on the number of interests and sects; and this may be presumed to depend on the extent of country and number of people comprehended under the same government. This view of the subject must particularly recommend a proper federal system to all the sincere and considerate friends of republican government: since it shows, that in exact proportion as the territory of the union may be formed into more circumscribed confederacies, or states, oppressive combinations of a majority will be facilitated; the best security under the republican form, for the rights of every class of citizens, will be diminished; and consequently, the stability and independence of some member of the government, the only other security, must be proportionally increased. Justice is the end of government. It is the end of civil society. It ever has been, and ever will be pursued, until it be obtained, or until liberty be lost in the pursuit. In a society, under the forms of which the stronger faction can readily unite and oppress the weaker, anarchy may as truly be said to reign, as in a state of nature, where the weaker individual is not secured against the violence of the stronger: and as in the latter state, even the stronger individuals are prompted, by the uncertainty of their condition, to submit to a government which may protect the weak, as well as themselves: so in the former state, will the more powerful factions or parties be gradually induced, by a like motive, to wish for a government which will protect all parties, the weaker as well as the more powerful. It can be little doubted, that if the state of Rhode Island was separated from the confederacy, and left to itself, the insecurity of rights under the popular form of government within such narrow limits, would be displayed by such reiterated oppressions of factious majorities, that some power altogether independent of the people, would soon be called for by the voice of the very factions whose misrule had proved the necessity of it. In the extended republic of the United States, and among the great variety of interests, parties, and sects, which it embraces, a coalition of a majority of the whole society could seldom take place upon any other principles than those of justice and the general good: whilst there being thus less danger to a minor from the will of a major party, there must be less pretext also, to provide for the security of the former, by introducing into the government a will not dependent on the latter: or, in other words, a will independent of the society itself. It is no less certain than it is important, notwithstanding the contrary opinions which have been entertained, that the larger the society, provided it lie within a practical sphere, the more duly capable it will be of self-government. And happily for the *republican cause,* the practicable sphere may be carried to a very great extent, by a judicious modification and mixture of the *federal principle.*

PUBLIUS

NO. LVII

CONCERNING THE HOUSE OF REPRESENTATIVES IN RELATION
TO THE SUPPOSED TENDENCY OF THE PLAN OF THE CONVENTION
TO ELEVATE THE FEW ABOVE THE MANY

The *third* charge against the house of representatives is, that it will be taken from that class of citizens which will have least sympathy with the mass of the people; and be most likely to aim at an ambitious sacrifice of the many, to the aggrandizement of the few.

Of all the objections which have been framed against the federal constitution, this is perhaps the most extraordinary. Whilst the objection itself is levelled against a pretended oligarchy, the principle of it strikes at the very root of republican government.

The aim of every political constitution is, or ought to be, first, to obtain for rulers men who possess most wisdom to discern, and most virtue to pursue, the common good of the society; and, in the next place, to take the most effectual precautions for keeping them virtuous, whilst they continue to hold their public trust. The elective mode of obtaining rulers, is the characteristic policy of republican government. The means relied on in this form of government for preventing their degeneracy, are numerous and various. The most effectual one, is such a limitation of the term of appointments, as will maintain a proper responsibility to the people.

Let me now ask, what circumstance there is in the constitution of the house of representatives, that violates the principles of republican government; or favours the elevation of the few, on the ruins of the many? Let me ask, whether every circumstance is not, on the contrary, strictly conformable to these principles; and scrupulously impartial to the rights and pretensions of every class and description of citizens?

Who are to be the electors of the federal representatives? Not the rich, more than the poor; not the learned, more than the ignorant; not the haughty heirs of distinguished names, more than the humble sons of obscurity and unpropitious fortune. The electors are to be the great body of the people of the United States. They are to be the same who exercise the right in every state of electing the correspondent branch of the legislature of the state.

Who are to be the objects of popular choice? Every citizen

whose merit may recommend him to the esteem and confidence of his country. No qualification of wealth, or birth, or religious faith, or of civil profession, is permitted to fetter the judgment or disappoint the inclination of the people.

If we consider the situation of the men on whom the free suffrages of their fellow-citizens may confer the representative trust, we shall find it involving every security which can be devised or desired for their fidelity to their constituents.

In the first place, as they will have been distinguished by the preference of their fellow-citizens, we are to presume, that in general they will be somewhat distinguished also by those qualities which entitle them to it, and which promise a sincere and scrupulous regard to the nature of their engagements.

In the second place, they will enter into the public service under circumstances which cannot fail to produce a temporary affection at least to their constituents. There is in every breast a sensibility to marks of honour, of favour, of esteem, and of confidence, which, apart from all considerations of interest, is some pledge for grateful and benevolent returns. Ingratitude is a common topic of declamation against human nature; and it must be confessed, that instances of it are but too frequent and flagrant, both in public and in private life. But the universal and extreme indignation which it inspires, is itself a proof of the energy and prevalence of the contrary sentiment.

In the third place, those ties which bind the representative to his constituents, are strengthened by motives of a more selfish nature. His pride and vanity attach him to a form of government which favours his pretensions, and gives him a share in its honours and distinctions. Whatever hopes or projects might be entertained by a few aspiring characters, it must generally happen, that a great proportion of the men deriving their advancement from their influence with the people, would have more to hope from a preservation of their favour, than from innovations in the government subversive of the authority of the people.

All these securities, however, would be found very insufficient without the restraint of frequent elections. Hence, in the fourth place, the house of representatives is so constituted, as to support in the members an habitual recollection of their dependence on the people. Before the sentiments impressed on their minds by the mode of their elevation can be effaced by the exercise of power, they will be compelled to anticipate the moment when their power is to cease, when their exercise of it is to be reviewed, and when they must descend to the level from which they were raised; there for ever to remain, unless a faithful discharge of their trust shall have established their title to a renewal of it.

I will add, as a fifth circumstance in the situation of the house of representatives, restraining them from oppressive measures, that they can make no law which will not have its full operation on themselves and their friends, as well as on the great mass of the society. This has always been deemed one of the strongest bonds by which human policy can connect the rulers and the people together. It creates between them that communion of interest, and sympathy of sentiments, of which few governments have furnished examples; but without which every government degenerates into tyranny. If it be asked, what is to restrain the house of representatives from making legal discriminations in favour of themselves, and a particular class of the society; I answer, the genius of the whole system; the nature of just and constitutional laws; and, above all, the vigilant and manly spirit which actuates the people of America; a spirit which nourishes freedom, and in return is nourished by it.

If this spirit shall ever be so far debased, as to tolerate a law not obligatory on the legislature, as well as on the people, the people will be prepared to tolerate any thing but liberty.

Such will be the relation between the house of representatives and their constituents. Duty, gratitude, interest, ambition itself, are the chords by which they will be bound to fidelity and sympathy with the great mass of the people. It is possible that these may all be insufficient to control the caprice and wickedness of men. But are they not all that government will admit, and that human prudence can devise? Are they not the genuine and the characteristic means, by which republican government provides for the liberty and happiness of the people? Are they not the identical means on which every state government in the union relies for the attainment of these important ends? What then are we to understand by the objection which this paper has combated? What are we to say to the men who profess the most flaming zeal for republican government, yet boldly impeach the fundamental principle of it; who pretend to be champions for the right and the capacity of the people to choose their own rulers, yet maintain that they will prefer those only who will immediately and infallibly betray the trust committed to them?

Were the objection to be read by one who had not seen the mode prescribed by the constitution for the choice of representatives, he could suppose nothing less, than that some unreasonable qualification of property was annexed to the right of suffrage; or that the right of eligibility was limited to persons of particular families or fortunes; or at least that the mode prescribed by the state constitutions was in some respect or other, very grossly departed from. We have seen, how far such a supposition would err, as to the two first points. Nor would it, in fact, be less erroneous as to the last. The only difference discoverable between the two cases is, that each representative of the United States will be elected by five or six thousand citizens: whilst in the individual states, the election of a representative is left to about as many hundred. Will it be pretended, that this difference is sufficient to justify an attachment to the state governments, and an abhorrence to the federal government? If this be the point on which the objection turns, it deserves to be examined.

Is it supported by *reason?* This cannot be said, without

maintaining that five or six thousand citizens are less capable of choosing a fit representative, or more liable to be corrupted by an unfit one, than five or six hundred. Reason, on the contrary, assures us, that as in so great a number, a fit representative would be most likely to be found; so the choice would be most likely to be found; so the choice would be less likely to be diverted from him, by the intrigues of the ambitious or the bribes of the rich.

Is the *consequence* from this doctrine admissible? If we say that five or six hundred citizens are as many as can jointly exercise their right of suffrage, must we not deprive the people of the immediate choice of their public servants, in every instance, where the administration of the government does not require as many of them as will amount to one for that number of citizens?

Is the doctrine warranted by *facts?* It was shown in the last paper, that the real representation in the British house of commons very little exceeds the proportion of one for every thirty thousand inhabitants. Besides a variety of powerful causes, not existing here, and which favour in that country the pretensions of rank and wealth, no person is eligible as a representative of a county, unless he possess real estate of the clear value of six hundred pounds sterling per year; nor of a city or borough, unless he possess a like estate of half that annual value. To this qualification, on the part of the county representatives, is added another on the part of the county electors, which restrains the right of suffrage to persons having a freehold estate of the annual value of more than twenty pounds sterling, according to the present rate of money. Notwithstanding these unfavourable circumstances, and notwithstanding some very unequal laws in the British code, it cannot be said, that the representatives of the nation have elevated the few on the ruins of the many.

But we need not resort to foreign experience on this subject. Our own is explicit and decisive. The districts in New Hampshire, in which the senators are chosen immediately by the people, are nearly as large as will be necessary for her representatives in the congress. Those of Massachusetts are larger than will be necessary for that purpose; and those of New York still more so. In the last state, the members of assembly, for the cities and counties of New York and Albany, are elected by very nearly as many voters as will be entitled to a representative in the congress, calculating on the number of sixty-five representatives only. It makes no difference, that in these senatorial districts and counties, a number of representatives are voted for by each elector at the same time. If the same electors, at the same time, are capable of choosing four or five representatives, they cannot be incapable of choosing one. Pennsylvania is an additional example. Some of her counties, which elect her state representatives, are almost as large as her districts will be by which her federal representatives will be elected. The city of Philadelphia is supposed to contain between fifty and sixty thousand souls. It will, therefore, form nearly two districts for the choice of federal representatives. It forms, however, but one county, in which every elector votes for each of its representatives in the state legislature. And what may appear to be still more directly to our purpose, the whole city actually elects a *single member* for the executive council. This is the case in all the other counties of the state.

Are not these facts the most satisfactory proofs of the fallacy which has been employed against the branch of the federal government under consideration? Has it appeared on trial, that the senators of New Hampshire, Massachusetts, and New York; or the executive council of Pennsylvania; or the members of the assembly in the two last states, have betrayed any peculiar disposition to sacrifice the many to the few; or are in any respect less worthy of their places, than the representatives and magistrates appointed in other states, by very small divisions of the people?

But there are cases of a stronger complexion than any which I have yet quoted. One branch of the legislature of Connecticut is so constituted, that each member of it is elected by the whole state. So is the governor of that state, of Massachusetts, and of this state, and the president of New Hampshire. I leave every man to decide, whether the result of any one of these experiments can be said to countenance a suspicion, that a diffusive mode of choosing representatives of the people tends to elevate traitors, and to undermine the public liberty.

PUBLIUS

NO. LXII

CONCERNING THE CONSTITUTION OF THE SENATE, WITH REGARD TO THE QUALIFICATIONS OF THE MEMBERS; THE MANNER OF APPOINTING THEM; THE EQUALITY OF REPRESENTATION; THE NUMBER OF THE SENATORS; AND THE DURATION OF THEIR APPOINTMENTS

Having examined the constitution of the house of representatives, and answered such of the objections against it as seemed to merit notice, I enter next on the examination of the senate.

The heads, under which this member of the government may be considered, are, 1. The qualifications of senators; 2. The appointment of them by the state legislatures; 3. The equality of representation in the senate; 4. The number of senators, and the term for which they are to be elected; 5. The powers vested in the senate.

1. The qualifications proposed for senators, as distinguished from those of representatives, consist in a more advanced age, and a longer period of citizenship: A senator must be thirty years of age at least; as a representative must be twenty-five. And the former must have been a citizen nine years; as seven years are required for the latter. The propriety of these distinctions is explained by the nature of the senatorial trust; which, requiring greater extent of information and stability of character, requires, at the same time, that the senator should have

reached a period of life most likely to supply these advantages; and which, participating immediately in transactions with foreign nations, ought to be exercised by none who are not thoroughly weaned from the prepossessions and habits incident to foreign birth and education. The term of nine years appears to be a prudent mediocrity between a total exclusion of adopted citizens, whose merit and talents may claim a share in the public confidence, and an indiscriminate and hasty admission of them, which might create a channel for foreign influence on the national councils.

2. It is equally unnecessary to dilate on the appointment of senators by the state legislatures. Among the various modes which might have been devised for constituting this branch of the government, that which has been proposed by the convention is probably the most congenial with the public opinion. It is recommended by the double advantage of favouring a select appointment, and of giving to the state governments such an agency in the formation of the federal government, as must secure the authority of the former, and may form a convenient link between the two systems.

3. The equality of representation in the senate is another point, which, being evidently the result of compromise between the opposite pretensions of the large and the small states, does not call for much discussion. If indeed it be right, that among a people thoroughly incorporated into one nation, every district ought to have a *proportional* share in the government; and that among independent and sovereign states, bound together by a simple league, the parties, however unequal in size, ought to have an *equal* share in the common councils; it does not appear to be without some reason, that in a compound republic, partaking both of the national and federal character, the government ought to be founded on a mixture of the principles of proportional and equal representation. But it is superfluous to try, by the standard of theory, a part of the constitution which

is allowed on all hands to be the result, not of theory, but "of a spirit of amity, and that mutual deference "and concession which the peculiarity of our political situation rendered indispensable." A common government, with powers equal to its objects, is called for by the voice, and still more loudly by the political situation, of America. A government, founded on principles more consonant to the wishes of the larger states, is not likely to be obtained from the smaller states. The only option, then, for the former, lies between the proposed government, and a government still more objectionable. Under this alternative, the advice of prudence must be, to embrace the lesser evil, and, instead of indulging a fruitless anticipation of the possible mischiefs which may ensue, to contemplate rather the advantageous consequences which may qualify the sacrifice.

In this spirit it may be remarked, that the equal vote allowed to each state, is at once a constitutional recognition of the portion of sovereignty remaining in the individual states, and an instrument for preserving that residuary sovereignty. So far the equality ought to be no less acceptable to the large than to the small states; since they are not less solicitous to guard, by every possible expedient, against an improper consolidation of the states into one simple republic.

Another advantage accruing from this ingredient in the constitution of the senate is, the additional impediment it must prove against improper acts of legislation. No law or resolution can now be past without the concurrence, first, of a majority of the people, and, then, of a majority of the states. It must be acknowledged that this complicated check on legislation may, in some instances, be injurious as well as beneficial; and *that* the peculiar defence which it involves in favour of the smaller states, would be more rational, if any interests common to them, and distinct from those of the other states, would otherwise be exposed to peculiar danger. But as the larger states will always be able, by their power over the supplies, to defeat unreasonable exertions of this prerogative of the lesser states; and as the facility and excess of law-making seem to be the diseases to which our governments are most liable, it is not impossible that this part of the constitution may be more convenient in practice, than it appears to many in contemplation.

4. The number of senators, and the duration of their appointment, come next to be considered. In order to form an accurate judgment on both these points, it will be proper to inquire into the purposes which are to be answered by a senate; and in order to ascertain these, it will be necessary to review the inconveniences which a republic must suffer from the want of such an institution.

First.   It is a misfortune incident to republican government, though in a less degree than to other governments, that those who administer it may forget their obligations to their constituents, and prove unfaithful to their important trust. In this point of view, a senate, as a second branch of the legislative assembly, distinct from, and dividing the power with, a first, must be in all cases a salutary check on the government. It doubles the security to the people, by requiring the concurrence of two distinct bodies in schemes of usurpation or perfidy, where the ambition or corruption of one would otherwise be sufficient. This is a precaution founded on such clear principles, and now so well understood in the United States, that it would be more than superfluous to enlarge on it. I will barely remark, that as the improbability of sinister combinations will be in proportion to the dissimilarity in the genius of the two bodies, it must be politic to distinguish them from each other by every circumstance which will consist with a due harmony in all proper measures, and with the genuine principles of republican government.

Second.   The necessity of a senate is not less indicated by the propensity of all single and numerous assemblies, to yield to the impulse of sudden and violent passions, and to be seduced by factious leaders into intemperate and pernicious reso-

lutions. Examples on this subject might be cited without
number; and from proceedings within the United States, as well
as from the history of other nations. But a position that will not
be contradicted, need not to be proved. All that need be remarked is, that a body which is to correct this infirmity, ought
itself to be free from it, and consequently ought to be less
numerous. It ought moreover to possess great firmness, and
consequently ought to hold its authority by a tenure of considerable duration.

Third.   Another defect to be supplied by a senate, lies in a
want of due acquaintance with the objects and principles of
legislation. It is not possible that an assembly of men, called for
the most part from pursuits of a private nature, continued in
appointment for a short time, and led by no permanent motive
to devote the intervals of public occupation to a study of the
laws, the affairs, and the comprehensive interests of their country, should, if left wholly to themselves, escape a variety of
important errors in the exercise of their legislative trust. It may
be affirmed, on the best grounds, that no small share of the
present embarrassments of America is to be charged on the
blunders of our governments; and that these have proceeded
from the heads rather than the hearts of most of the authors of
them. What indeed are all the repealing, explaining, and
amending laws, which fill and disgrace our voluminous codes,
but so many monuments of deficient wisdom; so many impeachments exhibited by each succeeding, against each preceding session; so many admonitions to the people, of the value
of those aids which may be expected from a well-constituted
senate.

A good government implies two things: first, fidelity to the
object of government, which is the happiness of the people;
secondly, a knowledge of the means by which that object can
be best attained. Some governments are deficient in both these
qualities: most governments are deficient in the first. I scruple
not to assert, that in American governments, too little attention

has been paid to the last. The federal constitution avoids this error: and what merits particular notice, it provides for the last in a mode which increases the security for the first.

Fourth.   The mutability in the public councils, arising from a rapid succession of new members, however qualified they may be, points out, in the strongest manner, the necessity of some stable institution in the government. Every new election in the states, is found to change one half of the representatives. From this change of men must proceed a change of opinions; and from a change of opinions, a change of measures. But a continual change even of good measures is inconsistent with every rule of prudence, and every prospect of success. The remark is verified in private life, and becomes more just, as well as more important in national transactions.

To trace the mischievous effects of a mutable government, would fill a volume. I will hint a few only, each of which will be perceived to be a source of innumerable others.

In the first place, it forfeits the respect and confidence of other nations, and all the advantages connected with national character. An individual who is observed to be inconsistent to his plans, or perhaps to carry on his affairs without any plan at all, is marked at once by all prudent people, as a speedy victim to his own unsteadiness and folly. His more friendly neighbours may pity him, but all will decline to connect their fortunes with his: and not a few will seize the opportunity of making their fortunes out of his. One nation is to another, what one individual is to another; with this melancholy distinction perhaps, that the former, with fewer of the benevolent emotions than the latter, are under fewer restraints also from taking undue advantage from the indiscretions of each other. Every nation, consequently, whose affairs betray a want of wisdom and stability, may calculate on every loss which can be sustained from the more systematic policy of its wiser neighbours. But the best instruction on this subject is unhappily conveyed to America by the example of her own situation. She finds that

she is held in no respect by her friends; that she is the derision
of her enemies; and that she is a prey to every nation which has
an interest in speculating on her fluctuating councils and embarrassed affairs.

The internal effects of a mutable policy are still more calami-
tous. It poisons the blessings of liberty itself. It will be of little
avail to the people, that the laws are made by men of their own
choice, if the laws be so voluminous that they cannot be read,
or so incoherent that they cannot be understood; if they be
repealed or revised before they are promulged, or undergo such
incessant changes, that no man, who knows what the law is
to-day, can guess, what it will be to-morrow. Law is defined to
be a rule of action: but how can that be a rule, which is little
known, and less fixed?

Another effect of public instability is the unreasonable advantage it gives to the sagacious, the enterprising, and the
moneyed few, over the industrious and uninformed mass of
the people. Every new regulation concerning commerce or revenue, or in any manner affecting the value of the different
species of property, presents a new harvest to those who watch
the change and can trace the consequences; a harvest, reared
not by themselves, but by the toils and cares of the great body
of their fellow-citizens. This is a state of things, in which it may
be said, with some truth, that laws are made for the *few*, not for
the *many*.

In another point of view, great injury results from an unstable government. The want of confidence in the public councils
damps every useful undertaking, the success and profit of
which may depend on a continuance of existing arrangements.
What prudent merchant will hazard his fortunes in any new
branch of commerce, when he knows not but that his plans may
be rendered unlawful before they can be executed? What
farmer or manufacturer will lay himself out for the encouragement given to any particular cultivation or establishment, when
he can have no assurance, that his preparatory labours and ad-

vances will not render him a victim to an inconstant government? In a word, no great improvement or laudable enterprise can go forward, which requires the auspices of a steady system of national policy.

But the most deplorable effect of all, is that diminution of attachment and reverence, which steals into the hearts of the people, towards a political system which betrays so many marks of infirmity, and disappoints so many of their flattering hopes. No government, any more than an individual, will long be respected, without being truly respectable; nor be truly respectable, without possessing a certain portion of order and stability.

PUBLIUS

NO. LXIII
A FURTHER VIEW OF THE CONSTITUTION OF THE SENATE, IN REGARD TO THE DURATION OF THE APPOINTMENT OF ITS MEMBERS

A fifth desideratum, illustrating the utility of a senate, is the want of a due sense of national character. Without a select and stable member of the government, the esteem of foreign powers will not only be forfeited by an unenlightened and variable policy, proceeding from the causes already mentioned; but the national councils will not possess that sensibility to the opinion of the world, which is perhaps not less necessary in order to merit, than it is to obtain its respect and confidence.

An attention to the judgment of other nations is important to every government, for two reasons: the one is, that independently of the merits of any particular plan or measure, it is desirable, on various accounts, that it should appear to other nations as the offspring of a wise and honourable policy: the second is, that in doubtful cases, particularly where the national councils may be warped by some strong passion, or momentary interest, the presumed or known opinion of the impartial world may be the best guide that can be followed. What has not America lost by her want of character with foreign nations; and how many errors and follies would she not have avoided, if the justice and propriety of her measures had, in every instance, been previously tried by the light in which they would probably appear to the unbiased part of mankind!

Yet however requisite a sense of national character may be, it is evident that it can never be sufficiently possessed by a numerous and changeable body. It can only be found in a number so small, that a sensible degree of the praise and blame of public measures may be the portion of each individual; or in an assembly so durably invested with public trust, that the pride and consequence of its members may be sensibly incorporated with the reputation and prosperity of the community. The half-yearly representatives of Rhode Island would probably have been little affected in their deliberations on the iniquitous measures of that state, by arguments drawn from the light in which such measures would be viewed by foreign nations, or even by the sister states; whilst it can scarcely be doubted, that if the concurrence of a select and stable body had been necessary, a regard to national character alone would have prevented the calamities under which that misguided people is now labouring.

I add, as a *sixth* defect, the want in some important cases of a due responsibility in the government to the people, arising from that frequency of elections, which in other cases produces this responsibility. The remarks will, perhaps, appear not only new, but paradoxical. It must nevertheless be acknowledged, when explained, to be as undeniable as it is important.

Responsibility, in order to be reasonable, must be limited to objects within the power of the responsible party; and, in order to be effectual, must relate to operations of that power, of which a ready and proper judgment can be formed by the constituents. The objects of government may be divided into two general classes: the one depending on measures, which have singly an immediate and sensible operation; the other depending on a succession of well-chosen and well-connected measures, which have a gradual and perhaps unobserved operation. The importance of the latter description to the collective and permanent welfare of every country, needs no explanation. And yet it is evident, that an assembly elected for so short a term as to be unable to provide more than one or two links in a chain of measures, on which the general welfare may essentially depend, ought not to be answerable for the final result, any more than a steward or tenant, engaged for one year, could be justly made to answer for plans or improvements which could not be accomplished in less than half a dozen years. Nor is it possible for the people to estimate the *share* of influence, which their annual assemblies may respectively have on events resulting from the mixed transactions of several years. It is sufficiently difficult, to preserve a personal responsibility in the members of a *numerous* body, for such acts of the body as have an immediate, detached, and palpable operation on its constituents.

The proper remedy for this defect must be an additional body in the legislative department, which, having sufficient permanency to provide for such objects as require a continued attention, and a train of measures, may be justly and effectually answerable for the attainment of those objects.

Thus far I have considered the circumstances which point out the necessity of a well-constructed senate, only as they relate to the representatives of the people. To a people as little blinded by prejudice, or corrupted by flattery, as those whom I address, I shall not scruple to add, that such an institution may be sometimes necessary, as a defence to the people against their own temporary errors and delusions. As the cool and deliberate sense of the community ought, in all governments, and actually will, in all free governments, ultimately prevail over the views of its rulers: so there are particular moments in public affairs, when the people, stimulated by some irregular passion, or some illicit advantage, or misled by the artful mis-representations of interested men, may call for measures which they themselves will afterwards be the most ready to lament and condemn. In these critical moments, how salutary will be the interference of some temperate and respectable body of citizens, in order to check the misguided career, and to suspend the blow meditated by the people against themselves, until reason, justice, and truth, can regain their authority over the public mind? What bitter anguish would not the people of Athens have often escaped, if their government had contained so provident a safeguard against the tyranny of their own passions! Popular liberty might then have escaped the indelible reproach of decreeing to the same citizens the hemlock on one day, and statues on the next.

It may be suggested, that a people spread over an extensive region cannot, like the crowded inhabitants of a small district, be subject to the infection of violent passions; or to the danger of combining in the pursuit of unjust measures. I am far from denying, that this is a distinction of peculiar importance. I have, on the contrary, endeavoured in a former paper to show, that it is one of the principal recommendations of a confederated republic. At the same time, this advantage ought not to be considered as superseding the use of auxiliary precautions. It may even be remarked, that the same extended situation, which will exempt the people of America from some of the dangers incident to lesser republics, will expose them to the inconveniency of remaining, for a longer time, under the influence of those misrepresentations which the combined industry of interested men may succeed in distributing among them.

It adds no small weight to all these considerations, to recollect, that history informs us of no longlived republic, which had not a senate. Sparta, Rome, and Carthage are, in fact, the only states to whom that character can be applied. In each of the two first, there was a senate for life. The constitution of the senate in the last is less known. Circumstantial evidence makes it probable, that it was not different in this particular from the two others. It is at least certain, that it had some quality or other, which rendered it an anchor against popular fluctuations; and that a smaller council, drawn out of the senate, was appointed not only for life, but filled up vacancies itself. These examples, though as unfit for the imitation, as they are repugnant to the genius, of America, are, notwithstanding, when compared with the fugitive and turbulent existence of other ancient republics, very instructive proofs of the necessity of some institution that will blend stability with liberty. I am not unaware of the circumstances which distinguish the American from other popular governments, as well ancient as modern; and which render extreme circumspection necessary, in reasoning from the one case to the other. But after allowing due weight to this consideration, it may still be maintained, that there are many points of similitude which render these examples not unworthy of our attention. Many of the defects, as we have seen, which can only be supplied by a senatorial institution, are common to a numerous assembly frequently elected by the people, and to the people themselves. There are others peculiar to the former, which require the control of such an institution. The people can never wilfully betray their own interests: but they may possibly be betrayed by the representatives of the people; and the danger will be evidently greater, where the whole legislative trust is lodged in the hands of one body of men, than where the concurrence of separate and dissimilar bodies is required in every public act.

The difference most relied on, between the American and other republics, consists in the principle of representation; which is the pivot on which the former move, and which is supposed to have been unknown to the latter, or at least to the ancient part of them. The use which has been made of this difference, in reasonings contained in former papers, will have shown, that I am disposed neither to deny its existence, nor to undervalue its importance. I feel the less restraint, therefore, in observing, that the position concerning the ignorance of the ancient governments on the subject of representation, is by no means precisely true, in the latitude commonly given to it. Without entering into a disquisition which here would be misplaced, I will refer to a few known facts, in support of what I advance.

In the most pure democracies of Greece, many of the executive functions were performed, not by the people themselves, but by officers elected by the people, and *representing* them in their *executive* capacity.

Prior to the reform of Solon, Athens was governed by nine archons, annually *elected by the people at large*. The degree of power, delegated to them, seems to be left in great obscurity. Subsequent to that period, we find an assembly, first of four, and afterwards of six hundred members, annually *elected by the people;* and *partially* representing them in their *legislative* capacity, since they were not only associated with the people in the function of making laws, but had the exclusive right of originating legislative propositions to the people. The senate of Carthage, also, whatever might be its power, or the duration of its appointment, appears to have been elective by the suffrages of the people. Similar instances might be traced in most, if not all the popular governments of antiquity.

Lastly, in Sparta, we meet with the ephori, and in Rome with the tribunes; two bodies, small indeed in number, but annually *elected by the whole body of the people,* and considered as the *representatives* of the people, almost in their *plenipotentiary* capacity. The cosmi of Crete were also annually *elected by the people;* and have been considered by some authors as an institution analogous to those of Sparta and Rome, with this difference only, that in the election of that representative body, the right of suffrage was communicated to a part only of the people.

From these facts, to which many others might be added, it is clear that the principle of representation was neither unknown to the ancients, nor wholly overlooked in their political constitutions. The true distinction between these and the American governments, lies *in the total exclusion of the people, in their collective capacity,* from any share in the *latter,* and not in the *total exclusion of the representatives of the people* from the administration of the *former.* The distinction, however, thus qualified, must be admitted to leave a most advantageous superiority in favour of the United States. But to ensure to this advantage its full effect, we must be careful not to separate it from the other advantage, of an extensive territory. For it cannot be believed, that any form of representative government could have succeeded within the narrow limits occupied by the democracies of Greece.

In answer to all these arguments, suggested by reason, illustrated by examples, and enforced by our own experience, the jealous adversary of the constitution will probably content himself with repeating, that a senate appointed not immediately by the people, and for the term of six years, must gradually acquire a dangerous preeminence in the government, and finally transform it into a tyrannical aristocracy.

To this general answer, the general reply ought to be sufficient; that liberty may be endangered by the abuses of liberty as well as by the abuses of power; that there are numerous instances of the former as well as of the latter; and that the former, rather than the latter, is apparently most to be apprehended by the United States. But a more particular reply may be given.

Before such a revolution can be effected, the senate, it is to be observed, must in the first place corrupt itself; must next corrupt the state legislatures; must then corrupt the house of representatives; and must finally corrupt the people at large. It is evident, that the senate must be first corrupted, before it can attempt an establishment of tyranny. Without corrupting the legislatures, it cannot prosecute the attempt, because the periodical change of members would otherwise regenerate the whole body. Without exerting the means of corruption with equal success on the house of representatives, the opposition of that coequal branch of the government would inevitably defeat the attempt; and without corrupting the people themselves, a succession of new representatives would speedily restore all things to their pristine order. Is there any man who can seriously persuade himself, that the proposed senate can, by any possible means within the compass of human address, arrive at the object of a lawless ambition, through all these obstructions?

If reason condemns the suspicion, the same sentence is pronounced by experience. The constitution of Maryland furnishes the most apposite example. The senate of that state is elected, as the federal senate will be, indirectly by the people; and for a term less by one year only than the federal senate. It is distinguished, also, by the remarkable prerogative of filling up its own vacancies within the term of its appointment; and at the same time, is not under the control of any such rotation as is provided for the federal senate. There are some other lesser distinctions, which would expose the former to colourable objections, that do not lie against the latter. If the federal senate, therefore, really contained the danger which has been so loudly proclaimed, some symptoms at least of a like danger ought by this time to have been betrayed by the senate of Maryland: but no such symptoms have appeared. On the contrary, the jealousies at first entertained by men of the same description with those who view with terror the correspondent part of the federal constitution, have been gradually extinguished by the progress of the experiment; and the Maryland constitution is daily deriving, from the salutary operation of this part of it, a reputation in which it will probably not be rivalled by that of any state in the union.

But if any thing could silence the jealousies on this subject, it ought to be the British example. The senate there, instead of being elected for a term of six years, and of being unconfined to particular families or fortunes, is an hereditary assembly of opulent nobles. The house of representatives, instead of being elected for two years, and by the whole body of the people, is elected for seven years; and, in very great proportion, by a very small proportion of the people. Here, unquestionably, ought to be seen in full display the aristocratic usurpations and tyranny which are at some future period to be exemplified in the United States. Unfortunately, however, for the anti-federal argument, the British history informs us, that this hereditary assembly has not even been able to defend itself against the continual encroachments of the house of representatives; and that it no sooner lost the support of the monarch, than it was actually crushed by the weight of the popular branch.

As far as antiquity can instruct us on this subject, its examples support the reasoning which we have employed. In Sparta the ephori, the annual representatives of the people, were found an overmatch for the senate for life; continually gained on its authority, and finally drew all power into their own hands. The tribunes of Rome, who were the representatives of the people, prevailed, it is well known, in almost every contest with the senate for life, and in the end gained the most complete triumph over it. This fact is the more remarkable, as unanimity was required in every act of the tribunes, even after their number was augmented to ten. It proves the irresistible force possessed by that branch of a free government, which has the people on its side. To these examples might be added that of Carthage, whose senate, according to the testimony of Polybius, instead of drawing all power into its vortex, had at the commencement of the second punic war, lost almost the whole of its original portion.

Besides the conclusive evidence resulting from this assemblage of facts, that the federal senate will never be able to transform itself, by gradual usurpations, into an independent and aristocratic body; we are warranted in believing, that if such a revolution should ever happen from causes which the foresight of man cannot guard against, the house of representatives, with the people on their side, will at all times be able to bring back the constitution to its primitive form and principles. Against the force of the immediate representatives of the people, nothing will be able to maintain even the constitutional authority of the senate, but such a display of enlightened policy, and attachment to the public good, as will divide with that branch of the legislature the affections and support of the entire body of the people themselves.

PUBLIUS

Part Three

OPPOSITION:
THE FEDERALIST ERA

13. A Bill of Rights:
Yes and No to Jefferson

It is rare indeed in American or any other history to find two great men, each strong-minded and ambitious, sustaining an unbroken personal and political partnership for half a century. The young Madison met Thomas Jefferson, his senior by eight years, in the Virginia House of Delegates during the momentous session of 1776. They quickly discovered common political ground and a remarkable harmony of mind and character. Every major public project of their lives, from establishing the Virginia republic on liberal foundations in the 1770s to creating the University of Virginia in the 1820s, became a joint enterprise, drawing the two leaders closer. At the end of his life, Jefferson left his good name and cause in Madison's hands: "Take care of me when dead," he wrote in February, 1826.

Such life-long intimacy cannot be explained short of a full dual biography. Certainly their common background as mem-

To Thomas Jefferson, October 17, 1788, in *Writings,* V, pp. 271–275.

bers of the enlightened Virginia gentry (literally as well as symbolically, their homes were a short thirty miles apart) provided an important bond. Still more significant was their profound agreement on the fundamentals of republican liberalism. Yet their differences of political style and temper, within the bounds of shared belief, might well have been the most powerful link of all. Although Jefferson was no mere ideologue, his mind seemed to find its full powers in the eloquent expression of grand principles: the Declaration of Independence is the true Jefferson, or at least the key to his unique identity. On the other side, Madison was no mere technician; yet his mind leaped forward when he faced the hard questions of political architecture: *The Federalist* is the true Madison. If Jefferson pulled Madison toward doctrinal commitments (as in their discussions of natural rights and the sovereignty of the living generation), Madison pulled Jefferson toward a kind of political prudence (as in their discussions of the new United States Constitution). At any rate, and for whatever reasons, Jefferson valued his prudent partner above all men of their generation.

Writing from Paris in 1787–1788, in response to news about the proposed Constitution, Jefferson gradually shifted his position from skepticism to conditional approval, influenced no doubt by Madison's careful explanations and arguments. On one point he remained firm: "a bill of rights is what the people are entitled to against every government on earth, general or particular; and what no just government should refuse, or rest on inference." In a letter of July 31, 1788, he specified to Madison the essential points of liberty, trial by jury, habeas corpus, no standing armies, free press and religion, and no monopolies. Madison's sympathetic yet critical reply of October 17 neatly illustrates the role of the prudent partner. In fact, Madison would be the one to formulate and secure passage of the federal Bill of Rights. (See Document 14.)

New York, October 17, 1788.

DEAR SIR,—The little pamphlet herewith inclosed will give you a collective view of the alterations which have been proposed [by the State Conventions] for the new Constitution. Various and numerous as they appear, they certainly omit many of the true grounds of opposition. The articles relating to Treaties, to paper money, and to contracts, created more enemies than all the errors in the system, positive and negative, put together.

It is true, nevertheless, that not a few, particularly in Virginia, have contended for the proposed alterations from the most honorable and patriotic motives; and that among the advocates for the Constitution there are some who wish for further guards to public liberty and individual rights. As far as these may consist of a constitutional declaration of the most essential rights, it is probable they will be added; though there are many who think such addition unnecessary, and not a few who think it misplaced in such a Constitution. There is scarce any point on which the party in opposition is so much divided as to its importance and its propriety. My own opinion has always been in favor of a bill of rights, provided it be so framed as not to imply powers not meant to be included in the enumeration. At the same time, I have never thought the omission a material defect, nor been anxious to supply it even by *subsequent* amendment, for any other reason than that it is anxiously desired by others. I have favored it because I supposed it might be of use, and, if properly executed, could not be of disservice.

I have not viewed it in an important light—1. Because I conceive that in a certain degree, though not in the extent argued by Mr. Wilson, the rights in question are reserved by the manner in which the federal powers are granted. 2. Because there is great reason to fear that a positive declaration of some of the most essential rights could not be obtained in the requisite latitude. I am sure that the rights of conscience in particular, if submitted to public definition, would be narrowed much more than they are likely ever to be by an assumed power. One of the objections in New England was, that the Constitution, by prohibiting religious tests, opened a door for Jews, Turks, and infidels. 3. Because the limited powers of the federal Government, and the jealousy of the subordinate Governments, afford a security which has not existed in the case of the State Governments, and exists in no other. 4. Because experience proves the inefficacy of a bill of rights on those occasions when its controul is most needed. Repeated violations of these parchment barriers have been committed by overbearing majorities in every State.

In Virginia, I have seen the bill of rights violated in every instance where it has been opposed to a popular current. Notwithstanding the explicit provision contained in that instrument for the rights of conscience, it is well known that a religious establishment would have taken place in that State, if the Legislative majority had found, as they expected, a majority of the people in favor of the measure; and I am persuaded that if a majority of the people were now of one sect, the measure would still take place, and on narrower ground than was then proposed, notwithstanding the additional obstacle which the law has since created.

Wherever the real power in a Government lies, there is the danger of oppression. In our Governments the real power lies in the majority of the community, and the invasion of private rights is *chiefly* to be apprehended, not from acts of Government contrary to the sense of its constituents, but from acts in which the Government is the mere instrument of the major number of the Constituents. This is a truth of great importance, but not yet sufficiently attended to; and is probably more strongly impressed on my mind by facts and reflections suggested by them than on yours, which has contemplated abuses of power issuing from a very different quarter. Wherever there is an interest and power to do wrong, wrong will generally be done, and not less readily by a powerful and interested party than by a powerful and interested prince. The difference, so far as it relates to the superiority of republics over monarchies, lies in the less degree of probability that interest may prompt abuses of power in the former than in the latter; and in the security in the former against an oppression of more than the smaller part of the Society, whereas, in the latter, it may be extended in a manner to the whole.

The difference, so far as it relates to the point in question— the efficacy of a bill of rights in controuling abuses of power —lies in this: that in a monarchy the latent force of the nation is superior to that of the Sovereign, and a solemn charter of popular rights must have a great effect as a standard for trying the validity of public acts, and a signal for rousing and uniting the superior force of the community; whereas, in a popular Government, the political and physical power may be considered as vested in the same hands, that is, in a majority of the people, and, consequently, the tyrannical will of the Sovereign is not to be controuled by the dread of an appeal to any other force within the community.

What use, then, it may be asked, can a bill of rights serve in popular Governments? I answer, the two following, which, though less essential than in other Governments, sufficiently recommend the precaution: 1. The political truths declared in that solemn manner acquire by degrees the character of fundamental maxims of free Government, and as they become incorporated with the National sentiment, counteract the impulses of interest and passion. 2. Although it be generally true, as above stated, that the danger of oppression lies in the interested majorities of the people rather than in usurped acts of the Government, yet there may be occasions on which the evil may spring from the latter source; and on such, a bill of rights will be a good ground for an appeal to the sense of the community. Perhaps, too, there may be a certain degree of danger that a succession of artful and ambitious rulers may, by gradual and well-timed advances, finally erect an independent Government on the subversion of liberty. Should this danger exist at all, it is prudent to guard against it, especially when the precaution can do no injury.

At the same time, I must own that I see no tendency in our Governments to danger on that side. It has been remarked that there is a tendency in *all* Governments to an augmentation of power at the expense of liberty. But the remark, as usually understood, does not appear to me well founded. Power, when it has attained a certain degree of energy and independence, goes on generally to further degrees. But when below that degree, the direct tendency is to further degrees of relaxation, until the abuses of liberty beget a sudden transition to an undue degree of power. With this explanation the remark may be true; and in the latter sense only is it, in my opinion, applicable to the existing Governments in America. It is a melancholy reflection that liberty should be equally exposed to danger whether the Government have too much or too little power, and that the line which divides these extremes should be so inaccurately defined by experience.

Supposing a bill of rights to be proper, the articles which ought to compose it admit of much discussion. I am inclined to think that *absolute* restrictions in cases that are doubtful, or where emergencies may overrule them, ought to be avoided. The restrictions, however strongly marked on paper, will never be regarded when opposed to the decided sense of the public; and after repeated violations, in extraordinary cases will lose even their ordinary efficacy. Should a Rebellion or insurrection alarm the people as well as the Government, and a suspension of the Habeas Corpus be dictated by the alarm, no written prohibitions on earth would prevent the measure. Should an army in time of peace be gradually established in our neighborhood by Britain or Spain, declarations on paper would have as little effect in preventing a standing force for the public safety. The best security against these evils is to remove the pretext for them.

With regard to Monopolies, they are justly classed among the greatest nuisances in Government. But is it clear that, as encouragements to literary works and ingenious discoveries, they are not too valuable to be wholly renounced? Would it not suffice to reserve in all cases a right to the public to abolish the privilege, at a price to be specified in the grant of it? Is there not, also, infinitely less danger of this abuse in our Governments than in most others? Monopolies are sacrifices of the many to the few. Where the power is in the few, it is natural for them to sacrifice the many to their own partialities and corruptions. Where the power, as with us, is in the many, not in the few, the danger cannot be very great that the few will be thus favored. It is much more to be dreaded that the few will be unnecessarily sacrificed to the many. . . .

14. Consent and Consensus:
Appeal for Amendments

Patrick Henry and the Virginia Antifederalists, after losing the fight against ratification of the Constitution, did their best to keep the brilliant leader of the Federalists out of the new government. They mustered the votes in the state legislature to reject Madison as U.S. Senator and to design for him a Congressional District loaded with presumed Antifederal voters. (Madison's reputation and family influence won him the House seat despite the stratagem.) They had good reason. Every scrap of evidence, dating at least from Madison's first appearance in the Continental Congress, indicated that he would be a stalwart of the nationalists in the new regime, with invaluable talents for making the system work. And so he was, emerging quickly as a leader of the House and a key advisor to Washington's administration.

Yet Madison's adversaries, and perhaps some friends as well, missed a quiet but decisive development in his view of the

Speech in the House of Representatives, June 8, 1789, in *Writings*, V, pp. 370–389.

new order. At Philadelphia, Madison had aimed at a federal government even more powerful and concentrated than the one adopted by the Convention. After the Virginia ratifying convention, he sensed that the American people had consented to the Constitution on the understanding that it would be substantially amended and strictly construed. The confining amendments proposed by Virginia, Massachusetts, and other divided states; the growing talk of a second convention, sponsored by New York and the Pennsylvania minority; rumblings in his own district: all persuaded Madison to take the lead in securing amendments that would win the loyalty of many who had opposed or grudgingly accepted the Constitution, without undermining the new system of government.

In 1789, Madison was not thinking of fomenting opposition but rather of preventing or taming it. On June 8 he introduced a series of amendments in the House and through the following months fought off delays and diversions. He saw the measures through a Senate-House conference, and finally, on September 25, 1789, could claim a major victory when both chambers, by a two-thirds vote, approved twelve amendments—basically corresponding to Madison's original proposals—for transmission to the states. He had successfully blocked attempts to amend away vital national powers; but he had failed to extend the protection of the rights of conscience, freedom of the press, and trial by jury against state governments.

Although the most hard-bitten Antifederalists in Virginia and elsewhere proved apathetic at best—they were more concerned with amendments limiting federal powers vis-a-vis the states—and some Federalists remained wary of amendments, the Bill of Rights was ratified by the eleventh state, Virginia, on December 13, 1791, becoming part of the supreme law of the land.

I am sorry to be accessary to the loss of a single moment of time by the House. If I had been indulged in my motion, and we had gone into a Committee of the Whole, I think we might have rose and resumed the consideration of other business before this time; that is, so far as it depended upon what I proposed to bring forward. As that mode seems not to give satisfaction, I will withdraw the motion, and move you, sir, that a select committee be appointed to consider and report such amendments as are proper for Congress to propose to the Legislatures of the several States, conformably to the fifth article of the Constitution.

I will state my reasons why I think it proper to propose amendments, and state the amendments themselves, so far as I think they ought to be proposed. If I thought I could fulfil the duty which I owe to myself and my constituents, to let the subject pass over in silence, I most certainly should not trespass upon the indulgence of this House. But I cannot do this, and am therefore compelled to beg a patient hearing to what I have to lay before you. And I do most sincerely believe, that if Congress will devote but one day to this subject, so far as to satisfy the public that we do not disregard their wishes, it will have a salutary influence on the public councils, and prepare the way for a favorable reception of our future measures. It appears to me that this House is bound by every motive of prudence, not to let the first session pass over without proposing to the State Legislatures, some things to be incorporated into the Constitution, that will render it as acceptable to the whole people of the United States, as it has been found acceptable to a majority of them. I wish, among other reasons why something should be done, that those who had been friendly to the adoption of this Constitution may have the opportunity of proving to those who were opposed to it that they were as sincerely devoted to liberty and a Republican Government, as those who charged them with wishing the adoption of this Constitution in order to lay the foundation of an aristocracy or despotism. It will be a desirable thing to extinguish from the bosom of every member of the community, any apprehensions that there are those among his countrymen who wish to deprive them of the liberty for which they valiantly fought and honorably bled. And if there are amendments desired of such a nature as will not injure the Constitution, and they can be ingrafted so as to give satisfaction to the doubting part of our fellow-citizens, the friends of the Federal Government will evince that spirit of deference and concession for which they have hitherto been distinguished.

It cannot be a secret to the gentlemen in this House, that, notwithstanding the ratification of this system of Government by eleven of the thirteen United States, in some cases unanimously, in others by large majorities; yet still there is a great number of our constituents who are dissatisfied with it, among whom are many respectable for their talents and patriotism, and respectable for the jealousy they have for their liberty, which, though mistaken in its object is laudable in its motive. There is a great body of the people falling under this description, who at present feel much inclined to join their support to the cause of Federalism, if they were satisfied on this one point. We ought not to disregard their inclination, but, on principles of amity and moderation, conform to their wishes, and expressly declare the great rights of mankind secured under this Constitution. The acquiescence which our fellow-citizens show under the Government, calls upon us for a like return of moderation. But perhaps there is a stronger motive than this for our going into a consideration of the subject. It is to provide those securities for liberty which are required by a part of the community; I allude in a particular manner to those two States that have not thought fit to throw themselves into the bosom of the Confederacy. It is a desirable thing, on our part as well as theirs, that a re-union should take place as soon as possible. I have no doubt, if we proceed to take those steps which would be prudent and requisite at this juncture, that in a short time we should see that disposition prevailing in those States which have not come in, that we have seen prevailing in those States which have embraced the Constitution.

But I will candidly acknowledge, that, over and above all these considerations, I do conceive that the Constitution may be amended; that is to say, if all power is subject to abuse, that then it is possible the abuse of the powers of the General Government may be guarded against in a more secure manner than is now done, while no one advantage arising from the exercise of that power shall be damaged or endangered by it. We have in this way something to gain, and, if we proceed with caution, nothing to lose. And in this case it is necessary to proceed with caution; for while we feel all these inducements to go into a revisal of the Constitution, we must feel for the Constitution itself, and make that revisal a moderate one. I should be unwilling to see a door opened for a reconsideration of the whole structure the Government—for a re-consideration of the principles and the substance of the powers given; because I doubt, if such a door were opened, we should be very likely to stop at that point which would be safe to the Government itself. But I do wish to see a door opened to consider, so far as to incorporate those provisions for the security of rights, against which I believe no serious objection has been made by any class of our constituents: such as would be likely to meet with the concurrence of two-thirds of both Houses, and the approbation of three-fourths of the State Legislatures. I will not propose a single alteration which I do not wish to see take place, as intrinsically proper in itself, or proper because it is wished for by a respectable number of my fellow-citizens; and therefore I shall not propose a single alteration but is likely to meet the concurrence required by the Constitution. There have been objections of various kinds made against the Constitution. Some were levelled against its structure because the President was without a council; because the Senate, which is a legislative body, had judicial powers in trials on impeachments; and because the powers of that body were compounded in other respects, in a manner that did not correspond with a particular theory; because it grants more power than is supposed to be necessary for every good purpose, and controls the ordinary powers of the State governments. I know some respectable characters who opposed this Government on these grounds; but I believe that the great mass of the people who opposed it, disliked it because it did not contain effectual provisions against the encroachments on particular rights, and those safe-guards which they have been long accustomed to have inter-posed between them and the magistrate who exercises the sovereign power; nor ought we to consider them safe, while a great number of our fellow-citizens think these securities necessary.

It is a fortunate thing that the objection to the Government has been made on the ground I stated; because it will be prac-ticable, on that ground, to obviate the objection, so far as to satisfy the public mind that their liberties will be perpetual, and this without endangering any part of the Constitution, which is considered as essential to the existence of the Govern-ment by those who promoted its adoption.

The amendments which have occurred to me, proper to be recommended by Congress to the State Legislatures, are these:

First. That there be prefixed to the Constitution a declara-tion, that all power is originally vested in, and consequently derived from, the people.

That Government is instituted and ought to be exercised for the benefit of the people; which consists in the enjoyment of life and liberty, with the right of acquiring and using property, and generally of pursuing and obtaining happiness and safety.

That the people have an indubitable, unalienable, and inde-feasible right to reform or change their Government, whenever it be found adverse or inadequate to the purposes of its insti-tution.

Secondly. That in article 1st, section 2, clause 3, these words be struck out, to wit: "The number of Representatives shall not exceed one for every thirty thousand, but each State shall have at least one Representative, and until such enumeration shall be made;" and that in place thereof be inserted these words, to wit: "After the first actual enumeration, there shall be one Representative for every thirty thousand, until the number amounts to ———, after which the proportion shall be so regulated by Congress, that the number shall never be less than ———, nor more than ———, but each State shall, after the first enumeration, have at least two Representatives; and prior thereto."

Thirdly.   That in article 1st, section 6, clause 1, there be added to the end of the first sentence, these words, to wit: "But no law varying the compensation last ascertained shall operate before the next ensuing election of Representatives."

Fourthly.   That in article 1st, section 9, between clauses 3 and 4, be inserted these clauses, to wit: The civil rights of none shall be abridged on account of religious belief or worship, nor shall any national religion be established, nor shall the full and equal rights of conscience be in any manner, or on any pretext, infringed.

The people shall not be deprived or abridged of their right to speak, to write, or to publish their sentiments; and the freedom of the press, as one of the great bulwarks of liberty, shall be inviolable.

The people shall not be restrained from peaceably assembling and consulting for their common good; nor from applying to the Legislature by petitions, or remonstrances, for redress of their grievances.

The right of the people to keep and bear arms shall not be infringed; a well armed and well regulated militia being the best security of a free country: but no person religiously scrupulous of bearing arms shall be compelled to render military service in person.

No soldiers shall in time of peace be quartered in any house without the consent of the owner; nor at any time, but in a manner warranted by law.

No person shall be subject, except in cases of impeachment, to more than one punishment or one trial for the same offence; nor shall be compelled to be a witness against himself; nor be deprived of life, liberty, or property, without due process of law; nor be obliged to relinquish his property, where it may be necessary for public use, without a just compensation.

Excessive bail shall not be required, nor excessive fines imposed, nor cruel and unusual punishments inflicted.

The rights of the people to be secured in their persons, their houses, their papers, and their other property, from all unreasonable searches and seizures, shall not be violated by warrants issued without probable cause, supported by oath or affirmation, or not particularly describing the places to be searched, or the persons or things to be seized.

In all criminal prosecutions, the accused shall enjoy the right to a speedy and public trial, to be informed of the cause and nature of the accusation, to be confronted with his accusers, and the witnesses against him; to have a compulsory process for obtaining witnesses in his favor; and to have the assistance of counsel for his defence.

The exceptions here or elsewhere in the Constitution, made in favor of particular rights, shall not be so construed as to diminish the just importance of other rights retained by the people, or as to enlarge the powers delegated by the Constitution; but either as actual limitations of such powers, or as inserted merely for greater caution.

Fifthly.   That in article 1st, section 10, between clauses 1 and 2, be inserted this clause, to wit:

No State shall violate the equal rights of conscience, or the freedom of the press, or the trial by jury in criminal cases.

Sixthly.   That, in article 3d, section 2, be annexed to the end of clause 2d, these words, to wit:

But no appeal to such court shall be allowed where the value in controversy shall not amount to ———— dollars: nor shall any fact triable by jury, according to the course of common law, be otherwise re-examinable than may consist with the principles of common law.

Seventhly.   That in article 3d, section 2, the third clause be struck out, and in its place be inserted the clauses following, to wit:

The trial of all crimes (except in cases of impeachments, and cases arising in the land or naval forces, or the militia when on actual service, in time of war or public danger) shall be by an impartial jury of freeholders of the vicinage, with the requisite of unanimity for conviction, of the right of challenge, and other accustomed requisites; and in all crimes punishable with loss of life or member, presentment or indictment by a grand jury shall be an essential preliminary, provided that in cases of crimes committed within any county which may be in possession of an enemy, or in which a general insurrection may prevail, the trial may by law be authorized in some other county of the same State, as near as may be to the seat of the offence.

In cases of crimes committed not within any county, the trial may by law be in such county as the laws shall have pre-scribed. In suits at common law, between man and man, the trial by jury, as one of the best securities to the rights of the people, ought to remain inviolate.

Eighthly.   That immediately after article 6th, be inserted, as article 7th, the clauses following, to wit:

The powers delegated by this Constitution are appropriated to the departments to which they are respectively distributed: so that the Legislative Department shall never exercise the powers vested in the Executive or Judicial, nor the Executive exercise the powers vested in the Legislative or Judicial, nor the Judicial exercise the powers vested in the Legislative or Executive Departments.

The powers not delegated by this Constitution, nor prohib-ited by it to the States, are reserved to the States respectively.

Ninthly.   That article 7th be numbered as article 8th.

The first of these amendments relates to what may be called a bill of rights. I will own that I never considered this provision so essential to the Federal Constitution as to make it improper to ratify it, until such an amendment was added; at the same time, I always conceived, that in a certain form, and to a certain extent, such a provision was neither improper nor altogether useless. I am aware that a great number of the most respectable friends to the Government, and champions for republican liberty, have thought such a provision not only unnecessary, but even improper; nay, I believe some have gone so far as to think it even dangerous. Some policy has been made use of, perhaps, by gentlemen on both sides of the question: I acknowledge the ingenuity of those arguments which were drawn against the Constitution, by a comparison with the policy of Great Britain, in establishing a declaration of rights; but there is too great a difference in the case to warrant the comparison: therefore, the arguments drawn from that source were in a great measure inapplicable. In the declaration of rights which that country has established, the truth is, they have gone no farther than to raise a barrier against the power of the Crown; the power of the Legislature is left altogether indefinite. Although I know whenever the great rights, the trial by jury, freedom of the press, or liberty of conscience, come in question in that body, the invasion of them is resisted by able advocates, yet their Magna Charta does not contain any one provision for the security of those rights, respecting which the people of America are most alarmed. The freedom of the press and rights of conscience, those choicest privileges of the people, are unguarded in the British Constitution.

But although the case may be widely different, and it may not be thought necessary to provide limits for the legislative power in that country, yet a different opinion prevails in the United States. The people of many States have thought it necessary to raise barriers against power in all forms and

departments of Government, and I am inclined to believe, if
once bills of rights are established in all the States as well as
the Federal Constitution, we shall find, that, although some
of them are rather unimportant, yet, upon the whole, they
will have a salutary tendency. It may be said, in some instances, they do no more than state the perfect equality of
mankind. This, to be sure, is an absolute truth, yet it is not
absolutely necessary to be inserted at the head of a Constitution.

In some instances they assert those rights which are exercised by the people in forming and establishing a plan of
Government. In other instances, they specify those rights
which are retained when particular powers are given up to be
exercised by the Legislature. In other instances, they specify
positive rights, which may seem to result from the nature of
the compact. Trial by jury cannot be considered as a natural
right, but a right resulting from a social compact, which regulates the action of the community, but is as essential to
secure the liberty of the people as any one of the pre-existent
rights of nature. In other instances, they lay down dogmatic
maxims with respect to the construction of the Government;
declaring that the Legislative, Executive, and Judicial branches,
shall be kept separate and distinct. Perhaps the best way of
securing this in practice is, to provide such checks as will prevent the encroachment of the one upon the other.

But, whatever may be the form which the several States
have adopted in making declarations in favor of particular
rights, the great object in view is to limit and qualify the
powers of Government, by excepting out of the grant of power
those cases in which the Government ought not to act, or to
act only in a particular mode. They point these exceptions
sometimes against the abuse of the Executive power, sometimes against the Legislative, and, in some cases, against the
community itself; or, in other words, against the majority in
favor of the minority.

In our Government it is, perhaps, less necessary to guard against the abuse in the Executive Department than any other; because it is not the stronger branch of the system, but the weaker. It therefore must be levelled against the Legislative, for it is the most powerful, and most likely to be abused, because it is under the least control. Hence, so far as a declaration of rights can tend to prevent the exercise of undue power, it cannot be doubted but such declaration is proper. But I confess that I do conceive, that in a Government modified like this of the United States, the great danger lies rather in the abuse of the community than in the Legislative body. The prescriptions in favor of liberty ought to be levelled against that quarter where the greatest danger lies, namely, that which possesses the highest prerogative of power. But this is not found in either the Executive or Legislative departments of Government, but in the body of the people, operating by the majority against the minority.

It may be thought that all paper barriers against the power of the community are too weak to be worthy of attention. I am sensible they are not so strong as to satisfy gentlemen of every description who have seen and examined thoroughly the texture of such a defence; yet, as they have a tendency to impress some degree of respect for them, to establish the public opinion in their favor, and rouse the attention of the whole community, it may be one means to control the majority from those acts to which they might be otherwise inclined.

It has been said, by way of objection to a bill of rights, by many respectable gentlemen out of doors, and I find opposition on the same principles likely to be made by gentlemen on this floor, that they are unnecessary articles of a Republican Government, upon the presumption that the people have those rights in their own hands, and that is the proper place for them to rest. It would be a sufficient answer to say, that this objection lies against such provisions under the State Governments, as well as under the General Government; and there are, I believe, but few gentlemen who are inclined to push their theory so far as to say that a declaration of rights in those cases is either ineffectual or improper. It has been said, that in the Federal Government they are unnecessary, because the powers are enumerated, and it follows, that all that are not granted by the Constitution are retained; that the Constitution is a bill of powers, the great residuum being the rights of the people; and, therefore, a bill of rights cannot be so necessary as if the residuum was thrown into the hands of the Government. I admit that these arguments are not entirely without foundation; but they are not conclusive to the extent which has been supposed. It is true, the powers of the General Government are circumscribed, they are directed to particular objects; but even if Government keeps within those limits, it has certain discretionary powers with respect to the means, which may admit of abuse to a certain extent, in the same manner as the powers of the State Governments under their constitutions may to an indefinite extent; because in the Constitution of the United States, there is a clause granting to Congress the power to make all laws which shall be necessary and proper for carrying into execution all the powers vested in the Government of the United States, or in any department or officer thereof; this enables them to fulfil every purpose for which the Government was established. Now, may not laws be considered necessary and proper by Congress, (for it is for them to judge of the necessity and propriety to accomplish those special purposes which they may have in contemplation,) which laws in themselves are neither necessary nor proper; as well as improper laws could be enacted by the State Legislatures, for fulfilling the more extended objects of those Governments? I will state an instance, which I think in point, and proves that this might be the case. The General Government has a right to pass all laws which shall be necessary to collect its revenue; the means for enforcing the collection are within the direction of the Legislature: may not general warrants be considered necessary for this purpose, as well as for some purposes which it was supposed at the framing of their constitutions the State Governments had in view? If there was reason for restraining the State Governments from exercising this power, there is like reason for restraining the Federal Government.

It may be said, indeed it has been said, that a bill of rights is not necessary, because the establishment of this Government has not repealed those declarations of rights which are added to the several State constitutions; that those rights of the people which had been established by the most solemn act, could not be annihilated by a subsequent act of that people, who meant and declared at the head of the instrument, that they ordained and established a new system, for the express purpose of securing to themselves and posterity the liberties they had gained by an arduous conflict.

I admit the force of this observation, but I do not look upon it to be conclusive. In the first place, it is too uncertain ground to leave this provision upon, if a provision is at all necessary to secure rights so important as many of those I have mentioned are conceived to be, by the public in general, as well as those in particular who opposed the adoption of this Constitution. Besides, some States have no bills of rights, there are others provided with very defective ones, and there are others whose bills of rights are not only defective, but absolutely improper; instead of securing some in the full extent which republican principles would require, they limit them too much to agree with the common ideas of liberty.

It has been objected also against a bill of rights, that, by enumerating particular exceptions to the grant of power, it would disparage those rights which were not placed in that enumeration; and it might follow by implication, that those rights which were not singled out, were intended to be assigned into the hands of the General Government, and were consequently insecure. This is one of the most plausible arguments I have ever heard urged against the admission of a bill of rights into this system; but, I conceive, that it may be guarded against. I have attempted it, as gentleman may see by turning to the last clause of the fourth resolution.

It has been said that it is unnecessary to load the Constitution with this provision, because it was not found effectual in the constitution of the particular States. It is true, there are a few particular States in which some of the most valuable articles have not, at one time or other, been violated; but it does not follow but they may have, to a certain degree, a salutary effect against the abuse of power. If they are incorporated into the Constitution, independent tribunals of justice will consider themselves in a peculiar manner the guardians of those rights; they will be an impenetrable bulwark against every assumption of power in the Legislative or Executive; they will be naturally led to resist every encroachment upon rights expressly stipulated for in the Constitution by the declaration of rights. Besides this security, there is a great probability that such a declaration in the federal system would be enforced; because the State Legislatures will jealously and closely watch the operations of this Government, and be able to resist with more effect every assumption of power, than any other power on earth can do; and the greatest opponents to a Federal Government admit the State Legislatures to be sure guardians of the people's liberty. I conclude, from this view of the subject, that it will be proper in itself, and highly politic, for the tranquillity of the public mind, and the stability of the Government, that we should offer something, in the form I have proposed, to be incorporated in the system of Government, as a declaration of the rights of the people.

In the next place, I wish to see that part of the Constitution revised which declares that the number of Representatives shall not exceed the proportion of one for every thirty thousand persons, and allows one Representative to every State which rates below that proportion. If we attend to the discussion of this subject, which has taken place in the State conventions, and even in the opinion of the friends to the Constitution, an alteration here is proper. It is the sense of the people of America, that the number of Representatives ought to be increased, but particularly that it should not be left in the discretion of the Government to diminish them, below that proportion, which certainly is in the power of the Legislature, as the Constitution now stands; and they may, as the population of the country increases, increase the House of Representatives to a very unwieldy degree. I confess I always thought this part of the Constitution defective, though not dangerous; and that it ought to be particularly attended to whenever Congress should go into the consideration of amendments.

There are several minor cases enumerated in my proposition, in which I wish also to see some alteration take place. That article which leaves it in the power of the Legislature to ascertain its own emolument, is one to which I allude. I do not believe this is a power which, in the ordinary course of Government, is likely to be abused. Perhaps of all the powers granted, it is least likely to abuse; but there is a seeming impropriety in leaving any set of men without control to put their hand into the public coffers, to take out money to put in their pockets; there is a seeming indecorum in such power, which leads me to propose a change. We have a guide to this alteration in several of the amendments which the different conventions have proposed. I have gone, therefore, so far as to fix it, that no law varying the compensation, shall operate until there is a change in the Legislature; in which case it cannot be for the particular benefit of those who are concerned in determining the value of the service.

I wish, also, in revising the Constitution, we may throw into that section, which interdicts the abuse of certain powers in the State Legislatures, some other provisions of equal, if not greater importance than those already made. The words, "No State shall pass any bill of attainder, *ex post facto* law," &c.,

were wise and proper restrictions in the Constitution. I think there is more danger of those powers being abused by the State Governments than by the Government of the United States. The same may be said of other powers which they possess, if not controlled by the general principle, that laws are unconstitutional which infringe the rights of the community. I should, therefore, wish to extend this interdiction, and add, as I have stated in the 5th resolution, that no State shall violate the equal right of conscience, freedom of the press, or trial by jury in criminal cases; because it is proper that every Government should be disarmed of powers which trench upon those particular rights. I know, in some of the State constitutions, the power of the Government is controlled by such a declaration; but others are not. I cannot see any reason against obtaining even a double security on those points; and nothing can give a more sincere proof of the attachment of those who opposed this Constitution to these great and important rights, than to see them join in obtaining the security I have now proposed; because it must be admitted, on all hands, that the State Governments are as liable to attack these invaluable privileges as the General Government is, and therefore ought to be as cautiously guarded against.

I think it will be proper, with respect to the judiciary powers, to satisfy the public mind on those points which I have mentioned. Great inconvenience has been apprehended to suitors from the distance they would be dragged to obtain justice in the Supreme Court of the United States, upon an appeal on an action for a small debt. To remedy this, declare that no appeal shall be made unless the matter in controversy amounts to a particular sum; this, with the regulations respecting jury trials in criminal cases, and suits at common law, it is to be hoped, will quiet and reconcile the minds of the people to that part of the Constitution.

I find, from looking into the amendments proposed by the State conventions, that several are particularly anxious that it should be declared in the Constitution, that the powers not therein delegated should be reserved to the several States. Perhaps other words may define this more precisely than the whole of the instrument now does. I admit they may be deemed unnecessary; but there can be no harm in making such a declaration, if gentlemen will allow that the fact is as stated. I am sure I understand it so, and do therefore propose it.

These are the points on which I wish to see a revision of the Constitution take place. How far they will accord with the sense of this body, I cannot take upon me absolutely to determine; but I believe every gentleman will readily admit that nothing is in contemplation, so far as I have mentioned, that can endanger the beauty of the Government in any one important feature, even in the eyes of its most sanguine admirers. I have proposed nothing that does not appear to me as proper in itself, or eligible as patronised by a respectable number of our fellow-citizens; and if we can make the Constitution better in the opinion of those who are opposed to it, without weakening its frame, or abridging its usefulness in the judgment of those who are attached to it, we act the part of wise and liberal men to make such alterations as shall produce that effect.

Having done what I conceived was my duty, in bringing before this House the subject of amendments, and also stated such as I wish for and approve, and offered the reasons which occurred to me in their support, I shall content myself, for the present, with moving "that a committee be appointed to consider of and report such amendments as ought to be proposed by Congress to the Legislatures of the States, to become, if ratified by three-fourths thereof, part of the Constitution of the United States." By agreeing to this motion, the subject may be going on in the committee, while other important business is proceeding to a conclusion in the House. I should advocate greater despatch in the business of amendments, if

I were not convinced of the absolute necessity there is of pursuing the organization of the Government; because I think we should obtain the confidence of our fellow-citizens, in proportion as we fortify the rights of the people against the encroachments of the Government.

15. Rights of the Living Generation: Prudent Counsels

A further example, among many possibilities, of the special dialogue between Jefferson and Madison is found in their exchange of views on the right of one generation to bind another. From revolutionary Paris, on September 6, 1789, Jefferson wrote Madison a long letter developing the idea that: "The earth belongs always to the living generation . . . They are masters, too, of their own persons, and consequently may govern them as they please . . . The Constitution and the laws of their predecessors are extinguished then, in their natural course, with those whose will gave them being." Jefferson calculated the legitimate duration of one generation's authority at exactly thirty-four years. (He would later reduce the period to nineteen years, on the basis of revised actuarial tables.) Madison's reply is a masterpiece of subtle instruction in the ways of political life, beginning with Jefferson's abstract premiss and ending with substantially different consequences. This contrast of political minds had already been pointed up

___
To Thomas Jefferson, February 4, 1790, in *Writings*, V, pp. 437–441.

in *Federalist* Number 49, a tactful but severe critique of Jefferson's 1783 proposal for a quick and easy way of amending constitutions: ". . . (F) requent appeals would, in a great measure, deprive the government of that veneration which time bestows on everything, and without which perhaps the wisest and freest governments would not possess the requisite stability."

New York, February 4, 1790.

DEAR SIR,—Your favor of January 9, inclosing one of September last, did not get to hand till a few days ago. The idea which the latter evolves is a great one, and suggests many interesting reflections to Legislators, particularly when contracting and providing for public debts. Whether it can be received in the extent to which your reasonings carry it is a question which I ought to turn more in my thoughts than I have yet been able to do before I should be justified in making up a full opinion on it. My first thoughts lead me to view the doctrine as not *in all respects* compatible with the course of human affairs. I will endeavour to sketch the grounds of my skepticism. "As the Earth belongs to the living, not to the dead, a living generation can bind itself only; in every Society, the will of the majority binds the whole; according to the laws of mortality, a majority of those ripe for the exercise of their will do not live beyond the term of 19 years; to this term, then, is limited the validity of every act of the society, nor can any act be continued beyond this term, without an *express* declaration of the public will." This I understand to be the outline of the argument.

The acts of a political society may be divided into three classes:

1. The fundamental constitution of the Government.
2. Laws involving some stipulation which renders them irrevocable at the will of the Legislature.
3. Laws involving no such irrevocable quality.

1. However applicable in theory the doctrine may be to a Constitution, it seems liable in practice to some weighty objec-- tions.

Would not a Government, ceasing of necessity at the end of a given term, unless prolonged by some Constitutional Act previous to its expiration, be too subject to the casualty and consequences of an interregnum?

Would not a Government so often revised become too mutable and novel to retain that share of prejudice in its favor which is a salutary aid to the most rational Government?

Would not such a periodical revision engender pernicious factions that might not otherwise come into existence, and agitate the public mind more frequently and more violently than might be expedient?

2. In the second class, of acts involving stipulations, must not exceptions, at least to the doctrine, be admitted?

If the earth be the gift of *nature* to the living, their title can extend to the earth in its *natural* state only. The *improvements* made by the dead form a debt against the living, who take the benefit of them. This debt cannot be otherwise discharged than by a proportionate obedience to the will of the Authors of the improvements.

But a case less liable to be controverted may, perhaps, be stated. Debts may be incurred with a direct view to the interests of the unborn, as well as of the living. Such are debts for repelling a Conquest, the evils of which descend through many generations. Debts may even be incurred principally for the benefit of posterity. Such, perhaps, is the debt incurred by the United States. In these instances the debts might not be dischargeable within the term of 19 years.

There seems, then, to be some foundation in the nature of things, in the relation which one generation bears to another, for the *descent* of obligations from one to another. Equity may require it. Mutual good may be promoted by it. And all that seems indispensable in stating the account between the dead and the living is, to see that the debts against the latter do not exceed the advances made by the former. Few of the incumbrances entailed on nations by their predecessors would bear a liquidation even on this principle.

3. Objections to the doctrine, as applied to the third class of acts, must be merely practical. But in that view alone they appear to be material.

Unless such temporary laws should be kept in force by acts regularly anticipating their expiration, all the rights depending on positive laws, that is, most of the rights of property, would become absolutely defunct, and the most violent struggles ensue between the parties interested in reviving, and those interested in reforming the antecedent state of property. Nor does it seem improbable that such an event might be suffered to take place. The checks and difficulties opposed to the passage of laws, which render the power of repeal inferior to an opportunity to reject, as a security against oppression, would here render the latter an insecure provision against anarchy. Add to this that the very possibility of an event so hazardous to the rights of property could not but depreciate its value; that the approach of the crisis would increase the effect; that the frequent return of periods superseding all the obligations dependent on antecedent laws and usages must, by weakening the sense of them, co-operate with motives to licenciousness already too powerful; and that the general uncertainty and vicissitudes of such a state of things would, on one side, discourage every useful effort of steady industry pursued under the sanction of existing laws, and, on the other, give an immediate advantage to the more sagacious over the less sagacious part of the Society.

I can find no relief from such embarrassments but in the received doctrine that a *tacit* assent may be given to established Governments and laws, and that this assent is to be inferred from the omission of an express revocation. It seems more practicable to remedy by well-constituted Governments the pestilent operation of this doctrine in the unlimited sense in which it is at present received, than it is to find a remedy for the evils necessarily springing from an unlimited admission of the contrary doctrine.

It is not doubtful whether it be possible to exclude wholly the idea of an implied or tacit assent, without subverting the very foundation of Civil Society?

On what principle is it that the voice of the majority binds the minority? It does not result, I conceive, from a law of nature, but from compact founded on utility. A greater proportion might be required by the fundamental Constitution of Society, if under any particular circumstances it were judged eligible. Prior, therefore, to the establishment of this principle, *unanimity* was necessary; and rigid Theory accordingly presupposes the assent of every individual to the rule which subjects the minority to the will of the majority. If this assent cannot be given tacitly, or be not implied where no positive evidence forbids, no person born in Society could, on attaining ripe age, be bound by any acts of the majority, and either a unanimous renewal of every law would be necessary as often as a new member should be added to the Society, or the express consent of every new member be obtained to the rule by which the majority decides for the whole.

If these observations be not misapplied, it follows that a limitation of the validity of all Acts to the computed life of the generation establishing them is in some cases not required by theory, and in others not consistent with practice. They are not meant, however, to impeach either the utility of the principle as applied to the cases you have particularly in view, or the general importance of it in the eye of the Philosophical Legislator. On the contrary, it would give me singular pleasure to see it first announced to the world in a law of the United States, and always kept in view as a salutary restraint on living generations from *unjust and unnecessary* burdens on their successors. This is a pleasure, however, which I have no hope of enjoying. The spirit of Philosophical legislation has not prevailed at all in some parts of America and is by no means the fashion of this part, or of the present Representative Body. The evils suffered on feared weakness in Government and licenciousness in the people have turned the attention more towards the means of strengthening the powers of the former, than of narrowing their extent in the minds of the latter. Besides this it is so much easier to descry the little difficulties immediately incident to every great plan than to comprehend its general and remote benefits, that further light must be added to the Councils of our Country before many truths which are seen through the medium of Philosophy become visible to the naked eye of the ordinary politician.

16.   Fear of Power:
Essays for the Party Press

As Secretary of the Treasury in the Washington administration, Alexander Hamilton quickly seized the governing initiative. Amidst the uncertainties of an untried system, he set out to shape the course of legislation and administration in the manner of a prime minister. His notable reports of 1790–1791 on public credit, banking, and manufactures represented far more than practical answers to the most urgent problems facing the first Congress: taken together, they defined a long-range program for achieving economic development and national power under the guidance of an ambitious central government. They presupposed a Constitution flexible enough to give Congress wide discretionary authority for meeting the emergent needs of the United States.

"Consolidation," *National Gazette*, December 5, 1791; "Spirit of Governments," *National Gazette*, February 20, 1792; "Republican Distribution of Citizens," *National Gazette*, March 5, 1792; "Property," *National Gazette*, March 29, 1792; "A Candid State of Parties," *National Gazette*, September 26, 1792; in *Letters*, IV, pp. 458–460, 474–476, 478–482.

Hamilton's Virginia collaborator in the nationalist movement of the 1780s might reasonably have been expected to lead a government party in Congress. In the Continental Congress, Madison had consistently advanced policies closely paralleling those that Hamilton now proposed: funding the national debt without discrimination between original and current creditors; assuming state debts; expanding federal power over taxation and trade; even, with some constitutional doubts, chartering a national bank. He had worked hard and brilliantly to create a new national regime capable of remedying the mortal diseases of bankruptcy, political and military impotence, separatism, and factional injustice. Madison, too, had a grand conception of federal policy to integrate, enrich, and strengthen the American union.

Yet, by the winter of 1791–92, Madison was becoming the Congressional leader of an opposition group that would soon harden into the Jeffersonian Republican party. If his particular objections to Hamiltonian measures—to funding, for example, or debt-assumption—seemed limited and moderate, a growing suspicion of the motives and consequences of the whole Hamiltonian system led him to see a fundamental attack on republican principles and popular interests. Among many signs, the most disturbing to Madison, perhaps, was the sight of stock jobbers in and out of Congress reaping speculative gains and, as it seemed, forming a "pretorian band" of Tory aristocrats around a power-hungry Secretary of the Treasury.

Madison and Jefferson (then Secretary of State) agreed that the opposition needed a reliable journal in Philadelphia to counteract the influence of John Fenno's *Gazette of the United States*, patronized by Hamilton and his friends. In 1791, they induced Madison's old Princeton friend, the poet and journalist Philip Fι∪neau, to establish a newspaper at the capital with the offer of financial backing by his New York publisher (Francis Childs), a modest translator's post in the State Department giving access to European news sources, and a share of the government printing. Madison among others solicited subscriptions in Virginia and generally helped to build a national circulation for Freneau's *National Gazette*, launched on October 31, 1791. After a year of publishing, Freneau claimed some 1700 subscribers. Between November 1791 and April 1792, Madison contributed more than a dozen unsigned essays that began to sketch the broad principles of a Republican opposition. By September 1792 his attacks became both more severe and more concrete, speaking of fixed party divisions in America. Republicans as well as Federalists found it difficult to conceive of a legitimate party competition for control of government: each commonly portrayed the other as enemies of the constitutional regime and, after the wars of the French Revolution began, as agents of a foreign power.

CONSOLIDATION

Much has been said, and not without reason, against the consolidation of the States into one government. Omitting lesser objections, two consequences would probably flow from such a change in our political system, which justify the cautions used against it. First, it would be impossible to avoid the dilemma of either relinquishing the present energy and responsibility of a *single* Executive Magistrate, for some *plural* substitute, which, by dividing so great a trust, might lessen the danger of it; or, suffering so great an accumulation of powers in the hands of that officer, as might by degrees transform him into a monarch. The incompetency of one Legislature to regulate all the various objects belonging to the local governments, would evidently force a transfer of many of them to the Executive department; whilst the increasing splendour and number of its prerogatives, supplied by this source, might prove excitements to ambition too powerful for a sober execution of the elective plan, and consequently strengthen the pretexts for an hereditary designation of the magistrate. Second. Were the State governments abolished, the same space of country that would produce an undue growth of the executive power, would prevent that control on the Legislative body which is essential to a faithful discharge of its trust; neither the voice nor the sense of ten or twenty millions of people, spread through so many latitudes as are comprehended within the United States, could ever be combined or called into effect, if deprived of those local organs, through which both can now be conveyed. In such a state of things, the impossibility of acting together might be succeeded by the inefficacy of partial expressions of the public mind, and this at length, by a universal silence and insensibility, leaving the whole government to that *self directed course* which, it must be owned, is the natural propensity of every government.

But if a consolidation of the States into one government be an event so justly to be avoided, it is not less to be desired, on the other hand, that a consolidation should prevail in their interests and affections; and this, too, as it fortunately happens, for the very reasons, among others, which lie against a governmental consolidation. For, in the first place, in proportion as uniformity is found to prevail in the interests and sentiments of the several States, will be the practicability of accommodating *Legislative* regulations to them, and thereby of withholding new and dangerous prerogatives from the Executive. Again, the greater the mutual confidence and affection of all parts of the Union, the more likely they will be to concur amicably, or to differ with moderation, in the elective-designation of the Chief Magistrate, and by such examples to guard and adorn the vital principle of our republican Constitution. Lastly, the less the supposed difference of interests, and the greater the concord and confidence throughout the great body of the people, the more readily must they sympathize with each other; the more seasonably can they interpose a common manifestation of their sentiments; the more certainly will they take the alarm at usurpation or oppression; and the more effectually will they consolidate their defence of the public liberty.

Here, then, is a proper object presented, both to those who are most jealously attached to the separate authority reserved to the States, and to those who may be more inclined to contemplate the people of America in the light of one nation. Let the former continue to watch against every encroachment which might lead to a gradual consolidation of the States into one government. Let the latter employ their utmost zeal, by eradicating local prejudices and mistaken rivalships, to consolidate the affairs of the States into one harmonious interest; and let it be the patriotic study of all to maintain the various authorities established by our complicated system, each in its respective constitutional sphere, and to erect over the whole one paramount empire of reason, benevolence and brotherly affection.

SPIRIT OF GOVERNMENTS

No government is perhaps reducible to a sole principle of operation. Where the theory approaches nearest to this character, different and often heterogeneous principles mingle their influence in the administration. It is useful, nevertheless, to analyze the several kinds of government, and to characterize them by the spirit which predominates in each.

Montesquieu has resolved the great operative principles of government into fear, honor, and virtue, applying the first to pure despotisms, the second to regular monarchies, and the third to republics. The portion of truth blended with the ingenuity of this system sufficiently justifies the admiration bestowed on its author. Its accuracy, however, can never be defended against the criticisms which it has encountered. Montesquieu was in politics not a Newton or a Locke, who established immortal systems—the one in matter, the other in mind.

He was in his particular science what Bacon was in universal science. He lifted the veil from the venerable errors which enslaved opinion, and pointed the way to those luminous truths of which he had but a glimpse himself.

May not governments be properly divided, according to their predominant spirit and principles, into three species, of which the following are examples:

First. A government operating by a permanent military force, which at once maintains the government and is maintained by it; which is at once the cause of burdens on the people, and of submission in the people to their burdens. Such have been the governments under which human nature has groaned through every age. Such are the governments which still oppress it in almost every country of Europe, the quarter of the globe which calls itself the pattern of civilization and the pride of humanity.

Secondly. A government operating by corrupt influence, substituting the motive of private interest in place of public duty, converting its pecuniary dispensations into bounties to favorites or bribes to opponents, accommodating its measures to the avidity of a part of the nation instead of the benefit of the whole; in a word, enlisting an army of interested partisans, whose tongues, whose pens, whose intrigues, and whose active combinations, by supplying the terror of the sword, may support a real domination of the few, under an apparent liberty of the many. Such a government, wherever to be found, is an impostor. It is happy for the New World that it is not on the west side of the Atlantic. It will be both happy and honorable for the United States if they never descend to mimic the costly pageantry of its form, not betray themselves into the venal spirit of its administration.

Thirdly. A government deriving its energy from the will of the society, and operating, by the reason of its measures, on the understanding and interest of the society. Such is the government for which philosophy has been searching and humanity been fighting from the most remote ages. Such are the republican governments which it is the glory of America to have invented, and her unrivalled happiness to possess. May her glory be completed by every improvement on the theory which experience may teach, and her happiness be perpetuated by a system of administration corresponding with the purity of the theory.

REPUBLICAN DISTRIBUTION OF CITIZENS

A perfect theory on this subject would be useful, not because it could be reduced to practice by any plan of legislation, or ought to be attempted by violence on the will or property of individuals; but because it would be a monition against empirical experiments by power, and a model to which the free choice of occupations by the people might gradually approximate the order of society.

The best distribution is that which would most favor *health, virtue, intelligence,* and *competency* in the *greatest number* of citizens. It is needless to add to these objects *liberty* and *safety.* The first is presupposed by them. The last must result from them.

The life of the husbandman is pre-eminently suited to the comfort and happiness of the individual. *Health,* the first of blessings, is an appertenance of his property and his employment. *Virtue,* the health of the soul, is another part of his patrimony, and no less favored by his situation. *Intelligence* may be cultivated in this as well as in any other walk of life. If the mind be less susceptible of polish in retirement than in a crowd, it is more capable of profound and comprehensive efforts. It is more ignorant of some things? It has a compensation in its ignorance of others. *Competency* is more universally the lot of those who dwell in the country where liberty is at the same time their lot. The extremes, both of want and of waste, have other abodes. 'Tis not the country that peoples either the Bridewells or the Bedlams. These mansions of wretchedness are tenanted from the distresses and vices of overgrown cities.

The condition to which the blessings of life are most denied is that of the sailor. His health is continually assailed and his span shortened by the stormy element to which he belongs. His virtue, at no time aided, is occasionally exposed to every scene that can poison it. His mind, like his body, is imprisoned within the bark that transports him. Though traversing and circumnavigating the globe, he sees nothing but the same vague objects of nature; the same monotonous occurrences in ports and docks; and at home in his vessel what new ideas can shoot from the unvaried use of the ropes and the rudder, or from the society of comrades as ignorant as himself? In the supply of his wants he often feels a scarcity, seldom more than a bare sustenance; and if his ultimate prospects do not embitter the present moment, it is because he never looks beyond it. How unfortunate, that in the intercourse by which nations are enlightened and refined, and their means of safety extended, the immediate agents should be distinguished by the hardest condition of humanity.

The great interval between the two extremes is, with a few exceptions, filled by those who work the materials furnished by the earth in its natural and cultivated state.

It is fortunate, in general, and particularly for this country, that so much of the ordinary and most essential consumption takes place in fabrics which can be prepared in every family, and which constitute, indeed, the natural ally of agriculture. The former is the work within doors, as the latter is without; and each being done by hands or at times that can be spared from the other, the most is made of everything.

The class of citizens who provide at once their own food and their own raiment, may be viewed as the most truly independent and happy. They are more; they are the best basis of public liberty and the strongest bulwark of public safety. It follows, that the greater the proportion of this class to the whole society, the more free, the more independent, and the more happy must be the society itself.

In appreciating the regular branches of manufacturing and mechanical industry, their tendency must be compared with the principles laid down, and their merit graduated accordingly. Whatever is least favorable to vigor of body, to the faculties of the mind, or to the virtues or to the utilities of life, instead of being forced or fostered by public authority, ought to be seen with regret, as long as occupations more friendly to human happiness lie vacant.

The several professions of more elevated pretensions, the merchant, the lawyer, the physician, the philosopher, the divine, form a certain proportion of every civilized society, and readily adjust their numbers to its demands and its circumstances.

PROPERTY

This term, in its particular application, means "that dominion which one man claims and exercises over the external things of the world, in exclusion of every other individual."

In its larger and juster meaning, it embraces everything to which a man may attach a value and have a right, and *which leaves to every one else the like advantage.*

In the former sense, a man's land, or merchandise, or money, is called his property.

In the latter sense, a man has a property in his opinions and the free communication of them.

He has a property of peculiar value in his religious opinions, and in the profession and practice dictated by them.

He has a property very dear to him in the safety and liberty of his person.

He has an equal property in the free use of his faculties, and free choice of the objects on which to employ them.

In a word, as a man is said to have a right to his property, he may be equally said to have a property in his rights.

Where an excess of power prevails, property of no sort is duly respected. No man is safe in his opinions, his person, his faculties, or his possessions.

Where there is an excess of liberty, the effect is the same, though from an opposite cause.

Government is instituted to protect property of every sort; as well that which lies in the various rights of individuals, as that which the term particularly expresses. This being the end of government, that alone is a *just* government which *impartially* secures to every man whatever is his *own*.

According to this standard of merit, the praise of affording a just security to property should be sparingly bestowed on a government which, however scrupulously guarding the possessions of individuals, does not protect them in the enjoyment and communication of their opinions, in which they have an equal, and, in the estimation of some, a more valuable property.

More sparingly should this praise be allowed to a government where a man's religious rights are violated by penalties, or fettered by tests, or taxed by a hierarchy.

Conscience is the most sacred of all property; other property depending in part on positive law, the exercise of that being a natural and unalienable right. To guard a man's house as his castle, to pay public and enforce private debts with the most exact faith, can give no title to invade a man's conscience, which is more sacred than his castle, or to withhold from it that debt of protection for which the public faith is pledged by the very nature and original conditions of the social pact.

That is not a just government, nor is property secure under it, where the property which a man has in his personal safety and personal liberty is violated by arbitrary seizures of one class of citizens for the service of the rest. A magistrate issuing his warrants to a press-gang would be in his proper functions in Turkey or Indostan, under appellations proverbial of the most complete despotism.

That is not a just government, nor is property secure under it, where arbitrary restrictions, exemptions, and monopolies deny to part of its citizens that free use of their faculties and free choice of their occupations which not only constitute their property in the general sense of the word, but are the means of acquiring property strictly so called.

What must be the spirit of legislation where a manufacturer of linen cloth is forbidden to bury his own child in a linen shroud, in order to favour his neighbour who manufactures woolen cloth; where the manufacturer and weaver of woolen cloth are again forbidden the economical use of buttons of that material, in favor of the manufacturer of buttons of other materials!

A just security to property is not afforded by that government, under which unequal taxes oppress one species of property and reward another species; where arbitrary taxes invade the domestic sanctuaries of the rich, and excessive taxes grind the faces of the poor; where the keenness and competitions of want are deemed an insufficient spur to labor, and taxes are again applied by an unfeeling policy, as another spur, in violation of that sacred property which Heaven, in decreeing man to earn his bread by the sweat of his brow, kindly reserved to him in the small repose that could be spared from the supply of his necessities.

If there be a government, then, which prides itself in maintaining the inviolability of property; which provides that none shall be taken *directly*, even for public use, without indemnification to the owner, and yet *directly* violates the property which individuals have in their opinions, their religion, their passions, and their faculties—nay, more, which *indirectly* violates their property in their actual possessions, in the labor that acquires their daily subsistence, and in the hallowed remnant of time which ought to relieve their fatigues and soothe their cares—the inference will have been anticipated that such a government is not a pattern for the United States.

If the United States mean to obtain or deserve the full praise due to wise and just governments, they will equally respect the rights of property and the property in rights; they will rival the government that most sacredly guards the former, and by repelling its example in violating the latter, will make themselves a pattern to that and all other governments.

A CANDID STATE OF PARTIES

As it is the business of the contemplative statesman to trace the history of parties in a free country, so it is the duty of the citizen at all times to understand the actual state of them. Whenever this duty is omitted, an opportunity is given to designing men, by the use of artificial or nominal distinctions, to oppose and balance against each other those who never differed as to the end to be pursued, and may no longer differ as to the means of attaining it. The most interesting state of parties in the United States may be referred to three periods. Those who espoused the cause of independence and those who adhered to the British claims, formed the parties of the first period; if, indeed, the disaffected class were considerable enough to deserve the name of a party. This state of things was superseded by the treaty of peace in 1783. From 1783 to 1787 there were parties in abundance, but being rather local than general, they are not within the present review.

The Federal Constitution, proposed in the latter year, gave birth to a second and most interesting division of the people. Every one remembers it, because every one was involved in it.

Among those who embraced the Constitution, the great body were unquestionably friends to republican liberty; though there were, no doubt, some who were openly or secretly attached to monarchy and aristocracy, and hoped to make the Constitution a cradle for these hereditary establishments.

Among those who opposed the Constitution, the great body were certainly well affected to the Union and to good government, though there might be a few who had a leaning unfavorably to both. This state of parties was terminated by the regular and effectual establishment of the Federal Government in 1788, out of the administration of which, however, has arisen a third division, which, being natural to most political societies, is likely to be of some duration in ours.

One of the divisions consists of those who, from particular interest, from natural temper, or from the habits of life, are more partial to the opulent than to the other classes of society; and having debauched themselves into a persuasion that mankind are incapable of governing themselves, it follows with them, of course, that government can be carried on only by the pageantry of rank, the influence of money and emoluments, and the tenor of military force. Men of those sentiments must naturally wish to point the measures of Government less to the interest of the many than of a few, and less to the reason of the many than to their weaknesses; hoping, perhaps, in proportion to the ardor of their zeal, that by giving such a turn to the administration, the Government itself may by degrees be narrowed into fewer hands, and approximated to an hereditary form. The other division consists of those who, believing in the doctrine that mankind are capable of governing themselves and hating hereditary power as an insult to the reason and an outrage to the rights of man, are naturally offended at every public measure that does not appeal to the understanding and to the general interest of the community, or that is not strictly conformable to the principles and conducive to the preservation of republican government.

This being the real state of parties among us, an experienced and dispassionate observer will be at no loss to decide on the probable conduct of each.

The anti-republican party, as it may be called, being the weaker in point of numbers, will be induced by the most obvious motives to strengthen themselves with the men of influence, particularly of moneyed, which is the most active and insinuating influence. It will be equally their true policy to weaken their opponents by reviving exploded parties, and taking advantage of all prejudices, local, political, and occupational, that may prevent or disturb a general coalition of sentiments.

The Republican party, as it may be termed, conscious that the mass of the people in every part of the Union, in every State, and of every occupation, must at bottom be with them, both in interest and sentiment, will naturally find their account in burying all antecedent questions, in banishing every other distinction than that between enemies and friends to republican government, and in promoting a general harmony among the latter, wherever residing or however employed.

Whether the republican or the rival party will ultimately establish its ascendence, is a problem which may be contemplated now, but which time alone can solve. On one hand, experience shows that in politics, as in war, stratagem is often an overmatch for numbers; and, among more happy characteristics of our political situation, it is now well understood that there are peculiarities, some temporary, others more durable, which may favour that side in the contest.

On the republican side, again, the superiority of numbers is so great, their sentiments are so decided, and the practice of making a common cause, where there is a common sentiment and common interest, in spite of circumstantial and artificial distinctions, is so well understood, that no temperate observer of human affairs will be surprised if the issue in the present instance should be reversed, and the Government be administered in the spirit and form approved by the great body of the people.

17.   Universal Peace

As Madison took up the role of opposition leader, his political thought turned toward simpler ideological categories, leaving aside much of the complex analysis of society and government that had characterized his earlier reasonings. He began to sound more like his friend Jefferson, although less eloquent and lofty. Madison's unsigned essay on "Universal Peace," published in the *National Gazette* (see Document 16 above), presents an interesting mixture of standard eighteenth-century rationalist and republican doctrine with his own special emphasis on balancing the interests and passions of men. Rousseau's "Paix Perpétuelle" (1761), representing the "new diplomacy" of the Enlightenment thinkers who sought to transcend traditional power politics, served Madison as a text. His objections to warm-hearted but soft-headed projects for eternal peace led

---

"Universal Peace," *National Gazette*, February 2, 1792, in *Letters*, IV, pp. 470–472.

him to submit a visionary project of his own, suited to an age advanced in "reason and reformation." By subjecting governments to the will of society, and society to the instructive discipline of paying promptly and painfully for its wars, men might yet secure the reign of peace on earth.

UNIVERSAL PEACE

Among the various reforms which have been offered to the world, the projects for universal peace have done the greatest honor to the hearts, though they seem to have done very little to the heads, of their authors.

Rousseau, the most distinguished of these philanthropists, has recommended a confederation of sovereigns, under a council of deputies, for the double purpose of arbitrating external controversies among nations, and of guarantying their respective governments against internal revolutions. He was aware neither of the impossibility of executing his pacific plan among governments which feel so many allurements to war, nor, what is more extraordinary, of the tendency of his plan to perpetuate arbitrary power wherever it existed; and, by extinguishing the hope of one day seeing an end of oppression, to cut off the only source of consolation remaining to the oppressed.

A universal and perpetual peace, it is to be feared, is in the catalogue of events which will never exist but in the imaginations of visionary philosophers, or in the breasts of benevolent enthusiasts. It is still, however, true, that war contains so much folly, as well as wickedness, that much is to be hoped from the progress of reason; and if anything is to be hoped, everything ought to be tried.

Wars may be divided into two classes: one flowing from the mere will of the government; the other according with the will of the society itself.

Those of the first class can no otherwise be prevented than

by such a reformation of the government as may identify its will with the will of the society. The project of Rousseau was, consequently, as preposterous as it was impotent. Instead of beginning with an external application, and even precluding internal remedies, he ought to have commenced with, and chiefly relied on, the latter prescription.

He should have said, whilst war is to depend on those whose ambition, whose revenge, whose avidity, or whose caprice may contradict the sentiment of the community, and yet be controlled by it; whilst war is to be declared by those who are to spend the public money, not by those who are to pay it; by those who are to direct the public forces, not by those who are to support them; by those whose power is to be raised, not by those whose chains may be riveted, the disease must continue to be *hereditary*, like the government of which it is the offspring. As the first step towards a cure, the government itself must be regenerated. Its will must be made subordinate to, or rather the same with, the will of the community.

Had Rousseau lived to see the Constitutions of the United States and of France, his judgment might have escaped the censure to which his project has exposed it.

The other class of wars, corresponding with the public will, are less susceptible of remedy.

There are antidotes, nevertheless, which may not be without their efficacy. As wars of the first class were to be prevented by subjecting the will of the government to the will of the society, those of the second can only be controlled by subjecting the will of the society to the reason of the society; by establishing permanent and constitutional maxims of conduct, which may prevail over occasional impressions, and inconsiderate pursuits.

Here our republican philosopher might have proposed as a model to lawgivers, that war should not only be declared by the authority of the people, whose toils and treasures are to support its burdens, instead of the government which is to reap its fruits; but that each generation should be made to bear the burden of its own wars, instead of carrying them on at the expense of other generations. And to give the fullest energy to his plan, he might have added, that each generation should not only bear its own burdens, but that the taxes composing them should include a due proportion of such as by their direct operation keep the people awake, along with those which, being wrapped up in other payments, may leave them asleep, to misapplications of their money.

To the objection, if started, that where the benefits of war descend to succeeding generations, the burdens ought also to descend, he might have answered, that the exceptions could not be easily made; that, if attempted, they must be made by one only of the parties interested; that in the alternative of sacrificing exceptions to general rules, or of converting exceptions into general rules, the former is the lesser evil; that the expense of *necessary* wars will never exceed the resources of an *entire* generation; that, in fine, the objection vanishes before the *fact*, that in every nation which has drawn on posterity for the support of its wars, *the accumulated interest* of its perpetual debts has soon become more than a *sufficient principal* for all its exigencies.

Were a nation to impose such restraints on itself, avarice would be sure to calculate the expenses of ambition; in the equipoise of these passions, reason would be free to decide for the public good, and an ample reward would accrue to the State—first, from the avoidance of all its wars of folly; secondly, from the vigor of its unwasted resources for wars of necessity and defence. Were all nations to follow the example, the reward would be doubled to each, and the temple of Janus might be shut, never to be opened more.

Had Rousseau lived to see the rapid progress of reason and reformation, which the present day exhibits, the philanthropy which dictated his project would find a rich enjoyment in the scene before him; and after tracing the past frequency of wars to a will in the government independent of the will of the

people, to the practice by each generation of taxing the principal of its debts on future generations, and to the facility with
which each generation is seduced into assumptions of the interest, by the deceptive species of taxes which pay it, he would
contemplate in a reform of every government subjecting its will
to that of the people, in a subjection of each generation to the
payment of its own debts, and in a substitution of a more palpable, in place of an imperceptible mode of paying them, the
only hope of UNIVERSAL AND PERPETUAL PEACE.

18. America and the French Revolution: The Voice of the People

Political parties were not created by immaculate conception. As Madison and Jefferson confirmed their hostility to the course of the Federalist administration in domestic and foreign affairs, they employed the political arts with great practical skill to foster opposition within the government and out of doors. Jefferson was no innocent in these matters, although his membership in the cabinet until the end of 1793 imposed on him a certain circumspection. (Madison and Jefferson had their own private cipher for communicating confidential information through the mails.) As the open leader of the dissidents in Congress, Madison felt no such restraints; and his shrewd tactical judgments, moreover, commanded the respect and often the deference of his senior partner. When the Third Congress convened in December 1793, Madison and Jefferson with their

---

To Thomas Jefferson, September 2, 1793, with enclosed Draft of County Resolutions, in *Writings,* VI, pp. 190–194, 192n–193n.

adept handy-man, John Beckley, Clerk of the House of Representatives and all-knowing confidential agent of the Republicans, had gone far toward transforming a political "connection"
of disaffected notables into an embryonic party.

If the Hamiltonian system first provoked opposition to the
Washington administration, the French Revolution and the
resulting declarations of war against the European powers in
1792–1793 widened and deepened political divisions in America. Madison, along with most Americans (including many
Federalists), had responded warmly to the Revolution of 1789
that seemed to promise a revival of liberty in France and all of
Europe. Indeed, Jefferson's sympathy for French culture, especially of the Enlightenment variety, and Madison's leanings
towards a French orientation in foreign economic policy ante-
dated the great Revolution. The Franco-American Alliance of
1778, through which the *Ancien Régime* befriended the new
revolutionary republic of the west, established continuing
claims of gratitude and obligation on the United States. Madison was one of eighteen "friends of liberty and universal
brotherhood"—his companions included, somewhat strangely,
Washington and Hamilton, as well as Tom Paine, Dr. Priestley,
and Jeremy Bentham from England—to whom the French National Assembly offered French citizenship in August 1792.
After a moment's prudent hesitation, in the face of Washington's Neutrality Proclamation and the unpredictable revolutions
in the Revolution, Madison gratefully accepted the honor with
Jefferson's approval.

The Virginians were eager to express their sympathy for the
Revolution by securing a cordial reception for the new French
Minister to the United States, Edmund Genêt. Genêt's reckless
meddling in domestic affairs aroused such wide hostility that
his American Republican friends were forced eventually to
abandon him. To preserve popular attachment to the French
cause and reverse the neutrality policy, as the following letter
of September 1793 explains, Madison supplied various friends

in Virginia with a draft of resolutions to express the spontaneous sentiments of the country folk.

September 2d, 1793.

DEAR SIR,—I dropped you a few lines this morning by a servant going to George Town with your horse. I had not time without detaining him to say more than that I had your two favors of the 11th ult. by Mr. D. R. [David Meade Randolph] and of the 18th by post. The former was communicated to Monroe as shall be the latter in case of opportunity. The conduct of Genet, as developed in these, and in his proceedings as exhibited in the newspapers, is as unaccountable as it is distressing. The effect is beginning to be strongly felt here in the surprise and disgust of those who are attached to the French cause, and viewed this minister as the instrument for cementing instead of alienating, the two Republics. These sensations are powerfully reinforced by the general and habitual veneration for the President. The Anglican party is busy as you may suppose in making the worst of everything, and in turning the public feelings against France, and thence in favor of England. The only antidote for their poison is to distinguish between the nation & its agent, between principles and events; and to impress the well meaning with the fact that the enemies of France & of Liberty are at work to lead them from their honorable connection with these into the arms and ultimately into the Government, of G. B. [Great Britain]. If the genuine sense of the people could be collected on the several points comprehended in the occasion, the calamity would be greatly alleviated if not absolutely controuled. But this is scarcely possible. The Country is too much uninformed, and too inert to speak for itself; and the language of the towns which are generally directed by an adverse interest will insidiously inflame the evil. It is however of such infinite importance to our own Government as well as to that of France, that the real sentiments of the people here should be understood, that something ought to be attempted on that head. I inclose a copy of a train of Ideas sketched on the first rumour of the war between the Executive & Genet, and particularly suggested by the Richmond Resolutions, as a groundwork for those who might take the lead in County meetings. It was intended that they should be modified in every particular according to the state of information and the particular temper of the place. A copy has been sent to Caroline with a hope that Mr. P. [Edmund Pendleton] might find it not improper to step forward. Another is gone to the District Court at Staunton in the hands of Monroe, who carried a letter from me on the subject to A. Stuart; and a third will be for consideration at the District Court at Charlottesville. If these examples should be set, there may be a chance of like proceedings elsewhere; and in themselves they will be respectable specimens of the principles and sensations of the Agricultural which is the commanding part of the Society. I am not sanguine however that the effort will succeed. If it does not, the State Legislatures, and the federal also if possible, must be induced to take up the matter in its true point of view. Monroe & myself read with attention your despatch by D. R. [David Randolph], and had much conversation on what passed between you & the P. [President]. It appeared to both of us that a real anxiety was marked to retain you in office, that over and above other motives, it was felt that your presence and implied sanction might be a necessary shield against certain criticisms from certain quarters; that the departure of the only counsellor possessing the confidence of the Republicans would be a signal for new & perhaps very disagreeable attacks; that in this point of view the respectful & conciliatory language of the P. [President] is worthy of particular attention; and that it affords a better hope than has existed of your being able to command attention, and to moderate the predominant tone. We agreed in opinion also that whilst this end is pursued, it would be wise to make as few concessions as possible that might embarrass the free pursuit of measures which may be dictated by Republican principles & required by the public good. In a word we think you ought to make the most of the value we perceive to be placed on your participation in the Executive Counsels. I am extremely glad to find that you are to remain another quarter. The season will be more apropos in several respects; and it will prevent any co-operation which a successor might be disposed to make towards a final breach with France. . . .

ENCLOSURE: DRAFT OF COUNTY RESOLUTIONS

It being considered that it is at all times the right & at certain periods the duty of the people to declare their principles & opinions on subjects which concern the National interest, that at the present conjuncture this duty is rendered the more indispensable by the prevailing practice of declaratory resolutions, in places where the inhabitants can more easily assemble & consult than in the Country at large, and where interests views & political opinions different from those of the great body of the people, may happen to predominate, whence there may be danger of unfair & delusive inferences concerning the true & general sense of the people. It being also considered that under the disadvantage a great proportion of the people labor in their distant & dispersed situation from the want of timely & correct knowledge of particular incidents, & the conduct of particular persons connected with public transactions, it is most prudent & safe, to wait with a decent reserve for full & satisfactory information in relation thereto, & in public declarations to abide by those great principles, just sentiments & established truths which can be little affected by personal or transitory occurrences:

Therefore as the sense of the present Meeting,

Resolved, That the Constitution of the U. S. ought to be

firmly & vigilantly supported against all direct or indirect attempts that may be made to subvert or violate the same:

That as it is the interest of the U. S. to cultivate the preservation of peace by all just and honorable means, the Executive Authority ought to be supported in the exercise of its constitutional powers & functions for enforcing the laws existing for that purpose:

That the eminent virtues & services of our illustrious fellow Citizen George Washington, President of U. S. entitle him to the highest respect & lasting gratitude of his Country, whose peace liberty, & safety must ever remind it of his distinguished agency in promoting the same.

That the eminent & generous aids rendered to the U. S. in their arduous struggle for liberty by the French Nation ought ever to be remembered & acknowledged with gratitude & that the spectacle exhibited by the severe & glorious contest in which it is now engaged for its own liberty, ought & must be peculiarly interesting to the wishes, the friendship & the sympathy of the people of America:

That all attempts which may be made in whatever form or disguise to alienate the good will of the people of America from the cause of liberty & republican Government in France have a tendency to weaken the affection to the free principles of their own Government, and manifest designs which ought to be narrowly watched & seasonably counteracted

That such attempts to disunite Nations mutually attached to the cause of liberty, & viewed with unfriendly eyes by all who hate it, ought more particularly to be reprobated at the present crisis, when such vast efforts are making by a combination of Princes & Nobles to crush an example that may open the eyes of all mankind to their natural & political rights:

That a dissolution of the honorable & beneficial connection between the U. S. & France would obviously tend to forward a plan of connecting them with Great Britain, as one great leading step towards assimilating our Government to the form

& spirit of the British Monarchy; and that this apprehension is greatly strengthened by the active zeal displayed by persons disaffected to the American Revolution & by others of known Monarchical principles, in propagating prejudices against the French Nation & Revolution.

19. War and the Executive: Helvidius Letters

In 1787 Madison and Hamilton had joined hands snugly under the toga of Publius. (See Document 12.) By 1793, they were veteran adversaries in the columns of the newspapers, anonymous but nonetheless well known. Washington's Neutrality Proclamation of April 22, 1793, largely reflecting the Hamiltonian line in a divided cabinet, drew them out again. Writing as Pacificus, the realistic defender of peace and the national interest against Francophile adventurism, Hamilton construed the neutrality policy in eight articles published in the *Gazette of the United States* between June 29 and July 27, 1793. Jefferson and Madison found the policy of the presidential proclamation bad enough, neglecting as they thought America's moral, political, and treaty obligations to revolutionary France. Hamilton's version of neutrality struck them as sheer heresy. Jefferson urged his friend to "cut him to pieces in the face of the public," and later was charmed by the performance.

"Letters of Helvidius," Numbers 1 and 4, *Gazette of the United States*, August 24 and September 14, 1793, in *Writings*, VI, pp. 138–151, 171–177.

Although Pacificus had examined a wide range of foreign policy questions raised by the Proclamation, Helvidius concentrated his attack on Hamilton's first essay, justifying far-reaching executive control over foreign relations. By taking a constitutional lawyer's approach to the burning issues of war and revolution, Madison's five Helvidius letters of August and September 1793 seemed to substitute form for substance, to avoid discussing the *merits* of American neutrality by harping on the *mode* of issuing the proclamation. Yet the constitutional power of the executive in foreign affairs, and in domestic concerns as well, was becoming for him the real test question of American politics, on which the future of republican government might well depend. Once more, as in the case of the national bank, he tried to base the opposition on the Constitution strictly construed according to the intentions of the ratifying conventions. Finding partial support in one of Hamilton's numbers of *The Federalist* added a nice twist to the argument. No doubt, too, he saw a better chance of settling policy decisions his own way in Congress than in the executive branch, as his relations with Washington deteriorated. Popular indignation over Citizen Genêt's arrogant interventions added a good political reason for skirting the French question as such.

It is not clear why Madison chose the mask of Helvidius, although one may guess that he was attracted by Tacitus' admiring portrait of Helvidius Priscus, a noble Roman imbued with the spirit of truth and liberty who suffered exile under Nero's tyranny and, after his recall, argued fiercely for the right of the Senate to appoint delegates to the Emperor and to regulate the conduct of the Treasury. (Curiously, Tacitus described Madison's pen-character, Helvidius, in language that Hamilton might well have borrowed for his discussion of the executive in *The Federalist* Number 72: "The love of fame," Tacitus wrote, "was by some objected to him as . . . his ruling passion. But the love of fame . . . is often . . . the great principle of the noble mind . . ." [*The History*, Book IV, S VI].

NO. I

Several pieces with the signature of PACIFICUS were lately published, which have been read with singular pleasure and applause, by the foreigners and degenerate citizens among us, who hate our republican government, and the French revolution; whilst the publication seems to have been too little regarded, or too much despised by the steady friends to both.

Had the doctrines inculcated by the writer, with the natural consequences from them, been nakedly presented to the public, this treatment might have been proper. Their true character would then have struck every eye, and been rejected by the feelings of every heart. But they offer themselves to the reader in the dress of an elaborate dissertation; they are mingled with a few truths that may serve them as a passport to credulity; and they are introduced with professions of anxiety for the preservation of peace, for the welfare of the government, and for the respect due to the present head of the executive, that may prove a snare to patriotism.

In these disguises they have appeared to claim the attention I propose to bestow on them: with a view to show, from the publication itself, that under colour of vindicating an important public act, of a chief magistrate who enjoys the confidence and love of his country, principles are advanced which strike at the vitals of its constitution, as well as at its honour and true interest.

As it is not improbable that attempts may be made to apply insinuations, which are seldom spared when particular purposes are to be answered, to the author of the ensuing observations, it may not be improper to premise, that he is a friend to the constitution, that he wishes for the preservation of peace, and that the present chief magistrate has not a fellow-citizen, who is penetrated with deeper respect for his merits, or feels a purer solicitude for his glory.

This declaration is made with no view of courting a more

favourable ear to what may be said than it deserves. The sole purpose of it is, to obviate imputations which might weaken the impressions of truth; and which are the more likely to be resorted to, in proportion as solid and fair arguments may be wanting.

The substance of the first piece, sifted from its inconsistencies and its vague expressions, may be thrown into the following propositions:

That the powers of declaring war and making treaties are, in their nature, executive powers:

That being particularly vested by the constitution in other departments, they are to be considered as exceptions out of the general grant to the executive department:

That being, as exceptions, to be construed strictly, the powers not strictly within them, remain with the executive.

That the executive consequently, as the organ of intercourse with foreign nations, and the interpreter and executor of treaties, and the law of nations, is authorized to expound all articles of treaties, those involving questions of war and peace, as well as others;—to judge of the obligations of the United States to make war or not, under any *casus fœderis* or eventual operation of the contract, relating to war; and to pronounce the state of things resulting from the obligations of the United States, as understood by the executive:

That in particular the executive had authority to judge, whether in the case of the mutual guaranty between the United States and France, the former were bound by it to engage in the war:

That the executive has, in pursuance of that authority, decided that the United States are not bound:—And

That its proclamation of the 22nd of April last, is to be taken as the effect and expression of that decision.

The basis of the reasoning is, we perceive, the extraordinary doctrine, that the powers of making war, and treaties, are in their nature executive; and therefore comprehended in the gencral grant of executive power, where not especially and strictly excepted out of the grant.

Let us examine this doctrine: and that we may avoid the possibility of mistaking the writer, it shall be laid down in his own words; a precaution the more necessary, as scarce any thing else could outweigh the improbability, that so extravagant a tenet should be hazarded at so early a day, in the face of the public.

His words are—"Two of these [exceptions and qualifications to the executive powers] have been already noticed—the participation of the senate in the *appointment of officers,* and the *making of treaties.* A *third* remains to be mentioned—the right of the legislature to *declare war, and grant letters of marque and reprisal.*"

Again—"It deserves to be remarked, that as the participation of the senate in the *making of treaties,* and the power of the legislature to *declare war,* are *exceptions* out of the general *executive power,* vested in the president; they are to be construed *strictly,* and ought to be extended no further than is *essential* to their execution."

If there be any countenance to these positions, it must be found either, first, in the writers of authority on public law; or, 2d, in the quality and operation of the powers to make war and treaties; or, 3d, in the constitution of the United States.

1. It would be of little use to enter far into the first source of information, not only because our own reason and our own constitution, are the best guides; but because a just analysis and discrimination of the powers of government, according to their executive, legislative, and judiciary qualities, are not to be expected in the works of the most received jurists, who wrote before a critical attention was paid to those objects, and with their eyes too much on monarchical governments, where all powers are confounded in the sovereignty of the prince. It will be found, however, I believe, that all of them, particularly Wol-

sius, Burlemaqui, and Vatel, speak of the powers to declare war, to conclude peace, and to form alliances, as among the highest acts of the sovereignty; of which the legislative power must at least be an integral and preeminent part.

Writers, such as Locke, and Montesquieu, who have discussed more the principles of liberty and the structure of government, lie under the same disadvantage, of having written before these subjects were illuminated by the events and discussions which distinguish a very recent period. Both of them, too, are evidently warped by a regard to the particular government of England, to which one of them owed allegiance;[1] and the other professed an admiration bordering on idolatry. Montesquieu, however, has rather distinguished himself by enforcing the reasons and the importance of avoiding a confusion of the several powers of government, than by enumerating and defining the powers which belong to each particular class. And Locke, notwithstanding the early date of his work on civil government, and the example of his own government before his eyes, admits that the particular powers in question, which, after some of the writers on public law he calls *federative,* are really *distinct* from the *executive,* though almost always united with it, and *hardly to be separated into distinct hands.* Had he not lived under a monarchy, in which these powers were united; or had he written by the lamp which truth now presents to lawgivers, the last observation would probably never have dropped from his pen. But let us quit a field of research which is more likely to perplex than to decide, and bring the question to other tests of which it will be more easy to judge.

2. If we consult, for a moment, the nature and operation of the two powers to declare war and to make treaties, it will be impossible not to see, that they can never fall within a proper definition of executive powers. The natural province of the

---

[1] The chapter on prerogative shows, how much the reason of the philosopher was clouded by the royalism of the Englishman.

executive magistrate is to execute laws, as that of the legislature is to make laws. All his acts, therefore, properly executive,
must presuppose the existence of the laws to be executed. A
treaty is not an execution of laws: it does not presuppose the
existence of laws. It is, on the contrary, to have itself the force
of a *law,* and to be carried into *execution,* like all *other laws,* by
the *executive magistrate.* To say then that the power of making
treaties, which are confessedly laws, belongs naturally to the
department which is to execute laws, is to say, that the executive department naturally includes a legislative power. In
theory this is an absurdity—in practice a tyranny.

The power to declare war is subject to similar reasoning. A
declaration that there shall be war, is not an execution of laws:
it does not suppose pre-existing laws to be executed: it is not,
in any respect, an act merely executive. It is, on the contrary,
one of the most deliberate acts that can be performed; and
when performed, has the effect of *repealing* all the *laws* operating in a state of peace, so far as they are inconsistent with a
state of war; and of *enacting,* as a *rule for the executive, a new
code* adapted to the relation between the society and its foreign enemy. In like manner, a conclusion of peace *annuls* all
the *laws* peculiar to a state of war, and *revives* the general
laws incident to a state of peace.

These remarks will be strengthened by adding, that treaties,
particularly treaties of peace, have sometimes the effect of
changing not only the external laws of the society, but operate
also on the internal code, which is purely municipal, and to
which the legislative authority of the country is of itself competent and complete.

From this view of the subject it must be evident, that
although the executive may be a convenient organ of preliminary communications with foreign governments, on the subjects
of treaty or war; and the proper agent for carrying into execution the final determinations of the competent authority; yet
it can have no pretensions, from the nature of the powers in

question compared with the nature of the executive trust, to that essential agency which gives validity to such determinations.

It must be further evident, that if these powers be not in their nature purely legislative, they partake so much more of that, than of any other quality, that under a constitution leaving them to result to their most natural department, the legislature would be without a rival in its claim.

Another important inference to be noted is, that the powers of making war and treaty being substantially of a legislative, not an executive nature, the rule of interpreting exceptions strictly must narrow, instead of enlarging, executive pretensions on those subjects.

3. It remains to be inquired, whether there be any thing in the constitution itself, which shows, that the powers of making war and peace are considered as of an executive nature, and as comprehended within a general grant of executive power.

It will not be pretended, that this appears from any *direct* position to be found in the instrument.

If it were *deducible* from any particular expressions, it may be presumed, that the publication would have saved us the trouble of the research.

Does the doctrine, then, result from the actual distribution of powers among the several branches of the government? or from any fair analogy between the powers of war and treaty, and the enumerated powers vested in the executive alone?

Let us examine:

In the general distribution of powers, we find that of declaring war expressly vested in the congress, where every other legislative power is declared to be vested; and without any other qualification than what is common to every other legislative act. The constitutional idea of this power would seem then clearly to be, that it is of a legislative and not an executive nature.

This conclusion becomes irresistible, when it is recollected, that the constitution cannot be supposed to have placed either any power legislative in its nature, entirely among executive powers, or any power executive in its nature, entirely among legislative powers, without charging the constitution, with that kind of intermixture and consolidation of different powers, which would violate a fundamental principle in the organization of free governments. If it were not unnecessary to enlarge on this topic here, it could be shown, that the constitution was originally vindicated, and has been constantly expounded, with a disavowal of any such intermixture.

The power of treaties is vested jointly in the president and in the senate, which is a branch of the legislature. From this arrangement merely, there can be no inference that would necessarily exclude the power from the executive class: since the senate is joined with the president in another power, that of appointing to offices, which, as far as relate to executive offices at least, is considered as of an executive nature. Yet on the other hand, there are sufficient indications that the power of treaties is regarded by the constitution as materially different from mere executive power, and as having more affinity to the legislative than to the executive character.

One circumstance indicating this, is the constitutional regulation under which the senate give their consent in the case of treaties. In all other cases, the consent of the body is expressed by a majority of voices. In this particular case, a concurrence of two-thirds at least is made necessary, as a substitute or compensation for the other branch of the legislature, which, on certain occasions, could not be conveniently a party to the transaction.

But the conclusive circumstance is, that treaties, when formed according to the constitutional mode, are confessedly to have force and operation of *laws,* and are to be a rule for the courts in controversies between man and man, as much as any *other laws.* They are even emphatically declared by the constitution to be "the supreme law of the land."

So far the argument from the constitution is precisely in opposition to the doctrine. As little will be gained in its favour from a comparison of the two powers, with those particularly vested in the president alone.

As there are but few, it will be most satisfactory to review them one by one.

"The president shall be commander in chief of the army and navy of the United States, and of the militia when called into the actual service of the United States."

There can be no relation worth examining between this power and the general power of making treaties. And instead of being analogous to the power of declaring war, it affords a striking illustration of the incompatibility of the two powers in the same hands. Those who are to *conduct a war* cannot in the nature of things, be proper or safe judges, whether a *war ought* to be *commenced, continued,* or *concluded.* They are barred from the latter functions by a great principle in free government, analogous to that which separates the sword from the purse, or the power of executing from the power of enacting laws.

"He may require the opinion in writing of the principal officers in each of the executive departments upon any subject relating to the duties of their respective offices; and he shall have power to grant reprieves and pardons for offences against the United States, except in case of impeachment." These powers can have nothing to do with the subject.

"The president shall have power to fill up vacancies that may happen during the recess of the Senate, by granting commissions which shall expire at the end of the next session." The same remark is applicable to this power, as also to that of "receiving ambassadors, other public ministers, and consuls." The particular use attempted to be made of this last power will be considered in another place.

"He shall take care that the laws shall be faithfully executed, and shall commission all officers of the United States." To see the laws faithfully executed constitutes the essence of the executive authority. But what relation has it to the power of making treaties and war, that is, of determining what the *laws shall be* with regard to other nations? No other certainly than what subsists between the powers of executing and enacting laws; no other, consequently, than what forbids a coalition of the powers in the same department.

I pass over the few other specified functions assigned to the president, such as that of convening the legislature, &c., &c., which cannot be drawn into the present question.

It may be proper however to take notice of the power of removal from office, which appears to have been adjudged to the president by the laws establishing the executive departments; and which the writer has endeavoured to press into his service. To justify any favourable inference from this case, it must be shown, that the powers of war and treaties are of a kindred nature to the power of removal, or at least are equally within a grant of executive power. Nothing of this sort has been attempted, nor probably will be attempted. Nothing can in truth be clearer, than that no analogy, or shade of analogy, can be traced between a power in the supreme officer responsible for the faithful execution of the laws, to displace a subaltern officer employed in the execution of the laws; and a power to make treaties and to declare war, such as these have been found to be in their nature, their operation, and their consequences.

Thus it appears that by whatever standard we try this doctrine, it must be condemned as no less vicious in theory than it would be dangerous in practice. It is countenanced neither by the writers on law; nor by the nature of the powers themselves; nor by any general arrangements, or particular expressions, or plausible analogies, to be found in the constitution.

Whence then can the writer have borrowed it?

There is but one answer to this question.

The power of making treaties and the power of declaring war, are *royal prerogatives* in the *British government,* and are accordingly treated as *executive prerogatives* by *British com-mentators*.

We shall be the more confirmed in the necessity of this solution of the problem, by looking back to the area of the constitution, and satisfying ourselves that the writer could not have been misled by the doctrines maintained by our own commentators on our own government. That I may not ramble beyond prescribed limits, I shall content myself with an extract from a work which entered into a systematic explanation and defence of the constitution; and to which there has frequently been ascribed some influence in con-ciliating the public assent to the government in the form proposed. Three circumstances conspire in giving weight to this contemporary exposition. It was made at a time when no application to *persons or measures* could bias: the opinion given was not transiently mentioned, but formally and criti-cally elucidated: it related to a point in the constitution which must consequently have been viewed as of importance in the public mind. The passage relates to the power of making treaties; that of declaring war, being arranged with such obvious propriety among the legislative powers, as to be passed over without particular discussion.

"Though several writers on the subject of government place that power [*of making treaties*] in the class of *executive authorities*, yet this is *evidently* an *arbitrary disposition*. For if we attend *carefully* to its operation, it will be found to par-take *more* of the *legislative* than of the *executive* character, though it does not seem strictly to fall within the definition of either of them. The essence of the legislative authority, is to enact laws; or, in other words, to prescribe rules for the regulation of the society: while the execution of the laws and the employment of the common strength, either for this purpose, or for the common defence, seem to comprise *all* the functions of the *executive magistrate*. The power of mak-ing treaties is *plainly* neither the one nor the other. It relates neither to the execution of the subsisting laws, nor to the enaction of new ones, and still less to an exertion of the common strength. Its objects are contracts with foreign nations, which have the *force of law,* but derive it from the obligations of good faith. They are not rules prescribed by the sovereign to the subject, but agreements between sovereign and sovereign. The power in question seems therefore to form a distinct department, and to belong properly neither to the legislative nor to the executive. The qualities elsewhere detailed as indispensable in the management of foreign *negotiations,* point out the executive as the most fit agent in those transactions; whilst the vast importance of the trust, and the operation of treaties as *laws,* plead strongly for the participation of the whole or a part of the *legislative body,* in the office of making them."—*Federalist,* p. 418.[2]

It will not fail to be remarked on this commentary, that whatever doubts may be started as to the correctness of its reasoning against the legislative nature of the power to make treaties; it is *clear, consistent,* and *confident,* in deciding that the power is *plainly* and *evidently* not an *executive power.*

NO. IV

The last papers completed the view proposed to be taken of the arguments in support of the new and aspiring doctrine, which ascribes to the executive the prerogative of judging and deciding, whether there be causes of war or not in the obligations of treaties; notwithstanding the express provision in the constitution, by which the legislature is made the organ of the national will, on questions, whether there be or be not a cause for declaring war. If the answer to these arguments has imparted the conviction which dic-

---

[2] No. 75, written by Mr. Hamilton.

tated it, the reader will have pronounced that they are generally superficial, abounding in contradictions, never in the least degree conclusive to the main point, and not unfrequently conclusive against the writer himself: whilst the doctrine—that the powers of treaty and war, are in their nature executive powers, which forms the basis of those arguments, is as indefensible and as dangerous as the particular doctrine to which they are applied.

But it is not to be forgotten that these doctrines, though ever so clearly disproved, or ever so weakly defended, remain before the public a striking monument of the principles and views which are entertained and propagated in the community.

It is also to be remembered, that however the consequences flowing from such premises, may be disavowed at this time, or by this individual, we are to regard it as morally certain, that in proportion as the doctrines make their way into the creed of the government, and the acquiescence of the public, every power that can be deduced from them, will be deduced, and exercised sooner or later by those who may have an interest in so doing. The character of human nature gives this salutary warning to every sober and reflecting mind. And the history of government in all its forms and in every period of time, ratifies the danger. A people, therefore, who are so happy as to possess the inestimable blessing of a free and defined constitution cannot be too watchful against the introduction, nor too critical in tracing the consequences, of new principles and new constructions, that may remove the landmarks of power.

Should the prerogative which has been examined, be allowed, in its most limited sense, to usurp the public countenance, the interval would probably be very short, before it would be heard from some quarter or other, that the prerogative either amounts to nothing, or means a right to judge and conclude that the obligations of treaty impose war, as well as that they permit peace; that it is fair reasoning to say, that if the prerogative exists at all, an operative rather than an *inert* character ought to be given to it.

In support of this conclusion, there would be enough to echo, "that the prerogative in this active sense, is connected with the executive in various capacities—as the organ of intercourse between the nation and foreign nations—as the interpreter of national treaties" (a violation of which may be a cause of war)—"as that power which is charged with the execution of the laws, or which treaties make a part—as that power, which is charged with *the command and application of the public force.*"

With additional force, it might be said, that the executive is as much the *executor* as the *interpreter* of treaties; that if by virtue of the *first* character, it is to judge of the *obligations* of treaties, it is, by virtue of the *second*, equally authorised to carry those obligations into *effect.* Should there occur, for example, a *casus fœderis,* claiming a military cooperation of the United States, and a military force should happen to be under the command of the executive, it must have the same right, as *executor of public treaties,* to *employ* the public force, as it has in quality of *interpreter of public treaties* to decide, whether it ought to be *employed.*

The case of a treaty of peace would be an auxiliary to comments of this sort: it is a condition annexed to every treaty, that an infraction even of an important article, on one side, extinguishes the obligations on the other: and the immediate consequence of a dissolution of a treaty of peace is a restoration of a state of war. If the executive is "to decide on the obligation of the nation with regard to foreign nations"—"to pronounce the *existing condition* (in the sense annexed by the writer) of the nation with regard to them; and to admonish the citizens of their obligations and duties, as founded upon *that condition* of things"—"to judge what are the *reciprocal rights* and obligations of the United States,

and of all and each of the powers at war;"—add, that if the
executive, moreover, possesses all powers relating to war,
not strictly within the power to *declare war,* which any pupil
of political casuistry could distinguish from a mere *relapse*
into a war that *had been declared:* with this store of materials,
and the example given of the use to be made of them, would
it be difficult to fabricate a power in the executive to plunge
the nation into war, whenever a treaty of peace might happen
to be infringed?

But if any difficulty should arise, there is another mode
chalked out, by which the end might clearly be brought
about, even without the violation of the treaty of peace;
especially if the other party should happen to change its
government at the crisis. The executive could *suspend* the
treaty of peace *by refusing to receive an ambassador* from the
new government; and the state of war *emerges of course.*

This is a sample of the use to which the extraordinary publication we are reviewing might be turned. Some of the inferences could not be repelled at all. And the least regular
of them must go smoothly down with those who had swallowed the gross sophistry which wrapped up the original dose.

Every just view that can be taken of this subject, admon-
ishes the public of the necessity of a rigid adherence to the
simple, the receive, and the fundamental doctrine of the constitution, that the power to declare war, including the power
of judging of the causes of war, is *fully* and *exclusively* vested
in the legislature; that the executive has no right, in any
case, to decide the question, whether there is or is not cause
for declaring war; that the right of convening and informing
congress, whenever such a question seems to call for a decision, is all the right which the constitution has deemed requisite or proper; and that for such, more than for any other
contingency, this right was especially given to the executive.

In no part of the constitution is more wisdom to be found,
than in the clause which confides the question of war or peace

to the legislature, and not to the executive department. Beside the objection to such a mixture to heterogeneous powers, the trust and the temptation would be too great for any one man; not such as nature may offer as the prodigy of many centuries, but such as may be expected in the ordinary successions of magistracy. War is in fact the true nurse of executive aggrandizement. In war, a physical force is to be created; and it is the executive will, which is to direct it. In war, the public treasures are to be unlocked; and it is the executive hand which is to dispense them. In war, the honours and emoluments of office are to be multiplied; and it is the executive patronage under which they are to be enjoyed. It is in war, finally, that laurels are to be gathered; and it is the executive brow they are to encircle. The strongest passions and most dangerous weaknesses of the human breast; ambition, avarice, vanity, the honourable or venial love of fame, are all in conspiracy against the desire and duty of peace.

Hence it has grown into an axiom that the executive is the department of power most distinguished by its propensity to war: hence it is the practice of all states, in proportion as they are free, to disarm this propensity of its influence.

As the best praise then that can be pronounced on an executive magistrate, is, that he is the friend of peace; a praise that rises in its value, as there may be a known capacity to shine in war: so it must be one of the most sacred duties of a free people, to mark the first omen in the society, of principles that may stimulate the hopes of other magistrates of another propensity, to intrude into questions on which its gratification depends. If a free people be a wise people also, they will not forget that the danger of surprise can never be so great, as when the advocates for the prerogative of war can sheathe it in a symbol of peace.

The constitution has manifested a similar prudence in refusing to the executive the *sole* power of making peace. The trust in this instance also, would be too great for the wisdom, and the temptations too strong for the virtue of a single citizen. The principle reasons on which the constitution proceeded in its regulation of the power of treaties, including treaties of peace, are so aptly furnished by the work already quoted more than once, that I shall borrow another comment from that source.

"However proper or safe it may be in a government where the executive magistrate is an hereditary monarch, to commit to him the entire power of making treaties, it would be utterly unsafe and improper to entrust that power to an elective magistrate of four years' duration. It has been remarked upon another occasion, and the remark is unquestionably just, that an hereditary monarch, though often the oppressor of his people, has personally too much at stake in the government to be in any material danger of being corrupted by foreign powers: but that a man raised from the station of a private citizen to the rank of chief magistrate, possessed of but a moderate or slender fortune, and looking forward to a period not very remote, when he may probably be obliged to return to the station from which he was taken, might sometimes be under temptations to sacrifice his duty to his interest, which it would require superlative virtue to withstand. An avaricious man might be tempted to betray the interests of the state to the acquisition of wealth. An ambitious man might make his own aggrandizement, by the aid of a foreign power, the price of his treachery to his constituents. The history of human conduct does not warrant that exalted opinion of human virtue, which would make it wise in a nation to commit interests of so delicate and momentous a kind, as *those which concern its intercourse* with the rest of the world, to the *sole* disposal of a magistrate created and circumstanced as would be a president of the United States." p. 418.[3]

---

[3] *Federalist*, No. 75, written by Mr. Hamilton.

I shall conclude this paper and this branch of the subject, with two reflections, which naturally arise from this view of the constitution.

The first is, that as the personal interest of an hereditary monarch in the government, is the *only* security against the temptation incident to the commitment of the delicate and momentous interests of the nation, which concern its intercourse with the rest of the world, to the disposal of a single magistrate, it is a plain consequence, that every addition that may be made to the *sole* agency and influence of the executive, in the intercourse of the nation with foreign nations, is an increase of the dangerous temptation to which an *elective and temporary* magistrate is exposed; and an *argument* and *advance* towards the security afforded by the personal interests of an *hereditary* magistrate.

Secondly, as the constitution has not permitted the executive *singly* to conclude or judge that peace ought to be made, it might be inferred from that circumstance alone, that it never meant to give it authority, *singly*, to judge and conclude that war ought not to be made. The trust would be precisely similar and equivalent in the two cases. The right to say that war ought not to go on, would be no greater than the right to say that war ought not to begin. Every danger of error or corruption, incident to such a prerogative in one case, is incident to it in the other. If the constitution therefore has deemed it unsafe or improper in the one case, it must be deemed equally so in the other case.

20. Bloodless War:
The Power of Commerce

In the modern liberal and republican tradition, war and political empire have been viewed as natural enemies of liberty, prosperity, and the increase of mankind. Visions of universal and perpetual peace run through the thought of the Enlightenment intellectuals; and their enthusiastic response to the American Revolution reveals the force of anti-imperialism as well. (See Document 17.) For many radical thinkers of the eighteenth century, the enlightened self-interest of the people working freely through the economic and political marketplace became the alternative to naked power struggles within society and among the nations.

Madison was peculiarly responsible for blending this large conception of the peaceful mission of republicanism with the traditional mercantilist policy of regulating foreign trade and navigation in the national economic and political interest.

Political Observations, April 20, 1795, in *Letters*, IV, pp. 485–489, 491–492, 496–502.

The product of the merger was a distinctive doctrine of bloodless commerical warfare as a substitute for fighting ships and
armies with all their train of evils: death and taxes, poverty
and despotism. In practical terms, of course, it was an attractive choice for a new nation with a limited industrial and
military capacity, a hatred of taxes, and a deep fear of military
establishments, particularly on the national level. Since the
1780s, moreover, Madison had added another concrete element
to the formula: the hope of breaking the British monopoly
over American trade and shipping, with its painful restrictions
and seemingly heavy costs, by developing alternative markets
in France and on the continent generally. Madison's profound
sympathy for the French Revolution, and his hostility to its
enemies, provided a further powerful motive. (See Document
18.)

In the first session of the First Congress, Madison had
pressed for discriminating tariff and tonnage charges against
nations not in treaty with the United States (chiefly, Great
Britain) and in favor of nations in treaty relations (chiefly,
France). In December, 1793, after the outbreak of war in
Europe, Secretary of State Jefferson submitted to the House of
Representatives a lengthy report cataloguing violations of
American commercial and shipping rights by the combatants,
with emphasis on British sins, and proposing a foreign policy
of economic coercion. Madison, on January 3, 1794, introduced
into the House a series of commerical resolutions implementing
Jefferson's report, and sustained his view in a lengthy and
sharp debate. Congress settled for a thirty-day embargo on
commerce, and Washington sent John Jay to negotiate a permanent settlement with London.

At this juncture, with American political tempers growing
short, Madison once more carried his opposition to the general
public with a long pamphlet, *Political Observations,* defending
his commercial resolutions, broadening his attack on the administration's pro-British policy, and preparing a hot reception

for John Jay (however his negotiations might turn out). He would soon lead a bitter struggle against Jay's treaty (signed in November, 1794, and taken up in secret by the Senate the following June). The doctrine of bloodless commerical warfare would characterize his foreign policy as Jefferson's Secretary of State (1801–1809) and as President, until he felt that he had exhausted the alternatives to military force in 1812. Then many of his old opposition arguments against militarism and national consolidation, debt and taxes, came home to roost. (See Part IV.)

A variety of publications, in pamphlets and other forms, have appeared in different parts of the Union since the session of Congress which ended in June, 1794; endeavoring, by discolored representations of our public affairs, and particularly of certain occurrences of that session, to turn the tide of public opinion into a party channel. The immediate object of the writers was either avowedly or evidently to operate on the approaching elections of Federal Representatives. As that crisis will have entirely elapsed before the following observations will appear, they will, at least, be free from a charge of the same views; and will, consequently, have the stronger claim to that deliberate attention and reflection to which they are submitted. . . .

Passing on then to the session of Congress preceding the last, we are met in the first place, by the most serious charges against the Southern members of Congress in general, and particularly against the Representatives of Virginia. They are charged with having supported a policy which would inevitably have involved the United States in the war of Europe, have reduced us from the rank of a free people to that of French colonies, and, possibly, have landed us in disunion, anarchy, and misery; and the policy from which these tremendous calamities was to flow, is referred to certain commercial resolutions moved by a member from Virginia in the House of Representatives [Madison].

To place in its true light the fallacy which infers such consequences from such a cause, it will be proper to review the circumstances which preceded and attended the resolution. . . .

It was natural to expect that one of the first objects of deliberation under the new Constitution would be that which had been first and most contemplated in forming it. Accordingly it was, at the first session, proposed that something should be done analogous to the wishes of the several States, and expressive of the efficiency of the new Government. A discrimination between nations in treaty and those not in treaty, the mode most generally embraced by the States, was agreed to in several forms, and adhered to in repeated votes by a very great majority of the House of Representatives. The Senate, however, did not concur with the House of Representatives, and our commercial arrangements were made up without any provision on the subject.

From that date to the session of Congress ending in June, 1794, the interval passed without any effective appeal to the interest of Great Britain. A silent reliance was placed on her voluntary justice or her enlightened interest.

This long and patient reliance being ascribed (as was foretold) to other causes than a generous forbearance on the part of the United States, had, at the commencement of the Third Congress, left us, with respect to a reciprocity of commercial regulations between the two countries, precisely where the commencement of the First Congress had found us. This was not all; the western posts, which entailed an expensive Indian war on us, continued to be withheld, although all pretext for it had been removed on our part. Depredations as derogatory to our rights as grievous to our interests, had been licensed by the British Government against our lawful commerce on the high seas. And it was believed, on the most probable grounds, that the measure by which the Algerine pirates were let loose on the Atlantic had not taken place without the participation of the same unfriendly counsels. In a word, to say nothing of the American victims to savages and barbarians, it was estimated that our annual damages from Great Britain were not less than three or four millions of dollars.

This distressing situation spoke the more loudly to the patriotism of the Representatives of the people, as the nature and manner of the communications from the President seemed to make a formal and affecting appeal on the subject to their co-operation. The necessity of some effort was palpable. The only room for different opinions seemed to lie in the different modes of redress proposed. On one side nothing was proposed beyond the eventual measures of defence, in which all concurred, except the building of six frigates, for the purpose of enforcing our rights against Algiers. The other side, considering this measure as pointed at one only of our evils, and as inadequate even to that, thought it best to seek for some safe but powerful remedy, that might be applied to the root of them; and with this view the commercial propositions were introduced.

They were at first opposed, on the ground that Great Britain was amicably disposed towards the United States, and that we ought to await the event of the depending negotiation. To this it was replied, that more than four years of appeal to that disposition had been tried in vain by the new Government; that the negotiation had been abortive and was no longer depending; that the late letters from Mr. Pinckney, the Minister at London, had not only cut off all remaining hope from that source, but had expressly pointed commercial regulations as the most eligible redress to be pursued.

Another ground of opposition was, that the United States were more dependent on the trade of Great Britain than Great Britain was on the trade of the United States. This will appear scarcely credible to those who understand the commerce between the two countries, who recollect that it supplies us chiefly with superfluities; whilst in return it employs the industry of one part of her people, sends to another part the very bread which keeps them from starving, and remits, moreover, an annual balance in specie of ten or twelve millions of dollars. It is true, nevertheless, as the debate shews, that this was the language, however strange, of some who combated the propositions.

Nay, what is still more extraordinary, it was maintained that the United States had, on the whole, little or no reason to complain of the footing of their commerce with Great Britain; although such complaints had prevailed in every State, among every class of citizens, ever since the year 1783; and although the Federal Constitution had originated in those complaints, and had been established with the known view of redressing them.

As such objections could have little effect in convincing the judgment of the House of Representatives, and still less that of the public at large, a new mode of assailing the propositions has been substituted. The American people love peace; and the cry of war might alarm when no hope remained of convincing them. The cry of war has accordingly been echoed through the continent with a loudness proportioned to the emptiness of the pretext; and to this cry has been added another still more absurd, that the propositions would, in the end, enslave the United States to their allies and plunge them into anarchy and misery.

It is truly mortifying to be obliged to tax the patience of the reader with an examination of such gross absurdities; but it may be of use to expose where there may be no necessity to refute them.

What were the commercial propositions? They discriminated between nations in treaty and nations not in treaty, by an additional duty on the manufactures and trade of the latter; and they reciprocated the navigation laws of all nations who excluded the vessels of the United States from a common right of being used in the trade between the United States and such nations.

Is there anything here that could afford a cause or a pretext for war to Great Britain or any other nation? If we hold at present the rank of a free people; if we are no longer Colonies of Great Britain; if we have not already relapsed into some dependence on that nation, we have the self-evident right to regulate our trade according to our own will and our own interest, not according to her will or her interest. This right can be denied to no independent nation. It has not been and will not be denied to ourselves, by any opponent of the propositions. . . .

One thing ought to be regarded as certain and conclusive on this head: whilst the war against France remains unsuccessful the United States are in no danger from any of the Powers engaged in it. In the event of a complete overthrow of that Republic, it is impossible to say what might follow. But if the hostile views of the combination should be turned towards this continent, it would clearly not be to vindicate the commercial interests of Great Britain against the commercial rights of the United States. The object would be, to root out Liberty from the face of the earth. No pretext would be wanted, or a better would be contrived than anything to be found in the commercial propositions.

On whatever other side we view the clamor against these propositions as inevitably productive of war, it presents neither evidence to justify it nor argument to colour it.

The allegation necessarily supposes either that the friends of the plan could discover no probability, where its opponents could see a certainty, or that the former were less averse to war than the latter.

The first supposition will not be discussed. A few observations on the other may throw new lights on the whole subject.

The members, in general, who espoused these propositions

have been constantly in that part of the Congress who have professed with most zeal, and pursued with most scruple, the characteristics of republican government. They have adhered to these characteristics in defining the meaning of the Constitution, in adjusting the ceremonial of public proceedings, and in marking out the course of the Administration. They have manifested, particularly, a deep conviction of the danger to liberty and the Constitution, from a gradual assumption or extension of discretionary powers in the executive department; from successive augmentations of a standing army; and from the perpetuity and progression of public debts and taxes. They have been sometimes reprehended in debate for an excess of caution and jealousy on these points. And the newspapers of a certain stamp, by distorting and discolouring this part of their conduct, have painted it in all the deformity which the most industrious calumny could devise.

Those best acquainted with the individuals who more particularly supported the propositions will be foremost to testify, that such are the principles which not only govern them in public life, but which are invariably maintained by them in every other situation. And it cannot be believed nor suspected, that with such principles they could view war as less an evil than it appeared to their opponents.

Of all the enemies to public liberty war is, perhaps, the most to be dreaded, because it comprises and develops the germ of every other. War is the parent of armies; from these proceed debts and taxes; and armies, and debts, and taxes are the known instruments for bringing the many under the domination of the few. In war, too, the discretionary power of the Executive is extended; its influence in dealing out offices, honors, and emoluments is multiplied; and all the means of seducing the minds, are added to those of subduing the force, of the people. The same malignant aspect in republicanism may be traced in the inequality of fortunes, and the opportunities of fraud, growing out of a state of war, and in the degeneracy of manners and of morals, engendered by both. No nation could preserve its freedom in the midst of continual warfare.

Those truths are well established. They are read in every page which records the progression from a less arbitrary to a more arbitrary government, or the transition from a popular government to an aristocracy or a monarchy.

It must be evident, then, that in the same degree as the friends of the propositions were jealous of armies, and debts, and prerogative, as dangerous to a republican Constitution, they must have been averse to war, as favourable to armies and debts, and prerogative.

The fact accordingly appears to be, that they were particularly averse to war. They not only considered the propositions as having no tendency to war, but preferred them, as the most likely means of obtaining our objects without war. They thought, and thought truly, that Great Britain was more vulnerable in her commerce than in her fleets and armies; that she valued our necessaries for her market, and our markets for her superfluities, more than she feared our frigates or our militia; and that she would, consequently, be more ready to make proper concessions under the influence of the former, than of the latter motive.

Great Britain is a commercial nation. Her power, as well as her wealth, is derived from commerce. The American commerce is the most valuable branch she enjoys. It is the more valuable, not only as being of vital importance to her in some respects, but of growing importance beyond estimate in its general character. She will not easily part with such a resource. She will not rashly hazard it. She would be particularly aware of forcing a perpetuity of regulations, which not merely diminish her share, but may favour the rivalship of other nations. If anything, therefore, in the power of the United States could overcome her pride, her avidity, and her repugnancy to this country, it was justly concluded to be, not the fear of our arms, which, though invincible in defence, are little formidable in a war of offence, but the fear of suffering in the most fruitful branch of her trade, and of seeing it distributed among her rivals. . . .

The next charge to be examined is, the tendency of the propositions to degrade the United States into French colonies.

As it is difficult to argue against suppositions made and multiplied at will, so it is happily impossible to impose on the good sense of this country by arguments which rest on suppositions only. In the present question it is first supposed that the exercise of the self-evident and sovereign right of regulating trade after the example of all independent nations, and that of the example of Great Britain towards the United States, would inevitably involve the United States in a war with Great Britain. It is then supposed that the other combined Powers, though some of them be favored by the regulations proposed, and all of them be jealous of the maritime predominance of Great Britain, would support the wrongs of Great Britain against the rights of the United States. It is, lastly, supposed that our allies, (the French,) in the event of success in establishing their own liberties, which they owe to our example, would be willing, as well as able, to rob us of ours, which they assisted us in obtaining; and that so malignant is their disposition on this head, that we should not be spared, even if embarked in a war against her own enemy. To finish the picture, it is intimated that in the character of allies we are the more exposed to this danger from the secret and hostile ambition of France.

It will not be expected that any formal refutation should be wasted on absurdities which answer themselves. None but those who have surrendered their reasoning faculties to the violence of their prejudices, will listen to suggestions implying that the freest nation in Europe is the basest people on the face of the earth; that instead of the friendly and festive sympathy indulged by the people of the United States, they ought to go into mourning at every triumph of the French arms; that instead of regarding the French revolution as a blessing to mankind and a bulwark to their own, they ought to anticipate its success as of all events the most formidable to their liberty and sovereignty; and that, calculating on the political connexion with that nation, as the source of additional danger from its enmity and its usurpation, the first favorable moment ought to be seized for putting an end to it.

It is not easy to dismiss this subject, however, without reflecting, with grief and surprise, on the readiness with which many launch into speculations unfriendly to the struggles of France, and regardless of the interesting relations in which that country stands to this. They seem to be more struck with every circumstance that can be made a topic of reproach or of chimerical apprehensions, than with all the splendid objects which are visible through the gloom of a revolution. But if there be an American who can see, without benevolent joy, the progress of that liberty to which he owes his own happiness, interest, at least, ought to find a place in his calculations. And if he cannot enlarge his views to the influence of the successes and friendship of France, or our safety as a nation, and particularly as a Republic, how can he be insensible to the benefits presented to the United States in her commerce? The French markets consume more of our best productions than are consumed by any other nation. If a balance in specie be as favorable as is usually supposed, the sum which supplies the immense drains of our specie is derived also from the same source more than from any other. And in the great and precious article of navigation, the share of American tonnage employed in the trade with the French dominions gives to that trade a distinguished value; as well to that part of the Union which most depends on ships and seamen for its prosperity, as to that which most requires them for its protection.

Whenever these considerations shall have that full weight which a calm review will not fail to allow them, none will wonder more than the mercantile class of citizens themselves, that whilst they so anxiously wait stipulations from Great Britain, which are always within our command, so much indifference should be felt to those more important privileges in the trade of France, which if not secured by a seasonable improvement of the commercial treaty with her, may possibly be forever lost to us.

Among the aspersions propagated against the friends, and the merits arrogated by the opponents, of the commercial propositions, much use has been made of the envoyship extraordinary to Great Britain. It has been affirmed that the former were averse to the measure on account of its pacific tendency; and that it was embraced by the latter as the proper substitute for all commercial operations on the policy of Great Britain. It is to be remembered, however,

1. That this measure originated wholly with the Executive.

2. That the opposition to it in the Senate (as far as the public have any knowledge of it) was made, not to the measure of appointing an envoy extraordinary, but to the appointment of the Chief Justice of the United States for that service.

3. That the House of Representatives never gave any opinion on the occasion, and that no opinion appears to have been expressed in debate by any individual of that House which can be tortured into a disapprobation of the measure on account of its pacific tendency.

4. That the measure did not take place until the commercial propositions had received all the opposition that could be given to them.

5. That there is no spark of evidence, that if the envoyship had never taken place or been thought of, the opponents of the propositions would have concurred in any commercial measures whatever, even after the West India spoliations had laid in their full claim to the public attention.

But it may be fairly asked of those who opposed first the commercial propositions, and then the non-importation bill, and who rest their justification on the appointment of an envoy extraordinary, wherein lay the inconsistency between these legislative and executive plans?

Was it thought best to appeal to the voluntary justice or liberal policy of Great Britain, and to these only? This was not certainly the case with those who opposed the commercial appeals to the interest and the apprehension of Great Britain, because they were the most zealous for appealing to her fears by military preparations and menaces. If these had any meaning, they avowed that Great Britain was not to be brought to reason otherwise than by the danger of injury to herself. And such being her disposition, she would, of course, be most influenced by measures, of which the comparative operation would be most against her. Whether that would be apprehended from measures of the one or the other kind will easily be decided. But in every view, if *fear* was a proper auxiliary to negotiation, the appeal to it in the commercial measures proposed could not be inconsistent with the envoyship. The inconsistency belongs to the reasoning of those who would pronounce it proper and effectual to say to Great Britain, do us justice or we will seize on Canada, though the loss will be trifling to you, while the cost will be immense to us; and who pronounce it improper and ineffectual to say to Great Britain, do us justice or you will suffer a wound where you will most of all feel it, in a branch of your commerce which feeds one part of your dominions, and sends annually to the other a balance in specie of more than ten millions of dollars.

The opponents of the commercial measures may be asked, in the next place, to what cause the issue of the envoyship, if successful, ought to be ascribed? . . .

Every well-informed and unprejudiced mind will answer, to the following:

1. The spirit of America expressed by the vote of the House of Representatives, on the subject of the commercial propositions, by the large majority of that house (overruled by the

casting voice in the Senate) in favour of the non importation bill, and by the act laying an embargo. Although these proceedings would, doubtless, have been more efficacious if the two former had obtained the sanction of laws, and if the last had not been so soon repealed, yet they must have had no little effect as warnings to the British Government, that if her obstinacy should take away the last pretext from the opponents of such measures, it might be impossible to divide or mislead our public councils with respect to them in future.

There is no room to pretend that her relaxation in this case, if she should relax, will be the effect, not of those proceedings, but of the ultimate defeat of them. Former defeats of a like policy had repeatedly taken place, and are known to have produced, instead of relaxation, a more confirmed perseverance on the part of Great Britain. Under the old Confederation, the United States had not the power over commerce: of that situation she took advantage. The new government which contained the power did not evince the will to exert it: of that situation she still took the advantage. Should she yield, then, at the present juncture, the problem ought not to be solved, without presuming her to be satisfied by what has lately passed—that the United States have now not only the power but the will to exert it.

The reasoning is short and conclusive. In the year 1783, when Great Britain apprehended commercial restrictions from the United States, she was disposed to concede and to accommodate. From the year 1783 to the year 1794, when she apprehended no commercial restrictions, she showed no disposition to concede or to accommodate. In the year 1794, when alarming evidence was given of the danger of commercial restrictions, she did concede and accommodate.

If anything can have weakened the operation of the proceedings above referred to on the British Government, it must be the laboured and vehement attempts of their opponents to show that the United States had little to demand and everything to dread from Great Britain; that the commerce between the two countries was more essential to us than to her; that our citizens would be less willing than her subjects to bear, and our Government less able than hers to enforce, restrictions or interruptions of it: in a word, that we were more dependent on her than she was on us; and, therefore, ought to court her not to withdraw from us her supplies, though chiefly luxuries, instead of threatening to withdraw from her our supplies, though mostly necessaries.

It is difficult to say whether the indiscretion or the fallacy of such arguments be the more remarkable feature in them. All that can be hoped is, that an antidote to their mischievous tendency in Great Britain may be found in the consciousness there of the errors on which they are founded, and the contempt which they will be known to have excited in this country.

2. The other cause will be, the posture into which Europe has been thrown by the war with France, and particularly by the campaign of 1794. The combined armies have everywhere felt the superior valour, discipline, and resources of their Republican enemies. Prussia, after heavy and perfidious [?] draughts on the British Treasury, has retired from the common standard to contend with new dangers peculiar to herself. Austria, worn out in unavailing resistence, her arms disgraced, her treasure exhausted, and her vassals discontented, seeks her last consolation in the same source of British subsidy. The Dutch, instead of continuing their proportion of aids for the war, have their whole faculties turned over to France. Spain, with all her wealth and all her pride, is palsied in every nerve, and forced to the last resorts of royalty, to a reduction of salaries and pensions, and to the hoards of superstition. Great Britain herself has seen her military glory eclipsed, her projects confounded, her hopes blasted, her marine threatened, her resources overcharged, and her Government in danger of losing its energy, by the despotic excesses into which it has been overstrained.

If, under such circumstances, she does not abandon herself to apathy and despair, it is because she finds her credit still alive, and in that credit sees some possibility of making terms with misfortune. But what is the basis of that credit? Her commerce. And what is the most valuable remnant of that resource? The commerce with the U. States. Will she risk this best part of her last resource, by persevering in her selfish and unjust treatment of the United States?

Time will give a final answer to this question. All that can be now pronounced is, that if, on the awful precipice to which Great Britain is driven, she will open neither her eyes to her danger nor her heart to her duty, her character must be a greater contrast to the picture of it drawn by the opponents of the commercial measures than could have easily been imagined. If, on the other hand, she should relent and consult her reason, the change will be accounted for by her prospects on the other side of the Atlantic, and the countenance exhibited on this; without supposing her character to vary in a single feature from the view of it entertained by the friends of such measures.

That the rising spirit of America, and the successes of France, will have been the real causes of any favorable terms obtained by the mission of Mr. Jay, cannot be controverted. Had the same forbearance which was tried for ten years on the part of the United States been continued, and had the combined Powers proceeded in the victorious career which has signalized the French arms, under this reverse of circumstances the most bigoted Englishman will be ashamed to say that any relaxing change in the policy of his Government was to be hoped for by the United States.

Such are the reflections which occur on the supposition of a successful issue to the envoyship. Should it unhappily turn out that neither the new countenance presented by America, nor the adverse fortunes of Great Britain, can bend the latter to a reasonable accommodation, it may be worth while to inquire what will probably be the evidence furnished by the friends and adversaries of commercial measures with respect to their comparative attachments to peace.?[1]

If any regard be paid to consistency, those who opposed all such measures must be for an instant resort to arms. With them there was no alternative but negotiation or war. Their language was, let us try the former, but be prepared for the latter; if the olive branch fail, let the sword vindicate our rights, as it has vindicated the rights of other nations. A real war is both more honourable and more eligible than commercial regulations. In these Great Britain is an over-match for us.

On the other side, the friends of commercial measures, if consistent, will prefer these measures, as an intermediate experiment between negotiation and war. They will persist in their language, that Great Britain is more dependent on us than we are on her; that this has ever been the American sentiment, and is the true basis of American policy; that war should not be resorted to till everything short of war has been tried; that if Great Britain be invulnerable to our attacks, it is in her fleets and armies; that if the United States can bring her to reason at all, the surest as well as the cheapest means will be a judicious system of commercial operations; that here the United States are unquestionably an over-match for Great Britain.

It must be the ardent prayer of all, that the occasion may not happen for such a test of the consistency and the disposition of those whose counsels were so materially different on the subject of a commercial vindication of our rights. Should it be otherwise ordained, the public judgment will pronounce on which side the politics were most averse to war, and most anxious for every pacific effort that might at the same time be an efficient one, in preference to that last and dreadful resort of injured nations. . . .

------

[1] When this was written the result of Mr. Jay's mission was wholly unknown.

21. Republican Manifesto: The Virginia Report

Only a decade after Madison helped to create the new federal regime, and little more than twenty years after Jefferson penned the Declaration of Independence, the two Virginia patriots were up to their necks in a demi-loyal opposition movement. Working behind an elaborately contrived screen of secrecy, Jefferson and Madison drafted the incendiary manifestos that the legislatures of Virginia and Kentucky adopted and broadcast among the states late in 1798. The Hamiltonian system of finance, with its broad construction of national powers, had already confirmed old Antifederalist suspicions and stirred fresh resentments, especially in the agrarian South. Bitter reactions to the Jay treaty of 1794 and then to John Adams' quasi-war with revolutionary France were channelled skillfully into the rising anti-administration party. When the Federalists, fright-

---

"Report on the Virginia Resolutions," 1799–1800, in Jonathan Elliot, ed., *The Debates in the Several State Conventions on the Adoption of the Federal Constitution* . . . (Philadelphia: J. B. Lippincott Co., 1836), IV, pp. 546–553, 561–580.

ened by the specter of French intrigue and "Jacobin" subversion, passed the Alien and Sedition Acts in 1798, Jefferson and
Madison saw at once a deadly threat to liberty and a priceless
political opportunity.

The studied ambiguity of the Virginia and Kentucky Resolutions reflected exactly this double-vision. At best, they could
make Republicans for the next elections. At worst, they could
prepare the sovereign states to exercise their ultimate right to
judge violations of the federal compact and to "interpose" their
power—in some unnamed but preferably mild way—in defense
of their "authorities, rights, and liberties." Jefferson character-
istically favored more extreme language—asserting the right of
a state to "nullify" Federal acts, for instance—and talked of
secession until Madison persuaded him that such threats were
imprudent and unnecessary. Repeated and enormous usurpations would be "cause enough in themselves" for separation
from the Union, Jefferson conceded after consulting with his
wary friend. (See letter to W. C. Nicholas, September 5, 1799.)

Between February and October, 1799, seven northern states
replied to the Virginia Resolutions; all flatly condemned the
protest. The Southern legislatures remained conspicuously silent. At the same time, local Republican partisans in Virginia,
Pennsylvania, and other states gathered thousands of signatures for petitions against the Alien and Sedition Acts. Madison's Virginia friends urged him to enter the State Assembly
in order to direct the further movements of the opposition.
There he drafted a long report justifying the original resolutions against the criticisms of the several states. In January,
1800, a substantial majority of the General Assembly endorsed
Madison's Report on the Virginia Resolutions and provided for
its publication.

The Virginia Report became the classic statement of Republican opposition principles. Stepping delicately between
the duties of national loyalty and the ultimate right of revolution, Madison emphasized the legitimate constitutional means
of "interposition" open to the states. Yet he softened none of

the charges of federal usurpation leading straight to monarchy. Presumably, the sequence of allegedly unconstitutional measures from the national bank law to the Alien and Sedition Acts, all unquestioned by a compliant federal judiciary, were just such "deliberate, palpable, and dangerous" violations of the compact as to give the states the right and duty to judge and act in their original sovereign capacity. The political case led Madison to a powerful defense of freedom of speech and press against federal controls (state regulation was another matter) anticipating a new libertarian interpretation of the First Amendment that would flourish in the next century.

Madison's Report figured prominently in the campaign of 1800, and in the long campaign of history over states' rights and nullification. He would never repudiate his Virginia doctrines, or even acknowledge any significant conflict between his Federalist arguments of the 1780s and his Republican arguments of the 1790s. Yet Madison's most strenuous denials during his last years could not convince the Old Republicans and nullifiers of the 1820s and 1830s—who were enlisting the sovereign states once more for the good fight against broad construction and consolidated power—that they were not the legitimate political heirs of Jefferson and Madison. The "spirit of '98" escaped Madison's control to assume a life of its own. (See Part V.)

House of Delegates, Session of 1799–1800.

REPORT OF THE COMMITTEE TO WHOM WERE REFERRED THE COMMUNICATIONS OF VARIOUS STATES, RELATIVE TO THE RESOLUTIONS OF THE LAST GENERAL ASSEMBLY OF THIS STATE, CONCERNING THE ALIEN AND SEDITION LAWS

Whatever room might be found in the proceedings of some of the states, who have disapproved of the resolutions of the General Assembly of this commonwealth, passed on the 21st day of December, 1798, for painful remarks on the spirit and manner of those proceedings, it appears to the committee most consistent with the duty, as well as dignity, of the General Assembly, to hasten an oblivion of every circumstance which might be construed into a diminution of mutual respect, confidence, and affection, among the members of the Union.

The committee have deemed it a more useful task to revise, with a critical eye, the resolutions which have met with their disapprobation; to examine fully the several objections and arguments which have appeared against them; and to inquire whether there can be any errors of fact, of principle, or of reasoning, which the candor of the General Assembly ought to acknowledge and correct.

The *first* of the resolutions is in the words following:—

Resolved, That the General Assembly of Virginia doth unequivocally express a firm resolution to maintain and defend the Constitution of the United States, and the Constitution of this state, against every aggression, either foreign or domestic; and that they will support the government of the United States in all measures warranted by the former.

No unfavorable comment can have been made on the sentiments here expressed. To maintain and defend the Constitution of the United States, and of their own state, against every aggression, both foreign and domestic, and to support the government of the United States in all measures warranted by their Constitution, are duties which the General Assembly ought always to feel, and to which, on such an occasion, it was evidently proper to express their sincere and firm adherence.

In their *next* resolution—

The General Assembly most solemnly declares a warm attachment to the union of the states, to maintain which it pledges all its powers; and that, for this end, it is their duty to watch over and oppose every infraction of those principles which constitute the only basis of that Union, because a faithful observance of them can alone secure its existence and the public happiness.

The observation just made is equally applicable to this solemn declaration of warm attachment to the Union, and this solemn pledge to maintain it; nor can any question arise among enlightened friends of the Union, as to the duty of watching over and opposing every infraction of those principles which constitute its basis, and a faithful observance of which can alone secure its existence, and the public happiness hereon depending.

The *third* resolution is in the words following:—

That this Assembly doth explicitly and peremptorily declare, that it views the powers of the federal government as resulting from the compact to which the states are parties, as limited by the plain sense and intention of the instrument constituting that compact—as no further valid than they are authorized by the grants enumerated in that compact; and that, in case of a deliberate, palpable, and dangerous exercise of other powers, not granted by the said compact, the states who are parties thereto have the right, and are in duty bound, to interpose, for arresting the progress of the evil, and for maintaining, within their respective limits, the authorities, rights, and liberties appertaining to them.

On this resolution the committee have bestowed all the attention which its importance merits. They have *scanned* it not merely with a strict, but with a severe eye; and they feel confidence in pronouncing that, in its just and fair construction, it is unexceptionably true in its several positions, as well as constitutional and conclusive in its inferences.

The resolution declares, *first,* that "it views the powers of the federal government as resulting from the compact to which the states are parties;" in other words, that the federal powers are derived from the Constitution: and that the Constitution is a compact to which the states are parties.

Clear as the position must seem, that the federal powers are derived from the Constitution, and from that alone, the committee are not unapprized of a late doctrine which opens another source of federal powers, not less extensive and important than it is new and unexpected. The examination of this doctrine will be most conveniently connected with a review of a succeeding resolution. The committee satisfy themselves here with briefly remarking that, in all the contemporary discussions and comments which the Constitution underwent, it was constantly justified and recommended on the ground that the powers not given to the government were withheld from it; and that, if any doubt could have existed on this subject, under the original text of the Constitution, it is removed, as far as words could remove it, by the 12th amendment, now a part of the Constitution, which expressly declares, "that the powers not delegated to the United States by the Constitution, nor prohibited by it to the states, are reserved to the states respectively, or to the people."[1]

The other position involved in this branch of the resolution, namely, "that the states are parties to the Constitution," or compact, is, in the judgment of the committee, equally free from objection. It is indeed true that the term "states" is sometimes used in a vague sense, and sometimes in different senses, according to the subject to which it is applied. Thus it sometimes means the separate sections of territory occupied by the political societies within each; sometimes the particular governments established by those societies; sometimes those societies as organized into those particular governments; and lastly, it means the people composing those political societies, in their highest sovereign capacity. Although it might be wished that the perfection of language admitted less diversity in the signification of the same words, yet little inconvenience is produced by it, where the true sense can be collected with certainty from the different applications. In the present instance, whatever different construction of the term "states," in the resolution, may have been entertained, all will at least concur in that last

---

[1] This article, submitted to the States as the Twelfth Amendment, was ratified as the Tenth Amendment. [Ed.]

mentioned; because in that sense the Constitution was submitted to the "states;" in that sense the "states" ratified it; and in that sense of the term "states," they are consequently parties to the compact from which the powers of the federal government result.

The next position is, that the General Assembly views the powers of the federal government "as limited by the plain sense and intention of the instrument constituting that compact," and "as no further valid than they are authorized by the grants therein enumerated." It does not seem possible that any just objection can lie against either of these clauses. The first amounts merely to a declaration that the compact ought to have the interpretation plainly intended by the parties to it; the other, to a declaration that it ought to have the execution and effect intended by them. If the powers granted be valid, it is solely because they are granted; and if the granted powers are valid because granted, all other powers not granted must not be valid.

The resolution, having taken this view of the federal compact, proceeds to infer, "That, in case of a deliberate, palpable, and dangerous exercise of other powers, not granted by the said compact, the states, who are parties thereto, have the right, and are in duty bound, to interpose for arresting the progress of the evil, and for maintaining, within their respective limits, the authorities, rights, and liberties, appertaining to them."

It appears to your committee to be a plain principle, founded in common sense, illustrated by common practice, and essential to the nature of compacts, that, where resort can be had to no tribunal superior to the authority of the parties themselves must be the rightful judges, in the last resort, whether the bargain made has been pursued or violated. The Constitution of the United States was formed by the sanction of the states, given by each in its sovereign capacity. It adds to the stability and dignity, as well as to the authority, of the Constitution, that it rests on this legitimate and solid foundation. The states, then, being the parties to the constitutional compact, and in their sovereign capacity, it follows of necessity that there can be no tribunal, above their authority, to decide, in the last resort, whether the compact made by them be violated; and consequently, that, as the parties to it, they must themselves decide, in the last resort, such questions as may be of sufficient magnitude to require their interposition.

It does not follow, however, because the states, as sovereign parties to their constitutional compact, must ultimately decide whether it has been violated, that such a decision ought to be interposed either in a hasty manner or on doubtful and inferior occasions. Even in the case of ordinary conventions between different nations, where, by the strict rule of interpretation, a breach of a part may be deemed a breach of the whole,—every part being deemed a condition of every other part, and of the whole,—it is always laid down that the breach must be both wilful and material, to justify an application of the rule. But in the case of an intimate and constitutional union, like that of the United States, it is evident that the interposition of the parties, in their sovereign capacity, can be called for by occasions only deeply and essentially affecting the vital principles of their political system.

The resolution has, accordingly, guarded against any misapprehension of its object, by expressly requiring, for such an interposition, "the case of a deliberate, palpable, and dangerous breach of the Constitution, by the exercise of powers not granted by it." It must be a case not of a light and transient nature, but of a nature dangerous to the great purposes for which the Constitution was established. It must be a case, moreover, not obscure or doubtful in its construction, but plain and palpable. Lastly, it must be a case not resulting from a partial consideration or hasty determination, but a case stamped with a final consideration and deliberate adherence. It is not necessary, because the resolution does not require, that the question should be discussed, how far the exercise of any particular power, ungranted by the Constitution, would justify the interposition of the parties to it. As cases might easily be stated, which none would contend ought to fall within that description,—cases, on the other hand, might, with equal ease, be stated, so flagrant and so fatal as to unite every opinion in placing them within the description.

But the resolution has done more than guard against misconstruction, by expressly referring to cases of a deliberate, palpable, and dangerous nature. It specifies the object of the interposition, which it contemplates to be solely that of arresting the progress of the evil of usurpation, and of maintaining the authorities, rights, and liberties, appertaining to the states as parties to the Constitution.

From this view of the resolution, it would seem inconceivable that it can incur any just disapprobation from those who, laying aside all momentary impressions, and recollecting the genuine source and object of the Federal Constitution, shall candidly and accurately interpret the meaning of the General Assembly. If the deliberate exercise of dangerous powers, palpably withheld by the Constitution, could not justify the parties to it in interposing even so far as to arrest the progress of the evil, and thereby to preserve the Constitution itself, as well as to provide for the safety of the parties to it, there would be an end to all relief from usurped power, and a direct subversion of the rights specified or recognized under all the state constitutions, as well as a plain denial of the fundamental principle on which our independence itself was declared.

But it is objected, that the judicial authority is to be regarded as the sole expositor of the Constitution in the last resort; and it may be asked for what reason the declaration by the General Assembly, supposing it to be theoretically true, could be required at the present day, and in so solemn a manner.

On this objection it might be observed, first, that there may be instances of usurped power, which the forms of the Constitution would never draw within the control of the judicial department; secondly, that, if the decision of the judiciary be raised above the authority of the sovereign parties to the Constitution, the decision of the other departments, not carried by the forms of the Constitution before the judiciary, must be equally authoritative and final with the decisions of that department. But the proper answer to the objection is, that the resolution of the General Assembly relates to those great and extraordinary cases, in which all the forms of the Constitution may prove ineffectual against infractions dangerous to the essential rights of the parties to it. The resolution supposes that dangerous powers, not delegated, may not only be usurped and executed by the other departments, but that the judicial department, also, may exercise or sanction dangerous powers beyond the grant of the Constitution; and, consequently, that the ultimate right of the parties to the Constitution, to judge whether the compact has been dangerously violated, must extend to violations by one delegated authority as well as by another—by the judiciary as well as by the executive, or the legislature.

However true, therefore, it may be, that the judicial department is, in all questions submitted to it by the forms of the Constitution, to decide in the last resort, this resort must necessarily be deemed the last in relation to the authorities of the other departments of the government; not in relation to the rights of the parties to the constitutional compact, from which the judicial, as well as the other departments, hold their delegated trusts. On any other hypothesis, the delegation of judicial power would annul the authority delegating it; and the concurrence of this department with the others in usurped powers, might subvert forever, and beyond the possible reach of any rightful remedy, the very Constitution which all were instituted to preserve.

The truth declared in the resolution being established, the expediency of making the declaration at the present day may safely be left to the temperate consideration and candid judgment of the American public. It will be remembered, that a frequent recurrence to fundamental principles is solemnly enjoined by most of the state constitutions, and particularly by our own, as a necessary safeguard against the danger of degeneracy, to which republics are liable, as well as other governments, though in a less degree than others. And a fair comparison of the political doctrines not unfrequent at the present day, with those which characterized the epoch of our revolution, and which form the basis of our republican constitutions, will best determine whether the declaratory recurrence here made to those principles ought to be viewed as unseasonable and improper, or as a vigilant discharge of an important duty. The authority of constitutions over governments, and of the sovereignty of the people over constitutions, are truths which are at all times necessary to be kept in mind; and at no time, perhaps, more necessary than at present.

The fourth resolution stands as follows:—

That the General Assembly doth also express its deep regret, that a spirit has, in sundry instances, been manifested by the federal government, to enlarge its powers by forced constructions of the constitutional charter which defines them; and that indications have appeared of a design to expound certain general phrases (which having been copied from the very limited grant of powers in the former Articles of Confederation, were the less liable to be misconstrued) so as to destroy the meaning and effect of the particular enumeration which necessarily explains and limits the general phrases, and so as to consolidate the states, by degrees, into one sovereignty, the obvious tendency and inevitable result of which would be to transform the present republican system of the United States into an absolute, or at best a mixed monarchy.

The *first* question here to be considered is, whether a spirit has, in sundry instances, been manifested by the federal government to enlarge its powers by forced constructions of the constitutional charter.

The General Assembly having declared their opinion, merely, by regretting, in general terms, that forced constructions for enlarging the federal powers have taken place, it does not appear to the committee necessary to go into a specification of every instance to which the resolution may allude. The Alien and Sedition Acts, being particularly named in a succeeding resolution, are of course to be understood as included in the allusion. Omitting others which have less occupied public attention, or been less extensively regarded as unconstitutional, the resolution may be presumed to refer particularly to the bank law, which, from the circumstances of its passage, as well as the latitude of construction on which it is founded, strikes the attention with singular force, and the carriage tax, distinguished also by circumstances in its history having a similar tendency. Those instances alone, if resulting from forced construction, and calculated to enlarge the powers of the federal government,—as the committee cannot but conceive to be the case,—sufficiently warrant this part of the resolution. The committee have not thought it incumbent on them to extend their attention to laws which have been objected to rather as varying the constitutional distribution of powers in the federal government, than as an absolute enlargement of them; because instances of this sort, however important in their principles and tendencies, do not appear to fall strictly within the text under view.

The other questions presenting themselves are, 1. Whether indications have appeared of a design to expound certain general phrases, copied from the "Articles of Confederation," so as to destroy the effect of the particular enumeration explaining and limiting their meaning; 2. Whether this exposition would, by degrees, consolidate the states into one sovereignty; 3. Whether the tendency and result of this consolidation would be to transform the republican system of the United States into a monarchy.

1. The general phrases here meant must be those "of providing for the common defence and general welfare."

In the "Articles of Confederation," the phrases are used as follows, in Art. VIII.: "All charges of war, and all other expenses that shall be incurred for the common defence and general welfare, and allowed by the United States in Congress assembled, shall be defrayed out of a common treasury, which shall be supplied by the several states, in proportion to the value of all land within each state, granted to or surveyed for any person, as such land, and the buildings and improvements thereon, shall be estimated, according to such mode as the United States in Congress assembled shall, from time to time, direct and appoint."

In the existing Constitution, they make the following part of sect. 8: "The Congress shall have power to lay and collect taxes, duties, imposts, and excises; to pay the debts, and provide for the common defence and general welfare, of the United States."

This similarity in the use of these phrases, in the two great federal charters, might well be considered as rendering their meaning less liable to be misconstrued in the latter; because it will scarcely be said, that in the former they were ever understood to be either a general grant of power, or to authorize the requisition or application of money, by the old Congress, to the common defence and general welfare, except in cases afterwards enumerated, which explained and limited their meaning; and if such was the limited meaning attached to these phrases in the very instrument revised and remodelled by the present Constitution, it can never be supposed that, when copied into this Constitution, a different meaning ought to be attached to them.

That, notwithstanding this remarkable security against misconstruction, a design has been indicated to expound these phrases, in the Constitution, so as to destroy the effect of the particular enumeration of powers by which it explains and limits them, must have fallen under the observation of those who have attended to the course of public transactions. Not to multiply proofs on this subject, it will suffice to refer to the debates of the federal legislature, in which arguments have, on different occasions, been drawn, with apparent effect, from these phrases, in their indefinite meaning.

To these indications might be added, without looking farther, the official report on manufactures by the late secretary of the treasury, made on the 5th of December, 1791, and the report of a committee of Congress, in January, 1797, on the promotion of agriculture. In the first of these it is expressly contended to belong "to the discretion of the national legislature to pronounce upon the objects which concern the general welfare, and for which, under that description, an appropriation of money is requisite and proper. And there seems to be no room for a doubt, that whatever concerns the general interests of learning, of agriculture, of manufactures, and of commerce, is within the sphere of national councils as far as regards an application of money." The latter report assumes the same latitude of power in the national councils, and applies it to the encouragement of agriculture, by means of a society to be established at the seat of government. Although neither of these reports may have received the sanction of a law carrying it into effect, yet, on the other hand, the extraordinary doctrine contained in both has passed without the slightest positive mark of disapprobation from the authority to which it was addressed.

Now, whether the phrases in question be construed to authorize every measure relating to the common defence and general welfare, as contended by some, or every measure only in which there might be an application of money, as suggested by the caution of others,—the effect must substantially be the same, in destroying the import and force of the particular enumeration of powers which follows these general phrases in the Constitution; for it is evident that there is not a single power whatever which may not have some reference to the common defence or the general welfare; nor a power of any magnitude which, in its exercise, does not involve, or admit, an application of money. The government, therefore, which possesses power in either one or other of these extents, is a government without the limitations formed by a particular enumeration of powers; and, consequently, the meaning and effect of this particular enumeration is destroyed by the exposition given to these general phrases.

This conclusion will not be affected by an attempt to qualify the power over the "general welfare," by referring it to cases where the general welfare is beyond the reach of the separate provisions by the individual states, and leaving to these their jurisdiction in cases to which their separate provisions may be competent; for, as the authority of the individual states must in all cases be incompetent to general regulations operating through the whole, the authority of the United States would be extended to every object relating to the general welfare, which might, by any possibility, be provided for by the general authority. This qualifying construction, therefore, would have little, if any, tendency to circumscribe the power claimed under the latitude of the term "general welfare."

The true and fair construction of this expression, both in the original and existing federal compacts, appears to the committee too obvious to be mistaken. In both, the Congress is authorized to provide money for the common defence and general welfare. In both is subjoined to this authority an enumeration of the cases to which their powers shall extend. Money cannot be applied to the general welfare, otherwise than by an application of it to some particular measure, conducive to the general welfare. Whenever, therefore, money has been raised by the general authority, and is to be applied to a particular measure, a question arises whether the particular measure be within the enumerated authorities vested in Congress. If it be, the money requisite for it may be applied to it. If it be not, no such application can be made. This fair and obvious interpretation coincides with, and is enforced by, the clause in the Constitution which declares that "no money shall be drawn from the treasury but in consequence of appropriations made by law." An appropriation of money to the general welfare would be deemed rather a mockery than an observance of this constitutional injunction.

2. Whether the exposition of the general phrases here combated would not, by degrees, consolidate the states into one sovereignty, is a question concerning which the committee can perceive little room for difference of opinion. To consolidate the states into one sovereignty nothing more can be wanted than to supersede their respective sovereignties, in the cases reserved to them, by extending the sovereignty of the United States to all cases of the "general welfare"—that is to say, to all cases whatever.

3. That the obvious tendency, and inevitable result, of a consolidation of the states into one sovereignty, would be to transform the republican system of the United States into a monarchy, is a point which seems to have been sufficiently decided by the general sentiment of America. In almost every instance of discussion relating to the consolidation in question, its certain tendency to pave the way to monarchy seems not to have been contested. The prospect of such a consolidation has formed the only topic of controversy. It would be unnecessary, therefore, for the committee to dwell long on the reasons which support the position of the General Assembly. It may not be improper, however, to remark two consequences, evidently flowing from an extension of the federal power to every subject falling within the idea of the "general welfare."

One consequence must be, to enlarge the sphere of discretion allotted to the executive magistrate. Even within the legislative limits properly defined by the Constitution, the difficulty of accommodating legal regulations to a country so great in extent, and so various in its circumstances, had been much felt, and has led to occasional investments of power in the executive, which involve perhaps as large a portion of discretion as can be deemed consistent with the nature of the executive trust. In proportion as the objects of legislative care might be multiplied, would the time allowed for each be diminished, and the difficulty of providing uniform and particular regulations for all be increased. From these sources would necessarily ensue a greater latitude to the agency of that department which is always in existence, and which could best mould regulations of a general nature, so as to suit them to the diversity of particular situations. And it is in this latitude, as a supplement to the deficiency of the laws, that the degree of executive prerogative materially consists.

The other consequence would be, that of an excessive augmentation of the offices, honors, and emoluments, depending on the executive will. Add to the present legitimate stock all those, of every description, which a consolidation of the states would take from them, and turn over to the federal government, and the patronage of the executive would necessarily be as much swelled, in this case, as its prerogative would be in the other.

This disproportionate increase of prerogative and patronage must evidently either enable the chief magistrate of the Union, by quiet means, to secure his reëlection from time to time, and finally to regulate the succession as he might please; or, by giving so transcendent an importance to the office, would render the election to it so violent and corrupt, that the public voice itself might call for an hereditary in place of an elective succession. Whichever of these events might follow, the transformation of the republican system of the United States into a monarchy, anticipated by the General Assembly from a consolidation of the states into one sovereignty, would be equally accomplished; and whether it would be into a mixed or an absolute monarchy, might depend on too many contingencies to admit of any certain foresight.

The resolution next in order is contained in the following terms:—

That the General Assembly doth particularly protest against the palpable and alarming infractions of the Constitution, in the two late cases of the 'Alien and Sedition Acts,' passed at the last session of Congress; the first of which exercises a power nowhere delegated to the federal government; and which, by uniting legislative and judicial powers to those of the executive, subverts the general principles of free government, as well as the particular organization and positive provisions of the Federal Constitution; and the other of which acts exercises, in like manner, a power not delegated by the Constitution, but, on the contrary, expressly and positively forbidden by one of the amendments thereto—a power which, more than any other, ought to produce universal alarm, because it is levelled against the right of freely examining public characters and measures, and of free communication among the people thereon, which has ever been justly deemed the only effectual guardian of every other right.

The subject of this resolution having, it is presumed, more particularly led the General Assembly into the proceedings which they communicated to the other states, and being in itself of peculiar importance, it deserves the most critical and faithful investigation; for the length of which no apology will be necessary.

The subject divides itself into,—

First, the "Alien Act."

Secondly, the "Sedition Act."

Of the "Alien Act," it is affirmed by the resolution—1. That it exercises a power nowhere delegated to the federal government; 2. That it unites legislative and judicial powers to those of the executive; 3. That this union of powers subverts the general principles of free government; 4. That it subverts the particular organization and positive provisions of the Federal Constitution [Madison's discussion of those four points is omitted.]

The *second* object, against which the resolution protests, is the Sedition Act.

Of this act it is affirmed—1. That it exercises, in like manner, a power not delegated by the Constitution; 2. That the power, on the contrary, is expressly and positively forbidden by one of the amendments to the Constitution; 3. That this is a power which, more than any other, ought to produce universal alarm, because it is levelled against that right of freely examining public characters and measures, and of free communication thereon, which has ever been justly deemed the only effectual guardian of every other right.

1. That it exercises a power not delegated by the Constitution.

Here, again, it will be proper to recollect that, the federal government being composed of powers specifically granted, with reservation of all others to the states or to the people, the positive authority under which the Sedition Act could be passed must be produced by those who assert its constitutionality. In what part of the Constitution, then, is this authority to be found?

Several attempts have been made to answer this question, which will be examined in their order. The committee will begin with one which has filled them with equal astonishment and apprehension; and which, they cannot but persuade themselves, must have the same effect on all who will consider it with coolness and impartiality, and with a reverence for our Constitution, in the true character in which it issued from the sovereign authority of the people. The committee refer to the doctrine lately advanced, as a sanction to the Sedition Act, "that the common or unwritten law"—a law of vast extent and complexity, and embracing almost every possible subject of legislation, both civil and criminal—makes a part of the law of these states, in their united and national capacity.

The novelty, and, in the judgment of the committee, the extravagance of this pretension, would have consigned it to the silence in which they have passed by other arguments which an extraordinary zeal for the act has drawn into the discussion; but the auspices under which this innovation presents itself have constrained the committee to bestow on it an attention which other considerations might have forbidden.

In executing the task, it may be of use to look back to the colonial state of this country prior to the revolution; to trace the effect of the revolution which converted the colonies into independent states; to inquire into the import of the Articles of Confederation, the first instrument by which the union of the states was regularly established; and, finally, to consult the Constitution of 1787, which is the oracle that must decide the important question.

In the state prior to the revolution, it is certain that the common law, under different limitations, made a part of the colonial codes. But, whether it be understood that the original colonists brought the law with them, or made it their law by adoption, it is equally certain that it was the separate law of each colony within its respective limits, and was unknown to them as a law pervading and operating through the whole, as one society.

It could not possibly be otherwise. The common law was not the same in any two of the colonies; in some, the modifications were materially and extensively different. There was no common legislature, by which a common will could be expressed in the form of a law; nor any common magistracy, by which such a law could be carried into practice. The will of each colony, alone and separately, had its organs for these purposes.

This stage of our political history furnishes no foothold for the patrons of this new doctrine.

Did, then, the principle or operation of the great event which made the colonies independent states, imply or introduce the common law, as a law of the Union?

The fundamental principle of the revolution was, that the

colonies were coördinate members with each other, and with Great Britain, of an empire united by a common executive sovereign, but not united by any common legislative sovereign. The legislative power was maintained to be as complete in each American Parliament, as in the British Parliament. And the royal prerogative was in force, in each colony, by virtue of its acknowledging the king for its executive magistrate, as it was in Great Britain, by virtue of a like acknowledgment there. A denial of these principles by Great Britain, and the assertion of them by America, produced the revolution.

There was a time, indeed, when an exception to the legislative separation of the several component and coëqual parts of the empire obtained a degree of acquiescence. The British Parliament was allowed to regulate the trade with foreign nations, and between the different parts of the empire. This was, however, mere practice without right, and contrary to the true theory of the Constitution. The convenience of some regulations, in both cases, was apparent, and, as there was no legislature with power over the whole, nor any constitutional preëminence among the legislatures of the several parts, it was natural for the legislature of that particular part which was the eldest and the largest, to assume this function, and for the others to acquiesce in it. This tacit arrangement was the less criticised, as the regulations established by the British Parliament operated in favor of that part of the empire which seemed to bear the principal share of the public burdens, and were regarded as an indemnification of its advances for the other parts. As long as this regulating power was confined to the two objects of conveniency and equity, it was not complained of, nor much inquired into. But no sooner was it perverted to the selfish views of the party assuming it, than the injured parties began to feel and to reflect; and the moment the claim to a direct and indefinite power was ingrafted on the precedent of the regulating power, the whole charm was dissolved, and every eye opened to the usurpation. The assertion by Great

Britain of a power to make laws for the other members of the empire, in all cases whatsoever, ended in the discovery that she had a right to make laws for them in no cases whatsoever.

Such being the ground of our revolution, no support or color can be drawn from it for the doctrine that the common law is binding on these states as one society. The doctrine, on the contrary, is evidently repugnant to the fundamental principle of the revolution.

The Articles of Confederation are the next source of information on this subject.

In the interval between the commencement of the revolution and the final ratification of these Articles, the nature and extent of the Union was determined by the circumstances of the crisis, rather than by any accurate delineation of the general authority. It will not be alleged that the "common law" could have any legitimate birth, as a law of the United States, during that state of things. If it came, as such, into existence at all, the charter of confederation must have been its parent.

Here, again, however, its pretensions are absolutely destitute of foundation. This instrument does not contain a sentence or a syllable that can be tortured into a countenance of the idea that the parties to it were, with respect to the objects of the common law, to form one community. No such law is named, or implied, or alluded to, as being in force, or as brought into force by that compact. No provision is made by which such a law could be carried into operation; whilst, on the other hand, every such inference or pretext is absolutely precluded by art. 2, which declares "that each state retains its sovereignty, freedom, and independence, and every power, jurisdiction, and right, which is not by this Confederation expressly delegated to the United States in Congress assembled."

Thus far it appears that not a vestige of this extraordinary doctrine can be found in the origin or progress of American institutions. The evidence against it has, on the contrary, grown stronger at every step, till it has amounted to a formal and positive exclusion, by written articles of compact among the parties concerned.

Is this exclusion revoked, and the common law introduced as national law, by the present Constitution of the United States? This is the final question to be examined.

It is readily admitted that particular parts of the common law may have a sanction from the Constitution, so far as they are necessarily comprehended in the technical phrases which express the powers delegated to the government; and so far, also, as such other parts may be adopted by Congress, as necessary and proper for carrying into execution the powers expressly delegated. But the question does not relate to either of these portions of the common law. It relates to the common law beyond these limitations.

The only part of the Constitution which seems to have been relied on in this case, is the 2d section of art. 3:—"The judicial power shall extend to all cases, in law and equity, arising under this Constitution, the laws of the United States, and treaties made, or which shall be made, under their authority."

It has been asked what cases, distinct from those arising under the laws and treaties of the United States, can arise under the Constitution, other than those arising under the common law; and it is inferred that the common law is, accordingly, adopted or recognized by the Constitution.

Never, perhaps, was so broad a construction applied to a text so clearly unsusceptible of it. If any color for the inference could be found, it must be in the impossibility of finding any other cases, in law and equity, within the provisions of the Constitution, to satisfy the expression; and rather than resort to a construction affecting so essentially the whole character of the government, it would perhaps be more rational to consider the expression as a mere pleonasm or inadvertence. But it is not necessary to decide on such a dilemma. The expression is fully satisfied, and its accuracy justified, by two descriptions of cases, to which the judicial authority is extended, and neither of which implies that the common law is the law of the United States. One of these descriptions comprehends the cases growing out of the restrictions on the legislative power of the states. For example, it is provided that "no state shall emit bills of credit," or "make any thing but gold and silver coin a tender for the payment of debts." Should this prohibition be violated, and a suit between citizens of the same state be the consequence, this would be a case arising under the Constitution before the judicial power of the United States. A second description comprehends suits between citizens and foreigners, of citizens of different states, to be decided according to the state or foreign laws, but submitted by the Constitution to the judicial power of the United States; the judicial power being, in several instances, extended beyond the legislative power of the United States.

To this explanation of the text, the following observations may be added:—

The expression "cases in law and equity" is manifestly confined to cases of a civil nature, and would exclude cases of criminal jurisdiction. Criminal cases in law and equity would be a language unknown to the law.

The succeeding paragraph in the same section is in harmony with this construction. It is in these words: "In all cases affecting ambassadors, or other public ministers, and consuls, and those in which a state shall be a party, the Supreme Court shall have original jurisdiction. *In all* the other cases, [including cases of law and equity arising under the Constitution,] the Supreme Court shall have *appellate* jurisdiction, both as to law and *fact*, with such exceptions, and under such regulations, as Congress shall make."

This paragraph, by expressly giving an *appellate* jurisdiction, in cases of law and equity arising under the Constitution, to *fact*, as well as to law, clearly excludes criminal cases, where the trial by jury is secured—because the fact, in such cases, is not a subject of appeal; and, although the appeal is liable to such *exceptions* and regulations as Congress may adopt, yet it is not to be supposed that an *exception* of *all* criminal cases could be contemplated, as well because a discretion in Congress to make or omit the exception would be improper, as because it would have been unnecessary. The exception could as easily have been made by the Constitution itself, as referred to the Congress.

Once more: The amendment last added to the Constitution deserves attention as throwing light on this subject. "The judicial power of the United States shall not be construed to extend to any suit in *law* or *equity,* commenced or prosecuted against one of the United States, by citizens of another state, or by citizens or subjects of any foreign power." As it will not be pretended that any criminal proceeding could take place against a state, the terms *law or equity* must be understood as appropriate to *civil,* in exclusion of *criminal* cases.

From these considerations, it is evident that this part of the Constitution, even if it could be applied at all to the purpose for which it has been cited, would not include any cases whatever of a criminal nature, and consequently would not authorize the inference from it, that the judicial authority extends to *offences* against the common law, as offences arising under the Constitution.

It is further to be considered that, even if this part of the Constitution could be strained into an application to every common-law case, criminal as well as civil, it could have no effect in justifying the Sedition Act, which is an act of legislative, and not of judicial power: and it is the judicial power only of which the extent is defined in this part of the Constitution.

There are two passages in the Constitution, in which a description of the law of the United States is found. The first is contained in art. 3, sect. 3, in the words following: "This Constitution, the laws of the United States, and treaties made, or which shall be made, under this authority." The second is contained in the second paragraph of art. 6, as follows: "This Constitution, and the laws of the United States which shall be made in pursuance thereof, and all treaties made, or which shall be made, under the authority of the United States, shall be the supreme law of the land." The first of these descriptions was meant as a guide to the judges of the United States; the second, as a guide to the judges of the several states. Both of them consist of an enumeration, which was evidently meant to be precise and complete. If the common law had been understood to be a law of the United States, it is not possible to assign a satisfactory reason why it was not expressed in the enumeration.

In aid of these objections, the difficulties and confusion inseparable from a constructive introduction of the common law would afford powerful reasons against it.

Is it to be the common law with or without the British statutes?

If without the statutory amendments, the vices of the code would be unsupportable.

If with these amendments, what period is to be fixed for limiting the British authority over our laws?

Is it to be the date of the eldest, or the youngest, of the colonies?

Or are the dates to be thrown together, and a medium deduced?

Or is our independence to be taken for the date?

Is, again, regard to be had to be various changes in the common law made by the local codes of America?

Is regard to be had to such changes subsequent as well as prior to the establishment of the Constitution?

Is regard to be had to future as well as past changes?

Is the law to be different in every state, as differently modified by its code; or are the modifications of any particular state to be applied to all?

And on the latter supposition, which among the state codes forms the standard?

Questions of this sort might be multiplied with as much ease as there would be difficulty in answering them.

These consequences, flowing from the proposed construction, furnish other objections equally conclusive; unless the text were peremptory in its meaning, and consistent with other parts of the instrument.

These consequences may be in relation to the legislative authority of the United States; to the executive authority; to the judicial authority; and to the governments of the several states.

If it be understood that the common law is established by the Constitution, it follows that no part of the law can be altered by the legislature. Such of the statutes already passed as may be repugnant thereto, would be nullified; particularly the Sedition Act itself, which boasts of being a melioration of the common law; and the whole code, with all its incongruities, barbarisms, and bloody maxims, would be inviolably saddled on the good people of the United States.

Should this consequence be rejected, and the common law be held, like other laws, liable to revision and alteration by the authority of Congress, it then follows that the authority of Congress is coëxtensive with the objects of common law; that is to say, with every object of legislation; for to every such object does some branch or other of the common law extend. The authority of Congress would, therefore, be no longer under the limitations marked out in the Constitution. They would be authorized to legislate in all cases whatsoever.

In the next place, as the President possesses the executive powers of the Constitution, and is to see that the laws be faithfully executed, his authority also must be coëxtensive with every branch of the common law. The additions which this would make to his power, though not readily to be estimated, claim the most serious attention.

This is not all: it will merit the most profound consideration, how far an indefinite admission of the common law, with a latitude in construing it equal to the construction by which it is deduced from the Constitution, might draw after it the various prerogatives, making part of the unwritten law of England. The English constitution itself is nothing more than a composition of unwritten laws and maxims.

In the third place, whether the common law be admitted as of legal or of constitutional obligation, it would confer on the judicial department a discretion little short of a legislative power.

On the supposition of its having a constitutional obligation, this power in the judges would be permanent and irremediable by the legislature. On the other supposition, the power would not expire until the legislature should have introduced a full system of statutory provisions. Let it be observed, too, that, besides all the uncertainties above enumerated, and which present an immense field for judicial discretion, it would remain with the same department to decide what parts of the common law would, and what would not, be properly applicable to the circumstances of the United States.

A discretion of this sort has always been lamented as incongruous and dangerous, even in the colonial and state courts, although so much narrowed by positive provisions in the local codes on all the principal subjects embraced by the common law. Under the United States, where so few laws exist on those subjects, and where so great a lapse of time must happen before the vast chasm could be supplied, it is manifest that the power of the judges over the law would, in fact, erect them into legislators, and that, for a long time, it would be impossible for the citizens to conjecture either what was, or would be, law.

In the last place, the consequence of admitting the common law as the law of the United States, on the authority of the individual states, is as obvious as it would be fatal. As this law relates to every subject of legislation, and would be paramount to the constitutions and laws of the states, the admission of it would overwhelm the residuary sovereignty of the states, and, by one constructive operation, new-model the whole political fabric of the country.

From the review thus taken of the situation of the American colonies prior to their independence; of the effect of this event on their situation; of the nature and import of the Articles of Confederation; of the true meaning of the passage in the existing Constitution from which the common law has been deduced; of the difficulties and uncertainties incident to the doctrine; and of its vast consequences in extending the powers of the federal government, and in superseding the authorities of the state governments,—the committee feel the utmost confidence in concluding that the common law never was, nor by any fair construction ever can be, deemed a law for the American people as one community; and they indulge the strongest expectation that the same conclusion will be finally drawn by all candid and accurate inquirers into the subject. It is, indeed, distressing to reflect that it ever should have been made a question, whether the Constitution, on the whole face of which is seen so much labor to enumerate and define the several objects of federal power, could intend to introduce in the lump, in an indirect manner, and by a forced construction of a few phrases, the vast and multifarious jurisdiction involved in the common law—a law filling so many ample volumes; a law overspreading the entire field of legislation; and a law that would sap the foundation of the Constitution as a system of limited and specified powers. A severer reproach could not, in the opinion of the committee, be thrown on the Constitution, on those who framed, or on those who established it, than such a supposition would throw on them.

The argument, then, drawn from the common law, on the ground of its being adopted or recognized by the Constitution, being inapplicable to the Sedition Act, the committee will proceed to examine the other arguments which have been founded on the Constitution.

They will waste but little time on the attempt to cover the

act by the preamble to the Constitution, it being contrary to every acknowledged rule of construction to set up this part of an instrument in opposition to the plain meaning expressed in the body of the instrument. A preamble usually contains the general motives or reason for the particular regulations or measures which follow it, and is always understood to be explained and limited by them. In the present instance, a contrary interpretation would have the inadmissible effect of rendering nugatory or improper every part of the Constitution which succeeds the preamble.

The paragraph in art. 1, sect. 8, which contains the power to lay and collect taxes, duties, imposts, and excises, to pay the debts, and provide for the common defence and general welfare, having been already examined, will also require no particular attention in this place. It will have been seen that, in its fair and consistent meaning, it cannot enlarge the enumerated powers vested in Congress.

The part of the Constitution which seems most to be recurred to, in defence of the Sedition Act, is the last clause of the above section, empowering Congress to make all laws which shall be necessary and proper for carrying into execution the foregoing powers, and all other powers vested by this Constitution in the government of the United States, or in any department or officer thereof."

The plain import of this clause is, that Congress shall have all the incidental or instrumental powers necessary and proper for carrying into execution all the express powers, whether they be vested in the government of the United States, more collectively, or in the several departments or officers thereof.

It is not a grant of new powers to Congress, but merely a declaration, or the removal of all uncertainty, that the means of carrying into execution those otherwise granted are included in the grant.

Whenever, therefore, a question arises concerning the constitutionality of a particular power, the first question is, whether the power be expressed in the Constitution. If it be, the question is decided. If it be not expressed, the next inquiry must be, whether it is properly an incident to an express power, and necessary to its execution. If it be, it may be exercised by Congress. If it be not, Congress cannot exercise it.

Let the question be asked, then, whether the power over the press, exercised in the Sedition Act, be found among the powers expressly vested in Congress. This is not pretended.

Is there any express power, for executing which it is a necessary and proper power?

The power which has been selected, as least remote, in answer to this question, is that "of suppressing insurrections;" which is said to imply a power to prevent insurrections, by punishing whatever may lead or tend to them. But it surely cannot, with the least plausibility, be said, that the regulation of the press, and punishment of libels, are exercises of a power to suppress insurrections. The most that could be said would be, that the punishment of libels, if it had the tendency ascribed to it, might prevent the occasion of passing or executing laws necessary and proper for the suppression of insurrections.

Has the federal government no power, then, to prevent as well as to punish resistance to the laws?

They have the power, which the Constitution deemed most proper, in their hands for the purpose. The Congress has power, before it happens, to pass laws for punishing it; and the executive and judiciary have power to enforce those laws when it does happen.

It must be recollected by many, and could be shown to the satisfaction of all, that the construction here put on the terms "necessary and proper" is precisely the construction which prevailed during the discussions and ratifications of the Constitution. It may be added, and cannot too often be repeated, that it is a construction absolutely necessary to maintain their consistency with the peculiar character of the government, as possessed of particular and definite powers only, not of the general and indefinite powers vested in ordinary governments; for, if the power to suppress insurrections includes the power to punish libels, or if the power to punish includes a power to prevent, by all the means that may have that tendency, such is the relation and influence among the most remote subjects of legislation, that a power over a very few would carry with it a power over all. And it must be wholly immaterial whether unlimited powers be exercised under the name of unlimited powers, or be exercised under the name of unlimited means of carrying into execution limited powers.

This branch of the subject will be closed with a reflection which must have weight with all, but more especially with those who place peculiar reliance on the judicial exposition of the Constitution, as the bulwark provided against an undue extension of the legislative power. If it be understood that the powers implied in the specified powers have an immediate and appropriate relation to them, as means necessary and proper for carrying them into execution, questions on constitutionality of laws passed for this purpose will be of a nature sufficiently precise and determinate for judicial cognizance and control. If, on the other hand, Congress are not limited, in the choice of means, by any such appropriate relation of them to the specified powers, but may employ all such means as they may deem fitted to prevent, as well as to punish, crimes subjected to their authority, (such as may have a tendency only to promote an object for which they are authorized to provide,) every one must perceive that questions relating to means of this sort must be questions for mere policy and expediency; on which legislative discretion alone can decide, and from which the judicial interposition and control are completely excluded.

2. The next point which the resolution requires to be proved is, that the power over the press, exercised by the Sedition Act, is positively forbidden by one of the amendments to the Constitution.

The amendment stands in these words: "Congress shall make no law respecting an establishment of religion, or prohibiting the free exercise thereof, or abridging the freedom of speech, or of the press, or of the right of the people peaceably to assemble, and to petition the government for a redress of grievances."

In the attempts to vindicate the Sedition Act, it has been contended, 1. That the "freedom of the press" is to be determined by the meaning of these terms in the common law; 2. That the article supposes the power over the press to be in Congress, and prohibits them only from abridging the freedom allowed to it by the common law.

Although it will be shown, on examining the second of these positions, that the amendment is a denial to Congress of all power over the press, it may not be useless to make the following observations on the first of them:—

It is deemed to be a sound opinion that the Sedition Act, in its definition of some of the crimes created, is an abridgment of the freedom of publication, recognized by principles of the common law in England.

The freedom of the press, under the common law, is, in the defences of the Sedition Act, made to consist in an exemption from all previous restraint on printed publications, by persons authorized to inspect or prohibit them. It appears to the committee that this idea of the freedom of the press can never be admitted to be the American idea of it; since a law inflicting penalties on printed publications would have a similar effect with a law authorizing a previous restraint on them. It would seem a mockery to say that no laws should be passed preventing publications from being made, but that laws might be passed for punishing them in case they should be made.

The essential difference between the British government and the American constitutions will place this subject in the clearest light.

In the British government, the danger of encroachments on

the rights of the people is understood to be confined to the executive magistrate. The representatives of the people in the legislature are not only exempt themselves from distrust, but are considered as sufficient guardians of the rights of their constituents against the danger from the executive. Hence it is a principle, that the Parliament is unlimited in its power; or, in their own language, is omnipotent. Hence, too, all the ramparts for protecting the rights of the people,—such as their Magna Charta, their bill of rights, &c.,—are not reared against the Parliament, but against the royal prerogative. They are merely legislative precautions against executive usurpation. Under such a government as this, an exemption of the press from previous restraint by licensers appointed by the king, is all the freedom that can be secured to it.

In the United States, the case is altogether different. The people, not the government, possess the absolute sovereignty. The legislature, no less than the executive, is under limitations of power. Encroachments are regarded as possible from the one as well as from the other. Hence, in the United States, the great and essential rights of the people are secured against legislative as well as executive ambition. They are secured, not by laws paramount to prerogative, but by constitutions paramount to laws. This security of the freedom of the press requires that it should be exempt, not only from previous restraint of the executive, as in Great Britain but from legislative restraint also; and this exemption, to be effectual must be an exemption, not only from the previous inspection of licensers, but from the subsequent penalty of laws.

The state of the press, therefore, under the common law, cannot, in this point of view, be the standard of its freedom in the United States.

But there is another view under which it may be necessary to consider this subject. It may be alleged that, although the security for the freedom of the press be different in Great Britain and in this country,—being a legal security only in the former, and a constitutional security in the latter,—and although there may be a further difference, in an extension of the freedom of the press, here, beyond an exemption from previous restraint, to an exemption from subsequent penalties also,—yet the actual legal freedom of the press, under the common law, must determine the degree of freedom which is meant by the terms, and which is constitutionally secured against both previous and subsequent restraints.

The committee are not unaware of the difficulty of all general questions, which may turn on the proper boundary between the liberty and licentiousness of the press. They will leave it, therefore, for consideration only, how far the difference between the nature of the British government, and the nature of the American government, and the practice under the latter, may show the degree of rigor in the former to be inapplicable to, and not obligatory in, the latter.

The nature of governments elective, limited, and responsible, in all their branches, may well be supposed to require a greater freedom of animadversion, than might be tolerated by the genius of such a government as that of Great Britain. In the latter, it is a maxim, that the king—an hereditary, not a responsible magistrate—can do no wrong; and that the legislature, which, in two thirds of its composition, is also hereditary, not responsible, can do what it pleases. In the United States, the executive magistrates are not held to be infallible, nor the legislatures to be omnipotent; and both, being elective, are both responsible. Is it not natural and necessary, under such different circumstances, that a different degree of freedom in the use of the press should be contemplated?

Is not such an inference favored by what is observable in Great Britain itself? Notwithstanding the general doctrine of the common law, on the subject of the press, and the occasional punishment of those who use it with a freedom offensive to the government, it is well known that, with respect to the responsible measures of the government, where the reasons operating here become applicable there, the freedom exercised by the press, and protected by public opinion, far exceeds the limits prescribed by the ordinary rules of law. The ministry, who are responsible to impeachment, are at all times animadverted on, by the press, with peculiar freedom; and during the elections for the House of Commons, the other responsible part of the government, the press is employed with as little reserve towards the candidates.

The practice in America must be entitled to much more respect. In every state, probably, in the Union, the press has exerted a freedom in canvassing the merits and measures of public men, of every description, which has not been confined to the strict limits of the common law. On this footing the freedom of the press has stood; on this foundation it yet stands; and it will not be a breach, either of truth or of candor, to say that no persons or presses are in the habit of more unrestrained animadversions on the proceedings and functionaries of the state governments than the persons and presses most zealous in vindicating the act of Congress for punishing similar animadversions on the government of the United States.

The last remark will not be understood as claiming for the state governments an immunity greater than they have heretofore enjoyed. Some degree of abuse is inseparable from the proper use of every thing; and in no instance is this more true than in that of the press. It has accordingly been decided, by the practice of the states, that it is better to leave a few of its noxious branches to their luxuriant growth, than, by pruning them away, to injure the vigor of those yielding the proper fruits. And can the wisdom of this policy be doubted by any one who reflects that to the press alone, checkered as it is with abuses, the world is indebted for all the triumphs which have been gained by reason and humanity over error and oppression; who reflects that to the same beneficent source the United States owe much of the lights which conducted them to the rank of a free and independent nation and which have improved their political system into a shape so auspicious to their happiness? Had Sedition Acts, forbidding every publication that might bring the constituted agents into contempt or disrepute, or that might excite the hatred of the people against the authors of unjust or pernicious measures, been uniformly enforced against the press, might not the United States have been languishing, at this day, under the infirmities of a sickly Confederation? Might they not, possibly, be miserable colonies, groaning under a foreign yoke?

To these observations one fact will be added, which demonstrates that the common law cannot be admitted as the universal expositor of American terms, which may be the same with those contained in that law. The freedom of conscience, and of religion, is found in the same instrument which asserts the freedom of the press. It will never be admitted that the meaning of the former, in the common law of England, is to limit their meaning in the United States.

Whatever weight may be allowed to these considerations, the committee do not, however, by any means intend to rest the question on them. They contend that the article of the amendment, instead of supposing in Congress a power that might be exercised over the press, provided its freedom was not abridged, meant a positive denial to Congress of any power whatever on the subject.

To demonstrate that this was the true object of the article, it will be sufficient to recall the circumstances which led to it, and to refer to the explanation accompanying the article.

When the Constitution was under the discussions which preceded its ratification, it is well known that great apprehensions were expressed by many, lest the omission of some positive exception, from the powers delegated, of certain rights, and of the freedom of the press particularly, might expose them to danger of being drawn, by construction, within some of the powers vested in Congress; more especially of the power to make all laws necessary and proper for carrying their other powers into execution. In reply to this objection, it was invariably urged to be a fundamental and characteristic principle of the Constitution, that all powers not given by it were reserved; that no powers were given beyond those enumerated in the Constitution, and such as were fairly incident to them; that the power over the rights in question, and particularly over the press, was neither among the enumerated powers, nor incident to any of them: and consequently that an exercise of any such power would be manifest usurpation. It is painful to remark how much the arguments now employed in behalf of the Sedition Act, are at variance with the reasoning which then justified the Constitution, and invited its ratification.

From this posture of the subject resulted the interesting question, in so many of the conventions, whether the doubts and dangers ascribed to the Constitution should be removed by any amendments previous to the ratification, or be postponed, in confidence that, as far as they might be proper, they would be introduced in the form provided by the Constitution. The latter course was adopted; and in most of the states, ratifications were followed by the propositions and instructions for rendering the Constitution more explicit, and more safe to the rights not meant to be delegated by it. Among those rights, the freedom of the press, in most instances, is particularly and emphatically mentioned. The firm and very pointed manner in which it is asserted in the proceedings of the Convention of this state will hereafter be seen.

In pursuance of the wishes thus expressed, the first Congress that assembled under the Constitution proposed certain amendments, which have since, by the necessary ratifications, been made a part of it; among which amendments is the article containing, among other prohibitions on the Congress, an express declaration that they should make no law abridging the freedom of the press.

Without tracing farther the evidence on this subject, it would seem scarcely possible to doubt that no power whatever over the press was supposed to be delegated by the Constitution, as it originally stood, and that the amendment was intended as a positive and absolute reservation of it.

But the evidence is still stronger. The proposition of amendments made by Congress is introduced in the following terms:—

"The conventions of a number of the states having, at the time of their adopting the Constitution, expressed a desire, in order to prevent misconstruction or abuse of its powers, that further declaratory and restrictive clauses should be added; and as extending the ground of public confidence in the government will best insure the beneficent ends of its institutions."

Here is the most satisfactory and authentic proof that the several amendments proposed were to be considered as either declaratory or restrictive, and, whether the one or the other, as corresponding with the desire expressed by a number of the states, and as extending the ground of public confidence in the government.

Under any other construction of the amendment relating to the press, than that it declared the press to be wholly exempt from the power of Congress, the amendment could neither be said to correspond with the desire expressed by a number of the states, nor be calculated to extend the ground of public confidence in the government.

Nay, more; the construction employed to justify the Sedition Act would exhibit a phenomenon without a parallel in the political world. It would exhibit a number of respectable states, as denying, first, that any power over the press was delegated by the Constitution; as proposing, next, that an amendment to it should explicitly declare that no such power was delegated; and, finally, as concurring in an amendment actually recognizing or delegating such a power.

Is, then, the federal government, it will be asked, destitute of every authority for restraining the licentiousness of the press, and for shielding itself against the libellous attacks which may be made on those who administer it?

The Constitution alone can answer this question. If no such power be expressly delegated, and if it be not both necessary and proper to carry into execution an express power; above all, if it be expressly forbidden, by a declaratory amendment to the Constitution,—the answer must be, that the federal government is destitute of all such authority.

And might it not be asked, in turn, whether it is not more probable, under all the circumstances which have been reviewed, that the authority should be withheld by the Constitution, than that it should be left to a vague and violent construction, whilst so much pains were bestowed in enumerating other powers, and so many less important powers are included in the enumeration?

Might it not be likewise asked, whether the anxious circumspection which dictated so many peculiar limitations on the general authority would be unlikely to exempt the press altogether from that authority? The peculiar magnitude of some of the powers necessarily committed to the federal government; the peculiar duration required for the functions of some of its departments; the peculiar distance of the seat of its proceedings from the great body of its constituents; and the peculiar difficulty of circulating an adequate knowledge of them through any other channel;—will not these considerations, some or other of which produced other exceptions from the powers of ordinary governments, altogether, account for the policy of binding the hands of the federal government from touching the channel which alone can give efficacy to its responsibility to its constituents, and of leaving those who administer it to a remedy, for their injured reputations, under the same laws, and in the same tribunals, which protect their lives, their liberties, and their properties?

But the question does not turn either on the wisdom of the

Constitution or on the policy which gave rise to its particular organization. It turns on the actual meaning of the instrument, by which it has appeared that a power over the press is clearly excluded from the number of powers delegated to the federal government.

3. And, in the opinion of the committee, well may it be said, as the resolution concludes with saying, that the unconstitutional power exercised over the press by the Sedition Act ought, "more than any other, to produce universal alarm; because it is levelled against that right of freely examining public characters and measures, and of free communication among the people thereon, which has ever been justly deemed the only effectual guardian of every other right."

Without scrutinizing minutely into all the provisions of the Sedition Act, it will be sufficient to cite so much of section 2d as follows:—"And be it further enacted, that if any shall write, print, utter, or publish, or shall cause or procure to be written, printed, uttered, or published, or shall knowingly and willingly assist or aid in writing, printing, uttering, or publishing, any false, scandalous, and malicious writing or writings against the government of the United States, or either house of the Congress of the United States, with an intent to defame the said government, or either house of the said Congress, or the President, or to bring them or either of them into contempt or disrepute, or to excite against them, or either or any of them, the hatred of the good people of the United States, &c.,—then such persons, being thereof convicted before any court of the United States having jurisdiction thereof, shall be punished by a fine not exceeding two thousand dollars, and by imprisonment not exceeding two years."

On this part of the act, the following observations present themselves:—

1. The Constitution supposes that the President, the Congress, and each of its Houses, may not discharge their trusts, either from

defect of judgment or other causes. Hence they are all made responsible to their constituents, at the returning periods of elections; and the President, who is singly intrusted with very great powers, is, as a further guard, subjected to an intermediate impeachment.

2. Should it happen, as the Constitution supposes it may happen, that either of these branches of the government may not have duly discharged its trust, it is natural and proper, that, according to the cause and degree of their faults, they should be brought into contempt or disrepute, and incur the hatred of the people.

3. Whether it has, in any case, happened that the proceedings of either or all of those branches evince such a violation of duty as to justify a contempt, a disrepute, or hatred among the people, can only be determined by a free examination thereof, and a free communication among the people thereon.

4. Whenever it may have actually happened that proceedings of this sort are chargeable on all or either of the branches of the government, it is the duty, as well as the right, of intelligent and faithful citizens to discuss and promulgate them freely—as well to control them by the censorship of the public opinion, as to promote a remedy according to the rules of the Constitution. And it cannot be avoided that those who are to apply the remedy must feel, in some degree, a contempt or hatred against the transgressing party.

5. As the act was passed on July 14, 1798, and is to be in force until March 3, 1801, it was of course that, during its continuance, two elections of the entire House of Representatives, an election of a part of the Senate, and an election of a President, were to take place.

6. That, consequently, during all these elections,—intended, by the Constitution, to preserve the purity or to purge the faults of the administration,—the great remedial rights of the people were to be exercised, and the responsibility of their public agents to be screened, under the penalties of this act.

May it not be asked of every intelligent friend to the liberties of his country, whether the power exercised in such an act as this ought not to produce great and universal alarm? Whether a rigid execution of such an act, in time past, would not have repressed that information and communication among the people which is indispensable to the just exercise of their electoral rights? And whether such an act, if made perpetual, and enforced with rigor, would not, in time to come, either destroy our free system of government, or prepare a convulsion that might prove equally fatal to it?

In answer to such questions, it has been pleaded that the writings and publications forbidden by the act are those only which are false and malicious, and intended to defame; and merit is claimed for the privilege allowed to authors to justify, by proving the truth of their publications, and for the limitations to which the sentence of fine and imprisonment is subjected.

To those who concurred in the act, under the extraordinary belief that the option lay between the passing of such an act, and leaving in force the common law of libels, which punishes truth equally with falsehood, and submits fine and imprisonment to the indefinite discretion of the court, the merit of good intentions ought surely not to be refused. A like merit may perhaps be due for the discontinuance of the corporal punishment, which the common law also leaves to the discretion of the court. This merit of intention, however, would have been greater, if the several mitigations had not been limited to so short a period; and the apparent inconsistency would have been avoided, between justifying the act, at one time, by contrasting it with the rigors of the common law otherwise in force; and at another time, by appealing to the nature of the crisis as requiring the temporary rigor exerted by the act.

But, whatever may have been the meritorious intentions of all or any who contributed to the Sedition Act, a very few reflections will prove that its baleful tendency is little diminished by the privilege of giving in evidence the truth of the matter contained in political writings.

In the first place, where simple and naked facts alone are in question, there is sufficient difficulty in some cases, and sufficient trouble and vexation in all, in meeting a prosecution from the government with the full and formal proof necessary in a court of law.

But in the next place, it must be obvious to the plainest minds, that opinions and inferences, and conjectural observations, are not only in many cases inseparable from the facts, but may often be more the objects of the prosecution than the facts themselves; or may even be altogether abstracted from particular facts; and that opinion, and inferences, and conjectural observations, cannot be subjects of that kind of proof which appertains to facts, before a court of law.

Again: it is no less obvious that the intent to defame, or bring into contempt, or disrepute, or hatred,—which is made a condition of the offence created by the act,—cannot prevent its pernicious influence on the freedom of the press. For, omitting the inquiry, how far the malice of the intent is an inference of the law from the mere publication, it is manifestly impossible to punish the intent to bring those who administer the government into disrepute or contempt, without striking at the right of freely discussing public characters and measures; because those who engage in such discussions must expect and intend to excite these unfavorable sentiments, so far as they may be thought to be deserved. To prohibit the intent to excite those unfavorable sentiments against those who administer the government, is equivalent to a prohibition of the actual excitement of them; and to prohibit the actual excitement of them is equivalent to a prohibition of discussions having that tendency and effect; which, again, is equivalent to a protection of those who administer the government, if they should at any time deserve the contempt or hatred of the people, against being exposed to it, by free animadversions on their characters and conduct. Nor can there be a doubt, if those in public trust be shielded by penal laws from such strictures of the press as may expose them to contempt, or disrepute, or hatred, where they may deserve it, that, in exact proportion as they may deserve to be exposed, will be the certainty and criminality of the intent to expose them, and the vigilance of prosecuting and punishing it; nor a doubt that a government thus intrenched in penal statutes against the just and natural effects of a culpable administration, will easily evade the responsibility which is essential to a faithful discharge of its duty.

Let it be recollected, lastly, that the right of electing the members of the government constitutes more particularly the essence of a free and responsible government. The value and efficacy of this right depends on the knowledge of the comparative merits and demerits of the candidates for public trust, and on the equal freedom, consequently, of examining and discussing these merits and demerits of the candidates respectively. It has been seen that a number of important elections will take place while the act is in force, although it should not be continued beyond the term to which it is limited. Should there happen, then, as is extremely probable in relation to some one or other of the branches of the government, to be competitions between those who are, and those who are not, members of the government, what will be the situations of the competitors? Not equal; because the characters of the former will be covered by the Sedition Act from animadversions exposing them to disrepute among the people, whilst the latter may be exposed to the contempt and hatred of the people without a violation of the act. What will be the situation of the people? Not free; because they will be compelled to make their election between competitors whose pretensions they are not permitted by the act equally to examine, to discuss, and to ascertain. And from both these situations will not those in power derive an undue advantage for continuing themselves in it: which, by impairing the right of election, endangers the blessings of the government founded on it?

It is with justice, therefore, that the General Assembly have affirmed, in the resolution, as well that the right of freely examining public characters and measures, and of communication thereon, is the only effectual guardian of every other right, as that this particular right is levelled at by the power exercised in the Sedition Act.

The resolution *next* in order is as follows:—

That this state having, by its Convention, which ratified the Federal Constitution, expressly declared that, among other essential rights, 'the liberty of conscience and of the press cannot be cancelled, abridged, restrained, or modified, by any authority of the United States; 'and, from its extreme anxiety to guard these rights from every possible attack of sophistry and ambition, having, with other states, recommended an amendment for that purpose, which amendment was in due time annexed to the Constitution, it would mark a reproachful inconsistency, and criminal degeneracy, if an indifference were now shown to the most palpable violation of one of the rights thus declared and secured, and to the establishment of a precedent which may be fatal to the other.

To place this resolution in its just light, it will be necessary to recur to the act of ratification by Virginia, which stands in the ensuing form:—

We, the delegates of the people of Virginia, duly elected in pursuance of a recommendation from the General Assembly, and now met in Convention, having fully and freely investigated and discussed the proceedings of the Federal Convention, and being prepared, as well as the most mature deliberation hath enabled us, to decide thereon,—DO, in the name and in behalf of the people of Virginia, declare and make known, that the powers granted under the Constitution, being derived from the people of the United States, may be resumed by them whensoever the same shall be perverted to their injury or oppression; and that every power not granted thereby remains with them, and at their will. That, therefore, no right of any denomination can be cancelled, abridged, restrained, or modified, by the Congress, by the Senate or the House of Representatives, acting in any capacity, by the President, or any department or officer of the United States, except in those instances in which power is given by the Constitution for those purposes; and that, among other essential rights, the liberty of conscience and of the press cannot be cancelled, abridged, restrained, or modified, by any authority of the United States.

Here is an express and solemn declaration by the Convention of the state, that they ratified the Constitution in the sense that no right of any denomination can be cancelled, abridged, restrained, or modified, by the government of the United States, or any part of it, except in those instances in which power is given by the Constitution; and in the sense, particularly, "that among other essential rights, the liberty of conscience and freedom of the press cannot be cancelled, abridged, restrained, or modified, by any authority of the United States."

Words could not well express, in a fuller or more forcible manner, the understanding of the Convention, that the liberty of conscience and freedom of the press were *equally* and *completely* exempted from all authority whatever of the United States.

Under an anxiety to guard more effectually these rights against every possible danger, the Convention, after ratifying the Constitution, proceeded to prefix to certain amendments proposed by them, a declaration of rights, in which are two articles providing, the one for the liberty of conscience, the other for the freedom of speech and of the press.

Similar recommendations having proceeded from a number of other states; and Congress, as has been seen, having, in consequence thereof, and with a view to extend the ground of public confidence, proposed, among other declaratory and restrictive clauses, a clause expressly securing the liberty of conscience and of the press; and Virginia having concurred in the ratifications which made them a part of the Constitution,— it will remain with a candid public to decide whether it would not mark an inconsistency and degeneracy, if an indifference were now shown to a palpable violation of one of those rights—

the freedom of the press; and to a precedent, therein, which may be fatal to the other—the free exercise of religion.

That the precedent established by the violation of the former of these rights may, as is affirmed by the resolution, be fatal to the latter, appears to be demonstrable by a comparison of the grounds on which they respectively rest, and from the scope of reasoning by which the power of the former has been vindicated.

First, Both of these rights, the liberty of conscience, and of the press, rest equally on the original ground of not being delegated by the Constitution, and consequently withheld from the government. Any construction, therefore, that would attack this original security for the one, must have the like effect on the other.

Secondly, They are both equally secured by the supplement to the Constitution, being both included in the same amendment, made at the same time and by the same authority. Any construction or argument, then, which would turn the amendment into a grant or acknowledgment of power, with respect to the press, might be equally applied to the freedom of religion.

Thirdly, If it be admitted that the extent of the freedom of the press, secured by the amendment, is to be measured by the common law on this subject, the same authority may be resorted to for the standard which is to fix the extent of the "free exercise of religion." It cannot be necessary to say what this standard would be—whether the common law be taken solely as the unwritten, or as varied by the written law of England.

Fourthly, If the words and phrases in the amendment are to be considered as chosen with a studied discrimination, which yields an argument for a power over the press, under the limitation that its freedom be not abridged, the same argument results from the same consideration, for a power over the exercise of religion, under the limitation that its freedom be not prohibited.

For, if Congress may regulate the freedom of the press, provided they do not abridge it, because it is said only, "they shall not abridge it," and is not said "they shall make no law respecting it," the analogy of reasoning is conclusive, that Congress may *regulate,* and even *abridge,* the free exercise of religion, provided they do not *prohibit* it; because it is said only "they shall not prohibit it;" and is *not* said, "they shall make no law *respecting,* or no law *abridging* it."

The General Assembly were governed by the clearest reason, then, in considering the Sedition Act, which legislates on the freedom of the press, as establishing a precedent that may be fatal to the liberty of conscience; and it will be the duty of all, in proportion as they value the security of the latter, to take the alarm at every encroachment on the former.

The two concluding resolutions only remain to be examined. They are in the words following:—

That the good people of this commonwealth, having ever felt, and continuing to feel, the most sincere affection for their brethren of the other states, the truest anxiety for establishing and perpetuating the union of all, and the most scrupulous fidelity to that Constitution which is the pledge of mutual friendship and the instrument of mutual happiness,—the General Assembly doth solemnly appeal to the like dispositions in the other states, in confidence that they will concur with this commonwealth in declaring, as it does hereby declare, that the acts aforesaid are unconstitutional; and that the necessary and proper measures will be taken, by each, for coöperating with this state, in maintaining, unimpaired, the authorities, rights, and liberties, reserved to the states respectively, or to the people.

That the governor be desired to transmit a copy of the foregoing resolutions to the executive authority of each of the other states, with a request that the same may be communicated to the legislature thereof; and that a copy be furnished to each of the senators and representatives representing this state in the Congress of the United States.

The fairness and regularity of the course of proceeding here pursued, have not protected it against objections even from sources too respectable to be disregarded.

It has been said that it belongs to the judiciary of the United

States, and not the state legislatures, to declare the meaning of the Federal Constitution.

But a declaration that proceedings of the federal government are not warranted by the Constitution, is a novelty neither among the citizens nor among the legislatures of the states; nor are the citizens or the legislature of Virginia singular in the example of it.

Nor can the declarations of either, whether affirming or denying the constitutionality of measures of the federal government, or whether made before or after judicial decisions thereon, be deemed, in any point of view, an assumption of the office of the judge. The declarations in such cases are expressions of opinion, unaccompanied with any other effect than what they may produce on opinion, by exciting reflection. The expositions of the judiciary, on the other hand, are carried into immediate effect by force. The former may lead to a change in the legislative expression of the general will—possibly to a change in the opinion of the judiciary; the latter enforces the general will, whilst that will and that opinion continue unchanged.

And if there be no impropriety in declaring the unconstitutionality of proceedings in the federal government, where can there be the impropriety of communicating the declaration to other states, and inviting their concurrence in a like declaration? What is allowable for one, must be allowable for all; and a free communication among the states, where the Constitution imposes no restraint, is as allowable among the state governments as among other public bodies or private citizens. This consideration derives a weight that cannot be denied to it, from the relation of the state legislatures to the federal legislature as the immediate constituents of one of its branches.

The legislatures of the states have a right also to originate amendments to the Constitution, by a concurrence of two thirds of the whole number, in applications to Congress for the purpose. When new states are to be formed by a junction of two or more states, or parts of states, the legislatures of the states concerned are, as well as Congress, to concur in the measure. The states have a right also to enter into agreements or compacts, with the consent of Congress. In all such cases a communication among them results from the object which is common to them.

It is lastly to be seen, whether the confidence expressed by the Constitution, that the *necessary and proper measures* would be taken by the other states for coöperating with Virginia in maintaining the rights reserved to the states, or to the people, be in any degree liable to the objections raised against it.

If it be liable to objections, it must be because either the object or the means are objectionable.

The object, being to maintain what the Constitution has ordained, is in itself a laudable object.

The means are expressed in the terms "the necessary and proper measures." A proper object was to be pursued by the means both necessary and proper.

To find an objection, then, it must be shown that some meaning was annexed to these general terms which was not proper; and, for this purpose, either that the means used by the General Assembly were an example of improper means, or that there were no proper means to which the terms could refer.

In the example, given by the state, of declaring the Alien and Sedition Acts to be unconstitutional, and of communicating the declaration to other states, no trace of improper means has appeared. And if the other states had concurred in making a like declaration, supported, too, by the numerous applications flowing immediately from the people, it can scarcely be doubted that these simple means would have been as sufficient as they are unexceptionable.

It is no less certain that other means might have been employed which are strictly within the limits of the Constitution. The legislatures of the states might have made a direct representation to Congress, with a view to obtain a rescinding of the two offensive acts; or they might have represented to their respective senators in Congress their wish that two thirds thereof would propose an explanatory amendment to the Constitution; or two thirds of themselves, if such had been their opinion, might, by an application to Congress, have obtained a convention for the same object.

These several means, though not equally eligible in themselves, nor probably to the states, were all constitutionally open for consideration. And if the General Assembly, after declaring the two acts to be unconstitutional, (the first and most obvious proceeding on the subject,) did not undertake to point out to the other states a choice among the further measures that might become necessary and proper, the reserve will not be misconstrued by liberal minds into any culpable imputation.

These observations appear to form a satisfactory reply to every objection which is not founded on a misconception of the terms employed in the resolutions. There is one other, however, which may be of too much importance not to be added. It cannot be forgotten that, among the arguments addressed to those who apprehended danger to liberty from the establishment of the general government over so great a country, the appeal was emphatically made to the intermediate existence of the state governments between the people and that government, to the vigilance with which they would descry the first symptoms of usurpation, and to the promptitude with which they would sound the alarm to the public. This argument was probably not without its effect; and if it was a proper one then to recommend the establishment of a constitution, it must be a proper one now to assist in its interpretation.

The only part of the two concluding resolutions that remains to be noticed, is the repetition, in the first, of that warm affection to the Union and its members, and of that scrupulous fidelity to the Constitution, which have been invariably felt by the people of this state. As the proceedings were introduced with these sentiments, they could not be more properly closed than in the same manner. Should there be any so far misled as to call in question the sincerity of these professions, whatever regret may be excited by the error, the General Assembly cannot descend into a discussion of it. Those who have listened to the suggestion can only be left to their own recollection of the part which this state has borne in the establishment of our national independence, or the establishment of our national Constitution, and in maintaining under it the authority and laws of the Union, without a single exception of internal resistance or commotion. By recurring to the facts, they will be able to convince themselves that the representatives of the people of Virginia must be above the necessity of opposing any other shield to attacks on their national patriotism, than their own conscientiousness, and the justice of an enlightened public; who will perceive in the resolutions themselves the strongest evidence of attachment both to the Constitution and the Union, since it is only by maintaining the different governments, and the departments within their respective limits, that the blessings of either can be perpetuated.

The extensive view of the subject, thus taken by the committee, has led them to report to the house, as *the result of the whole,* the following resolution:—

. *Resolved,* That the General Assembly, having carefully and respectfully attended to the proceedings of a number of the states, *in answer to the resolutions of December 21, 1798, and having accurately and fully reexamined and reconsidered the latter, find it to be their indispensable duty* to adhere to the same, as founded in truth, as consonant with the Constitution, and as conducive to its preservation; and more especially to be their duty to renew, as they do hereby renew, their PROTEST against Alien and Sedition Acts, as palpable and alarming infractions of the Constitution.

Part Four

POWER:
THE REPUBLICAN REGIME

22.   The Ambitious Republic: Louisiana Purchase

Jefferson's Inaugural Address of March 4, 1801, envisioned a free, prosperous and peaceful land that needed only wise and frugal government "to close the circle of our felicites." Madison shared his friend's bright hopes for the new Republican regime. Yet the sharp sense of political reality that had informed his earlier writings must have warned him to be wary. During most of the sixteen years when Madison served as Secretary of State (1801–1809) and President (1809–1817), the Napoleonic Wars raged over Europe and menaced the whole Atlantic world. The strategies of the great powers and the shifting fortunes of war set narrow bounds within which a vulnerable young nation could choose its course. From crisis to crisis, Madison moved cautiously toward a new nationalism recalling the spirit of his politics in the troubled decades of revolution and

---

Instruction to Robert R. Livingston and James Monroe, March 2, 1803, in *Writings*, VII, pp. 9–19.

founding. When the Virginia doctrines of his opposition years stood in the way of present political necessity, he often managed to slip quietly past them. Generally, on large questions of republican principle and national direction, Madison's public papers of this period speak a strangely opaque, wooden language. Perhaps a leader who must try to make high national claims and very little power go a long way in a hostile world is not inspired to teach memorable political lessons, especially when those lessons must fit within the narrow frame of Virginia Republican doctrine. The clarity and rigor of his mind, the sure command of fact and precedent, were best documented in the close inside work of negotiation.

Good fortune more than wise government gave Jefferson and Madison their first and only unqualified diplomatic success: the unplanned acquisition of a vast continental empire beyond the Mississippi. Early in the new administration Spain cut off American commercial rights at New Orleans. At the same time Napoleon, having regained Louisiana from Spain by treaty, prepared to build a great French empire in the West Indies and the American southwest. Westerners, goaded on by Federalist partisans, demanded that Jefferson strike boldly to re-open the Mississippi and anticipate the impending French occupation of Louisiana. Both Madison and Jefferson had long defended the western view of American rights and interests in the lower Mississippi country. Doubting that the United States could or should oppose the French by force, the Republican leaders searched for peaceful diplomatic means to avoid a crisis.

Madison's instructions of March 2 and April 18, 1803, exhausted the appeals to political and economic interest that might conceivably persuade France to sell New Orleans and (if it held the title) West Florida as well. Shrewd American arguments, unsupported by a credible show of power, did not impress Napoleon. American money did; but only after a disastrous French campaign against the black revolutionaries of

Santa Domingo convinced him simply to abandon his Western imperial design in favor of fresh European conquests. The startled American ministers at Paris, faced with an offer that Madison's instructions had never imagined, bought all of Louisiana reaching from New Orleans north to Canada and northwest to the Rockies for some $15 millions. Jefferson and Madison, swallowing their constitutional scruples, recommended the magnificent bargain to an eager Congress, and then set to work constructing a quasi-military government for the Orleans territory. A few years later (1810–1813), Madison would find it easier and cheaper to edge the Spanish garrisons out of West Florida. Strict Republican principles did not seem to exclude unprecedented stretches of national authority or the statecraft of *realpolitik*, so long as Madison believed that expansion eventually would spread free governments across the continent and secure the future of the American Republic.

Department of State, March 2d, 1803.

GENTLEMEN,—You will herewith receive a Commission and letters of credence, one of you as Minister Plenipotentiary, the other as Minister Extraordinary and Plenipotentiary, to treat with the Government of the French Republic, on the subject of the Mississippi and the Territory eastward thereof, and without the limits of the United States. The object in view is to procure by just and satisfactory arrangements a cession to the United States of New Orleans, and of West and East Florida, or as much thereof as the actual proprietor can be prevailed on to part with.

The French Republic is understood to have become the proprietor by a cession from Spain in the year [1800] of New Orleans, as part of Louisiana, if not of the Floridas also. If the Floridas should not have been then included in the Cession, it is not improbable that they will have been since added to it.

It is foreseen that you may have considerable difficulty in overcoming the repugnance and the prejudices of the French Government against a transfer to the United States of so important a part of the acquisition. The apparent solicitude and exertions amidst many embarrassing circumstances, to carry into effect the cession made to the French Republic, the reserve so long used on this subject by the French Government in its communications with the Minister of the United States at Paris, and the declaration finally made by the French Minister of Foreign relations, that it was meant to take possession before any overtures from the United States would be discussed, shew the importance which is attached to the territories in question. On the other hand as the United States have the strongest motives of interest and of a pacific policy to seek by just means the establishment of the Mississippi, down to its mouth as their boundary, so these are considerations which urge on France a concurrence in so natural and so convenient an arrangement.

Notwithstanding the circumstances which have been thought to indicate in the French Government designs of unjust encroachment, and even direct hostility on the United States, it is scarcely possible, to reconcile a policy of that sort, with any motives which can be presumed to sway either the Government or the Nation. To say nothing of the assurances given both by the French Minister at Paris, and by the Spanish Minister at Madrid, that the cession by Spain to France was understood to carry with it all the conditions stipulated by the former to the United States, the manifest tendency of hostile measures against the United States, to connect their Councils, and their Colosal growth with the great and formidable rival of France, can never escape her discernment, nor be disregarded by her prudence, and might alone be expected to produce very different views in her Government.

On the supposition that the French Government does not mean to force, or Court war with the United States; but on the contrary that it sees the interest which France has in cultivating their neutrality and amity, the dangers to so desirable a relation between the two countries which lurk under a neighbourhood modified as is that of Spain at present, must have great weight in recommending the change which you will have to propose. These dangers have been always sufficiently evident; and have moreover been repeatedly suggested by collisions between the stipulated rights or reasonable expectations of the United States, and the Spanish jurisdiction at New Orleans. But they have been brought more strikingly into view by the late proceeding of the Intendant at that place. The sensibility and unanimity in our nation which have appeared on this occasion, must convince France that friendship and peace with us must be precarious until the Mississippi shall be made the boundary between the United States and Louisiana; and consequently render the present moment favorable to the object with which your [are] charged.

The time chosen for the experiment is pointed out also by other important considerations. The instability of the peace of Europe, the attitude taken by Great Britain, the languishing state of the French finances, and the absolute necessity of either abandoning the West India Islands or of sending thither large armaments at great expence, all contribute at the present crisis to prepare in the French Government a disposition to listen to an arrangement which will at once dry up one source of foreign controversy, and furnish some aid in struggling with internal embarrassments. It is to be added, that the overtures committed to you coincide in great measure with the ideas of the person thro' whom the letter of the President of April 30–1802 was conveyed to Mr. Livingston, and who is presumed to have gained some insight into the present sentiments of the French Cabinet.

Among the considerations which have led the French Government into the project of regaining from Spain the province of Louisiana, and which you may find it necessary to meet in your discussions, the following suggest themselves as highly probable.

1st. A jealousy of the Minister as leaning to a coalition with Great Britain . . . [inconsistent?] with neutrality and amity towards France; and a belief that by holding the key to the commerce of the Mississippi, she will be able to command the interests and attachments of the Western portion of the United States; and thereby either controul the Atlantic portion also, or if that cannot be done, to seduce the former with a separate Government, and a close alliance with herself.

In each of these particulars the calculation is founded in error.

It is not true that the Atlantic states lean towards any connection with Great Britain inconsistent with their amicable relations to France. Their dispositions and their interests equally prescribe to them amity and impartiality to both of those nations. If a departure from this simple and salutary line of policy should take place, the causes of it will be found in the unjust or unfriendly conduct experienced from one or other of them. In general it may be remarked, that there are as many points on which the interests and views of the United States and of Great Britain may not be thought to coincide as can be discovered in relation to France. If less harmony and confidence should therefore prevail between France and the United States than may be maintained between Great Britain and the United States, the difference will be not in the want of motives drawn from the mutual advantage of the two nations; but in the want of favorable dispositions in the Governments of one or the other of them. That the blame in this respect will not justly fall on the Government of the United States, is sufficiently demonstrated by the Mission and the objects with which you are now charged.

The French Government is not less mistaken if it supposes that the Western part of the United States can be withdrawn from their present Union with the Atlantic part, into a separate Government closely allied with France.

Our Western fellow citizens are bound to the Union not only by the ties of kindred and affection which for a long time will derive strength from the stream of emigration peopling that region, but by two considerations which flow from clear and essential interests.

One of these considerations is the passage thro' the Atlantic ports of the foreign merchandize consumed by the Western inhabitants, and the payments thence made to a Treasury in which they would lose their participation by erecting a separate Government. The bulky productions of the Western Country may continue to pass down the Mississippi; but the difficulties of the ascending navigation of that river, however free it may be made, will cause the imports for consumption to pass thro' the Atlantic States. This is the course thro' which they are now received, nor will the impost to which they will be subject change the course even if the passage up the Mississippi should be duty free. It will not equal the difference in the freight thro' the latter channel. It is true that mechanical and other improvements in the navigation of the Mississippi may lessen the labour and expence of ascending the stream, but it is not the least probable, that savings of this sort will keep pace with the improvements in canals and roads, by which the present course of imports will be favored. Let it be added that the loss of the contributions thus made to a foreign Treasury would be accompanied with the necessity of providing by less convenient revenues for the expence of a separate Government, and of the defensive precautions required by the change of situation.

The other of these considerations results from the insecurity to which the trade from the Mississippi would be exposed, by such a revolution in the Western part of the United States. A connection of the Western people as a separate state with France, implies a connection between the Atlantic States and

Great Britain. It is found from long experience that France and Great Britain are nearly half their time at War. The case would be the same with their allies. During nearly one half the time therefore, the trade of the Western Country from the Mississippi, would have no protection but that of France, and would suffer all the interruptions which nations having the command of the sea could inflict on it.

It will be the more impossible for France to draw the Western Country under her influence, by conciliatory regulations of the trade thro' the Mississippi, because regulations which would be regarded by her as liberal and claiming returns of gratitude, would be viewed on the other side as falling short of justice. If this should not be at first the case, it soon would be so. The Western people believe, as do their Atlantic brethren, that they have a natural and indefeasible right to trade freely thro' the Mississippi. They are conscious of their power to enforce their right against any nation whatever. With these ideas in their minds, it is evident that France will not be able to excite either a sense of favor, or of fear, that would establish an ascendency over them. On the contrary, it is more than probable, that the different views of their respective rights, would quickly lead to disappointments and disgusts on both sides, and thence to collisions and controversies fatal to the harmony of the two nations. To guard against these consequences, is a primary motive with the United States, in wishing the arrangement proposed. As France has equal reasons to guard against them, she ought to feel an equal motive to concur in the arrangement.

2d. The advancement of the commerce of France by an establishment on the Mississippi, has doubtless great weight with the Government in espousing this project.

The commerce thro' the Mississippi will consist 1st of that of the United States, 2d of that of the adjacent territories to be acquired by France.

The 1st is now and must for ages continue the principal

commerce. As far as the faculties of France will enable her to share in it, the article to be proposed to her on the part of the United States on that subject promises every advantage she can desire. It is a fair calculation, that under the proposed arrangement, her commercial opportunities would be extended rather than diminished; inasmuch as our present right of deposit gives her the same competitors as she would then have, and the effect of the more rapid settlement of the Western Country consequent on that arrangement would proportionally augment the mass of commerce to be shared by her.

The other portion of commerce, with the exception of the Island of New Orleans and the contiguous ports of West Florida, depends on the Territory Westward of the Mississippi. With respect to this portion, it will be little affected by the Cession desired by the United States. The footing proposed for her commerce on the shore to be ceded, gives it every advantage she could reasonably wish, during a period within which she will be able to provide every requisite establishment on the right shore; which according to the best information, possesses the same facilities for such establishments as are found on the Island of New Orleans itself. These circumstances essentially distinguish the situation of the French commerce in the Mississippi after a Cession of New Orleans to the United States, from the situation of the commerce of the United States, without such a Cession; their right of deposit being so much more circumscribed and their territory on the Mississippi not reaching low enough for a commercial establishment on the shore, within their present limits.

There remains to be considered the commerce of the Ports in the Floridas. With respect to this branch, the advantages which will be secured to France by the proposed arrangement ought to be satisfactory. She will here also derive a greater share from the increase, which will be given by a more rapid settlement of a fertile territory, to the exports and imports thro' those ports, than she would obtain from any restrictive use she could make of those ports as her own property. But this is not all. The United States have a just claim to the use of the rivers which pass from their territories thro' the Floridas. They found their claim on like principles with those which supported their claim to the use of the Mississippi. If the length of these rivers be not in the same proportion with that of the Mississippi, the difference is balanced by the circumstance that both Banks in the former case belong to the United States.

With a view to perfect harmony between the two nations a cession of the Floridas is particularly to be desired, as obviating serious controversies that might otherwise grow even out of the regulations however liberal in the opinion of France, which she may establish at the Mouth of those rivers. One of the rivers, the Mobile, is said to be at present navigable for 400 miles above the 31° of latitude, and the navigation may no doubt be opened still further. On all of them, the Country within the Boundary of the United States, tho' otherwise between that and the sea, is fertile. Settlements on it are beginning; and the people have already called on the Government to procure the proper outlets to foreign Markets. The President accordingly, gave some time ago, the proper instructions to the Minister of the United States at Madrid. In fact, our free communication with the sea thro' these channels is so natural, so reasonable, and so essential that eventually it must take place, and in prudence therefore ought to be amicably and effectually adjusted without delay.

A further object with France may be, to form a Colonial establishment having a convenient relation to her West India Islands, and forming an independent source of supplies for them.

This object ought to weigh but little against the Cession we wish to obtain for two reasons, 1st. Because the Country which the Cession will leave in her hands on the right side of the Mississippi is capable of employing more than all the faculties she can spare for such an object and of yielding all the supplies which she could expect, or wish from such an establishment: 2d. Because in times of general peace, she will be sure of receiving whatever supplies her Islands may want from the United States, and even thro' the Mississippi if more convenient to her; because in time of peace with the United States, tho' of War with Great Britain, the same sources will be open to her, whilst her own would be interrupted; and because in case of war with the United States, which is not likely to happen without a concurrent war with Great Britain (the only case in which she could need a distinct fund of supplies) the entire command of the sea, and of the trade thro' the Mississippi, would be against her, and would cut off the source in question. She would consequently never need the aid of her new Colony, but when she could make little or no use of it.

There may be other objects with France in the projected acquisition; but they are probably such as would be either satisfied by a reservation to herself of the Country on the right side of the Mississippi, or are of too subordinate a character to prevail against the plan of adjustment we have in view; in case other difficulties in the way of it can be overcome. The principles and outlines of this plan are as follows viz.

Ist

France cedes to the United States forever, the Territory East of the River Mississippi, comprehending the two Floridas, the Island of New Orleans and the Island lying to the North and East of that channel of the said River, which is commonly called the Mississippi, together with all such other Islands as appertain to either West or East Florida; France reserving to herself all her territory on the West side of the Mississippi.

II

The boundary between the Territories ceded and reserved by France shall be a continuation of that already defined above the 31st degree of North Latitude viz, the middle of the channel or bed of the river, thro' the said South pass to the sea. The navigation of the river Mississippi in its whole breadth from its source to the ocean, and in all its passages to and from the same shall be equally free and common to citizens of the United States and of the French Republic.

III

The vessels and citizens of the French Republic may exercise commerce to and at such places on their respective shores below the said thirty first degree of North Latitude as may be allowed for that use by the parties to their respective citizens and vessels. And it is agreed that no other Nation shall be allowed to exercise commerce to or at the same or any other place on either shore, below the said thirty first degree of Latitude. For the term of ten years to be computed from the exchange of the ratifications hereof, the citizens, vessels and merchandizes of the United States and of France shall be subject to no other duties on their respective shores below the said thirty first degree of latitude than are imposed on their own citizens, vessels and merchandizes. No duty whatever shall, after the expiration of ten years be laid on Articles the growth or manufacture of the United States or of the ceded Territory exported thro' the Mississippi in French vessels, so long as such articles so exported in vessels of the United States shall be exempt from duty: nor shall French vessels exporting such articles, ever afterwards be subject to pay a higher duty than vessels of the United States.

IV

The citizens of France may, for the term of ten years, deposit their effects at New Orleans and at such other places on the ceded shore of the Mississippi, as are allowed for the commerce of the United States, without paying any other duty than a fair price for the hire of stores.

V

In the ports and commerce of West and East Florida, France shall never be on a worse footing than the most favored nations; and for the term of ten years her vessels and merchandize shall be subject therein to no higher duties than are paid by those of the United States and of the ceded Territory, exported in French vessels from any port in West or East Florida, [and] shall be exempt from duty as long as vessels of the United States shall enjoy this exemption.

VI

The United States, in consideration of the Cession of Territory made by this Treaty shall pay to France —————— millions of livres Tournois, in the manner following, viz, They shall pay ————— millions of livres tournois immediately on the exchange of the ratifications hereof: they shall assume in such order of priority as the Government of the United States may approve, the payment of claims, which have been or may be acknowledged by the French Republic to be due to American citizens, or so much thereof as with the payment to be made on the exchange of ratifications will not exceed the sum of ————— and in case a balance should remain due after such payment and assumption, the same shall be paid at the end of one year from the final liquidation of the claims hereby assumed, which shall be payable in three equal annual payments, the first of which is to take place one year after the exchange of ratifications or they shall bear interest at the rate of six per cent per annum from the date of such intended payments; until they shall be discharged. All the above mentioned payments shall be made at the Treasury of the United States and at the rate of one dollar and ten cents for every six livres tournois.

VII

To incorporate the inhabitants of the hereby ceded territory with the citizens of the United States on an equal footing, being a provision, which cannot now be made, it is to be expected, from the character and policy of the United States, that such incorporation will take place without unnecessary delay. In the meantime they shall be secure in their persons and property, and in the free enjoyment of their religion. . . .

23. Beyond Peaceable Coercion:
The Case for War

The ponderous sentences of Madison's war message suggest not so much a brave call to arms in a noble cause as a reluctant farewell to the Republican enterprise of "peace, commerce, and honest friendship with all nations," announced by Jefferson in 1801. According to Virginia teachings, Federalism had cursed America with a senseless war and its attendant evils of militarism and political oppression. The Republican administration at once confirmed the promise of a new departure in foreign policy by cutting the army and navy to the bone. If the belligerent European powers, perversely refusing the offer of impartial friendship and commerce, should violate America's neutral rights, the Republicans would try an experiment in "peaceable coercion" that Madison and Jefferson had first proposed in the 1790s. So long as the great powers, especially Great Britain

---

War Message to Congress, June 1, 1812, in James D. Richardson, ed., *A Compilation of the Messages and Papers of the Presidents, 1789–1897* (Washington: Government Printing Office, 1896), I, pp. 484–490.

with its western colonies, needed American agricultural staples and hungered after the growing American market for manufactures, the United States could use economic rewards and punishments, through the regulation of foreign commerce, in place of troops and frigates. (See Document 20.) For a few happy years, the country reaped the rich though risky profits of neutral trade without facing a critical test of the new foreign policy.

After 1805, the embattled French and British attacked neutral commerce with a vengeance, seizing American ships, cargoes, and—in the case of the British—sailors presumed to be deserters. The Republican policy of peaceful economic coercion, applied through Non-Importation, Embargo, and Non-Intercourse acts, failed to deter the belligerents, while imposing severe losses on the American economy and subjecting citizens to detailed and arbitrary controls beyond anything the Federalists had imposed. A rising Federalist opposition centered in New England fed on the administration's troubles, and a younger generation of Republican War Hawks urged aggressive action. Soon after his election to the presidency in 1809, Madison began to prepare for a final decision, proceeding on the silent premiss that British sea power posed a deadlier threat to American rights and interests than did Napoleon's domination of the European continent. With a flimsy French promise of concessions for justification, the United States broke off economic relations with Britain under the provisions of the Non-Intercourse Act. Hastily and clumsily the Republican administration tried to gather and organize fighting forces. New federal loans and taxes were painfully extracted. On June 1, 1812, Madison invited Congress to declare war. A strong anti-war minority in the Senate reflected the deep partisan and sectional antagonisms that would harass the President throughout the conflict. He signed the declaration on June 18, just a day after the British, in a sharp reversal of their American policy, repealed their offending trade restrictions. When the news from England reached Washington on July 27, it seemed too late to reverse the war decision.

Madison offered Americans a sober case for choosing to fight rather than surrender the maritime rights of a neutral nation and the honor of a free people. His public argument detached the American quarrel with Great Britain over impressment, blockades, and spoliations from the fundamental issues and consequences of the larger European conflict. Within such limited terms, he could formulate neither a grand strategy for the war within a war nor a long view of the ends and means of foreign policy. Of the Republican search for an alternative to traditional power politics, Madison could conclude only that British arrogance and greed had defeated the patient effort to find peace through the appeal to enlightened economic interest and the law of nations. (He believed, but did not say, that the arrogance and greed of Yankee Federalists had given essential aid and comfort to the British.) In short, avoiding serious political and military analysis of the crisis, Madison presented respectable legal and moral grounds for war.

Washington, June 1, 1812.

TO THE SENATE AND HOUSE OF REPRESENTATIVES
OF THE UNITED STATES

I communicate to Congress certain documents, being a continuation of those heretofore laid before them on the subject of our affairs with Great Britain.

Without going back beyond the renewal in 1803 of the war in which Great Britain is engaged, and omitting unrepaired wrongs of inferior magnitude, the conduct of her Government presents a series of acts hostile to the United States as an independent and neutral nation.

British cruisers have been in the continued practice of violating the American flag on the great highway of nations, and of seizing and carrying off persons sailing under it, not in the exercise of a belligerent right founded on the law of nations against an enemy, but of a municipal prerogative over British subjects. British jurisdiction is thus extended to neutral vessels in a situation where no laws can operate but the law of nations and the laws of the country to which the vessels belong, and a self-redress is assumed which, if British subjects were wrongfully detained and alone concerned, is that substitution of force for a resort to the responsible sovereign which falls within the definition of war. Could the seizure of British subjects in such cases be regarded as within the exercise of a belligerent right, the acknowledged laws of war, which forbid an article of captured property to be adjudged without a regular investigation before a competent tribunal, would imperiously demand the fairest trial where the sacred rights of persons were at issue. In place of such a trial these rights are subjected to the will of every petty commander.

The practice, hence, is so far from affecting British subjects alone that, under the pretext of searching for these, thousands of American citizens, under the safeguard of public law and of their national flag, have been torn from their country and from everything dear to them; have been dragged on board ships of war of a foreign nation and exposed, under the severities of their discipline, to be exiled to the most distant and deadly climes, to risk their lives in the battles of their oppressors, and to be the melancholy instruments of taking away those of their own brethren.

Against this crying enormity, which Great Britain would be so prompt to avenge if committed against herself, the United States have in vain exhausted remonstrances and expostulations, and that no proof might be wanting of their conciliatory dispositions, and no pretext left for a continuance of the practice, the British Government was formally assured of the readiness of the United States to enter into arrangements such as could not be rejected if the recovery of British subjects were the real and the sole object. The communication passed without effect.

British cruisers have been in the practice also of violating the rights and the peace of our coasts. They hover over and harass our entering and departing commerce. To the most insulting pretensions they have added the most lawless proceedings in our very harbors, and have wantonly spilt American blood within the sanctuary of our territorial jurisdiction. The principles and rules enforced by that nation, when a neutral nation, against armed vessels of belligerents hovering near her coasts and disturbing her commerce are well known. When called on, nevertheless, by the United States to punish the greater offenses committed by her own vessels, her Government has bestowed on their commanders additional marks of honor and confidence.

Under pretended blockades, without the presence of an adequate force and sometimes without the practicability of applying one, our commerce has been plundered in every sea, the great staples of our country have been cut off from their legitimate markets, and a destructive blow aimed at our agricultural and maritime interests. In aggravation of these predatory measures they have been considered as in force from the dates of their notification, a retrospective effect being thus added, as has been done in other important cases, to the unlawfulness of the course pursued. And to render the outrage the more signal these mock blockades have been reiterated and enforced in the face of official communications from the British Government declaring as the true definition of a legal blockade "that particular ports must be actually invested and previous warning given to vessels bound to them not to enter."

Not content with these occasional expedients for laying waste our neutral trade, the cabinet of Britain resorted at length to the sweeping system of blockades, under the name of orders in council, which has been molded and managed as might best suit its political views, its commercial jealousies, or the avidity of British cruisers.

To our remonstrances against the complicated and transcendent injustice of this innovation the first reply was that the orders were reluctantly adopted by Great Britain as a necessary retaliation on decrees of her enemy proclaiming a general blockade of the British Isles at a time when the naval force of that enemy dared not issue from his own ports. She was reminded without effect that her own prior blockades, unsupported by an adequate naval force actually applied and continued, were a bar to this plea; that executed edicts against millions of our property could not be retaliation on edicts confessedly impossible to be executed; that retaliation, to be just, should fall on the party setting the guilty example, not on an innocent party which was not even chargeable with an acquiescence in it.

When deprived of this flimsy veil for a prohibition of our trade with her enemy by the repeal of his prohibition of our trade with Great Britain, her cabinet, instead of a corresponding repeal or a practical discontinuance of its orders, formally avowed a determination to persist in them against the United States until the markets of her enemy should be laid open to British products, thus asserting an obligation on a neutral power to require one belligerent to encourage by its internal regulations the trade of another belligerent, contradicting her own practice toward all nations, in peace as well as in war, and betraying the insincerity of those professions which inculcated a belief that, having resorted to her orders with regret, she was anxious to find an occasion for putting an end to them.

Abandoning still more all respect for the neutral rights of the United States and for its own consistency, the British Government now demands as prerequisites to a repeal of its orders as they relate to the United States that a formality should be observed in the repeal of the French decrees nowise necessary to their termination nor exemplified by British usage, and that the French repeal, besides including that portion of the decrees which operates within a territorial jurisdiction, as well as that which operates on the high seas, against the commerce of the United States should not be a single and special repeal in relation to the United States, but should be extended to whatever other neutral nations unconnected with them may be affected by those decrees. And as an additional insult, they are called on for a formal disavowal of conditions and pretensions advanced by the French Government for which the United States are so far from having made themselves responsible that, in official explanations which have been published to the world, and in a correspondence of the American minister at London with the British minister for foreign affairs such a responsibility was explicitly and emphatically disclamed.

It has become, indeed, sufficiently certain that the commerce of the United States is to be sacrificed, not as interfering with the belligerent rights of Great Britain; not as supplying the wants of her enemies, which she herself supplies; but as interfering with the monopoly which she covets for her own commerce and navigation. She carries on a war against the lawful commerce of a friend that she may the better carry on a commerce with an enemy—a commerce polluted by the forgeries and perjuries which are for the most part the only passports by which it can succeed.

Anxious to make every experiment short of the last resort of injured nations, the United States have withheld from Great Britain, under successive modifications, the benefits of a free intercourse with their market, the loss of which could not but outweigh the profits accruing from her restrictions of our commerce with other nations. And to entitle these experiments to the more favorable consideration they were so framed as to enable her to place her adversary under the exclusive operation of them. To these appeals her Government has been equally inflexible, as if willing to make sacrifices of every sort rather than yield to the claims of justice or renounce the errors of a false pride. Nay, so far were the attempts carried to overcome the attachment of the British cabinet to its unjust edicts that it received every encouragement within the competency of the executive branch of our Government to expect that a repeal of them would be followed by a war between the United States and France, unless the French edicts should also be repealed. Even this communication, although silencing forever the plea of a disposition in the United States to acquiesce in those edicts originally the sole plea for them, received no attention.

If no other proof existed of a predetermination of the British Government against a repeal of its orders, it might be found in the correspondence of the minister plenipotentiary of the United States at London and the British secretary for foreign affairs in 1810, on the question whether the blockade of May, 1806, was considered as in force or as not in force. It had been ascertained that the French Government, which urged this blockade as the ground of its Berlin decree, was willing in the event of its removal to repeal that decree, which, being followed by alternate repeals of the other offensive edicts, might abolish the whole system on both sides. This inviting opportunity for accomplishing an object so important to the United States, and professed so often to be the desire of both the belligerents, was made known to the British Government. As that Government admits that an actual application of an adequate force is necessary to the existence of a legal blockade, and it was notorious that if such a force had ever been applied its long discontinuance had annulled the blockade in question, there could be no sufficient objection on the part of Great Britain to a formal revocation of it, and no imaginable objection to a declaration of the fact that the blockade did not exist. The declaration would have been consistent with her avowed principles of blockade, and would have enabled the United States to demand from France the pledged repeal of her decrees, either with success, in which case the way would have been opened for a general repeal of the belligerent edicts, or without success, in which case the United States would have been justified in turning their measures exclusively against France. The British Government would, however, neither rescind the blockade nor declare its nonexistence, nor permit its nonexistence to be inferred and affirmed by the American plenipotentiary. On the contrary, by representing the blockade to be comprehended in the orders in council, the United States were compelled so to regard it in their subsequent proceedings.

There was a period when a favorable change in the policy of the British cabinet was justly considered as established. The minister plenipotentiary of His Britannic Majesty here proposed an adjustment of the differences more immediately endangering the harmony of the two countries. The proposition was accepted with the promptitude and cordiality corresponding with the invariable professions of this Government. A foundation appeared to be laid for a sincere and lasting reconciliation. The prospect, however, quickly vanished. The whole proceeding was disavowed by the British Government without any explanations which could at that time repress the belief that the disavowal proceeded from a spirit of hostility to the commercial rights and prosperity of the United States; and it has since come into proof that at the very moment when the public minister was holding the language of friendship and inspiring confidence in the sincerity of the negotiation with which he was charged a secret agent of his Government was employed in intrigues having for their object a subversion of our Government and a dismemberment of our happy union.

In reviewing the conduct of Great Britain toward the United States our attention is necessarily drawn to the warfare just renewed by the savages on one of our extensive frontiers—a warfare which is known to spare neither age nor sex and to be distinguished by features peculiarly shocking to humanity. It is difficult to account for the activity and combinations which have for some time been developing themselves among tribes in constant intercourse with British traders and garrisons without connecting their hostility with that influence and without recollecting the authenticated examples of such interpositions heretofore furnished by the officers and agents of that Government.

Such is the spectacle of injuries and indignities which have been heaped on our country, and such the crisis which its unexampled forbearance and conciliatory efforts have not been able to avert. It might at least have been expected that an enlightened nation, if less urged by moral obligations or invited by friendly dispositions on the part of the United States, would have found in its true interest alone a sufficient motive to respect their rights and their tranquillity on the high seas; that an enlarged policy would have favored that free and general circulation of commerce in which the British nation is at all times interested, and which in times of war is the best alleviation of its calamities to herself as well as to other belligerents; and more especially that the British cabinet would not, for the sake of a precarious and surreptitious intercourse with hostile markets, have persevered in a course of measures which necessarily put at hazard the invaluable market of a great and growing country, disposed to cultivate the mutual advantages of an active commerce.

Other counsels have prevailed. Our moderation and conciliation have had no other effect than to encourage perseverance and to enlarge pretensions. We behold our seafaring citizens still the daily victims of lawless violence, committed on the great common and highway of nations, even within sight of the country which owes them protection. We behold our vessels, freighted with the products of our soil and industry, or returning with the honest proceeds of them, wrested from their lawful destinations, confiscated by prize courts no longer the organs of public law but the instruments of arbitrary edicts, and their unfortunate crews dispersed and lost, or forced or inveigled in British ports into British fleets, whilst arguments are employed in support of these aggressions which have no foundation but in a principle equally supporting a claim to regulate our external commerce in all cases whatsoever.

We behold, in fine, on the side of Great Britain a state of war against the United States, and on the side of the United States a state of peace toward Great Britain.

Whether the United States shall continue passive under these progressive usurpations and these accumulating wrongs, or, opposing force to force in defense of their national rights, shall commit a just cause into the hands of the Almighty Disposer of Events, avoiding all connections which might entangle it in the contest or views of other powers, and preserving a constant readiness to concur in an honorable reestablishment of peace and friendship, is a solemn question which the Constitution wisely confides to the legislative department of the Government. In recommending it to their early deliberations I am happy in the assurance that the decision will be worthy the enlightened and patriotic councils of a virtuous, a free, and a powerful nation.

Having presented this view of the relations of the United States with Great Britain and of the solemn alternative growing out of them, I proceed to remark that the communications last made to Congress on the subject of our relations with France will have shewn that since the revocation of her decrees, as they violated the neutral rights of the United States, her Government has authorized illegal captures by its privateers and public ships, and that other outrages have been practiced on our vessels and our citizens. It will have been seen also that no indemnity had been provided or satisfactorily pledged for the extensive spoliations committed under the violent and retrospective orders of the French Government against the property of our citizens seized within the jurisdiction of France. I abstain at this time from recommending to the consideration of Congress definitive measures with respect to that nation, in the expectation that the result of unclosed discussions between our minister plenipotentiary at Paris and the French Government will speedily enable Congress to decide with greater advantage on the course due to the rights, the interests, and the honor of our country.

24. Broad Construction: Lessons of the War

The Treaty of Ghent, signed on December 24, 1814, and ratified by the U. S. Senate the following February, simply closed hostilities and left all the issues of the war open to future negotiations. To the President and the nation, a peace restoring the pre-war status quo seemed a marvelous triumph. Madison's initial hopes for a better result were quickly doomed by the failure of his plan for a sudden invasion of Canada and, above all, by the wholly unexpected decline of French power, beginning with the destruction of Napoleon's Grand Army in Russia during the winter of 1812. After the fall of Paris in March, 1814, the British were free to throw their full strength into the American war. An empty treasury, widespread economic distress, ominous stirrings of resistance in New England—these together

Seventh Annual Message to Congress, December 5, 1815, in James D. Richardson, ed., *A Compilation of the Messages and Papers of the Presidents, 1789–1897* (Washington: Government Printing Office, 1896), I, pp. 547–554.

with the bleak military prospect in 1814 gave Americans every reason to welcome a peace without victory. Besides, the original issue of neutral maritime rights had lost its immediate significance with the close of the European war. On the British side, the accumulated burdens of a twenty-year struggle for Europe and the prohibitive cost of winning a decisive victory in America argued for the settlement.

Madison's Message to Congress of December 5, 1815, drew from the war experience both heartening and cautionary lessons that would turn Republican policy in new directions. In short retrospect, America's bumbling, half-hearted war became a source of national pride. The young republic had defied the awesome power of the British on a vital point of honor and interest and—if nothing more—survived the test intact. Yet Madison as war president had felt the alarming weakness of the nation under stress. Lacking effective military forces, and the financial, industrial, and transportation facilities and resources needed to sustain them, he had to lead a deeply divided country against a formidable enemy. The swelling sense of national pride demanded an ambitious view of the American future; the experience of national weakness pointed to a program that could realize the possibility. For Madison and many of his supporters, the old Virginia Republican doctrines, built on the fear of centralized power, faded into the background. In cautious, measured language he invoked the founding spirit that encouraged the broad use of federal authority to provide for the common defense, promote the general welfare, and link Americans in closer union. The most conspicuous products of post-war Republicanism were a moderate tariff to sustain the wartime growth of manufactures, especially cheap cottons, and the Second Bank of the United States, both approved by Madison in 1816. The creative force behind this post-war nationalism, however, came not from Madison but rather from a new breed of young Republicans, represented notably by John C. Calhoun.

Washington, December 5, 1815.

I have the satisfaction on our present meeting of being able to communicate to you the successful termination of the war which had been commenced against the United States by the Regency of Algiers. The squadron in advance on that service, under Commodore Decatur, lost not a moment after its arrival in the Mediterranean in seeking the naval force of the enemy then cruising in that sea, and succeeded in capturing two of his ships, one of them the principal ship, commanded by the Algerine admiral. The high character of the American commander was brilliantly sustained on the occasion which brought his own ship into close action with that of his adversary, as was the accustomed gallantry of all the officers and men actually engaged. Having prepared the way by this demonstration of American skill and prowess, he hastened to the port of Algiers, where peace was promptly yielded to his victorious force. In the terms stipulated the rights and honor of the United States were particularly consulted by a perpetual relinquishment on the part of the Dey of all pretensions to tribute from them. The impressions which have thus been made, strengthened as they will have been by subsequent transactions with the Regencies of Tunis and of Tripoli by the appearance of the larger force which followed under Commodore Bainbridge, the chief in command of the expedition, and by the judicious precautionary arrangements left by him in that quarter, afford a reasonable prospect of future security for the valuable portion of our commerce which passes within reach of the Barbary cruisers.

It is another source of satisfaction that the treaty of peace with Great Britain has been succeeded by a convention on the subject of commerce concluded by the plenipotentiaries of the two countries. In this result a disposition is manifested on the part of that nation corresponding with the disposition of the United States, which it may be hoped will be improved into liberal arrangements on other subjects on which the parties have mutual interests, or which might endanger their future harmony. Congress will decide on the expediency of promoting such a sequel by giving effect to the measure of confining the American navigation to American seamen—a measure which, at the same time that it might have that conciliatory tendency, would have the further advantage of increasing the independence of our navigation and the resources for our maritime defense.

In conformity with the articles in the treaty of Ghent relating to the Indians, as well as with a view to the tranquillity of our western and northwestern frontiers, measures were taken to establish an immediate peace with the several tribes who had been engaged in hostilities against the United States. Such of them as were invited to Detroit acceded readily to a renewal of the former treaties of friendship. Of the other tribes who were invited to a station on the Mississippi the greater number have also accepted the peace offered to them. The residue, consisting of the more distant tribes or parts of tribes, remain to be brought over by further explanations, or by such other means as may be adapted to the dispositions they may finally disclose.

The Indian tribes within and bordering on the southern frontier, whom a cruel war on their part had compelled us to chastise into peace, have latterly shown a restlessness which has called for preparatory measures for repressing it, and for protecting the commissioners engaged in carrying the terms of the peace into execution.

The execution of the act for fixing the military peace establishment has been attended with difficulties which even now can only be overcome by legislative aid. The selection of officers, the payment and discharge of the troops enlisted for the war, the payment of the retained troops and their reunion from detached and distant stations, the collection and security of the public property in the Quartermaster, Commissary, and Ordnance departments, and the constant medical assistance required in hospitals and garrisons rendered a complete execution of the act impracticable on the 1st of May, the period more immediately contemplated. As soon, however, as circumstances would permit, and as far as it has been practicable consistently with the public interests, the reduction of the Army has been accomplished; but the appropriations for its pay and for other branches of the military service having proved inadequate, the earliest attention to that subject will be necessary; and the expediency of continuing upon the peace establishment the staff officers who have hitherto been provisionally retained is also recommended to the consideration of Congress.

In the performance of the Executive duty upon this occasion there has not been wanting a just sensibility to the merits of the American Army during the late war; but the obvious policy and design in fixing an efficient military peace establishment did not afford an opportunity to distinguish the aged and infirm on account of their past services nor the wounded and disabled on account of their present sufferings. The extent of the reduction, indeed, unavoidably involved the exclusion of many meritorious officers of every rank from the service of their country; and so equal as well as so numerous were the claims to attention that a decision by the standard of comparative merit could seldom be attained. Judged, however, in candor by a general standard of positive merit, the Army Register will, it is believed, do honor to the establishment, while the case of those officers whose names are not included in it devolves with the strongest interest upon the legislative authority for such provision as shall be deemed the best calculated to give support and solace to the veteran and the invalid, to display the beneficence as well as the justice of the Government, and to inspire a martial zeal for the public service upon every future emergency.

Although the embarrassments arising from the want of an

uniform national currency have not been diminished since the adjournment of Congress, great satisfaction has been derived in contemplating the revival of the public credit and the efficiency of the public resources. The receipts into the Treasury from the various branches of revenue during the nine months ending on the 30th of September last have been estimated at $12,-500,000; the issues of Treasury notes of every denomination during the same period amounted to the sum of $14,000,000, and there was also obtained upon loan during the same period a sum of $9,000,000, of which the sum of $6,000,000 was subscribed in cash and the sum of $3,000,000 in Treasury notes. With these means, added to the sum of $1,500,000, being the balance of money in the Treasury on the 1st day of January, there has been paid between the 1st of January and the 1st of October on account of the appropriations of the preceding and of the present year (exclusively of the amount of the Treasury notes subscribed to the loan and of the amount redeemed in the payment of duties and taxes) the aggregate sum of $33,-500,000, leaving a balance then in the Treasury estimated at the sum of $3,000,000. Independent, however, of the arrearages due for military services and supplies, it is presumed that a further sum of $5,000,000, including the interest on the public debt payable on the 1st of January next, will be demanded at the Treasury to complete the expenditures of the present year, and for which the existing ways and means will sufficiently provide.

The national debt, as it was ascertained on the 1st of October last, amounted in the whole to the sum of $120,000,000, consisting of the unredeemed balance of the debt contracted before the late war ($39,000,000), the amount of the funded debt contracted in consequence of the war ($64,000,000), and the amount of the unfunded and floating debt, including the various issues of Treasury notes, $17,000,000, which is in a gradual course of payment. There will probably be some addition to the public debt upon the liquidation of various claims which are depending, and a conciliatory disposition on the part of

Congress may lead honorably and advantageously to an equitable arrangement of the militia expenses incurred by the several States without the previous sanction or authority of the Government of the United States; but when it is considered that the new as well as the old portion of the debt has been contracted in the assertion of the national rights and independence, and when it is recollected that the public expenditures, not being exclusively bestowed upon subjects of a transient nature, will long be visible in the number and equipments of the American Navy, in the military works for the defense of our harbors and our frontiers, and in the supplies of our arsenals and magazines the amount will bear a gratifying comparison with the objects which have been attained, as well as with the resources of the country.

The arrangements of the finances with a view to the receipts and expenditures of a permanent peace establishment will necessarily enter into the deliberations of Congress during the present session. It is true that the improved condition of the public revenue will not only afford the means of maintaining the faith of the Government with its creditors inviolate, and of prosecuting successfully the measures of the most liberal policy, but will also justify an immediate alleviation of the burdens imposed by the necessities of the war. It is, however, essential to every modification of the finances that the benefits of an uniform national currency should be restored to the community. The absence of the precious metals will, it is believed, be a temporary evil, but until they can again be rendered the general medium of exchange it devolves on the wisdom of Congress to provide a substitute which shall equally engage the confidence and accommodate the wants of the citizens throughout the Union. If the operation of the State banks can not produce this result, the probable operation of a national bank will merit consideration; and if neither of these expedients be deemed effectual it may become necessary to ascertain the terms upon which the notes of the Government (no longer required as an instrument of credit) shall be issued upon motives of general policy as a common medium of circulation.

Notwithstanding the security for future repose which the United States ought to find in their love of peace and their constant respect for the rights of other nations, the character of the times particularly inculcates the lesson that, whether to prevent or repel danger, we ought not to be unprepared for it. This consideration will sufficiently recommend to Congress a liberal provision for the immediate extension and gradual completion of the works of defense, both fixed and floating, on our maritime frontier, and an adequate provision for guarding our inland frontier against dangers to which certain portions of it may continue to be exposed.

As an improvement in our military establishment, it will deserve the consideration of Congress whether a corps of invalids might not be so organized and employed as at once to aid in the support of meritorious individuals excluded by age or infirmities from the existing establishment, and to procure to the public the benefit of their stationary services and of their exemplary discipline. I recommend also an enlargement of the Military Academy already established, and the establishment of others in other sections of the Union; and I can not press too much on the attention of Congress such a classification and organization of the militia as will most effectually render it the safeguard of a free state. If experience has shewn in the recent splendid achievements of militia the value of this resource for the public defense, it has shewn also the importance of that skill in the use of arms and that familiarity with the essential rules of discipline which can not be expected from the regulations now in force. With this subject is intimately connected the necessity of accommodating the laws in every respect to the great object of enabling the political authority of the Union to employ promptly and effectually the physical power of the Union in the cases designated by the Constitution.

The signal services which have been rendered by our Navy

and the capacities it has developed for successful cooperation in the national defense will give to that portion of the public force its full value in the eyes of Congress, at an epoch which calls for the constant vigilance of all governments. To preserve the ships now in a sound state, to complete those already contemplated, to provide amply the imperishable materials for prompt augmentations, and to improve the existing arrangements into more advantageous establishments for the construction, the repairs, and the security of vessels of war is dictated by the soundest policy.

In adjusting the duties on imports to the object of revenue the influence of the tariff on manufactures will necessarily present itself for consideration. However wise the theory may be which leaves to the sagacity and interest of individuals the application of their industry and resources, there are in this as in other cases exceptions to the general rule. Besides the condition which the theory itself implies of a reciprocal adoption by other nations, experience teaches that so many circumstances must concur in introducing and maturing manufacturing establishments, especially of the more complicated kinds, that a country may remain long without them, although sufficiently advanced and in some respects even peculiarly fitted for carrying them on with success. Under circumstances giving a powerful impulse to manufacturing industry it has made among us a progress and exhibited an efficiency which justify the belief that with a protection not more than is due to the enterprising citizens whose interests are now at stake it will become at an early day not only safe against occasional competitions from abroad, but a source of domestic wealth and even of external commerce. In selecting the branches more especially entitled to the public patronage a preference is obviously claimed by such as will relieve the United States from a dependence on foreign supplies, ever subject to casual failures, for articles necessary for the public defense or connected with the primary wants of individuals. It will be an additional recommendation of particular manufactures where the materials for them are extensively drawn from our agriculture, and consequently impart and insure to that great fund of national prosperity and independence an encouragement which can not fail to be rewarded.

Among the means of advancing the public interest the occasion is a proper one for recalling the attention of Congress to the great importance of establishing throughout our country the roads and canals which can best be executed under the national authority. No objects within the circle of political economy so richly repay the expense bestowed on them; there are none the utility of which is more universally ascertained and acknowledged; none that do more honor to the governments whose wise and enlarged patriotism duly appreciates them. Nor is there any country which presents a field where nature invites more the art of man to complete her own work for his accommodation and benefit. These considerations are strengthened, moreover, by the political effect of these facilities for intercommunication in bringing and binding more closely together the various parts of our extended confederacy. Whilst the States individually, with a laudable enterprise and emulation, avail themselves of their local advantages by new roads, by navigable canals, and by improving the streams susceptible of navigation, the General Government is the more urged to similar undertakings, requiring a national jurisdiction and national means, by the prospect of thus systematically completing so inestimable a work; and it is a happy reflection that any defect of constitutional authority which may be encountered can be supplied in a mode which the Constitution itself has providently pointed out.

The present is a favorable season also for bringing again into view the establishment of a national seminary of learning within the District of Columbia, and with means drawn from the property therein, subject to the authority of the General Government. Such an institution claims the patronage of Congress as a monument of their solicitude for the advancement of knowledge, without which the blessings of liberty can not be fully enjoyed or long preserved; as a model instructive in the formation of other seminaries; as a nursery of enlightened preceptors, and as a central resort of youth and genius from every part of their country, diffusing on their return examples of those national feelings, those liberal sentiments, and those congenial manners which contribute cement to our Union and strength to the great political fabric of which that is the foundation.

In closing this communication I ought not to repress a sensibility, in which you will unite, to the happy lot of our country and to the goodness of a superintending Providence, to which we are indebted for it. Whilst other portions of mankind are laboring under the distresses of war or struggling with adversity in other forms, the United States are in the tranquil enjoyment of prosperous and honorable peace. In reviewing the scenes through which it has been attained we can rejoice in the proofs given that our political institutions, founded in human rights and framed for their preservation, are equal to the severest trials of war, as well as adapted to the ordinary periods of repose. As fruits of this experience and of the reputation acquired by the American arms on the land and on the water, the nation finds itself possessed of a growing respect abroad and of a just confidence in itself, which are among the best pledges for its peaceful career. Under other aspects of our country the strongest features of its flourishing condition are seen in a population rapidly increasing on a territory as productive as it is extensive; in a general industry and fertile ingenuity which find their ample rewards, and in an affluent revenue which admits a reduction of the public burdens without withdrawing the means of sustaining the public credit, of gradually discharging the public debt, of providing for the necessary defensive and precautionary establishments, and of patronizing in every authorized mode undertakings conducive to the aggregate wealth and individual comfort of our citizens.

It remains for the guardians of the public welfare to persevere in that justice and good will toward other nations which invite a return of these sentiments toward the United States; to cherish institutions which guarantee their safety and their liberties, civil and religious; and to combine with a liberal system of foreign commerce an improvement of the national advantages and a protection and extension of the independent resources of our highly favored and happy country.

In all measures having such objects my faithful cooperation will be afforded.

25. Strict Construction: The Old Cause

Madison's veto of the Bonus bill, embodying a comprehensive plan for internal improvements, laid down the constitutional limits of Republican nationalism. His veto message, sent on March 3, 1817, was his farewell address to the American people: a quiet call to keep the old Republican faith. Once more, as in the 1790s, Madison warned against a rule of constitutional interpretation that could be used to sweep all legislative powers into the center, rob the states of their authority, and thus destroy the compact on which the federal union rested. Precisely because he favored internal improvements on policy grounds, his constitutional principles stood out in bold relief. Yet those principles were not so clear and fixed as his language suggested. Madison had not felt obliged to apply them to the national bank bill that he signed in 1816, although he could have cited his own constitutional arguments of 1791 against

Veto Message, March 3, 1817, in James D. Richardson, ed., *A Compilation of the Messages and Papers of the Presidents, 1789–1897* (Washington: Government Printing Office, 1896), I, pp. 569–570.

Hamilton's first bank. Consistent precedent and settled public opinion changed his view of the constitutional authority to create a bank.

There were precedents and sentiments favoring national support of internal improvements as well, and the Jefferson and Madison administrations supplied them. The National Road from Cumberland, Maryland, across the mountains to Wheeling, Virginia, was a Republican enterprise authorized by Congress in 1806 with Jefferson's consent, and built between 1811 and 1818 under Madison's direction. Secretary of the Treasury Gallatin, in his Report of 1808, projected a system of national roads and waterways that would have dazzled Hamilton. Nevertheless, Madison could plausibly claim that precedent was too equivocal and national opinion too divided—as the close congressional vote on the Bonus bill testified—to justify a loose reading of the Constitution in this case. At any rate, he much preferred an explicit grant of power by constitutional amendment. This would meet the demand for roads and canals, and save the principle of strict construction. After his retirement, he continued to advocate both the amendment procedure, and the national transportation network that it would make possible. In practice, his veto, re-enforced by Presidents Monroe and Jackson, shifted the major responsibility for financing and constructing great public works to the several states.

March 3, 1817.

TO THE HOUSE OF REPRESENTATIVES OF THE UNITED STATES

Having considered the bill this day presented to me entitled "An act to set apart and pledge certain funds for internal improvements," and which sets apart and pledges funds "for constructing roads and canals, and improving the navigation of water courses, in order to facilitate, promote, and give security to internal commerce among the several States, and to render more easy and less expensive the means and provisions for the common defense," I am constrained by the insuperable difficulty I feel in reconciling the bill with the Constitution of the United States to return it with that objection to the House of Representatives, in which it originated.

The legislative powers vested in Congress are specified and enumerated in the eighth section of the first article of the Constitution, and it does not appear that the power proposed to be exercised by the bill is among the enumerated powers, or that it falls by any just interpretation within the power to make laws necessary and proper for carrying into execution those or other powers vested by the Constitution in the Government of the United States.

"The power to regulate commerce among the several States" can not include a power to construct roads and canals, and to improve the navigation of water courses in order to facilitate, promote, and secure such a commerce without a latitude of construction departing from the ordinary import of the terms strengthened by the known inconveniences which doubtless led to the grant of this remedial power to Congress.

To refer the power in question to the clause "to provide for the common defense and general welfare" would be contrary to the established and consistent rules of interpretation, as rendering the special and careful enumeration of powers which follow the clause nugatory and improper. Such a view of the Constitution would have the effect of giving to Congress a general power of legislation instead of the defined and limited one hitherto understood to belong to them, the terms "common defense and general welfare" embracing every object and act within the purview of a legislative trust. It would have the effect of subjecting both the Constitution and laws of the several States in all cases not specifically exempted to be superseded by laws of Congress, it being expressly declared "that the Constitution of the United States and laws made in pursuance thereof shall be the supreme law of the land, and the judges of every State shall be bound thereby, anything in the constitution or laws of any State to the contrary notwithstanding." Such a view of the Constitution, finally, would have the effect of excluding the judicial authority of the United States from its participation in guarding the boundary between the legislative powers of the General and the State Governments, inasmuch as questions relating to the general welfare, being questions of policy and expediency, are unsusceptible of judicial cognizance and decision.

A restriction of the power "to provide for the common defense and general welfare" to cases which are to be provided for by the expenditure of money would still leave within the legislative power of Congress all the great and most important measures of Government, money being the ordinary and necessary means of carrying them into execution.

If a general power to construct roads and canals, and to improve the navigation of water courses, with the train of powers incident thereto, be not possessed by Congress, the assent of the States in the mode provided in the bill can not confer the power. The only cases in which the consent and cession of particular States can extend the power of Congress are those specified and provided for in the Constitution.

I am not unaware of the great importance of roads and canals and the improved navigation of water courses, and that a power in the National Legislature to provide for them might be exercised with signal advantage to the general prosperity. But seeing that such a power is not expressly given by the Constitution, and believing that it can not be deduced from any part of it without an inadmissible latitude of construction and a reliance on insufficient precedents; believing also that the permanent success of the Constitution depends on a definite partition of powers between the General and the State Governments, and that no adequate landmarks would be left by the constructive extension of the powers of Congress as proposed in the bill, I have no option but to withhold my signature from it, and to cherishing the hope that its beneficial objects may be attained by a resort for the necessary powers to the same wisdom and virtue in the nation which established the Constitution in its actual form and providently marked out in the instrument itself a safe and practicable mode of improving it as experience might suggest.

Part Five

**REFLECTIONS:
THE ELDER STATESMAN**

26. Long Road to Freedom:
Voluntary Emancipation and Colonization

After the inauguration of his Virginia friend and heir apparent, James Monroe, Madison retired from public life. His political labors had spanned and shaped the history of the new republic. For nearly twenty years he would live quietly at Montpelier, the great family estate in the Virginia Piedmont, mixing the business of a planter with the moderate pleasures of a country gentleman. Despite falling tobacco markets, crop failures, and the heavy debts of a wastrel stepson, he drew a comfortable income from his lands and slaves. An easy ride could bring him to Jefferson's Monticello. Their ancient friendship gained fresh meaning from the joint work of planning and creating the University of Virginia. As a living representative of the heroic generation Madison received and answered a steady flow of letters seeking his views on American history or the questions of the day. Old companions, travelling dignitaries, and curious

To Robert J. Evans, June 15, 1819, in *Writings*, VIII, pp. 439–447.

strangers regularly descended on Montpelier: Lafayette, the shocking Fanny Wright, Jared Sparks the historian, Webster, Jackson, and many more. Madison's conversation and correspondence reveal an elder statesman who cared more for politics than for the broad philosophical speculations that attracted Jefferson and Adams in their later years. Thus Madison's writings of the last two decades form a commentary on the changing state of the nation and a mature reconsideration of his own political views.

The problem of slavery demanded a kind of political genius and daring and conviction beyond the capacity even of Madison, Jefferson, and their great generation of enlightened Virginia planters. They made a revolution and founded a new society on republican principles of freedom and equality. They detested the idea of slavery in any form. The American republic, they believed, could not endure permanently half slave and half free. At the same time, they acknowledged the presence of the peculiar institution as a tragic legacy of history, and managed to live at ease in their private world of slaves and masters. Their hopes for abolition were checked by the constant fear that any radical attack on slavery would throw the South into a fatal race war and destroy the Union. In any case, as Jefferson wrote, explaining why he had not introduced an emancipation bill with his proposed revisal of the laws of Virginia: "But it was found that the public mind would not yet bear the proposition. . . ." The early banning of slave imports by Virginia and, in 1808, by Congress, seemed to Madison and his friends a prudent and promising first step toward freedom; but slavery only grew and spread more vigorously.

As the peculiar institution extended and deepened its hold on Southern society, Madison placed his faith in the organized movement for gradual, voluntary emancipation, and the colonization of freedmen in Africa or some other remote region. He became a life member of the American Colonization Society, formed in 1817, and served as a vice-president of the Colonization Society of Virginia. In response to an inquiry from Robert

J. Evans, an antislavery advocate from Philadelphia, he elaborated an ambitious scheme for subsidizing the purchase and colonization of slaves out of the proceeds of public land sales. Thus the nation, for some $600 millions, could buy its way out of the tragic dilemma and make America all free and all white. Madison, as usual, asked that his private views on the sensitive slavery question remain confidential.

Montpellier, June 15, 1819.

Sir,—I have received your letter of the 3d instant, requesting such hints as may have occurred to me on the subject of an eventual extinguishment of slavery in the U. S.

Not doubting the purity of your views, and relying on the discretion by which they will be regulated, I cannot refuse such a compliance as will at least manifest my respect for the object of your undertaking.

A general emancipation of slaves ought to be 1. gradual. 2. equitable & satisfactory to the individuals immediately concerned. 3. consistent with the existing & durable prejudices of the nation.

That it ought, like remedies for other deeprooted and widespread evils, to be gradual, is so obvious that there seems to be no difference of opinion on that point.

To be equitable & satisfactory, the consent of both the Master & the slave should be obtained. That of the Master will require a provision in the plan for compensating a loss of what he held as property guarantied by the laws, and recognised by the Constitution. That of the slave, requires that his condition in a state of freedom, be preferable in his own estimation, to his actual one in a state of bondage.

To be consistent with existing and probably unalterable prejudices in the U. S. the freed blacks ought to be permanently removed beyond the region occupied by or allotted to a White population. The objections to a thorough incorporation of the two people are, with most of the Whites insuperable; and are admitted by all of them to be very powerful. If the blacks, strongly marked as they are by Physical & lasting peculiarities, be retained amid the Whites, under the degrading privation of equal rights political or social, they must be always dissatisfied with their condition as a change only from one to another species of oppression; always secretly confederated against the ruling & privileged class; and always uncontroulled by some of the most cogent motives to moral and respectable conduct. The character of the free blacks, even where their legal condition is least affected by their colour, seems to put these truths beyond question. It is material also that the removal of the blacks be to a distance precluding the jealousies & hostilities to be apprehended from a neighboring people stimulated by the contempt known to be entertained for their peculiar features; to say nothing of their vindictive recollections, or the predatory propensities which their State of Society might foster. Nor is it fair, in estimating the danger of Collisions with the Whites, to charge it wholly on the side of the Blacks. There would be reciprocal antipathies doubling the danger.

The colonizing plan on foot, has as far as it extends, a due regard to these requisites; with the additional object of bestowing new blessings civil & religious on the quarter of the Globe most in need of them. The Society proposes to transport to the African Coast all free & freed blacks who may be willing to remove thither; to provide by fair means, &, it is understood with a prospect of success, a suitable territory for their reception; and to initiate them into such an establishment as may gradually and indefinitely expand itself.

The experiment, under this view of it, merits encouragement from all who regard slavery as an evil, who wish to see it diminished and abolished by peaceable & just means; and who have themselves no better mode to propose. Those who have most doubted the success of the experiment must at least have wished to find themselves in an error.

But the views of the Society are limited to the case of blacks already free, or who may be *gratuitously* emancipated. To provide a commensurate remedy for the evil, the plan must be extended to the great Mass of blacks, and must embrace a fund sufficient to induce the Master as well as the slave to concur in it. Without the concurrence of the Master, the benefit will be very limited as it relates to the Negroes; and essentially defective, as it relates to the United States; and the concurrence of Masters, must, for the most part, be obtained by purchase.

Can it be hoped that voluntary contributions, however adequate to an auspicious commencement, will supply the sums necessary to such an enlargement of the remedy? May not another question be asked? Would it be reasonable to throw so great a burden on the individuals, distinguished by their philanthropy and patriotism?

The object to be obtained, as an object of humanity, appeals alike to all; as a National object, it claims the interposition of the nation. It is the nation which is to reap the benefit. The nation therefore ought to bear the burden.

Must then the enormous sums required to pay for, to transport, and to establish in a foreign land all the slaves in the U. S. as their Masters may be willing to part with them, be taxed on the good people of the U. S. or be obtained by loans swelling the public debt to a size pregnant with evils next in degree to those of slavery itself?

Happily it is not necessary to answer this question by remarking that if slavery as a national evil is to be abolished, and it be just that it be done at the national expence, the amount of the expence is not a paramount consideration. It is the peculiar fortune, or, rather a providential blessing of the U. S. to possess a resource commensurate to this great object, without taxes on the people, or even an increase of the public debt.

I allude to the vacant territory the extent of which is so vast, and the vendible value of which is so well ascertained.

Supposing the number of slaves to be 1,500,000, and their

price to average 400 dollars, the cost of the whole would be
600 millions of dollars. These estimates are probably beyond
the fact; and from the number of slaves should be deducted   1.
those whom their Masters would not part with. 2. those who
may be gratuitously set free by their Masters. 3. those acquiring freedom under emancipating regulations of the States. 4.
those preferring slavery where they are, to freedom in an African settlement. On the other hand, it is to be noted that the
expence of removal & settlement is not included in the estimated sum; and that an increase of the slaves will be going on
during the period required for the execution of the plan.

On the whole the aggregate sum needed may be stated at
about 600 millions of dollars.

This will require 200 millions of Acres at 3 dollars per Acre;
or 300 millions at 2 dollars per Acre a quantity which tho'
great in itself, is perhaps not a third part of the disposable territory belonging to the U. S. And to what object so good so
great & so glorious, could that peculiar fund of wealth be appropriated? Whilst the sale of territory would, on one hand be
planting one desert with a free & civilized people, it would on
the other, be giving freedom to another people, and filling with
them another desert. And if in any instances, wrong has been
done by our forefathers to people of one colour, by dispossess-
ing them of their soil, what better atonement is now in our
power than that of making what is rightfully acquired a source
of justice & of blessings to a people of another colour?

As the revolution to be produced in the condition of the
negroes must be gradual, it will suffice if the sale of territory
keep pace with its progress. For a time at least the proceeds
would be in advance. In this case it might be best, after deduct-
ing the expence incident to the surveys & sales, to place the
surplus in a situation where its increase might correspond with
the natural increase of the unpurchased slaves. Should the
proceeds at any time fall short of the calls for their application,

anticipations might be made by temporary loans to be discharged as the land should find a Market.

But it is probable that for a considerable period, the sales would exceed the calls. Masters would not be willing to strip their plantations & farms of their laborers too rapidly. The slaves themselves, connected as they generally are by tender ties with others under other Masters, would be kept from the list of emigrants by the want of the multiplied consents to be obtained. It is probable indeed that for a long time a certain portion of the proceeds might safely continue applicable to the discharge of the debts or to other purposes of the Nation. Or it might be most convenient, in the outset, to appropriate a certain proportion only of the income from sales, to the object in view, leaving the residue otherwise applicable.

Should any plan similar to that I have sketched, be deemed eligible in itself no particular difficulty is foreseen from that portion of the nation which with a common interest in the vacant territory has no interest in slave property. They are too just to wish that a partial sacrifice should be made for the general good; and too well aware that whatever may be the intrinsic character of that description of property, it is one known to the constitution, and, as such could not be constitutionally taken away without just compensation. That part of the Nation has indeed shewn a meritorious alacrity in promoting, by pecuniary contributions, the limited scheme for colonizing the Blacks, & freeing the nation from the unfortunate stain on it, which justifies the belief that any enlargement of the scheme, if founded on just principles would find among them its earliest & warmest patrons. It ought to have great weight that the vacant lands in question have for the most part been derived from grants of the States holding the slaves to be redeemed & removed by the sale of them.

It is evident however that in effectuating a general emancipation of slaves, in the mode which has been hinted, difficulties of other sorts would be encountered. The provision for ascertaining the joint consent of the masters & slaves; for guarding against unreasonable valuations of the latter; and for the discrimination of those not proper to be conveyed to a foreign residence, or who ought to remain a charge on Masters in whose service they had been disabled or worn out and for the annual transportation of such numbers, would Require the mature deliberations of the National Councils. The measure implies also the practicability of procuring in Africa, an enlargement of the district or districts, for receiving the exiles, sufficient for so great an augmentation of their numbers.

Perhaps the Legislative provision best adapted to the case would be an incorporation of the Colonizing Society or the establishment of a similar one, with proper powers, under the appointment & superintendence of the National Executive.

In estimating the difficulties however incident to any plan of general emancipation, they ought to be brought into comparison with those inseparable from other plans, and be yielded to or not according to the result of the comparison.

One difficulty presents itself which will probably attend every plan which is to go into effect under the Legislative provisions of the National Government. But whatever may be the defect of existing powers of Congress, the Constitution has pointed out the way in which it can be supplied. And it can hardly be doubted that the requisite powers might readily be procured for attaining the great object in question, in any mode whatever approved by the Nation.

If these thoughts can be of any aid in your search of a remedy for the great evil under which the nation labors, you are very welcome to them. You will allow me however to add that it will be most agreeable to me, not to be publickly referred to in any use you may make of them.

27. Slavery in the West: The Missouri Crisis

The Missouri crisis of 1819–1821 put Madison's convictions on the slavery issue to a severe test. In letters to the President and several other correspondents—including the Philadelphia journalist and man of letters, Robert Walsh—he denied the power of Congress to attach an antislavery condition to the admission of a new state, or to control the migration of slaves within the United States. More tentatively, he questioned the constitutionality of laws excluding slavery from the national territories, despite the sweeping grant of federal power in the territorial clause and the long-standing precedent of the Northwest Ordinance as re-enacted by the First Congress. His strained legal and historical argument on this last point was hardly strengthened by the myopic prediction that the expansion and dispersion of slavery would improve the condition of the bondsmen and hasten the extinction of the peculiar institution. It is difficult to conceive how a man who lamented the first fatal introduction of slavery into Virginia could have written such

To Robert Walsh, November 27, 1819, in *Writings*, IX, pp. 1–13.

a prophecy. Madison and Jefferson—the most distinguished spokesmen for the Revolutionary tradition in the South—concluded that the real issue in the Missouri debates was not the spread of slavery across the Mississippi but rather the creation of a sectional party by disguised Federalists who appealed to Northern antislavery sentiments in order to divide and conquer the Republicans. The ultimate price of injecting slavery into national politics, they warned, would be the disruption of the Union.

The Compromise of 1820 admitted Missouri without antislavery conditions and, contrary to Madison's advice, banned slavery in the Louisiana Territory north of 36°30'. The *reversal* of that policy of exclusion by Congress and the Supreme Court in the 1850s finally precipitated the division that Madison had feared: the formation of a new Republican party in the North out of the antislavery elements of the major national parties.

Montpellier, November 27, 1819.

DEAR SIR,—Your letter of the 11th was duly received and I should have given it a less tardy answer, but for a succession of particular demands on my attention, and a wish to assist my recollections, by consulting both Manuscript & printed sources of information on the subjects of your enquiry. Of these, however, I have not been able to avail myself but very partially.

As to the intention of the framers of the Constitution in the clause relating to "the migration and importation of persons, &c" the best key may perhaps be found in the case which produced it. The African trade in slaves had long been odious to most of the States, and the importation of slaves into them had been prohibited. Particular States however continued the importation, and were extremely averse to any restriction on their power to do so. In the convention the former States were anxious, in framing a new constitution, to insert a provision for an immediate and absolute stop to the trade. The latter were not only averse to any interference on the subject; but solemnly declared that their constituents would never accede to a Constitution containing such an article. Out of this conflict grew the middle measure providing that Congress should not interfere until the year 1808; with an implication, that after that date, they might prohibit the importation of slaves into the States then existing, & previous thereto, into the States not then existing. Such was the tone of opposition in the States of South Carolina & Georgia, & such the desire to gain their acquiescence in a prohibitory power, that on a question between the epochs of 1800 & 1808, the States of New Hampshire, Massachusetts & Connecticut, (all the eastern States in the Convention), joined in the vote for the latter, influenced however by the collateral motive of reconciling those particular States to the power over commerce & navigation; against which they felt, as did some other States, a very strong repugnance. The earnestness of South Carolina & Georgia was farther manifested by their insisting on the security in the V article, against any amendment to the Constitution affecting the right reserved to them, & their uniting with the small states, who insisted on a like security for their equality in the Senate.

But some of the States were not only anxious for a Constitutional provision against the introduction of slaves. They had scruples against admitting the term "slaves" into the Instrument. Hence the descriptive phrase, "migration or importation of persons;" the term migration allowing those who were scrupulous of acknowledging expressly a property in human beings, to view *imported* persons as a species of emigrants, while others might apply the term to foreign malefactors sent or coming into the country. It is possible tho' not recollected, that some might have had an eye to the case of freed blacks, as well as malefactors.

But whatever may have been intended by the term "migration" or the term "persons," it is most certain, that they referred

exclusively to a migration or importation from other countries
into the United States; and not to a removal, voluntary or involuntary, of slaves or freemen, from one to another part of the
United States. Nothing appears or is recollected that warrants
this latter intention. Nothing in the proceedings of the State
conventions indicates such a construction there.[1] Had such
been the construction it is easy to imagine the figure it would
have made in many of the states, among the objections to the
constitution, and among the numerous amendments to it proposed by the State conventions[2] not one of which amendments

---

[1] The debates of the Pennsylvania Convention contain a speech of Mr.
Willson [James Wilson], (Dec. 3, 1787) who had been a member of the
general convention, in which, alluding to the clause tolerating for a time,
the farther importation of slaves, he consoles himself with the hope that,
in a few years it would be prohibited altogether; observing that in the
mean time, the new States which were to be formed would be under the
controul of Congress *in this particular,* and slaves would never be introduced among them. In another speech on the day following and alluding
to the same clause, his words are "yet the lapse of a few years & Congress will have power to *exterminate* slavery within our borders." How
far the language of Mr. W. may have been accurately reported is not
known. The expressions used, are more vague & less consistent than would
be readily ascribed to him. But as they stand, the fairest construction
would be, that he considered the power given to Congress, to arrest the
importation of slaves as "laying a foundation for banishing slavery out
of the country; & tho' at a period more distant than might be wished,
producing the same kind of gradual change which was pursued in Pennsylvania." (See his speech, page 90 of the Debates.) By this "change,"
after the example of Pennsylvania, he must have meant a change by the
other States influenced by that example, & yielding to the general way
of thinking & feeling, produced by the policy of putting an end to the
importation of slaves. He could not mean by "banishing slavery," more
than by a power "to exterminate it," that Congress were authorized to
do what is literally expressed.—*Madison's Note.*
[2] In the convention of Virginia the opposition to the Constitution comprised a number of the ablest men in the State. Among them were Mr.
Henry & Col. Mason, both of them distinguished by their acuteness, and
anxious to display unpopular constructions. One of them Col. Mason, had
been a member of the general convention and entered freely into accounts
of what passed within it. Yet neither of them, nor indeed any of the other
opponents, among the multitude of their objections, and farfetched interpretations, ever hinted, in the debates on the 9th Sect. of Art. I, at a

refers to the clause in question. Neither is there any indication that Congress have heretofore considered themselves as deriving from this Clause a power over the migration or removal of individuals, whether freemen or slaves, from one State to another, whether new or old: For it must be kept in view that if the power was given at all, it has been in force eleven years over all the States existing in 1808, and at all times over the States not then existing. Every indication is against such a construction by Congress of their constitutional powers. Their alacrity in exercising their powers relating to slaves, is a proof that they did not claim what they did not exercise. They punctually and unanimously put in force the power accruing in 1808 against the further importation of slaves from abroad. They had previously directed their power over American vessels on the high seas, against the African trade. They lost no time in applying the prohibitory power to Louisiana, which having maritime ports, might be an inlet for slaves from abroad. But they forebore to extend the prohibition to the introduction of slaves from other parts of the Union. They had even prohibited the importation of slaves into the Mississippi Territory from *without the limits of the U. S.* in the year 1798, without extending the prohibition to the introduction of slaves from *within those limits;* altho' at the time the ports of Georgia and South Carolina were open for the importation of slaves from abroad, and increasing the mass of slavery within the United States.

If these views of the subject be just, a power in Congress to controul the interior migration or removals of persons, must be derived from some other source than Sect. 9, Art. 1; either from the clause giving power to make all needful rules and regulations respecting the Territory or other property belonging to the U. S. or from that providing for the admission of New States into the Union.

---

power given by it to prohibit an interior migration of any sort. The meaning of the Section as levelled against migrations or importations from abroad, was not contested. [*Madison's Note*]

The terms in which the 1st of these powers is expressed, tho' of a ductile character, cannot well be extended beyond a power over the Territory as property, & a power to make the provisions really needful or necessary for the Government of settlers until ripe for admission as States into the Union. It may be inferred that Congress did not regard the interdict of slavery among the needful regulations contemplated by the constitution; since in none of the Territorial Governments created by them, is such an interdict found. The power, however, be its import what it may, is obviously limited to a Territory whilst remaining in that character as distinct from that of a State.

As to the power of admitting new States into the federal compact, the questions offering themselves are; whether congress can attach conditions, or the new States concur in conditions, which after admission, would abridge or *enlarge* the constitutional rights of legislation common to the other States; whether Congress can by a compact with a new member take power either to or from itself, or place the new member above or below the equal rank & rights possessed by the others; whether all such stipulations, expressed or implied would not be nullities, and so pronounced when brought to a practical test. It falls within the Scope of your enquiry, to state the fact, that there was a proposition in the convention to discriminate between the old and new States, by an Article in the Constitution declaring that the aggregate number of representatives from the States thereafter to be admitted should never exceed that of the States originally adopting the Constitution. The proposition happily was rejected. The effect of such a discrimination, is sufficiently evident.

In the case of Louisiana, there is a circumstance which may deserve notice. In the Treaty ceding it, a privilege was retained by the ceding party, which distinguishes between its ports & others of the U. S. for a special purpose & a short period. This privilege however was the result not of an ordinary legislative power in Congress; nor was it the result of an arrangement between Congress & the people of Louisiana. It rests on the ground that the same entire power, even in the nation, over that territory, as over the original territory of the U. S. never existed; the privilege alluded to being in the deed of cession carved by the foreign owner, out of the title conveyed to the purchaser. A sort of necessity therefore was thought to belong to so peculiar & extraordinary a case. Notwithstanding this plea it is presumable that if the privilege had materially affected the rights of other ports, or had been of a permanent or durable character, the occurrence would not have been so little regarded. Congress would not be allowed to effect through the medium of a Treaty, obnoxious discriminations between new and old States, more than among the latter.

With respect to what has taken place in the North West Territory, it may be observed, that the ordinance giving its distinctive character on the Subject of Slaveholding proceeded from the old Congress, acting, with the best intentions, but under a charter which contains no shadow of the authority exercised. And it remains to be decided how far the States formed within that Territory & admitted into the Union, are on a different footing from its other members, as to their legislative sovereignty.

For the grounds on which ⅗ of the slaves were admitted into the ratio of representation, I will with your permission, save trouble by referring to No. 54 of the Federalist. In addition, it may be stated that this feature in the Constitution was combined with that relating to the power over Commerce & navigation. In truth these two powers, with those relating to the importation of slaves, & the Articles establishing the equality of representation in the Senate & the rule of taxation, had a complicated influence on each other which alone would have justified the remark, that the Constitution was "the result of mutual deference & Concession."

It was evident that the large States holding slaves, and those not large which felt themselves so by anticipation, would not have concurred in a constitution, allowing them no more Representation in one legislative branch than the smallest States, and in the other less than their proportional contributions to the Common Treasury.

The considerations which led to this mixed ratio which had been very deliberately agreed on in April 1783, by the old Congress, make it probable that the Convention could not have looked to a departure from it, in any instance where slaves made a part of the local population.

Whether the Convention could have looked to the existence of slavery at all in the new States is a point on which I can add little to what has been already stated. The great object of the Convention seemed to be to prohibit the increase by the *importation* of slaves. A power to emancipate slaves was disclaimed; Nor is anything recollected that denoted a view to controul the distribution of those within the Country. The case of the North West Territory was probably superseded by the provision against the importation of slaves by South Carolina & Georgia, which had not then passed laws prohibiting it. When the existence of slavery in that territory was precluded, the importation of slaves was rapidly going on, and the only mode of checking it was by narrowing the space open to them. It is not an unfair inference that the expedient would not have been undertaken, if the power afterward given to terminate the importation everywhere, had existed or been even anticipated. It has appeared that the present Congress never followed the example during the twenty years preceding the prohibitory epoch.

The *expediency* of exercising a supposed power in Congress, to prevent a diffusion of the slaves actually in the Country, as far as the local authorities may admit them, resolves itself into the probable effects of such a diffusion on the interests of the slaves and of the Nation.

Will it or will it not better the condition of the slaves, by

lessening the number belonging to individual masters, and
intermixing both with greater masses of free people? Will partial manumissions be more or less likely to take place, and a
general emancipation be accelerated or retarded? Will the
moral & physical condition of slaves, in the mean time, be improved or deteriorated? What do experiences and appearances
decide as to the comparative rates of generative increase, in
their present, and, in a dispersed situation?

Will the aggregate strength, security, tranquillity, and harmony of the whole nation be advanced or impaired by lessening the proportion of slaves to the free people in particular
sections of it?

How far an occlusion of the space now vacant, against the
introduction of slaves may be essential to prevent compleatly a
smuggled importation of them from abroad, ought to influence
the question of expediency; [this] must be decided by a reasonable estimate of the degree in which the importation would
take place in spight of the spirit of the times, the increasing co-
operation of foreign powers against the slave trade, the increasing rigor of the Acts of Congress and the vigilant enforcement
of them by the Executive; and by a fair comparison of this estimate with the considerations opposed to such an occlusion.

Will a multiplication of States holding slaves, multiply advocates of the importation of foreign slaves, so as to endanger the
continuance of the prohibitory Acts of Congress? To such an
apprehension seem to be opposed the facts, that the States
holding fewest slaves are those which most readily abolished
slavery altogether; that of the 13 primitive States, Eleven had
prohibited the importation before the power was given to Congress, that all of them, with the newly added States, unanimously concurred in exerting that power; that most of the
present slaveholding States cannot be tempted by motives of
interest to favor the reopening of the ports to foreign slaves;
and that these, with the States which have even abolished

slavery within themselves, could never be outnumbered in the National Councils by new States wishing for slaves, and not satisfied with the supply attainable within the U. S.

On the whole, the Missouri question, as a constitutional one, amounts to the question whether the condition proposed to be annexed to the admission of Missouri would or would not be void in itself, or become void the moment the territory should enter as a State within the pale of the Constitution. And as a question of expediency & humanity, it depends essentially on the probable influence of such restrictions on the quantity & duration of slavery, and on the general condition of slaves in the U. S.

The question raised with regard to the tenor of the stipulation in the Louisiana Treaty, on the subject of its admission, is one which I have not examined, and on which I could probably throw no light if I had.

Under one aspect of the general subject, I cannot avoid saying, that apart from its merits under others, the tendency of what has passed and is passing, fills me with no slight anxiety. Parties under some denominations or other must always be expected in a Government as free as ours. When the individuals belonging to them are intermingled in every part of the whole Country, they strengthen the Union of the Whole, while they divide every part. Should a State of parties arise, founded on geographical boundaries and other Physical & permanent distinctions which happen to coincide with them, what is to controul those great repulsive Masses from awful shocks against each other?

The delay in answering your letter made me fear you might doubt my readiness to comply with its requests. I now fear you will think I have done more than these justified. I have been the less reserved because you are so ready to conform to my inclination formerly expressed, not to be drawn from my sequestered position into public view. . . .

28. Emancipation and Utopia:
On Fanny Wright's Experiment

In February of 1825 Madison welcomed Miss Frances Wright to Montpelier. (Madison sometimes used the variant spelling, Montpellier, in the French manner.) It is hard to imagine a stranger pair than the judicious elder statesman and the passionate young British radical who had attached herself to Lafayette and trailed the French hero on his triumphal tour of the United States. Fanny Wright sought Madison's advice and support for a scheme encouraging slaves to earn their freedom while acquiring the skills needed to support themselves. From Virginia she went on to visit the Utopian socialist community of New Harmony in Indiana and the abolitionist English colony in Illinois. Mixing the communitarian notions of the radical reformers with the cautionary counsels of Madison, she drafted *A Plan for the Gradual Abolition of Slavery in the United States Without Danger or Loss to the Citizens of the South* (1825). The pamphlet called for a series of experimental communities to be established throughout the South with the help of public land grants and capital subscriptions by antislavery philanthro-

---

To Frances Wright, September 1, 1825, in *Writings*, IX, pp. 224–229.

pists. By her enthusiastic calculations, the profits of cooperative slave labor under white management would pay the cost of emancipation within five to ten years. Nashoba, her model community in western Tennessee, was designed to demonstrate the practicability of the plan, and at the same time to offer a congenial home for free spirits.

Madison's response to her proposals in his letter of September 1, 1825, is a masterpiece of left-handed praise. He approved the conservative features consistent with his own ideas on gradual, voluntary emancipation and colonization (see Document 26); and he politely disparaged the novel doctrines of socialism. Perhaps deference to Fanny Wright's distinguished patron, more than genuine sympathy, elicited even this highly circumspect endorsement. Still, the idea of the experiment did not noticeably shock Madison; nor would the failure of the Nashoba enterprise a few years later surprise him. (The promoters did manage to colonize one small group of freedmen in Haiti.)

In 1828, Madison tactfully suggested to Lafayette why the General's protégé could expect no further encouragement from him or other respectable Americans: "With her rare talents and still rarer disinterestedness she has I fear created insuperable obstacles to the good fruits of which they might be productive by her disregard or rather defiance of the most established opinion and vivid feelings. Besides her views of amalgamating the white and black population so universally obnoxious, she gives an éclat to her notions on the subject of Religion and of marriage, the effect of which your knowledge of this Country can readily estimate." In the grosser argot of the press, Fanny Wright had become "the Red Harlot of infidelity."

Montpellier September 1, 1825.

DEAR MADAM,—Your letter to Mrs. Madison, containing observations addressed to my attention also, came duly to hand, as you will learn from her, with a printed copy of your plan for the gradual abolition of slavery in the United States.

The magnitude of this evil among us is so deeply felt, and so universally acknowledged, that no merit could be greater than that of devising a satisfactory remedy for it. Unfortunately the task, not easy under any other circumstances, is vastly augmented by the physical peculiarities[1] of those held in bondage, which preclude their incorporation with the white population; and by the blank in the general field of labour to be occasioned by their exile; a blank into which there would not be an influx of white labourers, successively taking the place of the exiles, and which, without such an influx, would have an effect distressing in prospect to the proprietors of the soil.

The remedy for the evil which you have planned is certainly recommended to favorable attention by the two characteristics, 1. that it requires the voluntary concurrence of the holders of the slaves with or without pecuniary compensation: 2. that it contemplates the removal of those emancipated, either to a foreign or distant region: And it will still further obviate objections, if the experimental establishments should avoid the neighbourhood of settlements where there are slaves.

Supposing these conditions to be duly provided for, particularly the removal of the emancipated blacks, the remaining questions relate to the aptitude & adequacy of the process by which the slaves are at the same time to earn the funds, entire or supplemental, required for their emancipation & removal; and to be sufficiently educated for a life of freedom and of social order.

With respect to a proper course of education no serious difficulties present themselves. And as they are to continue in a

---

[1] These peculiarities, it would seem are not of equal force in the South American States, owing in part perhaps to a former degradation produced by colonial vassalage, but principally to the lesser contrast of colours. The difference is not striking between that of many of the Spanish & Portuguese Creoles & that of many of the mixed breed. [*Madison's Note*]

state of bondage during the preparatory period, & to be within
the jurisdiction of States recognizing ample authority over
them, a competent discipline cannot be impracticable. The degree in which this discipline will enforce the needed labour,
and in which a voluntary industry will supply the defect of
compulsory labour, are vital points on which it may not be safe
to be very positive without some light from actual experiment.

Considering the probable composition of the labourers, &
the known fact that where the labour is compulsory, the greater
the number of labourers brought together (unless indeed where
a co-operation of many hands is rendered essential by a particular kind of work or of machinery) the less are the proportional profits, it may be doubted whether the surplus from that
source merely beyond the support of the establishment, would
sufficiently accumulate in five or even more years, for the objects in view. And candor obliges me to say that I am not satisfied either that the prospect of emancipation at a future day
will sufficiently overcome the natural and habitual repugnance
to labour, or that there is such an advantage of united over
individual labour as is taken for granted.

In cases where portions of time have been allotted to slaves,
as among the Spaniards, with a view to their working out their
freedom, it is believed that but few have availed themselves of
the opportunity, by a voluntary industry; And such a result
could be less relied on in a case where each individual would
feel that the fruit of his exertions would be shared by others
whether equally or unequally making them; and that the exertions of others would equally avail him, notwithstanding a deficiency in his own. Skilful arrangements might palliate this
tendency, but it would be difficult to counteract it effectually.

The examples of the Moravians, the Harmonites and the
Shakers in which the United labors of many for a common object have been successful, have no doubt an imposing character. But it must be recollected that in all these Establishments
there is a religious impulse in the members, and a religious

authority in the head, for which there will be no substitutes of equivalent efficacy in the Emancipating establishment. The code of rules by which Mr. Rap [George Rapp] manages his conscientious & devoted flock, & enriches a common treasury, must be little applicable to the dissimilar assemblage in question. His experience may afford valuable aid, in its general organization, and in the distribution & details of the work to be performed: But an efficient administration must, as is judiciously proposed, be in hands practically acquainted with the Propensities & habits of the members of the new Community.

With a reference to this dissimilarity & to the doubt as to the advantages of associated labour, it may deserve consideration whether the experiment would not be better commenced on a scale smaller than that assumed in the prospectus. A less expensive outfit would suffice; labourers in the proper proportions of sex & age would be more attainable; the necessary discipline, and the direction of their labour would be more simple & manageable; and but little time would be lost; or perhaps time gained, as success, for which the chance would according to my calculation be increased, would give an encouraging aspect to the plan, and suggest improvements better qualifying it for the larger scale proposed.

Such, Madam are the general ideas suggested by your interesting communication. If they do not coincide with yours, & imply less of confidence than may be due to the plan you have formed, I hope you will not question either my admiration of the generous philanthropy which dictated it, or my sense of the special regard it evinces for the honor & welfare of our expanding, & I trust rising Republic.

As it is not certain what construction would be put on the view I have taken of the subject, I leave it with your discretion to withhold it altogether, or to disclose it within the limits, you allude to; intimating only that it will be most agreeable to me on all occasions not to be brought before the Public, where there is no obvious call for it.

General Lafayette took his final leave of us a few days ago, expecting to embark about this time in the new frigate with an appropriate name. He carries with him the unanimous blessings of the free nation which has adopted him. If equal honors have not been his portion in that in which he had his birth, it is not because he did not deserve them. This hemisphere at least, & posterity in the other, will award what is due to the nobleness of his mind and the grandeur of his career.

He could add but little to the details explained in the Printed copy of the Abolition Plan, for want of a full knowledge of which justice may not have been done it. Mr. Davis has not yet favoured us with the promised call. I shall receive his communications on the subject, with attention & pleasure.

The date of this letter will shew some delay in acknowledging the favor of yours. But it is expected to be at Nashville by the time noted for your arrival there, and a prolonged stay in the post office was rather to be avoided than promoted.

I join Mrs. Madison in the hope that we shall not be without the opportunity of again welcoming you & your sister to Montpelier tendering you in the mean time my respectful salutations.

29. The New Proslavery School: Reply to Thomas Dew

The Nat Turner insurrection of 1831 touched off the first and last full-scale public debate over the future of slavery in Virginia. In the state legislature of 1831–1832, an overwhelming majority closed the controversy by voting down a resolution that aimed at gradual emancipation. Among 134 representatives, nine brave men from the Tidewater and Piedmont regions, plus another thirty-one from the predominantly white trans-Alleghany counties, went down with the antislavery cause. The specter of Nat Turner together with the moderate political challenge to slavery only deepened the commitment of Virginia—and the South—to the peculiar institution.

Professor Thomas R. Dew of William and Mary College, in his *Review of the Debate in the Virginia Legislature of 1831 and 1832* (1832), articulated a growing conviction that any conceivable abolition scheme must destroy the foundations of wealth and social order, of republican liberty and civilization

To Thomas R. Dew, February 23, 1833, in *Writings*, IX, pp. 498–502. The two opening paragraphs and the last are in *Letters*, IV, pp. 274–275, 279.

itself. The publication of his pamphlet marked an ominous shift in Southern opinion toward the positive defense of slavery. More immediately, his skillful economic and demographic analyses exposed grave flaws in the only antislavery program that Virginians would consider seriously: voluntary compensated emancipation and African colonization.

In his reply to Dew, Madison sadly acknowledged the force of this critique of gradual emancipation, even as he tried to answer it. He had always understood how difficult and dangerous the work of abolition would be. Indeed, largely for that reason, Madison and the liberal planters had skirted the slavery issue in Virginia for more than half a century. Yet he could not abandon the judgment of his own generation that slavery was "the greatest of our calamities." For Dew, "if, as really is the case, we cannot get rid of slavery without producing a greater injury to both the masters and slaves, there is no rule of conscience or revealed law of God which *can* condemn us." Madison—at 82 —quietly insisted that the possibilities of action were not yet exhausted. However dismal the prospect, men could not sink into "torpid acquiescence" in the perpetuation of slavery without condemning themselves. To blame the tariff or some other Northern outrage for Virginia's troubles, Madison warned the new proslavery school, was merely to evade the real issues, postpone the inevitable day of reckoning, and thus invite a bloody final solution.

Montpellier, February 23, 1833.

DEAR SIR,—I received, in due time, your letter of the 15th ultimo with copies of the two pamphlets; one on the "Restrictive System," the other on the "Slave Question."

The former I have not yet been able to look into, and in reading the latter with the proper attention I have been much retarded by many interruptions, as well as by the feebleness incident to my great age, increased as it is by the effects of an acute fever, preceded and followed by a chronic complaint under which I am still labouring. This explanation of the delay in acknowledging your favor will be an apology, also, for the brevity and generality of the answer. For the freedom of it, none, I am sure, will be required. In the views of the subject taken in the pamphlet, I have found much valuable and interesting information, with ample proof of the numerous obstacles to a removal of slavery from our country, and everything that could be offered in mitigation of its continuance; but I am obliged to say, that in not a few of the data from which you reason, and in the conclusion to which you are led, I cannot concur.

I am aware of the impracticability of an immediate or early execution of any plan, that combines deportation, with emancipation; and of the inadmissibility of emancipation without deportation. But I have yielded to the expediency of attempting a gradual remedy by providing for the double operation.

If emancipation was the sole object, the extinguishment of slavery, would be easy, cheap & compleat. The purchase by the public of all female children at their birth, leaving them in bondage, till it would defray the charge of rearing them, would within a limited period be a radical resort.

With the condition of deportation, it has appeared to me, that the great difficulty does not lie either in the expence of emancipation, or in the expence or the means of deportation, but in the attainment 1 of the requisite Asylums, 2, the consent of the individuals to be removed, 3, the labor for the vacuum to be created.

With regard to the expence. 1, much will be saved by voluntary emancipations, increasing under the influence of example, and the prospect of bettering the lot of the slaves. 2, much may be expected in gifts & legacies from the opulent the philanthropic and the conscientious, 3, more still from Legislative grants by the States, of which encouraging examples & indications have already appeared, 4, Nor is there any room for despair of aid from the indirect or direct proceeds of the public lands held in trust by Congress. With a sufficiency of pecuniary means, the facility of providing a naval transportation of the exiles is shewn by the present amount of our tonnage and the promptitude with which it can be enlarged; by the number of emigrants brought from Europe to North America within the last year; and by the greater number of slaves, which have been within single years brought from the Coast of Africa across the Atlantic.

In the attainment of adequate Asylums, the difficulty, though it may be considerable, is far from being discouraging. Africa is justly the favorite choice of the patrons of colonization; and the prospect there is flattering, 1, in the territory already acquired, 2 in the extent of Coast yet to be explored and which may be equally convenient, 3, the adjacent interior into which the littoral settlements can be expanded under the auspices of physical affinities between the new comers and the natives, and of the moral superiorities of the former, 4, the great inland Regions now ascertained to be accessible by navigable waters, & opening new fields for colonizing enterprises.

But Africa, tho' the primary, is not the sole asylum within contemplation. An auxiliary one presents itself in the islands adjoining this Continent where the colored population is already dominant, and where the wheel of revolution may from time to time produce the like result.

Nor ought another contingent receptacle for emancipated slaves to be altogether overlooked. It exists within the territory under the controul of the U. S. and is not too distant to be out of reach, whilst sufficiently distant to avoid for an indefinite period, the collisions to be apprehended from the vicinity of people distinguished from each other by physical as well as other characteristics.

The consent of the individuals is another pre-requisite in the plan of removal. At present there is a known repugnance in those already in a state of freedom to leave their native homes; and among the slaves there is an almost universal preference of their present condition to freedom in a distant & unknown land. But in both classes particularly that of the slaves the prejudices arise from a distrust of the favorable accounts coming to them through white channels. By degrees truth will find its way to them from sources in which they will confide, and their aversion to removal may be overcome as fast as the means of effectuating it shall accrue.

The difficulty of replacing the labour withdrawn by a removal of the slaves, seems to be urged as of itself an insuperable objection to the attempt. The answer to it is, 1, that notwithstanding the emigrations of the whites, there will be an annual and by degrees an increasing surplus of the remaining mass. 2, That there will be an attraction of whites from without, increasing with the demand, and, as the population elsewhere will be yielding a surplus to be attracted, 3 that as the culture of Tobacco declines with the contraction of the space within which it is profitable, & still more from the successful competition in the west, and as the farming system takes place of the planting, a portion of labour can be spared, without impairing the requisite stock, 4 that altho' the process must be slow, be attended with much inconvenience, and be not even certain in its result, is it not preferable to a torpid acquiescence in a perpetuation of slavery, or an extinguishment of it by convulsions more disastrous in their character & consequences than slavery itself.

In my estimate of the experiment instituted by the Colonization Society I may indulge too much my wishes & hopes, to be safe from error. But a partial success will have its value, and an entire failure will leave behind a consciousness of the laudable intentions with which relief from the greatest of our calamities was attempted in the only mode presenting a chance of effecting it.

I hope I shall be pardoned for remarking that in accounting

for the depressed condition of Virginia, you seem to allow too little to the existence of slavery; ascribe too much to the tariff laws, and not to have sufficiently taken into view the effect of the rapid settlement of the Western & South Western Country.

Previous to the Revolution, when, of these causes, slavery alone was in operation, the face of Virginia was in every feature of improvement & prosperity, a contrast to the Colonies where slavery did not exist, or in a degree only, not worthy of notice. Again, during the period of the tariff laws prior to the latter state of them, the pressure was little if at all, regarded as a source of the general suffering. And whatever may be the degree in which the extravagant augmentation of the tariff may have contributed to the depression the extent of this cannot be explained by the extent of the cause. The great & adequate cause of the evil is the cause last mentioned; if that be indeed an evil which improves the condition of our migrating citizens & adds more to the growth & prosperity of the whole than it subtracts from a part of the community.

Nothing is more certain than that the actual and prospective depression of Virginia, is to be referred to the fall in the value of her landed property, and in that of the staple products of the land. And it is not less certain that the fall in both cases, is the inevitable effect of the redundancy in the market both of land and of its products. The vast amount of fertile land offered at 125 Cents per acre in the West & South West could not fail to have the effect already experienced of reducing the land here to half its value; and when the labour that will here produce one Hogshead of Tobacco and ten barrels of flour, will there produce two Hogsheads and twenty barrels, now so cheaply transportable to the destined outlets, a like effect on these articles must necessarily ensue. Already more Tobacco is sent to New Orleans, than is exported from Virginia to foreign markets; Whilst the Article of flour exceeding for the most part the demand for it, is in a course of rapid increase from new sources as boundless as they are productive. The great staples of Virginia have but a limited market which is easily glutted. They have in fact sunk more in price, and have a more threatening prospect, than the more Southern staples of Cotton & Rice. The case is believed to be the same with her landed property. That it is so with her slaves is proved by the purchases made here for the market there.

The reflections suggested by this aspect of things will be more appropriate in your hands than in mine. They are also beyond the tether of my subject, which I fear I have already overstrained. I hasten, therefore, to conclude, with a tender of the high respect and cordial regards which I pray you to accept.

30. Complex Justice: Codification and the Common Law

Madison and his generation of American political leaders—
Federalists no less than Jeffersonians—were reformers in the
most profound sense. They framed the fundamental laws and
formed the institutions and policies of a radically new republican regime. Precisely because the enterprise of revolution and
founding seemed so audacious, so uncertain, Madison charac-
teristically cast a cool though curious eye on those reformers
who would break with all precedents and invite perpetual
revision of the rules and forms of political life. As he had
argued in *Federalist* No. 49—gently correcting Jefferson not for
the last time on a point of social order—frequent appeals to
the people on fundamental questions "would, in a great measure, deprive the government of that veneration which time
bestows on everything, and without which perhaps the wisest
and freest governments would not possess the requisite sta-

To Edward Livingston, July 10, 1822, in *Writings*, IX, pp. 98–103.

bility." (See Document 12.) If "blind veneration for antiquity, for custom, or for names" was in Madison's view a vice of slavish peoples, he equally insisted that "instability, injustice, and confusion" were the "mortal diseases" of all popular governments. Madison began as a reformer and continued to defend political experiments throughout his life; yet he always distinguished sharply between the theoretical schemes of "the wildest projectors" and the experiments of a people, at once daring and prudent, who followed "the suggestions of their own good sense, the knowledge of their own situation, and the lessons of their own experience." (See *The Federalist* Nos. 10 and 14, Document 12.)

Madison's response to Edward Livingston's draft of a *Report of the Plan of the Penal Code* for Louisiana nicely illustrates the view of a prudent reformer. Livingston proposed to reconstruct the criminal law for his adopted state of Louisiana, reducing the complex body of statutes, precedents and commentaries to a plain and systematic code. In this challenge to the Anglo-American common-law tradition, he reflected both the spirit of the English utilitarian reformer, Jeremy Bentham, and the French heritage of Louisiana's unique legal system. Madison no sooner praised Livingston for an interesting experiment than he warned him against the sin of rational pride. (Jefferson, in 1825, was not so cautious: Livingston's code, he wrote, "would certainly arrange his name with the sages of antiquity.") The precious standards and procedures of legal justice, deposited over centuries in the records of the common law, might well be distorted beyond recognition in a short, simple code. (A few years earlier, Madison had made the same sort of skeptical answer to Bentham himself after that philosophical gentleman coolly volunteered to codify the whole of American law.) But still: the federal system allowed the several states to experiment with uncertain reforms that might point the way to progress and, at worst, would only do limited damage. Fortunately, Livingston's code touched a favorite cause on which Madison could speak without reservations: freedom of conscience and the separation of Church and State. *That* reform, as Madison always believed, deserved universal and unqualified adoption. (See Documents 1 and 2.)

Edward Livingston (1764–1836), member of a wealthy and powerful New York clan, was an old Republican ally of Madison's who later fell out with the Jefferson administration. He made a second career (and fortune) in New Orleans as a lawyer, land speculator, and politician. From 1823 to 1835, he served as Congressman and Senator from Louisiana, and then as Jackson's Secretary of State and Minister to France. His speeches and writings against the South Carolina school, including the draft of the Nullification Proclamation (1832), won Madison's qualified praise. In Europe and America, his proposals for the reform of criminal law and prison discipline were widely read and respected. Young Tocqueville and Beaumont, for example, used Livingston's writings as an authoritative guide in their investigation of the American prison system.

Montpellier, July 10, 1822.

DEAR SIR,—I was favored some days ago with your letter of May 19, accompanied by a copy of your Report to the Legislature of the State on the subject of a penal Code.

I should commit a tacit injustice if I did not say that the Report does great honor to the talents and sentiments of the Author. It abounds with ideas of conspicuous value and presents them in a manner not less elegant than persuasive.

The reduction of an entire code of criminal jurisprudence, into statutory provisions, excluding a recurrence to foreign or traditional codes, and substituting for technical terms, more familiar ones with or without explanatory notes, cannot but be viewed as a very arduous task. I sincerely wish your execution of it may fulfil every expectation.

I cannot deny, at the same time, that I have been accustomed to doubt the practicability of giving all the desired simplicity to so complex a subject, without involving a discretion, inadmissible in free Government to those who are to expound and apply the law. The rules and usages which make a part of the law, tho' to be found only in elementary treatises, in respectable commentaries, and in adjudged cases, seem to be too numerous & too various to be brought within the requisite compass; even if there were less risk of creating uncertainties by defective abridgments, or by the change of phraseology.

This risk would seem to be particularly incident to a substitution of new words & definitions for a technical language, the meaning of which had been settled by long use and authoritative expositions. When a technical term may express a very simple idea, there might be no inconveniency or rather an advantage in exchanging it for a more familiar synonyme, if a precise one could be found. But where the technical terms & phrases have a complex import, not otherwise to be reduced to clearness & certainty, than by practical applications of them, it might be unsafe to introduce new terms & phrases, tho' aided by brief explanations. The whole law expressed by single terms, such as "trial by jury, evidence, &c, &c." fill volumes, when unfolded into the details which enter into their meaning.

I hope it will not be thought by this intimation of my doubts I wish to damp the enterprize from which you have not shrunk. On the contrary I not only wish that you may overcome all the difficulties which occur to me; but am persuaded that if compleat success should not reward your labors, there is ample room for improvements in the criminal jurisprudence of Louisiana as elsewhere which are well worthy the exertion of your best powers, and which will furnish useful examples to other members of the Union. Among the advantages distinguishing our compound Government it is not the least that it affords so many opportunities and chances in the local Legislatures, for salutary innovations by some, which may be adopted by others;

or for important experiments, which, if unsuccessful, will be of limited injury, and may even prove salutary as beacons to others. Our political system is found also to have the happy merit of exciting a laudable emulation among the States composing it, instead of the enmity marking competitions among powers wholly alien to each other.

I observe with particular pleasure the view you have taken of the immunity of Religion from civil jurisdiction, in every case where it does not trespass on private rights or the public peace. This has always been a favorite principle with me; and it was not with my approbation, that the deviation from it took place in Congress, when they appointed Chaplains, to be paid from the National Treasury. It would have been a much better proof to their Constituents of their pious feeling if the members had contributed for the purpose, a pittance from their own pockets. As the precedent is not likely to be rescinded, the best that can now be done, may be to apply to the Constitution the maxim of the law, de minimis non curat.

There has been another deviation from the strict principle in the Executive Proclamations of fasts & festivals, so far, at least, as they have spoken the language of *injunction,* or have lost sight of the equality of *all* religious sects in the eye of the Constitution. Whilst I was honored with the Executive Trust I found it necessary on more than one occasion to follow the example of predecessors. But I was always careful to make the Proclamations absolutely indiscriminate, and merely recommendatory; or rather mere *designations* of a day, on which all who thought proper might *unite* in consecrating it to religious purposes, according to their own faith & forms. In this sense, I presume you reserve to the Government a right to *appoint* particular days for religious worship throughout the State, without any penal sanction *enforcing* the worship. I know not what may be the way of thinking on this subject in Louisiana. I should suppose the Catholic portion of the people, at least, as a small & even unpopular sect in the U. S., would rally, as they did in

Virginia when religious liberty was a Legislative topic, to its broadest principle. Notwithstanding the general progress made within the two last centuries in favour of this branch of liberty, & the full establishment of it, in some parts of our Country, there remains in others a strong bias towards the old error, that without some sort of alliance or coalition between Government & Religion neither can be duly supported. Such indeed is the tendency to such a coalition, and such its corrupting influence on both the parties, that the danger cannot be too carefully guarded against. And in a Government of opinion, like ours, the only effectual guard must be found in the soundness and stability of the general opinion on the subject. Every new & successful example therefore of a perfect separation between ecclesiastical and civil matters, is of importance. And I have no doubt that every new example, will succeed, as every past one has done, in shewing that religion & Government will both exist in greater purity, the less they are mixed together. It was the belief of all sects at one time that the establishment of Religion by law, was right & necessary; that the true religion ought to be established in exclusion of every other; And that the only question to be decided was which was the true religion. The example of Holland proved that a toleration of sects, dissenting from the established sect, was safe & even useful. The example of the Colonies, now States, which rejected religious establishments altogether, proved that all Sects might be safely & advantageously put on a footing of equal & entire freedom; and a continuance of their example since the declaration of Independence, has shewn that its success in Colonies was not to be ascribed to their connection with the parent Country. If a further confirmation of the truth could be wanted, it is to be found in the examples furnished by the States, which have abolished their religious establishments. I cannot speak particularly of any of the cases excepting that of Virginia where it is impossible to deny that Religion prevails with more zeal, and a more exemplary priesthood than it ever did when established and patronised by Public authority. We are teaching the world the great truth that Governments do better without Kings & Nobles than with them. The merit will be doubled by the other lesson that Religion flourishes in greater purity, without than with the aid of Government.

My pen I perceive has rambled into reflections for which it was not taken up. I recall it to the proper object of thanking you for your very interesting pamphlet, and of tendering you my respects and good wishes. . . .

31. Public Education and the Classes: Virginia to Kentucky

The American public school and state university are the ambiguous monuments to an old republican faith in education. In Virginia, Jefferson had been since revolutionary times the moving spirit and eloquent advocate of educational reform. Madison, as usual, stood faithfully at his friend's right hand, giving political aid and prudent counsel. In 1822, answering the inquiries of the Kentucky Lieutenant Governor, William T. Barry, Madison added little to either the principles or the design of a republican educational system that Jefferson had first outlined more than forty years before in his "Bill for the General Diffusion of Knowledge," and had defended memorably in his *Notes on the State of Virginia* (1782–1785). (He had used Jefferson more critically when advising Kentuckians on constitutional matters in the 1780s. See Document 7.)

Sadly, Madison recognized that Virginia could not offer much in the way of practical achievement in public education

---

To William T. Barry, August 4, 1822, in *Writings*, IX, pp. 103–109.

to guide the Kentuckians. New England, the native ground of Federalism, provided a far better example. Few Virginians would have disputed Madison's statement of a common truth of republican politics: "A popular government, without popular information or the means of acquiring it, is but a prologue to a farce or a tragedy or, perhaps, both." Yet the representatives of the people, counting the costs, had provided only the barest beginnings of elementary education for the poor and, finally, in 1818, had reluctantly granted authorization and modest support for Jefferson's projected University of Virginia. (See Document 32.)

Writing from hard experience, Madison armed Barry, a professor as well as a politician, with arguments that might overcome popular prejudice against publicly supported higher education. Republicans of his generation never imagined, or wished, that significant numbers of "the labouring classes" would advance beyond elementary schooling. It was nevertheless essential for ordinary citizens to recognize their great stake in institutions that would interest the wealthy in public education, open present opportunities for gifted boys of modest means and future opportunities for the successful sons of the poor. For the rich, the poor, and the middling alike, "learned institutions" would broaden the sources of educated leadership for society, foster science and the useful arts to the greater glory of the American Republic, and would—above all—"throw that light over the public mind which is the best security against crafty and dangerous encroachments on the public liberty."

Although Barry's comprehensive report on education was not adopted by the Kentucky legislature, that commonwealth— unlike Virginia—did create a respectable public-school system by 1860. Discounting his Virginia pride, Madison might have seen this as another case of "salutary emulation" among the states of a federal system: a friendly competition in experimental reform.

August 4, 1822.

DEAR SIR,—I received some days ago your letter of June 30, and the printed Circular to which it refers.

The liberal appropriations made by the Legislature of Kentucky for a general system of Education cannot be too much applauded. A popular Government, without popular information, or the means of acquiring it, is but a Prologue to a Farce or a Tragedy; or, perhaps both. Knowledge will forever govern ignorance: And a people who mean to be their own Governors, must arm themselves with the power which knowledge gives.

I have always felt a more than ordinary interest in the destinies of Kentucky. Among her earliest settlers were some of my particular friends and Neighbors. And I was myself among the foremost advocates for submitting to the Will of the "District" the question and the time of its becoming a separate member of the American family. Its rapid growth & signal prosperity in this character have afforded me much pleasure; which is not a little enhanced by the enlightened patriotism which is now providing for the State a Plan of Education embracing every class of Citizens, and every grade & department of Knowledge. No error is more certain than the one proceeding from a hasty & superficial view of the subject: that the people at large have no interest in the establishment of Academies, Colleges, and Universities, where a few only, and those not of the poorer classes can obtain for their sons the advantages of superior education. It is thought to be unjust that all should be taxed for the benefit of a part, and that too the part least needing it.

If provision were not made at the same time for every part, the objection would be a natural one. But, besides the consideration when the higher Seminaries belong to a plan of general education, that it is better for the poorer classes to have the aid of the richer by a general tax on property, than that every parent should provide at his own expence for the education of his children, it is certain that every Class is interested in establishments which give to the human mind its highest improvements, and to every Country its truest and most durable celebrity.

Learned Institutions ought to be favorite objects with every free people. They throw that light over the public mind which is the best security against crafty & dangerous encroachments on the public liberty. They are the nurseries of skilful Teachers for the schools distributed throughout the Community. They are themselves schools for the particular talents required for some of the Public Trusts, on the able execution of which the welfare of the people depends. They multiply the educated individuals from among whom the people may elect a due portion of their public Agents of every description; more especially of those who are to frame the laws; by the perspicuity, the consistency, and the stability, as well as by the just & equal spirit of which the great social purposes are to be answered.

Without such Institutions, the more costly of which can scarcely be provided by individual means, none but the few whose wealth enables them to support their sons abroad can give them the fullest education; and in proportion as this is done, the influence is monopolized which superior information every where possesses. At cheaper & nearer seats of Learning parents with slender incomes may place their sons in a course of education putting them on a level with the sons of the Richest. Whilst those who are without property, or with but little, must be peculiarly interested in a System which unites with the more Learned Institutions, a provision for diffusing through the entire Society the education needed for the common purposes of life. A system comprizing the Learned Institutions may be still further recommended to the more indigent class of Citizens by such an arrangement as was reported to the General Assembly of Virginia, in the year 1779, by a Committee appointed to revise laws in order to adapt them to the genius of Republican Government. It made part of a "Bill for the more general diffusion of knowledge" that wherever a youth was ascertained to possess talents meriting an education which his parents could not afford, he should be carried forward at the public expence, from seminary to seminary, to the completion of his studies at the highest.

But why should it be necessary in this case, to distinguish the Society into classes according to their property? When it is considered that the establishment and endowment of Academies, Colleges, and Universities are a provision, not merely for the existing generation, but for succeeding ones also; that in Governments like ours a constant rotation of property results from the free scope to industry, and from the laws of inheritance, and when it is considered moreover, how much of the exertions and privations of all are meant not for themselves, but for their posterity, there can be little ground for objections from any class, to plans of which every class must have its turn of benefits. The rich man, when contributing to a permanent plan for the education of the poor, ought to reflect that he is providing for that of his own descendants; and the poor man who concurs in a provision for those who are not poor that at no distant day it may be enjoyed by descendants from himself. It does not require a long life to witness these vicissitudes of fortune.

It is among the happy peculiarities of our Union, that the States composing it derive from their relation to each other and to the whole, a salutary emulation, without the enmity involved in competitions among States alien to each other. This emulation, we may perceive, is not without its influence in several important respects; and in none ought it to be more felt than in the merit of diffusing the light and the advantages of Public Instruction. In the example therefore which Kentucky is presenting, she not only consults her own welfare, but is giving an impulse to any of her sisters who may be behind her in the noble career.

Throughout the Civilized World, nations are courting the

praise of fostering Science and the useful Arts, and are opening their eyes to the principles and the blessings of Representative Government. The American people owe it to themselves, and to the cause of free Government, to prove by their establishments for the advancement and diffusion of Knowledge, that their political Institutions, which are attracting observation from every quarter, and are respected as Models, by the newborn States in our own Hemisphere, are as favorable to the intellectual and moral improvement of Man as they are conformable to his individual & social Rights. What spectacle can be more edifying or more seasonable, than that of Liberty & Learning, each leaning on the other for their mutual & surest support?

The Committee, of which your name is the first, have taken a very judicious course in endeavouring to avail Kentucky of the experience of elder States, in modifying her Schools. I enclose extracts from the laws of Virginia on that subject; though I presume they will give little aid; the less as they have as yet been imperfectly carried into execution. The States where such systems have been long in operation will furnish much better answers to many of the enquiries stated in your Circular. But after all, such is the diversity of local circumstances, more particularly as the population varies in density & sparseness, that the details suited to some may be little so to others. As the population however, is becoming less & less sparse, and it will be well in laying the foundation of a Good System, to have a view to this progressive change, much attention seems due to examples in the Eastern States, where the people are most compact, & where there has been the longest experience in plans of popular education.

I know not that I can offer on the occasion any suggestions not likely to occur to the Committee. Were I to hazard one, it would be in favour of adding to Reading, Writing, & Arithmetic, to which the instruction of the poor, is commonly limited, some knowledge of Geography; such as can easily be conveyed by a Globe & Maps, and a concise Geographical Grammar. And how easily & quickly might a general idea even, be conveyed of the Solar System, by the aid of a Planatarium of the Cheapest construction. No information seems better calculated to expand the mind and gratify curiosity than what would thus be imparted. This is especially the case, with what relates to the Globe we inhabit, the Nations among which it is divided, and the characters and customs which distinguish them. An acquaintance with foreign Countries in this mode, has a kindred effect with that of seeing them as travellers, which never fails, in uncorrupted minds, to weaken local prejudices, and enlarge the sphere of benevolent feelings. A knowledge of the Globe & its various inhabitants, however slight, might moreover, create a taste for Books of Travels and Voyages; out of which might grow a general taste for History, an inexhaustible fund of entertainment & instruction. Any reading not of a vicious species must be a good substitute for the amusements too apt to fill up the leisure of the labouring classes.

I feel myself much obliged Sir by your expressions of personal kindness, and pray you to accept a return of my good wishes, with assurances of my great esteem & respect.

32. Political Creed for the University

The University of Virginia, Jefferson told an English correspondent, "will be based on the illimitable freedom of the
human mind." (Letter to William Roscoe, December 27, 1820.)
The *end* of a free university, as he always believed, was the
pursuit of knowledge for the physical and moral improvement
of the human condition, and of particular societies. Thus Jefferson's "Rockfish Gap" report to the Virginia legislature
(1818), endorsed by a commission including Madison, justified
public support of the new university on the grounds of public
utility: it would cultivate the learned sciences that advance the
prosperity, power, and happiness of a people; it would train
virtuous and enlightened citizens to lead society; and it would
spread sound (i.e. liberal and republican) principles of government, economy, and law through the state and nation.

In most fields of useful knowledge, Jefferson and Madison
agreed, the university's governing Board of Visitors should

To Thomas Jefferson, February 8, 1825, in *Writings*, IX, pp. 218–220.

seek the ablest available scholars and, within broad limits, leave them free to teach according to their lights. Two subjects of the highest importance stood outside that general rule. In order to preserve the separation of church and state and avoid dangerous denominational rivalries, the university should appoint no professor of divinity. Government and law, the branch of learning that most directly touched the public concerns of the university, must be assigned to a professor of orthodox Virginia-Republican views. Moreover, Jefferson wrote to Madison on February 1, 1825, the Board had a duty to guard against the dissemination of Federalist and consolidationist heresies among the future leaders of Virginia by a previous prescription of the texts to be adopted for the school of law. Locke and Sidney, the Declaration of Independence, *The Federalist,* and the Virginia Report of 1799: together these would define a political creed for Virginia and America.

Madison's reply, reprinted below, fully adopted the broad purpose of inculcating "the true doctrines of liberty as exemplified in our political system." Unlike the case of religion, the public right to frame a political creed raised no doubts for him. Yet the choice of texts and the mode of prescription would be a tricky political business for the university, Madison warned, and he offered several amendments that Jefferson readily accepted. On March 4, 1825, the Board of Visitors passed a resolution embodying the Jefferson-Madison proposals for the law school. The Board ensured a correct interpretation of the textbook by appointing, as Madison had advised, "an able and orthodox professor" of the Virginia strict-construction school. Yet one must add that Madison's own view of constitutional orthodoxy was not exactly Jefferson's, although he preferred to veil such differences. Significantly, just a few years earlier, he had encouraged Peter S. Du Ponceau in his proposal for a *national* "seminary of Jurisprudence": "This would be a species of consolidation having the happy tendency to diminish local prejudices, to cherish mutual confidence and to accommodate the intercourse of business between citizens of different states, without impairing the constitutional separation &c Independence of the states themselves. . . ." (To Du Ponceau, May, 1821.)

Montpellier, February 8, 1825.

DEAR SIR,—The letters from Mr. Cabell are herein returned. I just see that he has succeeded in defeating the project for removing the College from Williamsburg.

I hope your concurrence in what I said of Mr. Barbour will not divert your thoughts from others. It is possible that the drudgery of his profession, the uncertainty of Judicial appointment acceptable to him, and some other attractions at the University for his young family, might reconcile him to a removal thither; but I think the chance slender.

I have looked with attention over your intended proposal of a text book for the Law School. It is certainly very material that the true doctrines of liberty, as exemplified in our Political System, should be inculcated on those who are to sustain and may administer it. It is, at the same time, not easy to find standard books that will be both guides & guards for the purpose. Sidney & Locke are admirably calculated to impress on young minds the right of Nations to establish their own Governments, and to inspire a love of free ones; but afford no aid in guarding our Republican Charters against constructive violations. The Declaration of Independence, tho' rich in fundamental principles, and saying every thing that could be said in the same number of words, falls nearly under a like observation. The "Federalist" may fairly enough be regarded as the most authentic exposition of the text of the federal Constitution, as understood by the Body which prepared & the Authority which accepted it. Yet it did not foresee all the misconstructions which have occurred; nor prevent some that it did foresee. And what equally deserves remark, neither of the great rival Parties have acquiesced in all its comments. It may nevertheless be admissible as a School book, if any will be that goes so much into detail. It has been actually admitted into two Universities, if not more—those of Harvard and Rhode Island; but probably at the choice of the Professors, without any injunction from the superior authority. With respect to the Virginia Document of 1799, there may be more room for hesitation. Tho' corresponding with the predominant sense of the Nation; being of local origin & having reference to a state of Parties not yet extinct, an absolute prescription of it, might excite prejudices against the University as under Party Banners, and induce the more bigoted to withhold from it their sons, even when destined for other than the studies of the Law School. It may be added that the Document is not on every point satisfactory to all who belong to the same Party. Are we sure that to our brethren of the Board it is so? In framing a political creed, a like difficulty occurs as in the case of religion tho' the public right be very different in the two cases. If the Articles be in very general terms, they do not answer the purpose; if in very particular terms, they divide & exclude where meant to unite & fortify. The best that can be done in our case seems to be, to avoid the two extremes, by referring to selected Standards without requiring an unqualified conformity to them, which indeed might not in every instance be possible. The selection would give them authority with the Students, and might controul or counteract deviations of the Professor. I have, for your consideration, sketched a modification of the operative passage in your draught, with a view to relax the absoluteness of its injunction, and added to your list of Documents the Inaugural Speech and the Farewell Address of President Washington. They may help down what might be less readily swallowed, and contain nothing which is not good;

unless it be the laudatory reference in the Address to the Treaty of 1795 with Great Britain which ought not to weigh against the sound sentiments characterizing it.

After all, the most effectual safeguard against heretical intrusions into the School of Politics, will be an Able & Orthodox Professor, whose course of instruction will be an example to his successors, and may carry with it a sanction from the Visitors.

Affectionately yours.

Sketch

And on the distinctive principles of the Government of our own State, and of that of the United States, the best guides are to be found in—1. The Declaration of Independence, as the fundamental act of Union of these States. 2. the book known by the title of the "Federalist," being an Authority to which appeal is habitually made by all & rarely declined or denied by any, as evidence of the general opinion of those who framed & those who accepted the Constitution of the United States on questions as to its genuine meaning. 3. the Resolutions of the General Assembly of Virginia in 1799, on the subject of the Alien & Sedition laws, which appeared to accord with the predominant sense of the people of the U. S. 4. The Inaugural Speech & Farewell Address of President Washington, as conveying political lessons of peculiar value; and that in the branch of the School of law which is to treat on the subject of Government, these shall be used as the text & documents of the School.

33. Planters and Professors:
Toward Scientific Farming

Soil exhaustion, falling land values, and a general decline of the tobacco economy seemed to threaten ruin to the upper South in the early decades of the nineteenth century. Urgent economic necessity, as well as scientific curiosity and political concern, prompted such enlightened Virginia planters as Jefferson and Madison, John Taylor, and Edward Ruffin, to promote agricultural reforms. Although the prominent public men among the gentry were forced to entrust a large part of the direct management of their estates to subordinates—often with grievous results—they nevertheless directed a continuous experimentation with new crops and breeds, methods and implements, not only to solve their own problems but to influence the mass of ordinary farmers who clung stubbornly to old ways.

Madison, who had become the first president of the American Board of Agriculture (a national association of farm groups and agricultural reformers founded at Washington in 1803),

---

To the President of the Agricultural Society of _____, Virginia, October 21, 1822, in *Letters*, III, pp. 284–287.

served after his political retirement as president of the regional Agricultural Society of Albemarle (Virginia). His presidential address to the Society, published in 1818, knowingly discussed everything from manure to the place of agriculture in the balance of nature and the rise of civilization. The following appeal of 1822 to the several agricultural societies of the state for funds to endow a professorship of agriculture and "pattern farm" at the prospective University of Virginia did not succeed, although Jefferson as Rector charged the chemistry professor with responsibility for agricultural theory. A growing movement toward crop diversification and scientific farming—aided by the shameful profits of slave-breeding for the cotton states—did revive the economy of the Upper South in the pre-war decades.

[*Circular.*]

TO THE PRESIDENT OF THE AGRICULTURAL
SOCIETY OF ———, VIRGINIA

October 21, 1822.

Sir,—The enclosed Resolutions of the Agricultural Society of Albemarle explain the wish of the society to provide for agriculture the advantage of a professorship, to be incorporated into the University of Virginia; the means proposed for making the provision; and the hope entertained of a general co-operation in the scheme.

The present seems to be an important crisis in the agriculture of Virginia. The portions of her soil first brought into cultivation have, for the most part, been exhausted of its natural fertility, without being repaired by a meliorating system of husbandry; and much of what remains in forest, and can be spared from the demands of fuel and other rural wants, will need improvement on the first introduction of the plough.

These truths are now sufficiently impressed on the public attention, and have led to the establishment of the Agricultural Societies among us, which are so laudably promoting the work of reform.

As a further means of advancing the great object, it has occurred to the Albemarle Society that a distinct Professorship in the University of the State, if sanctioned by the proper authority, might be advantageously appropriated to the instruction of such as might attend in the theory and practice of rural economy in its several branches.

To the due success of agriculture, as of other arts, theory and practice are both requisite. They always reflect light on each other. If the former, without the test of the latter, be a vain science, the latter, without the enlightening precepts of the former, is generally enslaved to ancient modes, however erroneous, or is at best but too tardy and partial in adopting salutary changes. In no instance, perhaps, is habit more unyielding, or irrational practice more prevalent, than among those who cultivate the earth. And this is the more to be lamented, as agriculture is still so far below the attainments to which it may fairly aspire.

A professorship of agriculture may derive special advantage from the lights thrown out from the chair of Chemistry in that Institution. This science is every day penetrating some of the hidden laws of nature, and tracing the useful purposes to which they may be made subservient. Agriculture is a field on which it has already begun to shed its rays, and on which it promises to do much towards unveiling the processes of nature, to which the principles of agriculture are related. The professional lectures on chemistry, which are to embrace those principles, could not fail to be auxiliary to a professorship having lessons on agriculture for its essential charge.

The fund contemplated for the support of such a professorship is to consist of a sum drawn from unexpended subscriptions, from special donations, and from a diffusive contribution, not exceeding a dollar from an individual. It is hoped that, for a purpose of such general utility, the number of contributors will more than make up for the smallness of the respective sums; and that, with the other resources, means may be gathered not only adequate to the immediate views entertained, but justifying an enlargement of them.

Should this prove to be the case, it will be an enlargement of the plan of agricultural instruction to provide and place under the superintendence of the Professor a small farm in the vicinage, to be cultivated partly as a pattern farm, illustrating practically a system at once profitable and improving; partly as an experimental farm, not only bringing to the test new modes of culture and management, but introducing new plants and animals deemed worthy of experiment. In obtaining these, aid might be found in the patriotic attention of the public and private Naval Commanders, in their visits to foreign countries; and it might well happen that occasional success in rearing new species or varieties, of peculiar value, would yield in seeds and stocks a profit defraying the expenses incurred on this head.

A farm exhibiting an instructive model, observed, as it would be, by occasional visitors, and understood, as it would be, in its principles and plants by students returning to their dispersed homes, would tend to spread sound information on the subject of agriculture, and to cherish that spirit of imitation and emulation which is the source of improvement in every art and enterprise.

You will oblige, Sir, the Society of Albemarle by laying this communication before that over which you preside, and by transmitting its sentiments thereon; which will afford particular pleasure if they should accord with the views of this Society, and promise so valuable a co-operation in carrying them into effect.

By order of the Society.

JAMES MADISON, *President.*

34. Malthus and Utopia:
The New Harmony Experiment

Madison's skeptical remarks on the New Harmony (Indiana) community of Robert Dale Owen and his disciples remind one that the dismal population science of Thomas Robert Malthus was conceived in reaction to the earlier Utopian visions of William Godwin, Condorcet, and other revolutionary thinkers of the 1790s. To Godwin's enthusiastic faith in the perfection of human nature and society, Malthus opposed the grim "law of nature" determining "that the power of population is indefinitely greater than the power in the earth to produce subsistence for man." After all the means of reason and virtue had been exhausted, Malthus wrote in 1798, vice and misery and death must perpetually restore the precarious balance between hungry mouths (increasing geometrically) and scarce loaves (increasing arithmetically): such is man's fate. Presumably, enlightened republicans and hopeful reformers living in a land of plenty should have been, if not Godwinite Utopians, then at least firm anti-Malthusians.

To Nicholas P. Trist, April ——, 1827, in *Letters,* III, pp. 575–578.

Yet Jefferson called Malthus' work on population "one of the ablest I have ever seen" (Jefferson to Joseph Priestley, January 29, 1804); and Madison dismissed the statistical basis of Godwin's counterview as nonsense. (These judgments would have been remarkable even if they referred specifically to the softer view of the human prospect in the revised 1803 edition of Malthus' *Essay on the Principle of Population.*) Jefferson gave no clear explanation for his praise. He seemed to be more impressed by the re-statement of laissez-faire economic doctrines than by the distinctive population theory. Madison rather plainly declared himself to be a Malthusian, although with reservations in favor of the American future. The problem of population and poverty had concerned him as early as 1786, when he warned Jefferson that the best governed people in an old and fully developed country could not escape the evils of a labor surplus: "A certain degree of misery seems inseparable from a high degree of populousness." (Madison to Jefferson, June 19, 1786.) He later found in Malthus an able elaboration and application of a long familiar principle, "inherent in all the organized beings on the Globe," and necessary to maintain "the general symmetry and economy of nature." (Madison to Edward Everett, November 26, 1823.)

Writing to Nicholas P. Trist, a younger Virginian of the Jefferson circle, on Owen's New Harmony experiment, Madison's thoughts returned to Malthusian doctrine. The Utopian advocate had visited Madison in the Spring of 1825, and his *New Harmony Gazette* was received if not faithfully read by Madison. Once more, as in the case of Fanny Wright's Nashoba colony and other visionary projects, Madison found the venture "interesting," but doubtful. Even granting Owen the unlikely possibility of remaking man by creating a new social harmony, of making custom "nature itself," Madison could discover no convincing answer to the ultimate (Malthusian) dilemma. To Owen's "panacea" for the distress of the laboring classes, he preferred his own liberal "palliative": free trade, universal peace, and, of course, a free republican society.

Montpellier, January 29, 1828.

DEAR SIR,—The Harmony Gazette has been regularly sent me, but in the crowd of printed things I receive, I had not attended to the essays to which you refer me. The present situation of Great Britain, which gave rise to them, is full of instruction, and Mr. Owen avails himself of it with address in favour of his panacea. Such diseases are, however, too deeply rooted in human society to admit of more than great palliatives.

Every populous country is liable to contingencies that must distress a portion of its inhabitants. The chief of them are: 1. Unfruitful seasons, increasing the price of subsistence without increasing that of labour; and even reducing the price of labour by abridging the demand of those whose income depends on the fruits of the earth. 2. The sudden introduction of labour-saving machinery, taking employment from those whose labour is the only source of their subsistence. 3. The caprice of fashion, on which the many depend, who supply the wants of fancy. Take, for a sufficient illustration, a single fact: when the present King of England was Prince of Wales, he introduced the use of shoe-strings instead of shoe-buckles. The effect on the condition of the buckle-makers was such, that he received addresses from many thousands of them, praying him, as the arbiter of fashion, to save them from starving by restoring the taste for buckles in preference to strings. 4. To the preceding occurrences, to which an insulated community would be liable, must be added a loss of foreign markets to a manufacturing and commercial community, from whatever of the various causes it may happen. Among these causes may be named even the changeableness of foreign fashions. The substitution of shoe-strings for shoe-buckles in the United States had a like effect with that in England, on her buckle-makers.

Mr. Owen's remedy for these vicissitudes implies that labour will be relished without the ordinary impulses to it; that the love of equality will supersede the desire of distinction; and that the increasing leisure, from the improvements of machinery, will promote intellectual cultivation, moral enjoyment, and innocent amusements, without any of the vicious resorts, for the ennui of idleness. Custom is properly called a second nature; Mr. Owen makes it nature herself. His enterprise is, nevertheless, an interesting one. It will throw light on the maximum to which the force of education and habit can be carried; and, like Helvetius' attempt to show that all men come from the hand of nature perfectly equal, and owe every intellectual and moral difference to the education of circumstances, though failing of its entire object, that of proving the means to be all-sufficient, will lead to a fuller sense of their great importance.

The state of things promising most exemption from the distress exhibited in Great Britain, would be a freedom of commerce among all nations, and especially with the addition of universal peace. The *aggregate* fruits of the earth, which are little varied by the seasons, would then be accessible to all. The improvements of machinery not being adopted everywhere at once, would have a diminished effect where first introduced; and there being no interruptions to foreign commerce, the vicissitudes of fashion would be limited in their sudden effect in one country, by the numerous markets abroad for the same or similar articles.

After all, there is one indelible cause remaining, of pressure on the condition of the labouring part of mankind; and that is, the constant tendency of an increase of their number, after the increase of food has reached its term. The competition for employment then reduces wages to their minimum, and privation to its maximum; and whether the evil proceeding from this tendency be checked, as it must be, by either physical or moral causes, the checks are themselves but so many evils. With this knowledge of the impossibility of banishing evil altogether from human society, we must console ourselves with the belief that it is overbalanced by the good mixed with it, and direct our efforts to an increase of the good proportion of the mixture.

Even Mr. Owen's scheme, with all the success he assumes for it would not avoid the pressure in question. As it admits of marriages, and it would gain nothing by prohibiting them, I asked him, what was to be done after there should be a plenum of population for all the food his lots of ground could be made to produce. His answer was, that the earth could be made *indefinitely* productive by a deeper and deeper cultivation. Being easily convinced of this error, his resort was to colonizations to vacant regions. But your plan is to cover, and that rapidly, tho whole earth [with] flourishing communities. What is then to become of the increasing population? This was too remote a consideration to require present attention—an answer prudent, if not conclusive.

35. The Marshall Court and
the Virginia Opposition:
Three Letters to Judge Roane

During and after the War of 1812, Madison helped to guide
the Republican party and the country toward a cautious new
nationalism. (See Part IV.) Old Republicans of the states'-
rights and strict-construction school quickly regrouped their
forces, enlisted new recruits, and mounted a heavy counter-
attack. Their opposition to nationalist policies in the areas of
banking, tariffs, internal improvements, and the like led them
straight to the source of error: Chief Justice John Marshall and
the Supreme Court. If Marshall's loose reading of the Constitution prevailed, they warned, the state legislatures and courts
would be swallowed up by a consolidated central government
of unlimited powers.

In Virginia, Judge Spencer Roane of the State Supreme
Court of Appeals took a leading role in the political and legal
reaction. A prominent Jeffersonian politician and judge since

---

Madison to Spencer Roane, September 2, 1819, May 6, 1821, June 29,
1821, in *Writings*, VIII, pp. 447–453; IX, pp. 55–63, 65–68.

the 1790s. Roane was a veteran antagonist of Marshall's. The opinion of the Chief Justice in *McCulloch* v. *Maryland* (1819), laying down the principle of broad construction in the boldest Hamiltonian terms, provoked Roan to publish a series of impassioned letters in the Richmond *Enquirer*. Naturally, he turned to the Republican sages of Virginia for approval. Jefferson whole-heartedly endorsed Roane's attack on the Marshall court. Madison's reply of September 6, 1819, silently passed over the embarrassing fact that he agreed with the Court's judgment upholding the constitutionality of the national bank, and offered no clear objection to Marshall's finding that Maryland lacked the right to tax the federal branch bank at Baltimore. Nevertheless, his sharp critique of Marshall's "latitudinary mode of expounding the Constitution" gave some encouragement to Roane and his friends. At their urging, the Virginia legislature passed a resolution expressing its "most solemn protest" against the *McCulloch* decision and Marshall's judicial imperialism.

Two years later, Marshall's opinion in *Cohens* v. *Virginia* (1821) stirred Judge Roane to even greater fury, involving as it did a direct assertion of Supreme Court jurisdiction over a case originating in the courts and under the laws of his own state. Writing in the *Enquirer* under the name of "Algernon Sydney," he denounced the Supreme Court for a "most monstrous and unexampled decision." Again Roane appealed to the Republican patron saints, and again he drew enthusiastic praise from Jefferson, who considered Roane "our strongest bulwark" against the twin evils of judicial usurpation and national consolidation. Madison politely declined Roane's invitation to take up the public defense of the Virginia courts against the "fatal sophistries" of Marshall. His replies of May 6 and June 29, 1821, combined a moderate rebuke to the overbearing Marshall court with a tactful but stern rejection of Roane's main argument: without federal judicial review—and eventually a mutual accommodation of views among state and federal judges —the union would be reduced to legal and political chaos.

September 2, 1819.

DEAR SIR,—I have received your favor of the 22d ultimo inclosing a copy of your observations on the Judgment of the Supreme Court of the U. S. in the case of M'Culloch against the State of Maryland; and I have found their latitudinary mode of expounding the Constitution, combated in them with the ability and the force which were to be expected.

It appears to me as it does to you that the occasion did not call for the general and abstract doctrine interwoven with the decision of the particular case. I have always supposed that the meaning of a law, and for a like reason, of a Constitution, so far as it depends on Judicial interpretation, was to result from a course of particular decisions, and not these from a previous and abstract comment on the subject. The example in this instance tends to reverse the rule and to forego the illustration to be derived from a series of cases actually occurring for adjudication.

I could have wished also that the Judges had delivered their opinions seriatim. The case was of such magnitude, in the scope given to it, as to call, if any case could do so, for the views of the subject separately taken by them. This might either by the harmony of their reasoning have produced a greater conviction in the Public mind; or by its discordance have impaired the force of the precedent now ostensibly supported by a unanimous & perfect concurrence in every argument & dictum in the judgment pronounced.

But what is of most importance is the high sanction given to a latitude in expounding the Constitution which seems to break down the landmarks intended by a specification of the Powers of Congress, and to substitute for a definite connection between means and ends, a Legislative discretion as to the former to which no practical limit can be assigned. In the great system of Political Economy having for its general object the national welfare, everything is related immediately or remotely to every other thing; and consequently a Power over any one thing, if not limited by some obvious and precise affinity, may amount to a Power over every other. Ends & means may shift their character at the will & according to the ingenuity of the Legislative Body. What is an end in one case may be a means in another; nay in the same case, may be either an end or a means at the Legislative option. The British Parliament in collecting a revenue from the commerce of America found no difficulty in calling it either a tax for the regulation of trade, or a regulation of trade with a view to the tax, as it suited the argument or the policy of the moment.

Is there a Legislative power in fact, not expressly prohibited by the Constitution, which might not, according to the doctrine of the Court, be exercised as a means of carrying into effect some specified Power?

Does not the Court also relinquish by their doctrine, all controul on the Legislative exercise of unconstitutional powers? According to that doctrine, the expediency & constitutionality of means for carrying into effect a specified Power are convertible terms; and Congress are admitted to be Judges of the expediency. The Court certainly cannot be so; a question, the moment it assumes the character of mere expediency or policy, being evidently beyond the reach of Judicial cognizance.

It is true, the Court are disposed to retain a guardianship of the Constitution against legislative encroachments. "Should Congress," say they, "under the pretext of executing its Powers, pass laws for the accomplishment of objects not entrusted to the Government, it would become the painful duty of this Tribunal to say that such an act was not the law of the land." But suppose Congress should, as would doubtless happen, pass unconstitutional laws not to accomplish objects not specified in the Constitution, but the same laws as means expedient, convenient or conducive to the accomplishment of objects entrusted to the Government; by what handle could the Court take hold of the case? We are told that it was the policy of the old Government of France to grant monopolies, such as that of Tobacco, in order to create funds in particular hands from which loans could be made to the Public, adequate capitalists not being formed in that Country in the ordinary course of commerce. Were Congress to grant a like monopoly merely to aggrandize those enjoying it, the Court might consistently say, that this not being an object entrusted to the Government the grant was unconstitutional and void. Should Congress however grant the monopoly according to the French policy as a means judged by them to be necessary, expedient or conducive to the borrowing of money, which is an object entrusted to them by the Constitution, it seems clear that the Court, adhering to its doctrine, could not interfere without stepping on Legislative ground, to do which they justly disclaim all pretension.

It could not but happen, and was foreseen at the birth of the Constitution, that difficulties and differences of opinion might occasionally raise in expounding terms & phrases necessarily used in such a charter; more especially those which divide legislation between the General & local Governments; and that it might require a regular course of practice to liquidate & settle the meaning of some of them. But it was anticipated I believe by few if any of the friends of the Constitution, that a rule of construction would be introduced as broad & as pliant as what has occurred. And those who recollect, and still more those who shared in what passed in the State Conventions, thro' which the people ratified the Constitution, with respect to the extent of the powers vested in Congress, cannot easily be persuaded that the avowal of such a rule would not have prevented its ratification. It has been the misfortune, if not the reproach, of other nations, that their Governments have not been freely and deliberately established by themselves. It is the boast of ours that such has been its source and that it can be altered by the same authority only which established it. It is a further boast that a regular mode of making proper alterations has been providently inserted in the Constitution itself. It is anxiously to be wished therefore, that no innovations may take place in other modes, one of which would be a constructive assumption of powers never meant to be granted. If the powers be deficient, the legitimate source of additional ones is always open, and ought to be resorted to.

Much of the error in expounding the Constitution has its origin in the use made of the species of sovereignty implied in the nature of Government. The specified powers vested in Congress, it is said, are sovereign powers, and that as such they carry with them an unlimited discretion as to the means of executing them. It may surely be remarked that a limited Government may be limited in its sovereignty as well with respect to the means as to the objects of his powers; and that to give an extent to the former, superseding the limits to the latter, is in effect to convert a limited into an unlimited Government. There is certainly a reasonable medium between expounding the Constitution with the strictness of a penal law, or other ordinary statute, and expounding it with a laxity which may vary its essential character, and encroach on the local sovereignties with which it was meant to be reconcilable.

The very existence of these local sovereignties is a controul on the pleas for a constructive amplification of the powers of the General Government. Within a single State possessing the entire sovereignty, the powers given to the Government by the People are understood to extend to all the Acts whether as means or ends required for the welfare of the Community, and falling within the range of just Government. To withhold from such a Government any particular power necessary or useful in itself, would be to deprive the people of the good dependent on its exercise; since the power must be there or not exist at all. In the Government of the U. S. the case is obviously different. In establishing that Government the people retained other Governments capable of exercising such necessary and useful powers as were not to be exercised by the General Government.

No necessary presumption therefore arises from the importance of any particular power in itself, that it has been vested in that Government because tho' not vested there, it may exist elsewhere, and the exercise of it elsewhere might be preferred by those who alone had a right to make the distribution. The presumption which ought to be indulged is that any improvement of this distribution sufficiently pointed out by experience would not be withheld.

Altho' I have confined myself to the single question concerning the rule of interpreting the Constitution, I find that my pen has carried me to a length which would not have been permitted by a recollection that my remarks are merely for an eye to which no aspect of the subject is likely to be new. I hasten therefore to conclude with assurances &c &c.

Montpellier, May 6, 1821.

DEAR SIR,—I received more than two weeks ago, your letter of April 17. A visit to a sick friend at a distance, with a series of unavoidable attentions have prevented an earlier acknowledgment of it.

Under any circumstances I should be disposed rather to put such a subject as that to which it relates into your hands than to take it out of them. Apart from this consideration, a variety of demands on my time would restrain me from the task of unravelling the arguments applied by the Supreme Court of the U. S. to their late decision. I am particularly aware moreover that they are made to rest not a little on technical points of law, which are as foreign to my studies as they are familiar to yours.

It is to be regretted that the Court is so much in the practice of mingling with their judgments pronounced, comments & reasonings of a scope beyond them; and that there is often an apparent disposition to amplify the authorities of the Union at the expence of those of the States. It is of great importance as well as of indispensable obligation, that the constitutional boundary between them should be impartially maintained. Every deviation from it in practice detracts from the superiority of a Chartered over a traditional Government and mars the experiment which is to determine the interesting Problem whether the organization of the Political system of the U. S. establishes a just equilibrium; or tends to a preponderance of the National or the local powers, and in the latter case, whether of the national or of the local.

A candid review of the vicissitudes which have marked the progress of the General Government does not preclude doubts as to the ultimate & fixed character of a Political Establishment distinguished by so novel & complex a mechanism. On some occasions the advantage taken of favorable circumstances gave an impetus & direction to it which seemed to threaten subversive encroachments on the rights & authorities of the States. At a certain period we witnessed a spirit of usurpation by some of these on the necessary & legitimate functions of the former. At the present date, theoretic innovations at least are putting new weights into the scale of federal sovereignty which make it highly proper to bring them to the Bar of the Constitution.

In looking to the probable course and eventual bearing of the compound Government of our Country, I cannot but think that much will depend not only on the moral changes incident to the progress of society; but on the increasing number of the members of the Union. Were the members very few, and each very powerful, a feeling of self-sufficiency would have a relaxing effect on the bands holding them together. Were they numerous & weak, the Government over the whole world find less difficulty in maintaining & increasing subordination. It happens that whilst the power of some is swelling to a great size, the entire number is swelling also. In this respect a corresponding increase of centripetal & centrifugal forces, may be equivalent to no increase of either.

In the existing posture of things, my reflections lead me to infer that whatever may be the latitude of Jurisdiction assumed by the Judicial Power of the U. S. it is less formidable to the reserved sovereignty of the States than the latitude of power which it has assigned to the National Legislature; & that encroachments of the latter are more to be apprehended from impulses given to it by a majority of the States seduced by expected advantages, than from the love of Power in the Body itself, controuled as it *now* is by its responsibility to the Constituent Body.

Such is the plastic faculty of Legislation, that notwithstanding the firm tenure which judges have on their offices, they can by various regulations be kept or reduced within the paths of duty; more especially with the aid of their amenability to the Legislative tribunal in the form of impeachment. It is not probable that the Supreme Court would long be indulged in a career of usurpation opposed to the decided opinions & policy of the Legislature.

Nor do I think that Congress, even seconded by the Judicial Power, can, without some change in the character of the nation, succeed in *durable* violations of the rights & authorities of the States. The responsibility of one branch to the people, and of the other branch to the Legislatures, of the States, seem to be, in the present stage at least of our political history, an adequate barrier. In the case of the alien & sedition laws, which violated the general *sense* as well as the *rights* of the States, the usurping experiment was crushed at once, notwithstanding the co-operation of the federal Judges with the federal laws.

But what is to controul Congress when backed & even pushed on by a majority of their Constituents, as was the case in the late contest relative to Missouri, and as may again happen in the constructive power relating to Roads & Canals? Nothing within the pale of the Constitution but sound arguments & conciliatory expostulations addressed both to Congress & to their Constituents.

On the questions brought before the Public by the late doctrines of the Supreme Court of the U.S. concerning the extent of their own powers, and that of the exclusive jurisdiction of Congress over the ten miles square and other specified places, there is as yet no evidence that they express either the opinions of Congress or those of their Constituents. There is nothing therefore to discourage a development of whatever flaws the doctrines may contain, or tendencies they may threaten. Congress if convinced of these may not only abstain from the exercise of Powers claimed for them by the Court, but find the means of controuling those claimed by the Court for itself. And should Congress not be convinced, their Constituents, if so, can certainly under the forms of the Constitution effectuate a compliance with their deliberate judgment and settled determination.

In expounding the Constitution the Court seems not insensible that the intention of the parties to it ought to be kept in view; and that as far as the language of the instrument will permit, this intention ought to be traced in the contemporaneous expositions. But is the Court as prompt and as careful in citing and following this evidence, when against the federal Authority as when against that of the States? (See the partial reference of the Court to "The Federalist.")

The exclusive jurisdiction over the ten miles square is itself an anomaly in our Representative System. And its object being manifest, and attested by the views taken of it, at its date, there seems a peculiar impropriety in making it the fulcrum for a lever stretching into the most distant parts of the Union, and overruling the municipal policy of the States. The remark is still more striking when applied to the smaller places over which an exclusive jurisdiction was suggested by a regard to the defence & the property of the Nation.

Some difficulty, it must be admitted may result in particular cases from the impossibility of executing some of these powers within the defined spaces, according to the principles and rules enjoined by the Constitution; and from the want of a constitutional provision for the surrender of malefactors whose escape must be so easy, on the demand of the United States as

well as of the Individual States. It is true also that these exclusive jurisdictions are in the class of enumerated powers,
to which is subjoined the "power in Congress to pass all laws
necessary & proper for their execution." All however that could
be exacted by these considerations would be that the means
of execution should be of the most obvious & essential kind; &
exerted in the ways as little intrusive as possible on the powers
and police of the States. And, after all, the question would
remain whether the better course would not be to regard the
case as an omitted one, to be provided for by an amendment
of the Constitution. In resorting to legal precedents as sanctions
to power, the distinctions should ever be strictly attended to,
between such as take place under transitory impressions, or
without full examination & deliberation, and such as pass with
solemnities and repetitions sufficient to imply a concurrence of
the judgment & the will of those, who having granted the
power, have the ultimate right to explain the grant. Altho'
I cannot join in the protest of some against the validity of all
precedents, however uniform & multiplied, in expounding the
Constitution, yet I am persuaded that Legislative precedents
are frequently of a character entitled to little respect, and that
those of Congress are sometimes liable to peculiar distrust.
They not only follow the example of other Legislative assemblies in first procrastinating and then precipitating their acts;
but, owing to the termination of their session every other year
at a fixed day & hour, a mass of business is struck off, as it
were at shorthand, and in a moment. These midnight precedents of every sort ought to have little weight in any case.

On the question relating to involuntary submissions of the
States to the Tribunal of the Supreme Court, the Court seems
not to have adverted at all to the expository language when the
Constitution was adopted; nor to that of the Eleventh Amendment, which may as well import that it was declaratory, as
that it was restrictive of the meaning of the original text. It
seems to be a strange reasoning also that would imply that a

State in controversies with its own Citizens might have less of sovereignty, than in controversies with foreign individuals, by which the national relations might be affected. Nor is it less to be wondered that it should have appeared to the Court that the dignity of a State was not more compromitted by being made a party against a private person than against a co-ordinate Party.

The Judicial power of the U. S. over cases arising under the Constitution, must be admitted to be a vital part of the System. But that there are limitations and exceptions to its efficient character, is among the admissions of the Court itself. The Eleventh Amendment introduces exceptions if there were none before. A liberal & steady course of practice can alone reconcile the several provisions of the Constitution literally at variance with each other; of which there is an example in the Treaty Power & the Legislative Power on subjects to which both are extended by the words of the Constitution. It is particularly incumbent, in taking cognizance of cases arising under the Constitution, and in which the laws and rights of the States may be involved, to let the proceedings touch individuals only. Prudence enjoins this if there were no other motive, in consideration of the impracticability of applying coercion to States.

I am sensible Sir, that these ideas are too vague to be of value, and that they may not even hint for consideration anything not occurring to yourself. Be so good as to see in them at least an unwillingness to disregard altogether your request. Should any of the ideas be erroneous as well as vague, I have the satisfaction to know that they will be viewed by a friendly as well as a candid eye.

Montpellier, June 29, 1821.

DEAR SIR,—I have received, and return my thanks for your obliging communication of the 20th instant. The papers of "Algernon Sidney" have given their full lustre to the arguments against the suability of States by individuals, and against the projectile capacity of the power of Congress within the "ten miles square." The publication is well worthy of a Pamphlet form, but must attract Public attention in any form.

The Gordian Knot of the Constitution seems to lie in the problem of collision between the federal & State powers, especially as eventually exercised by their respective Tribunals. If the knot cannot be untied by the text of the Constitution it ought not, certainly, to be cut by any Political Alexander.

I have always thought that a construction of the instrument ought to be favoured, as far as the text would warrant, which would obviate the dilemma of a Judicial rencounter or a mutual paralysis; and that on the abstract question whether the federal or the State decisions ought to prevail, the sounder policy would yield to the claims of the former.

Our Governmental System is established by a compact, not between the Government of the United States, and the State Governments; but between the States, as sovereign communities, stipulating each with the others, a surrender of certain portions, of their respective authorities, to be exercised by a Common Government and a reservation, for their own exercise, of all their other Authorities. The possibility of disagreements concerning the line of division between these portions could not escape attention; and the existence of some Provision for terminating regularly & authoritatively such disagreements, [could] not but be regarded as a material desideratum.

Were this trust to be vested in the States in their individual characters, the Constitution of the U. S. might become different in every State, and would be pretty sure to do so in some; the State Governments would not stand all in the same relation to the General Government, some retaining more, others less of sovereignty; and the vital principle of equality, which cements their Union thus gradually be deprived of its virtue. Such a trust vested in the Government representing the whole and exercised by its tribunals, would not be exposed to these consequences; whilst the trust itself would be controulable by the States who directly or indirectly appoint the Trustees: whereas in the hands of the States no federal controul direct or indirect would exist the functionaries holding their appointments by tenures altogether independent of the General Government.

Is it not a reasonable calculation also that the room for jarring opinions between the National & State tribunals will be narrowed by successive decisions sanctioned by the Public concurrence; and that the weight of the State tribunals will be increased by improved organizations, by selections of abler Judges, and consequently by more enlightened proceedings? Much of the distrust of these departments in the States, which prevailed when the National Constitution was formed, has already been removed. Were they filled everywhere, as they are in some of the States, one of which I need not name, their decisions at once indicating & influencing the sense of their Constituents, and founded on united interpretations of constitutional points, could scarcely fail to frustrate an assumption of unconstitutional powers by the federal tribunals.

Is it too much to anticipate even that the federal & State Judges, as they become more & more co-ordinate in talents, with equal integrity, and feeling alike the impartiality enjoined by their oaths, will vary less & less also in their reasonings & opinions on all Judicial subjects; and thereby mutually contribute to the clearer & firmer establishment of the true boundaries of power, on which must depend the success & permanency of the federal republic, the best Guardian, as we believe, of the liberty, the safety, and the happiness of men. In these hypothetical views I may permit my wishes to sway too much my hopes. I submit the whole nevertheless to your perusal, well assured that you will approve the former, if you cannot join fully in the latter.

Under all circumstances I beg you to be assured of my distinguished esteem & sincere regard.

36. The Tariff and National Authority:
A Public Appeal

Passage of the "tariff of abominations" in 1828 touched off a chain of violent political reactions. Henceforth, the protective tariff would figure as a symbol of the great divisive issues in American public life: the political issue of sectional balance and centralized power; the constitutional issue of broad construction and states' rights; the economic issue of agrarian *vs.* industrial interests. Just beneath the surface of the tariff controversy lay the ominous moral issue of slavery. Under the leadership of John C. Calhoun, South Carolina moved toward nullification and the abyss that stretched beyond. Virginians of the states'-rights school, claiming the authority of the prophets of 1798, squinted in the same direction. Although Jefferson was dead, his word was broadcast by the anti-tariff forces in the form of a private letter of 1825, linking the tariff to a series of federal measures that would, if unchecked, leave Virginia

---

Madison to Joseph C. Cabell, September 18 and October 30, 1828; in *Writings*, IX, pp. 316–340, 317n–326n.

but two alternatives: "the dissolution of our Union . . . or submission to a government without limitation of powers." (Letter
to William Branch Giles, December 26, 1825.)

In this crisis, Joseph C. Cabell—a Virginia State Senator and
close collaborator in the founding of the university—appealed
to Madison to repudiate the use of his name by the states'-
rights faction and declare himself publicly on the tariff question. Madison's letter of September 18, 1828, arguing the
constitutionality of the tariff against the new heterodoxy out of
South Carolina, was at his request withheld from publication
until after the presidential election. A second letter of October
30 added an economic case for limited protection of American
industry, refuting the charge of naked exploitation of the
agrarian South made by Calhoun and his sympathizers. Cabell
arranged through U. S. Attorney General William Wirt for
publication of the two letters in the Washington *National
Intelligencer* of December 22, 23, and 25. Appearing almost
simultaneously with Calhoun's anonymous defense of nullification in the South Carolina Exposition and Protest, the
Madison letters raised a political storm in Washington and
Richmond.

Madison's analysis of the role of the tariff in the making of
the Constitution revived his old arguments of the 1780s on the
crucial importance of the federal commerce power to the establishment of an enduring nation. Moreover, his foreign policy
since the 1790s, and especially during the Jefferson-Madison
administrations, had depended essentially on peaceful coercion
through commercial regulations. The protective Tariff of 1816
reflected Madison's appeal for a program of national reconstruction after the war. (See Documents 24 and 25.) If he
doubted or denied some of John Marshall's sweeping constitutional dicta, and Marshall's very mode of legal reasoning from
abstract premises, Madison could not for a moment tolerate
the novel doctrines that would rob the national government of
a vital power. He could no more easily accept an iron dogma of

laissez-faire that would threaten the security and prosperity of the nation.

Montpellier, September 18, 1828.

DEAR SIR,—Your late letter reminds me of our Conversation on the constitutionality of the power in Congress to impose a tariff for the encouragement of Manufactures; and of my promise to sketch the grounds of the confident opinion I had expressed that it was among the powers vested in that Body. I had not forgotten my promise, & had even begun the task of fulfilling it; but frequent interruptions from other causes, being followed by a bilious indisposition, I have not been able sooner to comply with your request. The subjoined view of the subject, might have been advantageously expanded; but I leave that improvement to your own reflections and researches.

The Constitution vests in Congress expressly "the power to lay & collect taxes duties imposts & excises;" and "the power to regulate trade."

That the former Power, if not particularly expressed, would have been included in the latter, as one of the objects of a general power to regulate trade, is not necessarily impugned, as has been alledged, by its being so expressed. Examples of this sort, cannot sometimes be easily avoided, and are to be seen elsewhere in the Constitution. Thus the power "to define & punish offences against the law of Nations" includes the power, afterward particularly expressed "to make rules concerning captures &c., from offending Neutrals." So also, a power "to coin money," would doubtless include that of "regulating its value," had not the latter power been expressly inserted. The term taxes, if standing *alone*, would certainly have included, duties, imposts & excises. In another clause it is said, "no tax or duty shall be laid on imports [exports)]," &c. Here the two terms are used as synonymous. And in another clause where it is said, "no State shall lay any imposts or duties" &c,

the terms imposts & duties are synonymous. Pleonasms, tautologies & the promiscuous use of terms & phrases differing in their shades of meaning, (always to be expounded with reference to the context and under the controul of the general character & manifest scope of the Instrument in which they are found) are to be ascribed sometimes to the purpose of greater caution; sometimes to the imperfections of language; & sometimes to the imperfection of man himself. In this view of the subject, it was quite natural, however certainly the general power to regulate trade might include a power to impose duties on it, not to omit it in a clause enumerating the several modes of revenue authorized by the Constitution. In few cases could the *"ex majori cautela"* occur with more claim to respect.

Nor can it be inferred, as has been ingeniously attempted, that a power to regulate trade does not involve a power to tax it, from the distinction made in the original controversy with Great Britain, between a power to regulate trade with the Colonies & a power to tax them. A power to regulate trade between different parts of the Empire was confessedly *necessary;* and was admitted to lie, as far as that was the case in the British Parliament, the taxing part being at the same time denied to the Parliament, & asserted to be necessarily inherent in the Colonial Legislatures, as sufficient & the only safe depositories of the taxing power. So difficult was it nevertheless to maintain the distinction in practice, that the ingredient of revenue was occasionally overlooked or disregarded in the British regulations; as in the duty on sugar & Molasses imported into the Colonies. And it was fortunate that the attempt at an internal and direct tax in the case of the Stamp Act, produced a radical examination of the subject, before a regulation of trade with a view to revenue had grown into an established Authority. One thing at least is certain, that the main & admitted object of the Parliamentary *regulations* of trade with the Colonies, was the encouragement of *manufactures* in Great Britain.

But the present question is unconnected, with the former relations between Great Britain and her Colonies, which were of a peculiar, a complicated, and, in several respects, of an undefined character. It is a simple question under the Constitution of the U. S. whether "the power to regulate trade with foreign nations" as a distinct & substantive item in the enumerated powers, embraces the object of encouraging by duties restrictions and prohibitions the manufactures & products of the Country? And the affirmative must be inferred from the following considerations:

1. The meaning of the Phrase "to regulate trade" must be sought in the general use of it, in other words in the objects to which the power was generally understood to be applicable, when the Phrase was inserted in the Constitution.

2. The power has been understood and used by all commercial & manufacturing Nations as embracing the object of encouraging manufactures. It is believed that not a single exception can be named.

3. This has been particularly the case with Great Britain, whose commercial vocabulary is the parent of ours. A primary object of her commercial regulations is well known to have been the protection and encouragement of her manufactures.

4. Such was understood to be a proper use of the power by the States most prepared for manufacturing industry, while retaining the power over their foreign trade. It was the aim of Virginia herself, as will presently appear, though at the time among the least prepared for such a use of her power to regulate trade.

5. Such a use of the power by Congress accords with the intention and expectation of the States in transferring the power over trade from themselves to the Government of the U. S. This was emphatically the case in the Eastern, the more manufac-

turing members of the Confederacy. Hear the language held in the Convention of Massachusetts, p. 84, 86, 136.

By Mr. Dawes an advocate for the Constitution, it was observed: "our manufactures are another great subject which has received no encouragement by national Duties on foreign manufactures, and they never can by any authority in the Old Confederation"; again "If we wish to *encourage our own manufactures,* to preserve our own commerce, to raise the value of our own lands, we must give Congress the powers in question."

By Mr. Widgery, an opponent, "All we hear is, that the merchant & farmer will flourish, & that the mechanic & tradesman are to make their fortunes directly, if the Constitution goes down."

The Convention of Massachusetts was the only one in New England whose debates have been preserved. But it cannot be doubted that the sentiment there expressed was common to the other States in that quarter, more especially to Connecticut & Rhode Island, the most thickly peopled of all the States, and having of course their thoughts most turned to the subject of manufactures. A like inference may be confidently applied to New Jersey, whose debates in Convention have not been preserved. In the populous and manufacturing State of Pennsylvania, a partial account only of the debates having been published, nothing certain is known of what passed in her Convention on this point. But ample evidence may be found elsewhere, that regulations of trade for the encouragement of manufactures, were considered as within the power to be granted to the new Congress, as well as within the scope of the National Policy. Of the States south of Pennsylvania, the only two in whose Conventions the debates have been preserved are Virginia & North Carolina, and from these no adverse inferences can be drawn. Nor is there the slightest indication that either of the two States farthest South, whose debates in Convention if preserved have not been made public, viewed the encouragement of manufactures as not within the general power over trade to be transferred to the Government of the U. S.

6. If Congress have not the power it is annihilated for the nation; a policy without example in any other nation, and not within the reason of the solitary one in our own. The example alluded to is the prohibition of a tax on exports which resulted from the apparent impossibility of raising in that mode a revenue from the States proportioned to the ability to pay it; the ability of some being derived in a great measure, not from their exports, but from their fisheries, from their freights and from commerce at large, in some of its branches altogether external to the U. S.; the profits from all which being invisible & intangible would escape a tax on exports. A tax on imports, on the other hand, being a tax on consumption which is in proportion to the ability of the consumers whencesoever derived was free from that inequality.

7. If revenue be the sole object of a legitimate impost, and the encouragement of domestic articles be not within the power of regulating trade it would follow that no monopolizing or unequal regulations of foreign Nations could be counteracted; that neither the staple articles of subsistence nor the essential implements for the public safety could under any circumstances be ensured or fostered at home by regulations of commerce, the usual & most convenient mode of providing for both; and that the American navigation, tho the source of naval defence, of a cheapening competition in carrying our valuable & bulky articles to Market, and of an independent carriage of them during foreign wars, when a foreign navigation might be withdrawn, must be at once abandoned or speedily destroyed; it being evident that a tonnage duty merely in foreign ports against our vessels, and an exemption from such a duty in our ports in favor of foreign vessels, must have the inevitable effect of banishing ours from the Ocean.

To assume a power to protect our navigation, & the cultivation & fabrication of all articles requisite for the Public safety as incident to the war power, would be a more latitudinary construction of the text of the Constitution, than to consider it as embraced by the specified power to regulate trade; a power which has been exercised by all Nations for those purposes; and which effects those purposes with less of interference with the authority & conveniency of the States, than might result from internal & direct modes of encouraging the articles, any of which modes would be authorized as far as deemed "necessary & proper," by considering the Power as an incidental Power.

8. That the encouragement of Manufactures, was an object of the power, to regulate trade, is proved by the use made of the power for that object, in the first session of the first Congress under the Constitution; when among the members present were so many who had been members of the federal Convention which framed the Constitution, and of the State Conventions which ratified it; each of these classes consisting also of members who had opposed & who had espoused, the Constitution in its actual form. It does not appear from the printed proceedings of Congress on that occasion that the power was denied by any of them. And it may be remarked that members from Virginia in particular, as well of the anti-federal as the federal party, the names then distinguishing those who had opposed and those who had approved the Constitution, did not hesitate to propose duties, & to suggest even prohibitions, in favor of several articles of her production. By one a duty was proposed on mineral Coal in favor of the Virginia Coal-Pits; by another a duty on Hemp was proposed to encourage the growth of that article; and by a third a prohibition even of foreign Beef was suggested as a measure of sound policy. (See *Lloyd's Debates.*)

A further evidence in support of the Congress' power to protect & foster manufactures by regulations of trade, an evidence that ought of itself to settle the question, is the uniform & practical sanction given to the power, by the General Government for nearly 40 years with a concurrence or acquiescence of every State Government throughout the same period; and it may be added thro all the vicissitudes of Party, which marked the period. No novel construction however ingeniously devised, or however respectable and patriotic its Patrons, can withstand the weight of such authorities, or the unbroken current of so prolonged & universal a practice. And well it is that this cannot be done without the intervention of the same authority which made the Constitution. If it could be so done, there would be an end to that stability in Government and in Laws which is essential to good Government & good Laws; a stability, the want of which is the imputation which has at all times been levelled against Republicanism with most effect by its most dexterous adversaries. The imputation ought never therefore to be countenanced, by innovating constructions, without any plea of a precipitancy or a paucity of the constructive precedents they oppose; without any appeal to material facts newly brought to light; and without any claim to a better knowledge of the original evils & inconveniences, for which remedies were needed, the very best keys to the true object & meaning of all laws & constitutions.

And may it not be fairly left to the unbiased judgment of all men of experience & of intelligence, to decide which is most to be relied on for a sound and safe test of the meaning of a Constitution, a uniform interpretation by all the successive authorities under it, commencing with its birth, and continued for a long period, thro' the varied state of political contests, or the opinion of every new Legislature heated as it may be by the strife of parties, or warped as often happens by the eager pursuit of some favourite object; or carried away possibly by the powerful eloquence, or captivating address of a few popular Statesmen, themselves influenced, perhaps, by the same misleading causes. If the latter test is to prevail, every new Legislative opinion might make a new Constitution; as the foot of every new Chancellor would make a new standard of measure.

It is seen with no little surprize, that an attempt has been made, in a highly respectable quarter, and at length reduced to a resolution formally proposed in Congress, to substitute for the power of Congress to regulate trade so as to encourage manufactures, a power in the several States to do so, with the consent of that Body; and this expedient is derived from a clause in the 10 sect. of Art: I. of the Const; which says: ["No State shall, without the consent of Congress, lay any imposts or duties on imports or exports, except what may be absolutely necessary for executing its inspection laws; and the net produce of all duties and imposts laid by any State on imports and exports shall be for the use of the Treasury of the United States; and all such laws shall be subject to the revision and control of the Congress."]

To say nothing of the clear indications in the Journal of the Convention of 1787, that the clause was intended merely to provide for expences incurred by particular States in their inspection laws, and in such improvements as they might chuse to make in their Harbours & rivers with the sanction of Congress, objects to which the reserved power has been applied in several instances, at the request of Virginia & of Georgia, how could it ever be imagined that any State would wish to tax its own trade for the encouragement of manufactures, if possessed of the authority, or could in fact do so, if wishing it?

A tax on imports would be a tax on its own consumption; and the nett proceeds going, according to the clause, not into its own treasury, but into the treasury of the U. S., the State would tax itself separately for the equal gain of all the other States; and as far as the manufactures so encouraged might succeed in ultimately increasing the Stock in Market, and lowering the price by competition, this advantage also, procured at the sole expence of the State, would be common to all the others.

But the very suggestion of such an expedient to any State

would have an air of mockery, when its *experienced* impracticability is taken into view. No one who recollects or recurs to the
period when the power over Commerce was in the individual
States, & separate attempts were made to tax or otherwise
regulate it, needs be told that the attempts were not only
abortive, but by demonstrating the necessity of general & uniform regulations gave the original impulse to the Constitutional
reform which provided for such regulations.

To refer a State therefore to the exercise of a power as reserved to her by the Constitution, the impossibility of exercising which was an inducement to adopt the Constitution, is,
of all remedial devices the last that ought to be brought forward. And what renders it the more extraordinary is that, as
the tax on commerce as far as it could be separately collected,
instead of belonging to the treasury of the State as previous to
the Constitution would be a tribute to the U. S.; the State
would be in a worse condition, after the adoption of the Constitution, than before, in relation to an important interest, the
improvement of which was a particular object in adopting the
Constitution.

Were Congress to make the proposed declaration of consent
to State tariffs in favour of State manufactures, and the permitted attempts did not defeat themselves, what would be the
situation of States deriving their foreign supplies through the
ports of other States? It is evident that they might be compelled to pay, in their consumption of particular articles imported, a tax for the common treasury not common to all the
States, without having any manufacture or product of their
own to partake of the contemplated benefit.

Of the impracticability of separate regulations of trade, & the
resulting necessity of general regulations, no State was more
sensible than Virginia. She was accordingly among the most
earnest for granting to Congress a power adequate to the object. On more occasions than one in the proceedings of her
Legislative Councils, it was recited, "that the relative situation

of the States had been found on *trial* to require *uniformity* in their comercial regulations as the *only* effectual policy for obtaining in the ports of foreign nations a stipulation of privileges reciprocal to those enjoyed by the subjects of such nations in the ports of the U. S., for preventing animosities which cannot fail to arise among the several States from the interference of partial & separate regulations; and for *deriving from comerce* such aids to the public *revenue* as it ought to contribute," &c.

During the delays & discouragements experienced in the attempts to invest Congress with the necessary powers, the State of Virginia made various trials of what could be done by her individual laws. She ventured on duties & imposts as a source of Revenue; Resolutions were passed at one time to encourage & protect her own navigation & ship-building; and in consequence of complaints & petitions from Norfolk, Alexandria & other places, against the monopolizing navigation laws of Great Britain, particularly in the trade *between the U. S. & the British W. Indies*, she deliberated with a purpose controuled only by the inefficacy of separate measures, on the experiment of forcing a reciprocity by prohibitory regulations of her own. (See Journal of House of Delegates in 1785.)

The effect of her separate attempts to raise revenue by duties on imports, soon appeared in Representations from her Merchants, that the commerce of the State was banished by them into other channels, especially of Maryland, where imports were less burdened than in Virginia. (See ditto 1786.)

Such a tendency of separate regulations was indeed too manifest to escape anticipation. Among the projects prompted by the want of a federal authority over Commerce, was that of a concert, first proposed on the part of Maryland for a uniformity of regulations between the 2 States, and comissioners were appointed for that purpose. It was soon perceived however that the concurrence of Pennsylvania was as necessary to Maryland as of Maryland to Virginia, and the concurrence of Pennsylvania was accordingly invited. But Pennsylvania could no more

482 THE MIND OF THE FOUNDER

concur without N. Y. than Maryland without Pennsylvania nor
N. Y. without the concurrence of Boston &c.

These projects were superseded for the moment by that of
the Convention at Annapolis in 1786, and forever by the Convention at Philadelphia in 1787, and the Constitution which
was the fruit of it.

There is a passage in Mr. Necker's work on the finances of
France which affords a signal illustration of the difficulty of
collecting, in contiguous communities, indirect taxes when not
the same in all, by the violent means resorted to against
smuggling from one to another of them. Previous to the late
revolutionary war in that Country, the taxes were of very different rates in the different Provinces; particularly the tax on salt
which was high in the interior Provinces & low in the maritime;
and the tax on Tobacco, which was very high in general whilst
in some of the Provinces the use of the article was altogether
free. The consequence was that the standing army of Patrols
against smuggling, had swollen to the number of twenty three
thousand; the annual arrests of men women & children engaged in smuggling, to five thousand five hundred & fifty; and
the number annually arrested on account of Salt & Tobacco
alone, to seventeen or eighteen hundred, more than three hundred of whom were consigned to the terrible punishment of the
Galleys.

May it not be regarded as among the Providential blessings
to these States, that their geographical relations multiplied as
they will be by artificial channels of intercourse, give such
additional force to the many obligations to cherish that Union
which alone secures their peace, their safety, and their prosperity. Apart from the more obvious & awful consequences of
their entire separation into Independent Sovereignties, it is
worthy of special consideration, that divided from each other
as they must be by narrow waters & territorial lines merely, the
facility of surreptitious introductions of contraband articles,
would defeat every attempt at revenue in the easy and indirect

modes of impost and excise; so that whilst their expenditures would be necessarily & vastly increased by their new situation, they would, in providing for them, be limited to direct taxes on land or other property, to arbitrary assessments on invisible funds, & to the odious tax on persons.

You will observe that I have confined myself, in what has been said to the constitutionality & expediency of the power in congress to encourage domestic products by regulations of commerce. In the exercise of the power, they are responsible to their Constituents, whose right & duty it is, in that as in all other cases, to bring their measures to the test of justice & of the general good.

October 30, 1828.

Dear Sir,—In my letter of September 18th, I stated briefly the grounds on which I rested my opinion that a power to impose duties & restrictions on imports with a view to encourage domestic productions, was constitutionally lodged in Congress. In the observations then made was involved the opinion also, that the power was properly there lodged. As this last opinion necessarily implies that there are cases in which the power may be usefully exercised by Congress, the only Body within our political system capable of exercising it with effect, you may think it incumbent on me to point out cases of that description.

I will premise that I concur in the opinion that, as a *general* rule, individuals ought to be deemed the best judges, of the best application of their industry and resources.

I am ready to admit also that there is no Country in which the application may, with more safety, be left to the intelligence and enterprize of individuals, than the United States.

Finally, I shall not deny that, in all doubtful cases, it becomes every Government to lean rather to a confidence in the judgment of individuals, than to interpositions controuling the free exercise of it.

With all these concessions, I think it can be satisfactorily shewn, that there are exceptions to the general rule, now expressed by the phrase "Let us alone," forming cases which call for interpositions of the competent authority, and which are not inconsistent with the generality of the rule.

1. The Theory of "Let us alone," supposes that all nations concur in a perfect freedom of commercial intercourse. Were this the case, they would, in a commercial view, be but one nation, as much as the several districts composing a particular nation; and the theory would be as applicable to the former, as to the latter. But this golden age of free trade has not yet arrived; nor is there a single nation that has set the example. No Nation can, indeed, safely do so, until a reciprocity at least be ensured to it. Take for a proof, the familiar case of the navigation employed in a foreign commerce. If a nation adhering to the rule of never interposing a countervailing protection of its vessels, admits foreign vessels into its ports free of duty, whilst its own vessels are subject to a duty in foreign ports, the ruinous effect is so obvious, that the warmest advocate for the theory in question, must shrink from a *universal* application of it.

A nation leaving its foreign trade, in all cases, to regulate itself, might soon find it regulated by other nations, into a subserviency to a foreign interest. In the interval between the peace of 1783, and the establishment of the present Constitution of the United States, the want of a General Authority to regulate trade, is known to have had this consequence. And have not the pretensions & policy latterly exhibited by Great Britain, given warning of a like result from a renunciation of all countervailing regulations, on the part of the United States. Were she permitted, by conferring on certain portions of her Domain the name of Colonies, to open from these a trade for herself, to foreign Countries, and to exclude, at the same time, a reciprocal trade to such colonies by foreign Countries, the use to be made of the monopoly needs not be traced. Its character will be placed in a just relief, by supposing that one of the Colonial Islands, instead of its present distance, happened to be in the vicinity of Great Britain, or that one of the Islands in that vicinity should receive the name & be regarded in the light of a Colony, with the peculiar privileges claimed for colonies. It is not manifest, that in this case, the favored Island might be made the sole medium of the commercial intercourse with foreign nations, and the parent Country thence enjoy every essential advantage, as to the terms, of it, which would flow from an *unreciprocal* trade from her other ports with other nations.

Fortunately the British claims, however speciously coloured or adroitly managed were repelled at the commencement of our comercial career as an Independent people; and at successive epochs under the existing Constitution, both in legislative discussions and in diplomatic negotations. The claims were repelled on the solid ground, that the Colonial trade as a *rightful monopoly*, was limited to the intercourse between the parent Country & its Colonies, and between one Colony and another; the whole being, strictly in the nature of a coasting trade from one to another port of the same nation; a trade with which no other nation has a right to interfere. It follows of necessity, that the Parent Country, whenever it opens a Colonial port for a direct trade to a foreign Country, departs itself from the principle of Colonial Monopoly, and entitles the foreign Country to the same reciprocity in every respect, as in its intercourse with any other ports of the nation.

This is common sense, and common right. It is still more, if more could be required; it is in conformity with the established usage of all nations, other than Great Britain, which have Colonies; notwithstanding British representations to the contrary. Some of those Nations are known to adhere to the monopoly of their Colonial trade, with all the rigor & constancy which circumstances permit. But it is also known, that whenever, and from whatever cause, it has been found necessary or expedient, to open their Colonial ports to a foreign trade, the

rule of reciprocity in favour of the foreign party was not refused, nor, as is believed, a right to refuse it ever pretended.

It cannot be said that the reciprocity was dictated by a deficiency of the commercial marine. France, at least could not
be, in every instance, governed by that consideration; and Holland still less; to say nothing of the navigating States of Sweden
and Denmark, which have rarely if ever, enforced a colonial
monopoly. The remark is indeed obvious, that the shipping
liberated from the usual conveyance of supplies from the parent Country to the Colonies, might be employed in the new
channels opened for them in supplies from abroad.

Reciprocity, or an equivalent for it, is the only rule of intercourse among Independent communities; and no nation ought
to admit a doctrine, or adopt an invariable policy, which would
preclude the counteracting measures necessary to enforce the
rule.

2. The Theory supposes moreover a perpetual peace, not
less chimerical, it is to be feared, than a universal freedom of
commerce.

The effect of war among the commercial and manufacturing
nations of the World, in raising the wages of labour and the
cost of its products, with a like effect on the charges of freight
and insurance, needs neither proof nor explanation. In order to
determine, therefore, a question of economy between depending on foreign supplies, and encouraging domestic substitutes,
it is necessary to compare the probable periods of war, with
the probable periods of peace; and the cost of the domestic encouragement in times of peace, with the cost added to foreign
articles in times of War.

During the last century the periods of war and peace have
been nearly equal. The effect of a state of war in raising the
price of imported articles, cannot be estimated with exactness.
It is certain, however, that the increased price of particular
articles, may make it cheaper to manufacture them at home.

Taking, for the sake of illustration, an equality in the two periods, and the cost of an imported yard of cloth in time of war to be 9½ dollars, and in time of peace to be 7 dollars, whilst the same could, at all times, be manufactured at home, for 8 dollars; it is evident that a tariff of 1¼ dollar on the imported yard, would protect the home manufacture in time of peace, and avoid a tax of 1½ dollars imposed by a state of war.

It cannot be said that the manufactories, which could not support themselves in periods of peace, would spring up of themselves at the recurrence of war prices. It must be obvious to every one, that, apart from the difficulty of great & sudden changes of employment, no prudent capitalists would engage in expensive establishments of any sort, at the commencement of a war of uncertain duration, with a certainty of having them crushed by the return of peace.

The strictest economy, therefore, suggests, as exceptions to the general rule, an estimate, in every given case, of war & peace periods and prices, with inferences therefrom, of the amount of a tariff which might be afforded during peace, in order to avoid the tax resulting from war. And it will occur at once, that the inferences will be strengthened, by adding to the supposition of wars wholly foreign, that of wars in which our own country might be a party.

3. It is an opinion in which all must agree, that no nation ought to be unnecessarily dependent on others for the munitions of public defence, or for the materials essential to a naval force, where the nation has a maritime frontier or a foreign commerce to protect. To this class of exceptions to the theory may be added the instruments of agriculture and of mechanic arts, which supply the other primary wants of the community. The time has been when many of these were derived from a foreign source, and some of them might relapse into that dependence were the encouragement to the fabrication of them at home withdrawn. But, as all foreign sources must be liable to interruptions too inconvenient to be hazarded, a provident

policy would favour an internal and independent source as a reasonable exception to the general rule of consulting cheapness alone.

4. There are cases where a nation may be so far advanced in the pre-requisites for a particular branch of manufactures, that this, if once brought into existence, would support itself; and yet, unless aided in its nascent and infant state by public encouragement and a confidence in public protection, might remain, if not altogether, for a long time unattempted, or attempted without success. Is not our cotton manufacture a fair example? However favoured by an advantageous command of the raw material and a machinery which dispenses in so extraordinary a proportion with manual labour, it is quite probable that, without the impulse given by a war cutting off foreign supplies and the patronage of an early tariff, it might not even yet have established itself; and pretty certain that it would be far short of the prosperous condition which enables it to face, in foreign markets, the fabrics of a nation that defies all other competitors. The number must be small that would now pronounce this manufacturing boon not to have been cheaply purchased by the tariff which nursed it into its present maturity.

5. Should it happen, as has been suspected, to be an object, though not of a foreign Government itself, of its great manufacturing capitalists, to strangle in the cradle the infant manufactures of an extensive customer or an anticipated rival, it would surely, in such a case, be incumbent on the suffering party so far to make an exception to the "let alone" policy as to parry the evil by opposite regulations of its foreign commerce.

6. It is a common objection to the public encouragement of particular branches of industry, that it calls off labourers from other branches found to be more profitable; and the objection is, in general, a weighty one. But it loses that character in pro-

portion to the effect of the encouragement in attracting skilful labourers from abroad. Something of this sort has already
taken place among ourselves, and much more of it is in prospect; and as far as it has taken or may take place, it forms an
exception to the general policy in question.

The history of manufactures in Great Britain, the greatest
manufacturing nation in the world, informs us, that the woollen
branch, till of late her greatest branch, owed both its original
and subsequent growths to persecuted exiles from the Netherlands; and that her silk manufactures, now a flourishing and
favourite branch, were not less indebted to emigrants flying
from the persecuting edicts of France. [*Anderson's History of
Commerce.*]

It appears, indeed, from the general history of manufacturing industry, that the prompt and successful introduction of it
into new situations has been the result of emigrations from
countries in which manufactures had gradually grown up to a
prosperous state; as into Italy, on the fall of the Greek Empire;
from Italy into Spain and Flanders, on the loss of liberty in
Florence and other cities; and from Flanders and France into
England, as above noticed. [*Franklin's Canadian Pamphlet.*]

In the selection of cases here made, as exceptions to the "let
alone" theory, none have been included which were deemed
controvertible; and if I have viewed them, or a part of them
only, in their true light, they show what was to be shown, that
the power granted to Congress to encourage domestic products
by regulations of foreign trade was properly granted, inasmuch
as the power is, in effect, confined to that body, and may, when
exercised with a sound legislative discretion, provide the better
for the safety and prosperity of the nation.

NOTES.

It does not appear that any of the strictures on the letters
from J. Madison to J. C. Cabell have in the least invalidated

the constitutionality of the power in Congress to favour domestic manufactures by regulating the commerce with foreign
nations.

1. That this regulating power embraces the object remains
fully sustained by the uncontested fact that it has been so
understood and exercised by all commercial and manufacturing
nations, particularly by Great Britain; nor is it any objection
to the inference from it, that those nations, unlike the Congress
of the United States, had all other powers of legislation as well
as the power of regulating foreign commerce, since this was
the particular and appropriate power by which the encouragement of manufactures was effected.

2. It is equally a fact that it was generally understood among
the States previous to the establishment of the present Constitution of the United States, that the encouragement of domestic manufactures by regulations of foreign commerce,
particularly by duties and restrictions on foreign manufactures,
was a legitimate and ordinary exercise of the power over
foreign commerce; and that, in transferring this power to the
Legislature of the United States, it was anticipated that it
would be exercised more effectually than it could be by the
States individually. [See Lloyd's Debates and other publications of the period.]

It cannot be denied that a right to vindicate its commercial,
manufacturing, and agricultural interests against unfriendly
and unreciprocal policy of other nations, belongs to every
nation; that it has belonged at all times to the United States as
a nation; that, previous to the present Federal Constitution,
the right existed in the governments of the individual States,
not in the Federal Government; that the want of such an
authority in the Federal Government was deeply felt and deplored; that a supply of this want was generally and anxiously
desired; and that the authority has, by the substituted Constitution of the Federal Government, been expressly or virtu-

ally taken from the individual States; so that, if not transferred to the existing Federal Government it is lost and annihilated for the United States as a nation. Is not the presumption irresistible, that it must have been the intention of those who framed and ratified the Constitution, to vest the authority in question in the substituted Government? and does not every just rule of reasoning allow to a presumption so violent a proportional weight in deciding on a question of such a power in Congress, not as a source of power distinct from and additional to the constitutional source, but as a source of light and evidence as to the true meaning of the Constitution?

3. It is again a fact, that the power was so exercised by the first session of the first Congress, and by every succeeding Congress, with the sanction of every other branch of the Federal Government, and with universal acquiescence, till a very late date. [See the Messages of the Presidents and the Reports and Letters of Mr. Jefferson.]

4. That the surest and most recognized evidence of the meaning of the Constitution, as of a law, is furnished by the evils which were to be cured or the benefits to be obtained; and by the immediate and long-continued application of the meaning to these ends. This species of evidence supports the power in question in a degree which cannot be resisted without destroying all stability in social institutions, and all the advantages of known and certain rules of conduct in the intercourse of life.

5. Although it might be too much to say that no case could arise of a character overruling the highest evidence of precedents and practice in expounding a constitution, it may be safely affirmed that no case which is not of a character far more exorbitant and ruinous than any now existing or that has occurred, can authorize a disregard of the precedents and practice which sanction the constitutional power of Congress

to encourage domestic manufactures by regulations of foreign commerce.

The importance of the question concerning the authority of precedents, in expounding a constitution as well as a law, will justify a more full and exact view of it.

It has been objected to the encouragement of domestic manufactures by a tariff on imported ones, that duties and imposts are in the clause specifying the sources of revenue, and therefore cannot be applied to the encouragement of manufactures when not a source of revenue.

But, 1. It does not follow from the applicability of duties and imposts under one clause for one usual purpose, that they are excluded from an applicability under another clause to another purpose, also requiring them, and to which they have also been usually applied. 2. A history of that clause, as traced in the printed journal of the Federal Convention, will throw light on the subject.

It appears that the clause, as it originally stood, simply expressed "a power to lay taxes, duties, imposts, and exercises," without pointing out the objects; and, of course, leaving them applicable in carrying into effect the other specified powers. It appears, farther, that a solicitude to prevent any constructive danger to the validity of public debts contracted under the superseded form of government, led to the addition of the words "to pay the debts."

This phraseology having the appearance of an appropriation limited to the payment of debts, an express appropriation was added "for the expenses of the Government," &c.

But even this was considered as short of the objects for which taxes, duties, imposts, and excises might be required; and the more comprehensive provision was made by substituting "for expenses of Government" the terms of the old Confederation, viz.: and provide for the common defence and general welfare, making duties and imposts, as well as taxes and excises, applicable not only to payment of debts, but to the common defence and general welfare.

The question then is, What is the import of that phrase, common defence and general welfare, in its actual connexion? The import which Virginia has always asserted, and still contends for, is, that they are explained and limited to the enumerated objects subjoined to them, among which objects is the regulation of foreign commerce; as far, therefore, as a tariff of duties is necessary and proper in regulating foreign commerce for any of the usual purposes of such regulations, it may be imposed by Congress, and, consequently, for the purpose of encouraging manufactures, which is a well-known purpose for which duties and imposts have been usually employed. This view of the clause providing for revenue, instead of interfering with or excluding the power of regulating foreign trade, corroborates the rightful exercise of power for the encouragement of domestic manufactures.

It may be thought that the Constitution might easily have been made more explicit and precise in its meaning. But the same remark might be made on so many other parts of the instrument, and, indeed, on so many parts of every instrument of a complex character, that, if completely obviated, it would swell every paragraph into a page and every page into a volume; and, in so doing, have the effect of multiplying topics for criticism and controversy.

The best reason to be assigned, in this case, for not having made the Constitution more free from a charge of uncertainty in its meaning, is believed to be, that it was not suspected that any such charge would ever take place; and it appears that no such charge did take place, during the early period of the Constitution, when the meaning of its authors could be best ascertained, nor until many of the contemporary lights had in the lapse of time been extinguished. How often does it happen, that a notoriety of intention diminishes the caution against its being misunderstood or doubted! What would be the effect of the Declaration of Independence, or of the Virginia Bill of Rights, if not expounded with a reference to that view of their meaning?

Those who assert that the encouragement of manufactures is not within the scope of the power to regulate foreign commerce, and that a tariff is exclusively appropriated to revenue, feel the difficulty of finding authority for objects which they cannot admit to be unprovided for by the Constitution; such as ensuring internal supplies of necessary articles of defence, the countervailing of regulations of foreign countries, &c., unjust and injurious to our navigation or to our agricultural products. To bring these objects within the constitutional power of Congress, they are obliged to give to the power "to regulate foreign commerce" an extent that at the same time necessarily embraces the encouragement of manufactures; and how, indeed, it is possible to suppose that a tariff is applicable to the extorting from foreign Powers of a reciprocity of privileges and not applicable to the encouragement of manufactures, an object to which it has been far more frequently applied?

37. The Force of Precedent: Changing Views on the Bank

Once drawn into the tariff controversy of 1828, Madison could not easily escape the role of public antagonist. Sympathizers sought the counsel and seal of the patriarch; adversaries tried to undermine his authority by charging inconsistency and even hinting at senility. As he commented ruefully to N.P. Trist on February 15, 1830: "A man whose years have but reached the canonical three-score-and-ten (and mine are much beyond the number) should distrust himself, whether distrusted by his friends or not, and should never forget that his arguments . . . will be answered by allusions to the date of his birth." Still, reading the alarming signs of the new antifederalist spirit, Madison was not ready for quiet retirement.

Charles Jared Ingersoll, an influential Democratic lawyer and politician from Philadelphia, solicited Madison's opinion on the national bank to help persuade the Pennsylvania legis-

Madison to Charles Jared Ingersoll, June 25, 1831, in *Letters*, IV, pp. 183–187.

lature to pass a pro-bank resolution. Madison's second reply of June 25, 1831, met the common charge of inconsistency with a short discourse on the force of constitutional precedent. Undeniably, he had changed his original position of 1791 on the constitutionality of the national bank. Legislators, like judges, were bound to recognize constructions established by a long course of precedents "amounting to the requisite evidence of the national judgment and intention." If each new set of public authorities were free to exercise their own "abstract and individual opinions" on constitutional questions, there could be no settled and known rules to guide the conduct of the community. Significantly, Madison did not (as he had in the case of the tariff) argue from the original intentions of the Philadelphia and ratifying conventions, or from the language and logic of the Constitution; indeed he made no case either way on the intrinsic legal merits of the bank question. Precedent decided the issue. Thus he affirmed at once the values of consistency and stability in the fundamental laws, and the legitimacy of change (exemplified by his own changing views) that was grounded in solemn, uniform, persistent expressions of national opinion.

Montpellier, June 25, 1831.

DEAR SIR,—I have received your friendly letter of the 18th instant. The few lines which answered your former one of the 21 January last were written in haste and in bad health, but they expressed, though without the attention, in some respects, due to the occasion, a dissent from the views of the President as to a Bank of the United States, and a substitute for it, to which I cannot but adhere. The objections to the latter have appeared to me to preponderate greatly over the advantages expected from it, and the constitutionality of the power I still regard as sustained by the considerations to which I yielded in giving my assent to the existing Bank.

The charge of inconsistency between my objection to the constitutionality of such a bank in 1791 and my assent in 1817, turns on the question how far legislative precedents, expounding the Constitution, ought to guide succeeding Legislatures and overrule individual opinions.

Some obscurity has been thrown over the question by confounding it with the respect due from one Legislature to laws passed by preceding Legislatures. But the two cases are essentially different. A Constitution being derived from a superior authority, is to be expounded and obeyed, not controlled or varied, by the subordinate authority of a Legislature. A law, on the other hand, resting on no higher authority than that possessed by every successive Legislature, its expediency as well as its meaning is within the scope of the latter.

The case in question has its true analogy in the obligation arising from judicial expositions of the law on succeeding judges; the Constitution being a law to the legislator, as the law is a rule of decision to the judge.

And why are judicial precedents, when formed on due discussion and consideration, and deliberately sanctioned by reviews and repetitions, regarded as of binding influence, or, rather, of authoritative force in settling the meaning of a law? It must be answered; 1st. Because it is a reasonable and established axiom, that the good of society requires that the rules of conduct of its members should be certain and known, which would not be the case if any judge, disregarding the decision of his predecessors, should vary the rule of law according to his individual interpretation of it. *Misera est servitus ubi jus est aut vagum aut incognitum.* 2. Because an exposition of the law publicly made, and repeatedly confirmed by the constituted authority, carries with it, by fair inference, the sanction of those who, having made the law through their legislative organ, appear, under such circumstances, to have determined its meaning through their judiciary organ.

Can it be of less consequence that the meaning of a Constitution should be fixed and known, than that the meaning of a law should be so? Can, indeed, a law be fixed in its meaning and operation unless the Constitution be so? On the contrary, if a particular Legislature, differing in the construction of the Constitution from a series of preceding constructions, proceed to act on that difference, they not only introduce uncertainty and instability in the Constitution, but in the laws themselves; inasmuch as all laws preceding the new construction and inconsistent with it are not only annulled for the future, but virtually pronounced nullities from the beginning.

But it is said that the legislator having sworn to support the Constitution, must support it in his own construction of it, however different from that put on it by his predecessors, or whatever be the consequences of the construction. And is not the judge under the same oath to support the law? Yet, has it ever been supposed that he was required or at liberty to disregard all precedents, however solemnly repeated and regularly observed, and, by giving effect to his own abstract and individual opinions, to disturb the established course of practice in the business of the community? Has the wisest and most conscientious judge ever scrupled to acquiesce in decisions in which he has been overruled by the matured opinions of the majority of his colleagues, and subsequently to conform himself thereto, as to authoritative expositions of the law? And is it not reasonable that the same view of the official oath should be taken by a legislator, acting under the Constitution, which is his guide, as is taken by a judge, acting under the law, which is his?

There is, in fact and in common understanding, a necessity of regarding a course of practice, as above characterized, in the light of a legal rule of interpreting a law, and there is a like necessity of considering it a constitutional rule of interpreting a Constitution.

That there may be extraordinary and peculiar circumstances controlling the rule in both cases, may be admitted; but with such exceptions the rule will force itself on the practical judgment of the most ardent theorist. He will find it impossible to adhere, and act officially upon, his solitary opinions as to the meaning of the law or Constitution, in opposition to a construction reduced to practice during a reasonable period of time; more especially when no prospect existed of a change of construction by the public or its agents. And if a reasonable period of time, marked with the usual sanctions, would not bar the individual prerogative, there could be no limitation to its exercise, although the danger of error must increase with the increasing oblivion of explanatory circumstances, and with the continual changes in the import of words and phrases.

Let it, then, be left to the decision of every intelligent and candid judge, which, on the whole, is most to be relied on for the true and safe construction of a constitution; that which has the uniform sanction of successive legislative bodies, through a period of years and under the varied ascendency of parties; or that which depends upon the opinions of every new Legislature, heated as it may be by the spirit of party, eager in the pursuit of some favourite object, or led astray by the eloquence and address of popular statesmen, themselves, perhaps, under the influence of the same misleading causes.

It was in conformity with the view here taken, of the respect due to deliberate and reiterated precedents, that the Bank of the United States, though on the original question held to be unconstitutional, received the Executive signature in the year 1817. The act originally establishing a bank had undergone ample discussions in its passage through the several branches of the Government. It had been carried into execution throughout a period of twenty years with annual legislative recognitions; in one instance, indeed, with a positive ramification of it into a new State; and with the entire acquiescence of all the local authorities, as well as of the nation at large; to all of which may be added, a decreasing prospect of any change in the public opinion adverse to the constitutionality of such an institution. A veto from the Executive, under these circumstances, with an admission of the expediency and almost necessity of the measure, would have been a defiance of all the obligations derived from a course of precedents amounting to the requisite evidence of the national judgment and intention.

It has been contended that the authority of precedents was in that case invalidated by the consideration that they proved only a respect for the stipulated duration of the bank, with a toleration of it until the law should expire; and by the casting vote given in the Senate by the Vice President, in the year 1811, against a bill for establishing a National Bank, the vote being expressly given on the ground of unconstitutionality. But if the law itself was unconstitutional, the stipulation was void, and could not be constitutionally fulfilled or tolerated. And as to the negative of the Senate by the casting vote of the Presiding Officer, it is a fact, well understood at the time, that it resulted, not from an equality of opinions in that assembly on the power of Congress to establish a bank, but from a junction of those who admitted the power, but disapproved the plan with those who denied the power. On a simple question of constitutionality there was a decided majority in favour of it.

38. Property and Suffrage: Second Thoughts on the Constitutional Convention

The Constitutional Convention of 1787 met behind closed doors under a pledge of secrecy and, at the end, placed its journal and other confidential records in the custody of Washington subject to the directions of the Congress-to-be. By common consent, their work would be known simply by its product: the Constitution signed by fifty-five delegates. Madison bore a peculiar and heavy responsibility of his own. His notes represented incomparably the best record of the convention debates. (See Document 11.) As the nation confronted difficult constitutional questions, men continually appealed to the intentions of the founders. Madison refused to reveal his notes to the public, knowing that they contained politically embarrassing evidence of his high Federalist views at Philadelphia. To his credit, he also resisted (with minor lapses) the temptation to re-touch his

Note on Madison's Speech of August 7, 1787, ca. 1821, in *Documentary History of the Constitution of the United States* (Washington: Government Printing Office, 1894–1905) V, pp. 440–449.

self-portrait as he prepared the notes of the great convention for posthumous publication.

About 1821, while correcting and expanding his notes from recently printed sources, Madison recorded a modest but significant change in his views of democracy. In a convention speech of August 7, 1787, he had tentatively recommended a property qualification for electors of the House of Representatives: "Viewing the subject in its merits alone, the freeholders of the Country would be the safest depositories of Republican liberty." More than three decades later, he still believed that government in civilized communities must secure the rights of property as well as persons. The long-run prospect of a property-less majority seemed to him no less certain, or dangerous. Suffrage qualifications, extensive electoral districts, and prolonged terms of office remained legitimate republican defenses against the interests and passions of a dominating faction. Now, however, Madison explicitly rejected voting conditions that would in time exclude the mass of society from any political representation. Indeed, he recognized, the democratic tendencies of the American people as evidenced in recent state conventions probably would not long permit even moderate limitations of universal white manhood suffrage. Thus the final hopes for justice and minority rights would have to rest with popular enlightenment, the natural influence and merit of the propertied, and—as always—with the large republic of many diverse interests. The democratization of American politics demanded a still more perfect union.

These observations (in the speech of J. M. See debates in the Convention of 1787 on the [7] day of [August]) do not convey the speaker's more full & matured view of the subject, which is subjoined. He felt too much at the time the example of Virginia.

The right of suffrage is a fundamental Article in Republican Constitutions. The regulation of it is, at the same time, a task of peculiar delicacy. Allow the right exclusively to property, and the rights of persons may be oppressed. The feudal polity alone sufficiently proves it. Extend it equally to all, and the rights of property or the claims of justice may be overruled by a majority without property, or interested in measures of injustice. Of this abundant proof is afforded by other popular Governments and is not without examples in our own, particularly in the laws impairing the obligation of contracts.

In civilized communities, property as well as personal rights is an essential object of the laws, which encourage industry by securing the enjoyment of its fruits: that industry from which property results, & that enjoyment which consists not merely in its immediate use, but in its posthumous destination to objects of choice and of kindred affection.

In a just & a free, Government, therefore, the rights both of property & of persons ought to be effectually guarded. Will the former be so in case of a universal & equal suffrage? Will the latter be so in case of a suffrage confined to the holders of property?

As the holders of property have at stake all the other rights common to those without property, they may be the more restrained from infringing, as well as the less tempted to infringe the rights of the latter. It is nevertheless certain, that there are various ways in which the rich may oppress the poor; in which property may oppress liberty; and that the world is filled with examples. It is necessary that the poor should have a defence against the danger.

On the other hand, the danger to the holders of property can not be disguised, if they be undefended against a majority without property. Bodies of men are not less swayed by interest than individuals, and are less controlled by the dread of reproach and the other motives felt by individuals. Hence the liability of the rights of property, and of the impartiality of laws affecting it, to be violated by Legislative majorities having an interest real or supposed in the injustice: Hence agrarian laws, and other leveling schemes: Hence the cancelling or evading of debts, and other violations of contracts. We must not shut our eyes to the nature of man, nor to the light of experience. Who would rely on a fair decision from three individuals if two had an interest in the case opposed to the rights of the third? Make the number as great as you please, the impartiality will not be increased, nor any further security against justice be obtained, than what may result from the greater difficulty of uniting the wills of a greater number.

In all Governments there is a power which is capable of oppressive exercise. In Monarchies and Aristocracies oppression proceeds from a want of sympathy & responsibility in the Government towards the people. In popular Governments the danger lies in an undue sympathy among individuals composing a majority, and a want of responsibility in the majority to the minority. The characteristic excellence of the political System of the U. S. arises from a distribution and organization of its powers, which at the same time that they secure the dependence of the Government on the will of the nation, provides better guards than are found in any other popular Government against interested combinations of a Majority against the rights of a Minority.

The United States have a precious advantage also in the actual distribution of property particularly the landed property; and in the universal hope of acquiring property. This latter peculiarity is among the happiest contrasts in their situation to that of the old world, where no anticipated change in this respect, can generally inspire a like sympathy with the rights of property. There may be at present, a Majority of the Nation, who are even freeholders, or the heirs, or aspirants to Freeholds. And the day may not be very near when such will cease to make up a Majority of the community. But they cannot always so continue. With every admissible subdivision of the Arable lands, a populousness not greater than that of England or France, will reduce the holders to a Minority. And whenever the Majority shall be without landed or other equivalent property and without the means or hope of acquiring it, what is to secure the rights of property against the danger from an equality & universality of suffrage, vesting compleat power over property in hands without a share in it: not to speak of a danger in the mean time from a dependence of an increasing number on the wealth of a few? In other Countries this dependence results in some from the relations between Landlords & Tenants in other both from that source, & from the relations between wealthy capitalists & indigent labourers. In the U. S. the occurrence must happen from the last source; from the connection between the great Capitalists in Manufactures & Commerce and the members employed by them. Nor will accumulations of Capital for a certain time be precluded by our laws of descent & of distribution; such being the enterprize inspired by free Institutions, that great wealth in the hands of individuals and associations, may not be unfrequent. But it may be observed, that the opportunities, may be diminished, and the permanency defeated by the equalizing tendency of the laws.

No free Country has ever been without parties, which are a natural offspring of Freedom. An obvious and permanent division of every people is into the owners of the Soil, and the other inhabitants. In a certain sense the Country may be said to belong to the former. If each landholder has an exclusive property in his share, the Body of Landholders have an exclusive property in the whole. As the Soil becomes subdivided, and actually cultivated by the owners, this view of the subject derives force from the principle of natural law, which vests in individuals an exclusive right to the portions of ground with which he has incorporated his labour & improvements. Whatever may be the rights of others derived from their birth in the Country, from their interest in the high ways & other parcels left open for common use as well, as in the national Edifices and monuments; from their share in the public defence, and from their concurrent support of the Government, it would seem unreasonable to extend the right so far as to give them when become the majority, a power of Legislation over the landed property without the consent of the proprietors. Some barrier against the invasion of their rights would not be out of place in a just & provident System of Government. The principle of such an arrangement has prevailed in all Governments where peculiar privileges or interests held by a part were to be secured against violation, and in the various associations where pecuniary or other property forms the stake. In the former case a defensive right has been allowed; and if the arrangement be wrong, it is not in the defense, but in the kind of privilege to be defended. In the latter case, the shares of suffrage allotted to individuals, have been with acknowledged justice apportioned more or less to their respective interests in the Common Stock.

These reflections suggest the expediency of such a modification of Government as would give security to the part of the Society having most at stake and being most exposed to danger. Three modifications present themselves.

1. *Confining* the right of suffrage to freeholders, & to such as hold an equivalent property, convertible of course into freeholds. The objection to this regulation is obvious. It violates the vital principle of free Government that those who are to be bound by laws, ought to have a voice in making them. And the violation would be more strikingly unjust as the lawmakers become the minority: The regulation would be as unpropitious also as it would be unjust. It would engage the numerical & physical force in a constant struggle against the public authority; unless kept down by a standing army fatal to all parties.

2. Confining the right of suffrage for one Branch to the holders of property, and for the other Branch to those without property. This arrangement which would give a mutual defence, where there might be mutual danger of encroachment,

has an aspect of equality & fairness. But it would not be in fact either equal or fair, because the rights to be defended would be unequal, being on one side those of property as well as of persons, and on the other those of persons only. The temptation also to encroach tho' in a certain degree mutual, would be felt more strongly on one side than on the other; It would be more likely to beget an abuse of the Legislative Negative in extorting concessions at the expence of property, than the reverse. The division of the State into the two Classes, with distinct & independent Organs of power, and without any intermingled Agency whatever, might lead to contests & antipathies not dissimilar to those between the Patricians & Plebeians at Rome.

3. Confining the right of electing one Branch of the Legislature to freeholders, and admitting all others to a common right with holders of property, in electing the other Branch. This would give a defensive power to holders of property, and to the class also without property when becoming a majority of electors, without depriving them in the mean time of a participation in the public Councils. If the holders of property would thus have a twofold share of representation, they would have at the same time a twofold stake in it, the rights of property as well as of persons the twofold object of political Institutions. And if no exact & safe equilibrium can be introduced, it is more reasonable that a preponderating weight should be allowed to the greater interest than to the lesser. Experience alone can decide how far the practice in this case would correspond with the Theory. Such a distribution of the right of suffrage was tried in New York and has been abandoned whether from experienced evils, or party calculations, may possibly be a question. It is still on trial in North Carolina, with what practical indications is not known. It is certain that the trial, to be satisfactory ought to be continued for no inconsiderable period; untill in fact the non freeholders should be the majority.

4. Should Experience or public opinion require an equal & universal suffrage for each branch of the Government such as prevails generally in the U. S., a resource favorable to the rights of landed & other property, when its possessors become the Minority, may be found in an enlargement of the Election Districts for one branch of the Legislature, and an extension of its period of service. Large districts are manifestly favorable to the election of persons of general respectability, and of probable attachment to the rights of property, over competitors depending on the personal solicitations practicable on a contracted theatre. And altho' an ambitious candidate, of personal distinction, might occasionally recommend himself to popular choice by espousing a popular though unjust object, it might rarely happen to many districts at the same time. The tendency of a longer period of service would be, to render the Body more stable in its policy, and more capable of stemming popular currents taking a wrong direction, till reason & justice could regain their ascendancy.

5. Should even such a modification as the last be deemed inadmissible, and universal suffrage and very short periods of elections within contracted spheres be required for each branch of the Government, the security for the holders of property when the minority, can only be derived from the ordinary influence possessed by property, & the superior information incident to its holders; from the popular sense of justice enlightened & enlarged by a diffusive education; and from the difficulty of combining & effectuating unjust purposes throughout an extensive country; a difficulty essentially distinguishing the U. S. and even most of the individual States, from the small communities where a mistaken interest or contagious passion, could readily unite a majority of the whole under a factious leader, in trampling on the rights of the Minor party.

Under every view of the subject, it seems indispensable that the Mass of Citizens should not be without a voice, in making the laws which they are to obey, & in chusing the Magistrates, who are to administer them, and if the only alternative be between an equal & universal right of suffrage for each branch of the Government and a confinement of the *entire* right to a part of the Citizens, it is better that those having the greater interest at stake namely that of property & persons both, should be deprived of half their share in the Government; than, that those having the lesser interest, that of personal rights only, should be deprived of the whole.

39. Partnership of Power:
The Virginia Convention of 1829–1830

In an autobiographical sketch, Madison explained his return to public duties for the last time during the fall and winter of 1829–1830: "In 1829 he was prevailed on, notwithstanding his age and very feeble health . . . , to serve as a member of the Convention which revised the Constitution of the State. . . . His main object was to promote a compromise of ideas between parties fixed in their hot opinion by their local interests, and threatening an abortive result to an experiment closely connected with the tranquillity of the State, and the capacity of man for self-government." On the principal questions that divided this assembly of Virginia notables at Richmond, Madison recalled: "His personal opinion[s] . . . were either controuled by the known will and *meditated* instructions of his Constituents or by the necessity of securing an effective and tranquil result by indulging the party, whose defeat would have been

Speech in the Virginia Constitutional Convention, December 2, 1829, with Memorandum on Suffrage, in *Writings*, IX, pp. 358–364, 358n–36on.

most pregnant with danger to it." That party, plainly, comprised the planters of the Tidewater and Piedmont counties who resisted any change in suffrage qualifications, the basis of apportioning representatives, or in other provisions of the 1776 Constitution that would seriously endanger their control of the state.

As the sole survivor of the Virginia Convention of 1776 and the Philadelphia Convention of 1787, Madison was an awesome, almost mythic figure even in the company of such dignitaries as ex-President Monroe, Chief Justice Marshall, and assorted past and future national and state leaders. His speech of December 2, 1829, revived once more the familiar problem of securing minority rights under popular government, in order to prepare the way for a compromise proposal that would base representation in the lower house on white population (as the Western reformers demanded) and use the "Federal ratio" of whites plus three-fifths of the slaves for apportioning Senate seats (as the Eastern conservatives insisted). The effect of the speech, however, was to strengthen the conservative position in the Convention. Madison's concern for the slaves themselves was no doubt sincere but incidental, although a westward shift of political power beyond the Blue Ridge Mountains (where slaves represented a small minority of the population) would improve the chances of eventual emancipation.

During the debates, Madison circulated a memorandum on voting rights that helped to win support for the extension of the suffrage from freeholders to renters and taxpaying householders and heads of families. His argument refined and expanded the reflections of his note of 1821 on the fate of democracy in a mature and densely populated America. (See Document 38.) An amended constitution, he hoped, would endure for a century and more if Virginians carefully expanded "the partnership of power." His confidence dropped considerably when he saw the one-sided compromise that the convention adopted, and the bitter resentment of the Western minority, although he still believed that Virginians would accept the verdict of the lawful majority.

December 2, 1829.

[MR. MADISON NOW ROSE AND ADDRESSED THE CHAIR: THE MEMBERS RUSHED FROM THEIR SEATS, AND CROWDED AROUND HIM.]

Although the actual posture of the subject before the Committee might admit a full survey of it, it is not my purpose, in rising, to enter into the wide field of discussion, which has called forth a display of intellectual resources and varied powers of eloquence, that any country might be proud of, and which I have witnessed with the highest gratification. Having been, for a very long period, withdrawn from any participation in proceedings of deliberative bodies, and under other disqualifications now of which I am deeply sensible, though perhaps less sensible than others may perceive that I ought to be, I shall not attempt more than a few observations, which may suggest the views I have taken of the subject, and which will consume but little of the time of the Committee, become precious. It is sufficiently obvious, that persons now and property are the two great subjects on which Governments are to act; and that the rights of persons, and the rights of property, are the objects, for the protection of which Government was instituted. These rights cannot well be separated. The personal right to acquire property, which is a natural right, gives to property, when acquired, a right to protection, as a social right. The essence of Government is power; and power, lodged as it must be in human hands, will ever be liable to abuse. In monarchies, the interests and happiness of all may be sacrificed to the caprice and passions of a despot. In aristocracies, the rights and welfare of the many may be sacrificed to the pride and cupidity of the few. In republics, the great danger is, that the majority may not sufficiently respect the rights of the minority.

Some gentlemen, consulting the purity and generosity of their own minds, without adverting to the lessons of experience, would find a security against that danger, in our social feelings; in a respect for character; in the dictates of the monitor within; in the interests of individuals; in the aggregate interests of the community. But man is known to be a selfish, as well as a social being. Respect for character, though often a salutary restraint, is but too often overruled by other motives. When numbers of men act in a body, respect for character is often lost, just in proportion as it is necessary to control what is not right. We all know that conscience is not a sufficient safe-guard; and besides, that conscience itself may be deluded; may be misled, by an unconscious bias, into acts which an enlightened conscience would forbid. As to the permanent interest of individuals in the aggregate interests of the community, and in the proverbial maxim, that honesty is the best policy, present temptation is often found to be an overmatch for those considerations. These favourable attributes of the human character are all valuable, as auxiliaries; but they will not serve as a substitute for the coercive provision belonging to Government and Law. They will always, in proportion as they prevail, be favourable to a mild administration of both: but they can never be relied on as a guaranty of the rights of the minority against a majority disposed to take unjust advantage of its power. The only effectual safeguard to the rights of the minority, must be laid in such a basis and structure of the Government itself, as may afford, in a certain degree, directly or indirectly, a defensive authority in behalf of a minority having right on its side.

To come more nearly to the subject before the Committee, viz.: that peculiar feature in our community, which calls for a peculiar division in the basis of our government, I mean the coloured part of our population. It is apprehended, if the power of the Commonwealth shall be in the hands of a majority, who have no interest in this species of property, that, from the facility with which it may be oppressed by excessive taxation, injustice may be done to its owners. It would seem, therefore, if we can incorporate that interest into the basis of our system, it will be the most apposite and effectual security that can be devised. Such an arrangement is recommended to me by many very important considerations. It is due to justice; due to humanity; due to truth; to the sympathies of our nature; in fine, to our character as a people, both abroad and at home, that they should be considered, as much as possible, in the light of human beings, and not as mere property. As such, they are acted upon by our laws, and have an interest in our laws. They may be considered as making a part, though a degraded part, of the families to which they belong.

If they had the complexion of the Serfs in the North of Europe, or of the Villeins formerly in England; in other terms, if they were of our own complexion, much of the difficulty would be removed. But the mere circumstance of complexion cannot deprive them of the character of men. The Federal number, as it is called, is particularly recommended to attention in forming a basis of Representation, by its simplicity, its certainty, its stability, and its permanency. Other expedients for securing justice in the case of taxation, while they amount in pecuniary effect, to the same thing, have been found liable to great objections: and I do not believe that a majority of this Convention is disposed to adopt them, if they can find a substitute they can approve. Nor is it a small recommendation of the Federal number, in my view, that it is in conformity to the ratio recognized in the Federal Constitution. The cases, it is true, are not precisely the same, but there is more of analogy than might at first be supposed. If the coloured population were equally diffused through the State, the analogy would fail; but existing as it does, in large masses, in particular parts of it, the distinction between the different parts of the State, resembles that between the slave-holding and non-slave-holding States: and, if we reject a doctrine in our own State, whilst we claim the benefit of it in our relations to other States, other disagreeable consequences may be added to the charge of inconsistency, which will be brought against us. If the example of our sister States is to have weight, we find that in Georgia, the Federal number is made the basis of Representation in both branches of their Legislature; and I do not learn, that any dissatisfaction or inconvenience has flowed from its adoption. I wish we could know more of the manner in which particular organizations of Government operate in other parts of the United States. There would be less danger of being misled into error, and we should have the advantage of their experience, as well as our own. In the case I mention, there can, I believe, be no error.

Whether, therefore, we be fixing a basis of Representation, for the one branch or the other of our Legislature, or for both, in a combination with other principles, the Federal ratio is a favourite resource with me. It entered into my earliest views of the subject, before this Convention was assembled: and though I have kept my mind open, have listened to every proposition which has been advanced, and given to them all a candid consideration, I must say, that in my judgment, we shall act wisely in preferring it to others, which have been brought before us. Should the Federal number be made to enter into the basis in one branch of the Legislature, and not into the other, such an arrangement might prove favourable to the slaves themselves. It may be, and I think it has been suggested, that those who have themselves no interest in this species of property, are apt to sympathise with the slaves, more than may be the case with their masters; and would, therefore, be disposed, when they had the ascendancy, to protect them from laws of an oppressive character, whilst the masters, who have a common interest with the slaves, against undue taxation, which must be paid out of their labour, will be their protectors when they have the ascendancy.

The Convention is now arrived at a point, where we must

agree on some common ground, all sides relaxing in their opinions, not changing, but mutually surrendering a part of them. In framing a Constitution, great difficulties are necessarily to be overcome; and nothing can ever overcome them, but a spirit of compromise. Other nations are surprised at nothing so much as our having been able to form Constitutions in the manner which has been exemplified in this country. Even the union of so many States, is, in the eyes of the world, a wonder; the harmonious establishment of a common Government over them all, a miracle. I cannot but flatter myself, that without a miracle, we shall be able to arrange all difficulties. I never have despaired, notwithstanding all the threatening appearances we have passed through. I have now more than a hope—a consoling confidence, that we shall at last find, that our labours have not been in vain.

NOTE DURING THE CONVENTION FOR AMENDING
THE CONSTITUTION OF VIRGINIA

The right of suffrage being of vital importance, and approving an extension of it to House keepers & heads of families, I will suggest a few considerations which govern my judgment on the subject.

Were the Constitution on hand to be adapted to the present circumstances of our Country, without taking into view the changes which time is rapidly producing, an unlimited extension of the right would probably vary little the character of our public councils or measures. But as we are to prepare a system of Government for a period which it is hoped will be a long one, we must look to the prospective changes in the condition and composition of the society on which it is to act.

It is a law of nature, now well understood, that the earth under a civilized cultivation is capable of yielding subsistence for a large surplus of consumers, beyond those having an immediate interest in the soil; a surplus which must increase with the increasing improvements in agriculture, and the labor-saving arts applied to it. And it is a lot of humanity that of this surplus a large proportion is necessarily reduced by a competition for employment to wages which afford them the bare necessaries of life. That proportion being without property, or the hope of acquiring it, can not be expected to sympathize sufficiently with its rights, to be safe depositories of power over them.

What is to be done with this unfavored class of the community? If it be, on one hand, unsafe to admit them to a full share of political power, it must be recollected, on the other, that it cannot be expedient to rest a Republican Government on a portion of the society having a numerical & physical force excluded from, and liable to be turned against it; and which would lead to a standing military force, dangerous to all parties & to liberty itself.

This view of the subject makes it proper to embrace in the partnership of power, every description of citizens having a sufficient stake in the public order, and the stable administration of the laws; and particularly the House keepers & Heads of families, most of whom "having given hostages to fortune," will have given them to their Country also.

This portion of the community, added to those, who although not possessed of a share of the soil, are deeply interested in other species of property, and both of them added to the territorial proprietors, who in a certain sense may be regarded as the owners of the Country itself, form the safest basis of free Government. To the security for such a Government afforded by these combined numbers, may be further added, the political & moral influence emanating from the actual possession of authority and a just & beneficial exercise of it.

It would be happy if a State of Society could be found or framed, in which an equal voice in making the laws might be allowed to every individual bound to obey them. But this is a

Theory, which like most Theories, confessedly requires limitations & modifications, and the only question to be decided in
this as in other cases, turns on the particular degree of departure, in practice, required by the essence & object of the
Theory itself.

It must not be supposed that a crowded state of population,
of which we have no example here, and which we know only
by the image reflected from examples elsewhere, is too remote
to claim attention.

The ratio of increase in the U. S. shows that the present

12 Millions will in	25 years be	24 Mils.		
24 "	" " 50	" " 48 "		
48 "	" " 75	" " 96 "		
96 "	" " 100	" 192 "		

There may be a gradual decrease of the rate of increase: but
it will be small as long as agriculture shall yield its abundance.
Great Britain has doubled her population in the last 50 years;
notwithstanding its amount in proportion to its territory at the
commencement of that period, and Ireland is a much stronger
proof of the effect of an increasing product of food, in multiplying the consumers.

How far this view of the subject will be affected by the Republican laws of descent and distribution, in equalizing the
property of the citizens and in reducing to the minimum mutual
surplusses for mutual supplies, cannot be inferred from any
direct and adequate experiment. One result would seem to be
a deficiency of the capital for the expensive establishments
which facilitate labour and cheapen its products on one hand,
and, on the other, of the capacity to purchase the costly and
ornamental articles consumed by the wealthy alone, who must
cease to be idlers and become labourers. Another the increased
mass of labourers added to the production of necessaries by the
withdrawal for this object, of a part of those now employed in

producing luxuries, and the addition to the labourers from the class of present consumers of luxuries. To the effect of these changes, intellectual, moral, and social, the institutions and laws of the Country must be adapted, and it will require for the task all the wisdom of the wisest patriots.

Supposing the estimate of the growing population of the U.S. to be nearly correct, and the extent of their territory to be 8 or 9 hundred Millions of acres, and one fourth of it to consist of inarable surface, there will in a century or a little more, be nearly as crowded a population in the U. S. as in Great Britain or France, and if the present Constitution (of Virginia) with all its flaws, lasted more than half a century, it is not an unreasonable hope that an amended one will last more than a century.

If these observations be just, every mind will be able to develop & apply them.

40. Defense of Majority Rule:
The Least Imperfect Government

Madison's lifelong concern with the dangers of majority rule has sometimes obscured the source of that concern: his prior commitment to popular government. As he explained in *Federalist* No. 10: "If a faction consists of less than a majority, relief is supplied by the republican principle, which enables the majority to defeat its sinister views by regular vote. . . . When a majority is included in a faction, the form of popular government on the other hand enables it to sacrifice to its ruling passion or interest, both the public good and the rights of other citizens. To secure the public good, and private rights, against the danger of such a faction, and at the same time to preserve the spirit and the form of popular government, is then the great object to which our enquiries are directed." After 1828, the new doctrines of Calhoun and his school forcefully reminded Madison that the American commitment to "the vital principle of republican government"—the *lex majoris partis*—could no longer be taken for granted.

Madison to _____, [1833], [Majority Governments], in *Writings*, IX, pp. 520–528.

Madison's draft of a letter on "Majority Governments" (1833) named no addressee and probably was not sent. The style suggests that, like other notes and memoranda of his last years, it was intended as a position paper rather than a personal communication. The letter serves as an important commentary on the problem of factions and the large republic—the problem of *Federalist* 10—viewed in the new light of Calhoun's formidable challenge and illustrated from the present and prospective condition of Virginia. If Americans were to accept the constitutional argument for nullification joined to the political argument for a "concurrent majority" of organized interests, they would in the end have to abandon popular government for the states as well as the nation and "seek a refuge under an authority master of both." Diverse class and local interests with conflicting demands were the very elements of free political life. Only the large republic founded on the principle of majority rule—however qualified and guarded—could resolve such conflicts in favor of the public good. Republican government remained the best of all regimes, not simply, but as "the least imperfect."

[1833.]

[MAJORITY GOVERNMENTS.]

DEAR SIR,—You justly take alarm at the new doctrine that a majority Government is of all other Governments the most oppressive. The doctrine strikes at the root of Republicanism, and if pursued into its consequences, must terminate in absolute monarchy, with a standing military force; such alone being impartial between its subjects, and alone capable of overpowering majorities as well as minorities.

But it is said that a majority Government is dangerous only where there is a difference in the interest of the classes or sections composing the community; that this difference will generally be greatest in communities of the greatest extent; and that such is the extent of the U.S. and the discordance of interests in them, that a majority cannot be trusted with power over a minority.

Formerly, the opinion prevailed that a Republican Government was in its nature limited to a small sphere; and was in its true character only when the sphere was so small that the people could, in a body, exercise the Government over themselves.

The history of the ancient Republics, and those of a more modern date, had demonstrated the evils incident to popular assemblages, so quickly formed, so susceptible of contagious passions, so exposed to the misguidance of eloquent & ambitious leaders; and so apt to be tempted by the facility of forming interested majorities, into measures unjust and oppressive to the minor parties.

The introduction of the representative principle into modern Governments particularly of Great Britain and her colonial offsprings, had shown the practicability of popular Governments in a larger sphere, and that the enlargement of the sphere was a cure for many of the evils inseparable from the popular forms in small communities.

It remained for the people of the U. S., by combining a federal with a republican organization, to enlarge still more the sphere of representative Government and by convenient partitions & distributions of power, to provide the better for internal justice & order, whilst it afforded the best protection against external dangers.

Experience & reflection may be said not only to have exploded the old error, that republican Governments could only exist within a small compass, but to have established the important truth, that as representative Governments are necessary substitutes for popular assemblages; so an association of free communities, each possessing a responsible Government under a collective authority also responsible, by enlarging the practicable sphere of popular governments, promises a consummation of all the reasonable hopes of the patrons of free Government.

It was long since observed by Montesquieu, has been often repeated since, and, may it not be added, illustrated within the U. S. that in a confederal system, if one of its members happens to stray into pernicious measures, it will be reclaimed by the frowns & the good examples of the others, before the evil example will have infected the others.

But whatever opinions may be formed on the general subjects of confederal systems, or the interpretation of our own, every friend to Republican Government ought to raise his voice against the sweeping denunciation of majority Governments as the most tyrannical and intolerable of all Governments.

The Patrons of this new heresy will attempt in vain to mask its anti-republicanism under a contrast between the extent and the discordant interests of the Union, and the limited dimensions and sameness of interests within its members. Passing by the great extent of some of the States, and the fact that these cannot be charged with more unjust & oppressive majorities than the smaller States, it may be observed that the extent of the Union, divided as the powers of Government are between it and its members, is found to be within the compass of a successful administration of all the departments of Government notwithstanding the objections & anticipations founded on its extent when the Constitution was submitted to the people. It is true that the sphere of action has been and will be not a little enlarged by the territories embraced by the Union. But it will not be denied, that the improvements already made in internal navigation by canals & steamboats, and in turnpikes & railroads, have virtually brought the most distant parts of the Union, in its present extent, much closer together than they were at the date of the Federal Constitution. It is not too much to say, that the facility and quickness of intercommunication throughout the Union is greater now than it formerly was between the remote parts of the State of Virginia.

But if majority Governments as such, are so formidable, look at the scope for abuses of their power within the individual States, in their division into creditors & debtors, in the distribution of taxes, in the conflicting interests, whether real or supposed, of different parts of the State, in the case of improving roads, cutting canals, &c., to say nothing of many other sources of discordant interests or of party contests, which exist or would arise if the States were separated from each other. It seems to be forgotten, that the abuses committed within the individual States previous to the present Constitution, by interested or misguided majorities, were among the prominent causes of its adoption, and particularly led to the provision contained in it which prohibits paper emissions and the violations of contracts, and which gives an appellate supremacy to the judicial department of the U. S. Those who framed and ratified the Constitution believed that as power was less likely to be abused by majorities in representative Governments than in democracies, where the people assembled in mass, and less likely in the larger than in the smaller communities, under a representative Government, inferred also, that by dividing the powers of Government and thereby enlarging the practicable sphere of Government, unjust majorities would be formed with still more difficulty, and be therefore the less to be dreaded, and whatever may have been the just complaints of unequal laws and sectional partialities under the majority Government of the U. S. it may be confidently observed that the abuses have been less frequent and less palpable than those which disfigured the administrations of the State Governments while all the effective powers of sovereignty were separately exercised by them. If bargaining interests and views have created majorities under the federal system, what, it may be asked, was the case in this respect antecedent to this system, and what but for this would now be the case in the State Governments. It has been said that all Government is an evil. It would be more proper to say that the necessity of any Government is a misfortune. This necessity however exists; and the problem to be solved is, not what form of Government is perfect, but which of the forms is least imperfect; and here the general question must be between a republican Government in which the majority rule the minority, and a Government in which a lesser number or the least number rule the majority. If the republican form is, as all of us agree, to be preferred, the final question must be, what is the structure of it that will best guard against precipitate counsels and factious combinations for unjust purposes, without a sacrifice of the fundamental principle of Republicanism. Those who denounce majority Governments altogether because they may have an interest in abusing their power, denounce at the same time all Republican Government and must maintain that minority governments would feel less of the bias of interest or the seductions of power.

As a source of discordant interests within particular States, reference may be made to the diversity in the applications of agricultural labour, more or less visible in all of them. Take for example Virginia herself. Her products for market are in one district Indian corn and cotton; in another, chiefly tobacco; in another, tobacco and wheat; in another, chiefly wheat, rye, and live stock. This diversity of agricultural interests, though greater in Virginia than elsewhere, prevails in different degrees within most of the States.

Virginia is a striking example also of a diversity of interests, real or supposed, in the great and agitating subjects of roads and water communications, the improvements of which are little needed in some parts of the State, tho' of the greatest importance in others; and in the parts needing them much disagreement exists as to the times, modes, & the degrees of the public patronage; leaving room for an abuse of power by majorities, and for majorities made up by affinities of interests, losing sight of the just & general interest.

Even in the great distinctions of interest and of policy generated by the existence of slavery, is it much less between the Eastern & Western districts of Virginia than between the Southern & Northern sections of the Union? If proof were necessary, it would be found in the proceedings of the Virginia Convention of 1829–30, and in the Debates of her Legislature in 1830–31. Never were questions more uniformly or more tenaciously decided between the North & South in Congress, than they were on those occasions between the West & the East of Virginia.

But let us bring this question to the test of the tariff itself [out of which it has grown,] and under the influences of which it has been inculcated, that a permanent incompatibility of interests exists in the regulations of foreign commerce between the agricultural and the manufacturing population, rendering it unsafe for the former to be under a majority power when patronizing the latter.

In all countries, the mass of people become, sooner or later, divided mainly into the class which raises food and raw materials, and the class which provides clothing & the other necessaries and conveniences of life. As hands fail of profitable employment in the culture of the earth, they enter into the latter class. Hence, in the old world, we find the nations everywhere formed into these grand divisions, one or the other being a decided majority of the whole, and the regulations of their relative interests among the most arduous tasks of the Government. Although the mutuality of interest in the interchanges useful to both may, in one view, be a bond of amity & union, yet when the imposition of taxes whether internal or external takes place, as it must do, the difficulty of equalizing the burden and adjusting the interests between the two classes is always more or less felt. When imposts on foreign commerce have a protective as well as a revenue object, the task of adjustment assumes a peculiar arduousness.

This view of the subject is exemplified in all its features by the fiscal & protective legislation of Great Britain and it is worthy of special remark that there the advocates of the protective policy belong to the landed interest; and not as in the U. S. to the manufacturing interest; though in some particulars both interests are suitors for protection against foreign competition.

But so far as abuses of power are engendered by a division of a community into the agricultural & manufacturing interests and by the necessary ascendency of one or the other as it may comprize the majority, the question to be decided is whether the danger of oppression from this source must not soon arise within the several States themselves, and render a majority Government as unavoidable an evil in the States individually; as it is represented to be in the States collectively.

That Virginia must soon become manufacturing as well as agricultural, and be divided into these two great interests, is obvious & certain. Manufactures grow out of the labour not needed for agriculture, and labour will cease to be so needed or employed as its products satisfy & satiate the demands for domestic use & for foreign markets. Whatever be the abundance or fertility of the soil, it will not be cultivated when its fruits must perish on hand for want of a market. And is it not manifest that this must be henceforward more & more the case in this State particularly? The earth produces at this time as much as is called for by the home & the foreign markets; while the labouring population, notwithstanding the emigration to the West and the South West, is fast increasing. Nor can we shut our eyes to the fact, that the rapid increase of the exports of flour & Tobacco from a new & more fertile soil will be continually lessening the demand on Virginia for her two great staples, and be forcing her, by the inability to pay for imports by exports, to provide within herself substitutes for the former.

Under every aspect of the subject, it is clear that Virginia must be speedily a manufacturing as well as an agricultural State; that the people will be formed into the same great classes here as elsewhere; that the case of the tariff must of course among other conflicting cases real or supposed be decided by the republican rule of majorities; and, consequently, if majority governments as such, be the worst of Governments those who think & say so cannot be within the pale of the republican faith. They must either join the avowed disciples of aristocracy oligarchy or monarchy, or look for a Utopia exhibiting a perfect homogeneousness of interests, opinions & feelings nowhere yet found in civilized communities. Into how many parts must Virginia be split before the semblance of such a condition could be found in any of them. In the smallest of the fragments, there would soon be added to previous sources of discord a manufacturing and an agricultural class, with the difficulty experienced in adjusting their relative interests in the regulation of foreign commerce if any, or if none in equalising the burden of internal improvement and of taxation within them. On the supposition that these difficulties could be surmounted, how many other sources of discords to be decided by the majority would remain. Let those who doubt it consult the records of corporations of every size such even as have the greatest apparent simplicity & identity of pursuits and interests.

In reference to the conflicts of interests between the agricultural and manufacturing States, it is a consoling anticipation that, as far as the legislative encouragements to one may not involve an actual or early compensation to the other, it will accelerate a state of things in which the conflict between them will cease and be succeeded by an interchange of the products profitable to both; converting a source of discord among the States into a new cement of the Union, and giving to the country a supply of its essential wants independent of contingencies and vicissitudes incident to foreign commerce.

It may be objected to majority governments, that the majority, as formed by the Constitution, may be a minority when compared with the popular majority. This is likely to be the case more or less in all elective governments. It is so in many of the States. It will always be so where property is combined with population in the election and apportionment of representation. It must be still more the case with confederacies, in which the members, however unequal in population, have equal votes in the administration of the government. In the compound system of the United States, though much less than in mere confederacies, it also necessarily exists to a certain extent. That this departure from the rule of equality, creating a political and constitutional majority in contradistinction to a numerical majority of the people, may be abused in various degrees oppressive to the majority of the people, is certain; and in modes and degrees so oppressive as to justify ultra or anti-constitutional resorts to adequate relief is equally certain. Still the constitutional majority must be acquiesced in by the constitutional minority, while the Constitution exists. The moment that arrangement is successfully frustrated, the Constitution is at an end. The only remedy, therefore, for the oppressed minority is in the amendment of the Constitution or a subversion of the Constitution. This inference is unavoidable. While the Constitution is in force, the power created by it, whether a popular minority or majority, must be the legitimate power, and obeyed as the only alternative to the dissolution of all government. It is a favourable consideration, in the impossibility of securing in all cases a coincidence of the constitutional and numerical majority, that when the former is the minority, the existence of a numerical majority with justice on its side, and its influence on public opinion, will be a salutary control on the abuse of power by a minority constitutionally possessing it: a control generally of adequate force, where a military force, the disturber of all the ordinary movements of free governments, is not on the side of the minority.

The result of the whole is, that we must refer to the monitory reflection that no government of human device and human ad-

ministration can be perfect; that that which is the least imperfect is therefore the best government; that the abuses of all
other governments have led to the preference of republican
government as the best of all governments, because the least
imperfect; that the vital principle of republican government is
the *lex majoris partis,* the will of the majority; that if the will of
a majority cannot be trusted where there are diversified and
conflicting interests, it can be trusted nowhere, because such
interests exist everywhere; that if the manufacturing and agricultural interests be of all interests the most conflicting in the
most important operations of government, and a majority government over them be the most intolerable of all governments,
it must be as intolerable within the States as it is represented to
be in the United States; and, finally, that the advocates of the
doctrine, to be consistent, must reject it in the former as well as
in the latter, and seek a refuge under an authority master of
both.

41. The Nullification Heresy:
Letter to the North American Review

Madison's Virginia Resolutions of 1798 and the *Report* of 1799–
1800 came back to haunt him more than once. (See Document
21.) Although his authorship had been carefully concealed (as
had Jefferson's hand in the corresponding Kentucky Resolutions), Federalist opponents saw more than a hint of the truth
when they sharpened their knives on the Virginia and Kentucky doctrines for attacks on Mr. Jefferson's Embargo and Mr.
Madison's War. A few years later, unreconstructed Old Republicans and new Nullifiers claimed Jefferson and Madison as
their masters and the Virginia and Kentucky protests of 1798–
1800 as their canonical texts. In the famous Webster-Hayne
debate of 1830 over nullification and the nature of the Union,
the South Carolina Senator appealed directly to Madison's
teachings and confidently sent a copy of his speech to Montpelier for approval. Madison respectfully declined responsibil-

Madison to Edward Everett, August 28, 1830, published in the *North American Review*, October 1830, in *Writings*, IX, pp. 383–403.

ity for any such view of the Constitution, enclosing a copy of his reply to Edward Everett, Congressman from Massachusetts and editor of the *North American Review*.

Alarmed by the spread of the nullification heresy and deeply disturbed by the use of his Virginia doctrines, Madison agreed to publish his critique of Hayne in the *North American Review*, revised in the form of a letter to Everett. The essay, printed in the issue of October 1830, heartened adversaries of nullification throughout the country and inspired Chief-Justice Marshall to welcome the founder back into the fold. "Madison," he wrote to Justice Story, "is himself again." Marshall might well have recognized the firm logic and high national spirit that he had encountered more than forty years earlier at the Virginia Ratifying Convention. On the other side, states'-rights radicals like Hayne, Calhoun, and William B. Giles were now compelled to claim that they understood the Virginia doctrines of '98 better than the venerable author did. They were rather unconvincing, yet not entirely wrong. The spirit of '98 made the studied ambiguities of the Virginia Resolutions and Report mean something more than the appeal to sober second thought that Madison now remembered. Saving the Jefferson of '98 from the embrace of the nullifiers required of Madison a kind of dexterity that bordered on deception.

August 28, 1830.

DEAR SIR,—I have duly received your letter in which you refer to the "nullifying doctrine," advocated as a constitutional right by some of our distinguished fellow citizens; and to the proceedings of the Virginia Legislature in '98 & '99, as appealed to in behalf of that doctrine; and you express a wish for my ideas on those subjects.

I am aware of the delicacy of the task in some respects; and the difficulty in every respect of doing full justice to it. But having in more than one instance complied with a like request from other friendly quarters, I do not decline a sketch of the views which I have been led to take of the doctrine in question, as well as some others connected with them; and of the grounds from which it appears that the proceedings of Virginia have been misconceived by those who have appealed to them. In order to understand the true character of the Constitution of the U. S. the error, not uncommon, must be avoided, of viewing it through the medium either of a consolidated Government or of a confederated Government whilst it is neither the one nor the other, but a mixture of both. And having in no model the similitudes & analogies applicable to other systems of Government it must more than any other be its own interpreter, according to its text & *the facts of the case.*

From these it will be seen that the characteristic peculiarities of the Constitution are 1. The mode of its formation, 2. The division of the supreme powers of Government between the States in their united capacity and the States in their individual capacities.

1. It was formed, not by the Governments of the component States, as the Federal Government for which it was substituted was formed; nor was it formed by a majority of the people of the U. S. as a single community in the manner of a consolidated Government.

It was formed by the States—that is by the people in each of the States, acting in their highest sovereign capacity; and formed, consequently by the same authority which formed the State Constitutions.

Being thus derived from the same source as the Constitutions of the States, it has within each State, the same authority as the Constitution of the State; and is as much a Constitution, in the strict sense of the term, within its prescribed sphere, as the Constitutions of the States are within their respective spheres; but with this obvious & essential difference, that being a compact among the States in their highest sovereign capacity, and constituting the people thereof one people for certain purposes, it cannot be altered or annulled at the will of the States individually, as the Constitution of a State may be at its individual will.

2. And that it divides the supreme powers of Government between the Government of the United States, & the Governments of the individual States, is stamped on the face of the instrument; the powers of war and of taxation, of commerce & of treaties, and other enumerated powers vested in the Government of the U. S. being of as high & sovereign a character as any of the powers reserved to the State Governments.

Nor is the government of the U. S. created by the Constitution, less a Government in the strict sense of the term, within the sphere of its powers, than the governments created by the constitutions of the States are within their several spheres. It is like them organized into Legislative, Executive, & Judiciary Departments. It operates like them, directly on persons & things. And, like them, it has at command a physical force for executing the powers committed to it. The concurrent operation in certain cases is one of the features marking the peculiarity of the system.

Between these different constitutional Governments—the one operating in all the States, the others operating separately in each, with the aggregate powers of Government divided between them, it could not escape attention that controversies would arise concerning the boundaries of jurisdiction; and that some provision ought to be made for such occurrences. A political system that does not provide for a peaceable & authoritative termination of occurring controversies, would not be more than the shadow of a Government; the object & end of a real Government being the substitution of law & order for uncertainty confusion, and violence.

That to have left a final decision in such cases to each of the States, then 13 & already 24, could not fail to make the Constitution & laws of the U. S. different in different States was obvious; and not less obvious, that this diversity of independent decisions, must altogether distract the Government of the Union & speedily put an end to the Union itself. A uniform authority of the laws, is in itself a vital principle. Some of the most important laws could not be partially executed. They must be executed in all the States or they could be duly executed in none. An impost or an excise, for example, if not in force in some States, would be defeated in others. It is well known that this was among the lessons of experience which had a primary influence in bringing about the existing Constitution. A loss of its general authority would moreover revive the exasperating questions between the States holding ports for foreign commerce and the adjoining States without them, to which are now added all the inland States necessarily carrying on their foreign commerce through other States.

To have made the decisions under the authority of the individual States, co-ordinate in all cases with decisions under the authority of the U. S. would unavoidably produce collisions incompatible with the peace of society, & with that regular & efficient administration which is the essence of free Governments. Scenes could not be avoided in which a ministerial officer of the U. S. and the correspondent officer of an individual State, would have rencounters in executing conflicting decrees, the result of which would depend on the comparative force of the local posse attending them, and that a casualty depending on the political opinions and party feelings in different States.

To have referred every clashing decision under the two authorities for a final decision to the States as parties to the Constitution, would be attended with delays, with inconveniences, and with expenses amounting to a prohibition of the expedient, not to mention its tendency to impair the salutary veneration for a system requiring such frequent interpositions, nor the delicate questions which might present themselves as to the form of stating the appeal, and as to the Quorum for deciding it.

To have trusted to negociation, for adjusting disputes between the Government of the U. S. and the State Governments as between independent & separate sovereignties, would have lost sight altogether of a Constitution & Government for the Union; and opened a direct road from a failure of that resort, to the ultima ratio between nations wholly independent of and alien to each other. If the idea had its origin in the process of adjustment between separate branches of the same Government the analogy entirely fails. In the case of disputes between independent parts of the same Government neither part being able to consummate its will, nor the Government to proceed without a concurrence of the parts, necessity brings about an accommodation. In disputes between a State Government and the Government of the United States the case is practically as well as theoretically different; each party possessing all the Departments of an organized Government, Legislative, Executive & Judiciary; and having each a physical force to support its pretensions. Although the issue of negociation might sometimes avoid this extremity, how often would it happen among so many States, that an unaccommodating spirit in some would render that resource unavailing? A contrary supposition would not accord with a knowledge of human nature or the evidence of our own political history.

The Constitution, not relying on any of the preceding modifications for its safe & successful operation, has expressly declared on the one hand; 1. "That the Constitution, and the laws made in pursuance thereof, and all Treaties made under the authority of the U. S. shall be the supreme law of the land; 2. That the judges of every State shall be bound thereby, anything in the Constitution or laws of any State to the contrary notwithstanding; 3. That the judicial power of the U. S. shall extend to all cases in law & equity arising under the Constitution, the laws of the U. S. and Treaties made under their authority &c."

On the other hand, as a security of the rights & powers of the States in their individual capacities, against an undue preponderance of the powers granted to the Government over them in their united capacity, the Constitution has relied on, 1. The responsibility of the Senators and Representatives in the Legislature of the U. S. to the Legislatures & people of the States. 2. The responsibility of the President to the people of the United States; & 3. The liability of the Executive and Judiciary functionaries of the U. S. to impeachment by the Representatives of the people of the States, in one branch of the Legislature of the U. S. and trial by the Representatives of the States, in the other branch; the State functionaries, Legislative, Executive, & Judiciary, being at the same time in their appointment & responsibility, altogether independent of the agency or authority of the United States.

How far this structure of the Government of the U. S. be adequate & safe for its objects, time alone can absolutely determine. Experience seems to have shown that whatever may grow out of future stages of our national career, there is as yet a sufficient controul in the popular will over the Executive & Legislative Departments of the Government. When the Alien & Sedition laws were passed in contravention to the opinions and feelings of the community, the first elections that ensued put an end to them. And whatever may have been the character of other acts in the judgment of many of us, it is but true that they have generally accorded with the views of a majority of the States and of the people. At the present day it seems well understood that the laws which have created most dissatisfaction have had a like sanction without doors; and that whether continued varied or repealed, a like proof will be given of the sympathy & responsibility of the Representative Body to the Constituent Body. Indeed, the great complaint now is, not against the want of this sympathy and responsibility, but against the results of them in the legislative policy of the nation.

With respect to the Judicial power of the U. S. and the authority of the Supreme Court in relation to the boundary of jurisdiction between the Federal & the State Governments I may be permitted to refer to the [thirty-ninth] number of the "Federalist" for the light in which the subject was regarded by its writer, at the period when the Constitution was depending; and it is believed that the same was the prevailing view then taken of it, that the same view has continued to prevail, and that it does so at this time notwithstanding the eminent exceptions to it.

But it is perfectly consistent with the concession of this power to the Supreme Court, in cases falling within the course of its functions, to maintain that the power has not always been rightly exercised. To say nothing of the period, happily a short one, when judges in their seats did not abstain from intemperate & party harangues, equally at variance with their duty and their dignity, there have been occasional decisions from the Bench which have incurred serious & extensive disapprobation. Still it would seem that, with but few exceptions, the course of the judiciary has been hitherto sustained by the predominant sense of the nation.

Those who have denied or doubted the supremacy of the judicial power of the U. S. & denounce at the same time nullifying power in a State, seem not to have sufficiently adverted to the utter inefficiency of a supremacy in a law of the land, without a supremacy in the exposition & execution of the law; nor to the destruction of all equipoise between the Federal Government and the State governments, if, whilst the functionaries of the Federal Government are directly or indirectly elected by and responsible to the States & the functionaries of the States are in their appointments & responsibility wholly independent of the U. S. no constitutional control of any sort belonged to the U. S. over the States. Under such an organization it is evident that it would be in the power of the States individually, to pass unauthorized laws, and to carry them into complete effect, anything in the Constitution and laws of the U. S. to the contrary notwithstanding. This would be a nullifying power in its plenary character; and whether it had its final effect, thro the

Legislative, Executive or Judiciary organ of the State, would be equally fatal to the constitutional relation between the two Governments.

Should the provisions of the Constitution as here reviewed be found not to secure the Government & rights of the States against usurpations & abuses on the part of the U. S. the final resort within the purview of the Constitution lies in an amendment of the Constitution according to a process applicable by the States.

And in the event of a failure of every constitutional resort, and an accumulation of usurpations & abuses, rendering passive obedience & non-resistence a greater evil, than resistence & revolution, there can remain but one resort, the last of all, an appeal from the cancelled obligations of the constitutional compact, to original rights & the law of self-preservation. This is the ultima ratio under all Government whether consolidated, confederated, or a compound of both; and it cannot be doubted that a single member of the Union, in the extremity supposed, but in that only, would have a right, as an extra & ultra constitutional right, to make the appeal.

This brings us to the expedient lately advanced, which claims for a single State a right to appeal against an exercise of power by the Government of the U. S. decided by the State to be unconstitutional, to the parties of the Constitutional compact; the decision of the State to have the effect of nullifying the act of the Government; of the U. S. unless the decision of the State be reversed by three-fourths of the parties.

The distinguished names & high authorities which appear to have asserted and given a practical scope to this doctrine, entitle it to a respect which it might be difficult otherwise to feel for it.

If the doctrine were to be understood as requiring the three-fourths of the States to sustain, instead of that proportion to reverse, the decision of the appealing State, the decision to be without effect during the appeal, it would be sufficient to remark, that this extra constitutional course might well give way to that marked out by the Constitution which authorizes ⅔ of the States to institute and ¾ to effectuate, an amendment of the Constitution establishing a permanent rule of the highest authority in place of an irregular precedent of construction only.

But it is understood that the nullifying doctrine imports that the decision of the State is to be presumed valid, and that it overrules the law of the U. S. unless overuled by ¾ of the States.

Can more be necessary to demonstrate the inadmissibility of such a doctrine than that it puts it in the power of the smallest fraction over ¼ of the U. S.—that is, of 7 States out of 24—to give the law and even the Constitution to 17 States, each of the 17 having as parties to the Constitution an equal right with each of the 7 to expound it & to insist on the exposition. That the 7 might, in particular instances be right and the 17 wrong, is more than possible. But to establish a positive & permanent rule giving such a power to such a minority over such a majority, would overturn the first principle of free Government and in practice necessarily overturn the Government itself.

It is to be recollected that the Constitution was proposed to the people of the States as a *whole,* and unanimously adopted by the States as a *whole,* it being a part of the Constitution that not less than ¾ of the States should be competent to make any alteration in what had been unanimously agreed to. So great is the caution on this point, that in two cases when peculiar interests were at stake, a proportion even of ¾ is distrusted, and unanimity required to make an alteration.

When the Constitution was adopted as a whole, it is certain that there were many parts which if separately proposed, would have been promptly rejected. It is far from impossible, that every part of the Constitution might be rejected by a majority, and yet, taken together as a whole be unanimously accepted. Free constitutions will rarely if ever be formed without reciprocal concessions; without articles conditioned on & balancing each other. Is there a constitution of a single State out of the 24 that would bear the experiment of having its component parts submitted to the people & separately decided on?

What the fate of the Constitution of the U. S. would be if a small proportion of States could expunge parts of it particularly valued by a large majority, can have but one answer.

The difficulty is not removed by limiting the doctrine to cases of construction. How many cases of that sort, involving cardinal provisions of the Constitution, have occurred? How many now exist? How many may hereafter spring up? How many might be ingeniously created, if entitled to the privilege of a decision in the mode proposed?

Is it certain that the principle of that mode would not reach farther than is contemplated. If a single State can of right require ¾ of its co-States to overrule its exposition of the Constitution, because that proportion is authorized to amend it, would the plea be less plausible that, as the Constitution was unanimously established, it ought to be unanimously expounded?

The reply to all such suggestions seems to be unavoidable and irresistible, that the Constitution is a compact; that its text is to be expounded according to the provision for expounding it, making a part of the compact; and that none of the parties can rightfully renounce the expounding provision more than any other part. When such a right accrues, as it may accrue, it must grow out of abuses of the compact releasing the sufferers from their fealty to it.

In favour of the nullifying claim for the States individually, it appears, as you observe, that the proceedings of the Legislature of Virginia in '98 & '99 against the Alien and Sedition Acts are much dwelt upon.

It may often happen, as experience proves, that erroneous constructions, not anticipated, may not be sufficiently guarded against in the language used; and it is due to the distinguished individuals who have misconceived the intention of those proceedings to suppose that the meaning of the Legislature, though well comprehended at the time, may not now be obvious to those unacquainted with the contemporary indications and impressions.

But it is believed that by keeping in view the distinction between the Government of the States & the States in the sense in which they were parties to the Constitution; between the rights of the parties, in their concurrent and in their individual capacities; between the several modes and objects of interposition against the abuses of power, and especially between interpositions within the purview of the Constitution & interpositions appealing from the Constitution to the rights of nature paramount to all Constitutions; with these distinctions kept in view, and an attention, always of explanatory use, to the views & arguments which were combated, a confidence is felt, that the Resolutions of Virginia, as vindicated in the Report on them, will be found entitled to an exposition, showing a consistency in their parts and an inconsistency of the whole with the doctrine under consideration.

That the Legislature could not have intended to sanction such a doctrine is to be inferred from the debates in the House of Delegates, and from the address of the two Houses to their constituents on the subject of the resolutions. The tenor of the debates which were ably conducted and are understood to have been revised for the press by most, if not all, of the speakers, discloses no reference whatever to a constitutional right in an individual State to arrest by force the operation of a law of the U. S. Concert among the States for redress against the alien & sedition laws, as acts of usurped power, was a leading sentiment, and the attainment of a concert the immediate object of the course adopted by the Legislature, which was that of inviting the other States "to *concur* in declaring the acts to be unconstitutional, and to *co-operate* by the necessary & proper measures in maintaining unimpaired the authorities rights & liberties reserved to the States respectively & to the people." That by the necessary and proper measures to be *concurrently* and co-operatively taken, were meant measures known to the Constitution, particularly the ordinary controul of the people and Legislatures of the States over the Government of the U. S. cannot be doubted; and the interposition of this controul as the event showed was equal to the occasion.

It is worthy of remark, and explanatory of the intentions of the Legislature, that the words "not law, but utterly null, void, and of no force or effect," which had followed, in one of the Resolutions, the word "unconstitutional," were struck out by common consent. Tho the words were in fact but synonymous with "unconstitutional," yet to guard against a misunderstanding of this phrase as more than declaratory of opinion, the word unconstitutional alone was retained, as not liable to that danger.

The published address of the Legislature to the people their constituents affords another conclusive evidence of its views. The address warns them against the encroaching spirit of the General Government, argues the unconstitutionality of the alien & sedition acts, points to other instances in which the constitutional limits had been overleaped; dwells upon the dangerous mode of deriving power by implications; and in general presses the necessity of watching over the consolidating tendency of the Federal policy. But nothing is said that can be understood to look to means of maintaining the rights of the States beyond the regular ones within the forms of the Constitution.

If any farther lights on the subject could be needed, a very strong one is reflected in the answers to the Resolutions by the States which protested against them. The main objection to these, beyond a few general complaints against the inflammatory tendency of the resolutions was directed against the assumed authority of a State Legislature to declare a law of the

544   THE MIND OF THE FOUNDER

U. S. unconstitutional, which they pronounced an unwarrantable interference with the exclusive jurisdiction of the Supreme Court of the U. S. Had the resolutions been regarded as avowing & maintaining a right in an individual State, to arrest by force the execution of a law of the U. S. it must be presumed that it would have been a conspicuous object of their denunciation.

42. The Nature of the Union: A Final Reckoning

Even in his eighties, Madison allowed himself to be drawn into painful public controversies with the nullifiers and continued to give invaluable counsel and support to friends of the Union. Yet one senses that he was less profoundly concerned with current issues than he was with thoughts of death and immortality. For a philosophical statesman of the eighteenth century, and a founder of the new American Republic, that meant above all balancing his political accounts and clearing his reputation for posterity. Early in 1833, he drafted a long note on nullification and during 1835 and 1836—at the very end—revised the text. Significantly, in this final comprehensive statement on the nature of the Union, Madison dwelt almost compulsively on his Virginia Resolutions and Report. Practically, as we have seen, it was important to deny historical legitimacy to the Carolina heresy. Madison's explicaton of his texts went beyond that. It was as if he feared that his name would endure not as the founder of a free nation but as the prophet of anarchy and ruin.

Notes on Nullification, 1835–1836, in *Writings*, IX, pp. 573–607.

THE MIND OF THE FOUNDER

In this perspective, his friendly quarrel with nationalists like Daniel Webster seemed trivial. Whether one interpreted "we the people" to mean the pre-existing collective American people, or the aggregate peoples of the several states joined in compact, no state could claim the constitutional right to determine and enforce for itself the supreme law of the land. For extreme cases without legal remedy, there remained only the ultimate appeal to the right of revolution that belonged to every man by nature. "Prudence," Jefferson had said in 1776, "indeed, will dictate that governments long established should not be changed for light and transient causes . . ." And Madison remained as always the prudent partner.

Altho' the Legislature of Virginia declared at a late session almost unanimously, that South Carolina was not supported in her doctrine of nullification by the Resolutions of 1798, it appears that those resolutions are still appealed to as expressly or constructively favoring the doctrine.

That the doctrine of nullification may be clearly understood it must be taken as laid down in the Report of a special committee of the House of Representatives of South Carolina in 1828. In that document it is asserted, that a single State has a constitutional right to arrest the execution of a law of the U. S. within its limits; that the arrest is to be presumed right and valid, and is to remain in force unless ¾ of the States, in a Convention, shall otherwise decide.

The forbidding aspect of a naked creed, according to which a process instituted by a single State is to terminate in the ascendancy of a minority of 7, over a majority of 17, has led its partizans to disguise its deformity under the position that a single State may rightfully resist an unconstitutional and tyrannical law of the U. S., keeping out of view the essential distinction between a constitutional right and the natural and universal right of resisting intolerable oppression. But the true question is whether a single state has a constitutional right to annul or suspend the operation of a law of the U. S. within its limits, the State remaining a member of the Union, and admitting the Constitution to be in force.

With a like policy, the nullifiers pass over the state of things at the date of the proceedings of Virginia and the particular doctrines and arguments to which they were opposed; without an attention to which the proceedings in this as in other cases may be insecure against a perverted construction.

It must be remarked also that the champions of nullification, attach themselves exclusively to the 3rd Resolution, averting their attention from the 7th Resolution which ought to be coupled with it, and from the Report also, which comments on both, & gives a full view of the object of the Legislature on the occasion.

Recurring to the epoch of the proceedings, the facts of the case are that Congress had passed certain acts, bearing the name of the alien and sedition laws, which Virginia & some of the other States, regarded as not only dangerous in their tendency, but unconstitutional in their text; and as calling for a remedial interposition of the States. It was found also that not only was the constitutionality of the acts vindicated by a predominant party, but that the principle was asserted at the same time, that a sanction to the acts given by the supreme Judicial authority of the U. S. was a bar to any interposition whatever on the part of the States, even in the form of a legislative declaration that the acts in question were unconstitutional.

Under these circumstances, the subject was taken up by Virginia in her resolutions, and pursued at the ensuing session of the Legislature in a comment explaining and justifying them; her main and immediate object, evidently being, to produce a conviction everywhere, that the Constitution had been violated by the obnoxious acts and to procure a concurrence and cooperation of the other States in effectuating a repeal of the acts. She accordingly asserted and offered her proofs at great length, that the acts were unconstitutional. She asserted moreover & offered her proofs that the States had a right in such cases, to interpose, first in their constituent character to which the government of the U. S. was responsible and otherwise as specially provided by the Constitution; and further, that the States, in their capacity of parties to and creators of the Constitution, had an ulterior right to interpose, notwithstanding any decision of a constituted authority; which, however it might be the *last resort* under the forms of the Constitution in cases falling within the scope of its functions, could not preclude an interposition of the States as the parties which made the Constitution and, as such, possessed an authority paramount to it.

In this view of the subject there is nothing which excludes a natural right in the States individually, more than in any portion of an individual State, suffering under palpable and insupportable wrongs, from seeking relief by resistance and revolution.

But it follows, from no view of the subject, that a nullification of a law of the U. S. can as is now contended, belong rightfully to a single State, as one of the parties to the Constitution; the State not ceasing to avow its adherence to the Constitution. A plainer contradiction in terms, or a more fatal inlet to anarchy, cannot be imagined.

And what is the text in the proceedings of Virginia which this spurious doctrine of nullification claims for its parentage? It is found in the 3rd of the Resolutions of –98, which is in the following words.

"That in case of a deliberate, a palpable & dangerous exercise of powers not granted by the [constitutional] compact, the *States* who are parties thereto have a right and are in duty bound to interpose for arresting the progress of the evil, & for maintaining within their respective limits, the authorities rights & liberties appertaining to them."

Now is there anything here from which a *single* State can infer a right to arrest or annul an act of the General Government which it may deem unconstitutional? So far from it, that the obvious & proper inference precludes such a right on the part of a single State; *plural* number being used in every application of the term.

In the next place, the course & scope of the reasoning requires that by the rightful authority to interpose in the cases & for the purposes referred to, was meant, not the authority of the States *singly* & *separately,* but their authority as the *parties* to the Constitution, the authority which, in fact, made the Constitution; the authority which being paramount to the Constitution was paramount to the authorities constituted by it, to the Judiciary as well as the other authorities. The resolution derives the asserted right of interposition for arresting the progress of usurpations by the Federal Government from the fact, that its powers were limited to the grant made by the States; a grant certainly not made by a *single* party to the grant, but by the *parties* to the compact containing the grant. The mode of their interposition, in extraordinary cases, is left by the Resolution to the parties themselves; as the mode of interposition lies with the parties to other Constitutions, in the event of usurpations of power not remediable, under the forms and by the means provided by the Constitution. If it be asked why a claim by a single party to the constitutional compact, to arrest a law, deemed by it a breach of the compact, was not expressly guarded against the simple answer is sufficient that a pretension so novel, so anomalous & so anarchical, was not & could not be anticipated.

In the third place, the nullifying claim for a single State is probably irreconcilable with *the effect* contemplated by the interposition claimed by the Resolution for the parties to the Constitution namely that of "maintaining within the respective limits of the States the authorities rights & liberties appertaining to them." Nothing can be more clear than that these authorities &c., &c., of the States, in other words, the authority & laws of the U. S. must be the same in all; or that this cannot continue to be the case, if there be a right in each to annul or suspend within itself the operation of the laws & authority of the whole. There cannot be different laws in different states on subjects within the compact without subverting its fundamental principles, and rendering it as abortive in practice as it would be incongruous in theory. A concurrence & co-operation of the States in favor of each, would have the effect of preserving the necessary uniformity in all, which the Constitution so carefully & so specifically provided for in cases where the rule might be in most danger of being violated. Thus the citizens of every State are to enjoy reciprocally the privileges of citizens in every other State. Direct taxes are to be apportioned on all, according to a fixed rule. Indirect taxes are to be the same in all the States. The duties on imports are to be uniform: No preference is to be given to the ports of one State over those of another. Can it be believed, that with these provisions of the Constitution illustrating its vital principles fully in view of the Legislature of Virginia, that its members could in the Resolution quoted, intend to countenance a right in a single State to distinguish itself from its co-States, by avoiding the burdens, or restrictions borne by them; or indirectly giving the law to them.

These startling consequences from the nullifying doctrine have driven its partizans to the extravagant presumption that no State would ever be so unreasonable, unjust & impolitic as to avail itself of its right in any case not so palpably just and fair as to ensure a concurrence of the others, or at least the requisite proportion of them.

Omitting the obvious remark that in such a case the law would never have been passed or immediately repealed; and the surprize that such a defence of the nullifying right should come from South Carolina in the teeth & at the time of her own example, the presumption of such a forbearance in each of the States, or such a pliability in all, among 20 or 30 independent sovereignties, must be regarded as a mockery by those who reflect for a moment on the human character, or consult the lessons of experience, not the experience of other countries & times, but that among ourselves; and not only under the former defective Confederation, but since the improved system took place of it. Examples of differences, persevering differences among the States on the constitutionality of Federal acts, will readily occur to every one; and which would, e'er this, have defaced and demolished the Union, had the nullifying claim of South Carolina been indiscriminately exercisable. In some of the States, the carriage-tax would have been collected, in others unpaid. In some, the tariff on imports would be collected; in others, openly resisted. In some, lighthouses would be established; in others denounced. In some States there might be war with a foreign power; in others, peace and commerce. Finally, the appellate authority of the Supreme Court of the U. S. would give effect to the Federal laws in some States, whilst in others they would be rendered nullities by the State Judiciaries. In a word, the nullifying claims if reduced to practice, instead of being the conservative principle of the Constitution, would necessarily, and it may be said obviously, be a deadly poison.

Thus, from the 3rd resolution itself, whether regard be had to the employment of the term *States* in the plural number, the argumentative use of it, or to the object namely the "maintaining the authority & rights of each, which must be the same in all as in each, it is manifest that the adequate interposition to which it relates, must be not a single, but a concurrent interposition.

If we pass from the 3rd to the 7th Resolution, which, tho' it repeats and re-enforces the 3rd and which is always skipped over by the nullifying commentators, the fallacy of their claim will at once be seen. The resolution is in the following words. ["That the good people of the common-wealth having ever felt and continuing to feel the most sincere affection to their brethren of the other states, the truest anxiety for establishing and perpetuating the union of all, and the most scrupulous fidelity to that Constitution which is the pledge of mutual friendship and the instrument of mutual happiness, the General Assembly doth solemnly appeal to the like dispositions in the other states, in confidence that they will concur with this commonwealth in declaring, as it does hereby declare, that the acts aforesaid are unconstitutional, and that the necessary and proper measures will be taken by each for co-operating with this state in maintaining unimpaired the authorities, rights, and liberties reserved in the states respectively or to the people."] Here it distinctly appears, as in the 3rd resolution that the course contemplated by the Legislature, "for maintaining the authorities, rights, & liberties reserved to the States respectively," was not a *solitary* or *separate* interposition, but a *co-operation* in the means necessary & proper for the purpose.

If a further elucidation of the view of the Legislature could be needed, it happens to be found in its recorded proceedings. In the 7th Resolution as originally proposed, the term *"unconstitutional,"* was followed by null void, &c. These added words being considered by some as giving pretext for some disorganizing misconstruction, were unanimously stricken out, or rather withdrawn by the mover of the Resolutions.

An attempt has been made, by ascribing to the words stricken out, a nullifying signification, to fix on the reputed draftsman of the Resolution the character of a nullifier. Could this have been effected, it would only have vindicated the Legislature the more effectually from the imputation of favoring the doctrine of South Carolina. The unanimous erasure of nullifying expressions was a protest by the House of Delegates, in the most emphatic form against it.

But let us turn to the "Report," which explained and vindicated the Resolutions; and observe the light in which it placed first the third and then the 7th.

It must be recollected that this Document proceeded from Representatives chosen by the people some months after the

Resolutions had been before them, with a longer period for manifesting their sentiments before the Report was adopted; and without any evidence of disapprobation in the Constituent Body. On the contrary, it is known to have been received by the Republican party, a decided majority of the people, with the most entire approbation. The Report therefore must be regarded as the most authoritative evidence of the meaning attached by the State to the Resolutions. This consideration makes it the more extraordinary, and let it be added the more inexcusable, in those, who in their zeal to extract a particular meaning from a particular resolution, not only shut their eyes to another Resolution, but to an authentic exposition of both.

And what is the comment of the Report on that particular resolution?, namely, the 3rd.

In the first place, it conforms to the resolution in using the term which expresses the interposing authority of the States, in the *plural* number *States*, not in the singular number *State*. It is indeed impossible not to perceive that the entire current & complexion of the observations explaining & vindicating the resolutions imply necessarily, that by the interposition of the States for arresting the evil of usurpation, was meant a concurring authority not that of a *single* state; whilst the collective meaning of the term, gives consistency & effect to the reasoning & the object.

But besides this general evidence that the Report in the invariable use of the plural term *States*, withheld from a single State the right expressed in the Resolution a still more precise and decisive inference, to the same effect, is afforded by several passages in the document.

Thus the report observes "The States then being the parties to the constitutional compact, and in their highest sovereign capacity, it follows of necessity, that there can be no tribunal above *their* authority to decide in the *last* resort, whether the compact made by them be violated; and, consequently that as the parties to it, they must *themselves* decide in the last resort such questions as may be of sufficient magnitude to require their interposition."

Now apart from the palpable insufficiency of an interposition by a single State to effect the declared object of the interposition namely, to maintain authorities & rights which must be the same in all the States, it is not true that there would be no tribunal above the authority of a state as a single party; the aggregate authority of the parties being a tribunal above it to decide in the *last* resort.

Again the language of the Report is, "If the deliberate exercise of dangerous powers palpably withheld by the Constitution could not justify the parties to it in interposing even so far as to arrest the progress of the evil, & thereby preserve the Constitution itself, as well as to provide for the safety of the parties to it, there would be an end to all relief from usurped power"— Apply here the interposing power of a single State, and it would not be true that there would be no relief from usurped power. A sure & adequate relief would exist in the interposition of the *States,* as the *co-parties* to the Constitution, with a power paramount to the Constitution itself.

It has been said that the right of interposition asserted for the states by the proceedings of Virginia could not be meant a right for them in their collective character of parties to and creators of the Constitution, because that was a right by none denied. But as a simple truth or truism, its assertion might not be out of place when applied as in the resolution, especially in an avowed recurrence to fundamental principles, as in duty called for by the occasion. What is a portion of the Declaration of Independence but a series of simple and undeniable truths or truisms? what but the same composed a great part of the Declarations of Rights prefixed to the state constitutions? It appears, however, from the report itself, which explains the resolutions, that the last *resort* claimed for the Supreme Court of the United States, in the case of the alien and sedition laws, was understood to require a recurrence to the ulterior resort in the authority from which that of the court was derived. "But, (continues the Report) it is objected[1] that the judicial authority is to be regarded as the sole expositor of the Constitution in the last resort."

In answering this objection the Report observes, "that however true it may be that the judicial department, in all questions submitted to it by the forms of the Constitution to decide in the last resort, this resort must necessarily *not* be the last—in relation to the rights of the parties to the constitutional compact from which the Judicial as well as the other Departments hold their *delegated trusts*. On any other hypothesis, the Delegation of judicial power would annul the authority delegating it, and the concurrence of this Department with the others in usurped power, might subvert for ever, and beyond the possible reach of any rightful remedy, the very Constitution which all were instituted to preserve." Again observes the report, "The truth declared in the resolution being established, the expediency of making the declaration at the present day may safely be left to the temperate consideration and candid judgment of the American public. It will be remembered that a frequent recurrence to fundamental principles is solemnly enjoined by most of the State constitutions, and particularly by our own, as a necessary safeguard against the danger of degeneracy, to which republics are liable as well as other governments, though in a less degree than others. And a fair comparison of the political doctrines, not unfrequent at the present day, with those which characterized the epoch of our revolution, and which form the basis of our republican constitutions, will best determine whether the declaratory recurrence here made to those principles ought to be viewed as unreasonable and improper, or as a vigilant discharge of an important duty. The authority of

---

[1] There is a direct proof that the authority of the Supreme Court of the U. S. was understood by the Legislature of Virginia to have been an asserted bar to an interposition by the states against the alien and sedition laws. [*Madison's Note*]

constitutions over governments, and of the sovereignty of the people over constitutions, are truths which are at all times necessary to be kept in mind; and at no time, perhaps, more necessary than at present."

Who can avoid seeing the necessity of understanding by the *"parties"* to the constitutional compact, the authority, which made the compact and from which all the Departments held their delegated trusts. These trusts were certainly not delegated by a *single* party. By regarding the term *parties* in its plural, not individual meaning, the answer to the objection is clear and satisfactory. Take the term as meaning *a party*, and not *the parties*, and there is neither truth nor argument in the answer. But further, on the hypothesis, that the rights of the *parties* meant the rights of *a party*, it would not be true as affirmed by the Report, that "the Delegation of Judicial power would annul the authority delegating it, and that the concurrence of this Department with others in usurped power might subvert for ever, & beyond the reach of any rightful remedy, the very Constitution which all were instituted to preserve." However deficient a remedial right in a *single State* might be to preserve the Constitution against usurped power an ultimate and adequate remedy would always exist in the rights of the *parties* to the Constitution in whose hands the Constitution is at all times but clay in the hands of the potter, and who could apply a remedy by explaining, amending, or remaking it, as the one or the other mode might be the most proper remedy.

Such being the comment of the Report on the 3rd. Resolution, it fully demonstrates the meaning attached to it by Virginia when passing it, and rescues it from the nullifying misconstruction into which the Resolution has been distorted.

Let it next be seen, how far the comment of the Report on the 7th. Resolution above inserted accords with that on the 3rd; and that this may the more conveniently be scanned by every eye, the comment is subjoined at full length. . . .[2]

---

[2] See Document 21, pp. 345–349 above.

Here is certainly not a shadow of countenance to the doctrine of nullification. Under every aspect, it enforces the arguments and authority against such an apocryphal version of the text.

From this view of the subject, those who will duly attend to the tenour of the proceedings of Virginia and to the circumstances of the period when they took place will concur in the fairness of disclaiming the inference from the undeniableness of a truth, that it could not be the truth meant to be asserted in the Resolution. The employment of the truth asserted, and the reasons for it, are too striking to be denied or misunderstood.

More than this, the remark is obvious, that those who resolve the nullifying claim into the *natural* right to resist intolerable oppression, are precluded from inferring that to be the right meant by the Resolution, since that is as little denied, as the paramountship of the authority, creating a Constitution over an authority derived from it.

The true question therefore is whether there be a *constitutional* right in a single state to nullify a law of the U. S. We have seen the absurdity of such a claim in its naked and suicidal form. Let us turn to it as modified by South Carolina, into a right in every State to resist within itself, the execution of a Federal law deemed by it to be unconstitutional; and to demand a Convention of the States to decide the question of constitutionality, the annulment of the law to continue in the mean time, and to be permanent, unless ¾ of the states concur in over-ruling the annulment.

Thus, during the temporary nullification of the law, the results would be the same from those proceeding from an unqualified nullification, and the result of a convention might be, that 7 out of the 24 states, might make the temporary results permanent. It follows, that any State which could obtain the concurrence of six others, might abrogate any law of the U. S. constructively whatever, and give to the Constitution any shape they please, in opposition to the construction and will of the other seventeen, each of the 17 having an equal right

& authority with each of the 7. Every feature in the Constitution, might thus be successively changed; and after a scene of unexampled confusion & distraction, what had been unanimously agreed to as a whole, would not as a whole be agreed to by a single party. The amount of this modified right of nullification is, that a single State may arrest the operation of a law of the United States, and institute a process which is to terminate in the ascendency of a minority over a large majority, in a Republican System, the characteristic rule of which is that the major will is the ruling will. And this newfangled theory is attempted to be fathered on Mr. Jefferson the apostle of republicanism, and whose own words declare that "acquiescence in the decision of the majority is the vital principle of it." [See his Inaugural Address.]

Well might Virginia declare, as her Legislature did by a resolution of 1833 "that the resolutions of 98–99, gave no support to the nullifying doctrine of South Carolina." And well may the friends of Mr. J. disclaim any sanction to it or to any *constitutional* right of nullification from his opinions. His memory is fortunately rescued from such imputations, by the very Document procured from his files and so triumphantly appealed to by the nullifying partisans of every description. In this Document, the remedial right of nullification is expressly called a *natural* right, and, consequently, not a right derived from the Constitution, but from abuses or usurpations, releasing the parties to it from their obligation.[3]

---

[3] No example of the inconsistency of party zeal can be greater than is seen in the value allowed to Mr. Jefferson's authority by the nullifying party; while they disregard his repeated assertions of the Federal authority, even under the articles of confederation, to stop the commerce of a refractory State, while they abhor his opinions & propositions on the subject of slavery & overlook his declaration, that in a republick, it is a vital principle that the minority must yield to the majority—they seize on an expression of Mr. Jefferson that nullification is the rightful remedy, as the Shiboleth of their party, & almost a sanctification of their cause. But in *addition* to their inconsistency, their zeal is guilty of the subterfuge of

It is said that in several instances the authority & laws of the U. S. have been successfully nullified by the particular States. This may have occurred possibly in urgent cases, and in confidence that it would not be at variance with the construction of the Federal Government or in cases where, operating within the Nullifying State alone it might be connived at as a lesser evil than a resort to force; or in cases not falling within the Federal jurisdiction; or finally in cases, deemed by the States, subversive of their *essential rights*, and justified therefore, by the *natural* right of self-preservation. Be all this as it may, examples of nullification, tho' passing off without any immediate disturbance of the public order, are to be deplored, as weakening the common Government and as undermining the Union. One thing seems to be certain, that the States which have exposed themselves to the charge of nullification, have, with the exception of South Carolina disclaimed it as a *constitutional* right, and have moreover protested against it as *modified* by the process of South Carolina.

---

droping a part of the language of Mr. Jefferson, which shews his meaning to be entirely at variance with the nullifying construction. His words in the document appealed to as the infallible test of his opinions are: [. . . "but, when powers are assumed which have not been delegated, a nullification of the act is the rightful remedy: that every state has a natural right in cases not within the compact (*casus non fœderis*), to nullify" etc.]

Thus the right of nullification meant by Mr. Jefferson is the natural right, which all admit to be a remedy against insupportable oppression. It cannot be supposed for a moment that Mr. Jefferson would not revolt at the doctrine of South Carolina, that a single state could constitutionally resist a law of the Union while remaining within it, and that with the accession of a small minority of the others, overrule the will of a great majority of the whole, & constitutionally annul the law everywhere.

If the right of nullification meant by him had not been thus guarded against a perversion of it, let him be his own interpreter in his letter to Mr. Giles in December 1826 in which he makes the rightful remedy of a state in an extreme case to be a separation from the Union, not a resistance to its authority while remaining in it. The authority of Mr. Jefferson, therefore, belongs not, but is directly opposed to, the nullifying party who have so unwarrantably availed themselves of it. [*Madison's Note*]

The conduct of Pennsylvania and the opinions of Judge McKean & Tilgman have been particularly dwelt on by the nullifiers. But the final acquiescence of the state in the authority of the Federal Judiciary transfers their authority to the other scale, and it is believed that the opinions of the two judges, have been superseded by those of their brethren, which have been since & at the present time are, opposed to them.

Attempts have been made to shew that the resolutions of Virginia contemplated a forcible resistance to the alien & sedition laws and as evidence of it, the laws relating to the armory, and a Habeas corpus for the protection of members of her Legislature, have been brought into view. It happens however, as has been ascertained by the recorded dates that the first of these laws was enacted prior to the alien and sedition laws. As to the last, it appears that it was a general law, providing for other emergencies as well as federal arrests and its applicability never tested by any occurrence under the alien and sedition laws. The law did not necessarily preclude an acquiescence in the supervising decision of the Federal Judiciary should that not sustain the Habeas corpus which it might be calculated would be sustained. And all must agree, that cases might arise, of such violations of the security & privileges of representatives of the people, as would justify the states in a resort to the *natural* law of self-preservation. The extent of the privileges of the federal & State representatives of the people, against criminal charges by the 2 authorities reciprocally, involves delicate questions which it may be better to leave for those who are to decide on them, than unnecessarily to discuss them in advance. The moderate views of Virginia on the critical occasion of the alien and sedition laws, are illustrated by the terms of the 7th Resolution with an eye to which the 3rd Resolution ought always to be expounded, by the unanimous erasure of the terms "null void" &c., from the 7th article as it stood; and by the condemnation & imprisonment of Callender under the law, without the slightest opposition on the part of the State. So far was the State from countenancing the nullifying doctrine, that the occasion was viewed as a proper one for exemplifying its devotion to public order, and acquiescence in laws which it deemed unconstitutional, whilst those laws were not constitutionally repealed. The language of the Governor in a letter to a friend, will best attest the principles & feelings which dictated the course pursued on the occasion.[4]

It is sometimes asked in what mode the States could interpose in their collective character as parties to the Constitution against usurped power. It was not necessary for the object & reasoning of the resolutions & report, that the mode should be pointed out. It was sufficient to shew that the authority to interpose existed, and was a resort beyond that of the Supreme Court of the U. S. or any authority derived from the Constitution. The authority being plenary, the mode was of its own choice, and it is obvious, that, if employed by the States as

---

[4] Extract of a letter from Monroe to Madison, dated Albemarle, May 15, 1800: "Besides, I think there is cause to suspect the sedition law will be carried into effect in this state at the approaching federal court, and I ought to be there [Richmond] to aid in preventing trouble. A camp is formed of about 400 men at Warwick, four miles below Richmond, and no motive for it assigned except to proceed to Harper's Ferry, to sow cabbage-seed. But the gardening season is passing, and this camp remains. I think it possible an idea may be entertained of opposition, and by means whereof the fair prospect of the republican party may be overcast. But in this they are deceived, as certain characters in Richmond and some neighbouring counties are already warned of their danger, so that an attempt to excite a hotwater insurrection will fail."

Extract from another letter from J. Monroe to J. M., dated Richmond, June 4, 1800: "The conduct of the people on this occasion was exemplary, and does them the highest honour. They seemed aware the crisis demanded of them a proof of their respect for law and order, and resolved to show they were equal to it. I am satisfied a different conduct was expected from them, for everything that could was done to provoke it. It only remains that this business be closed on the part of the people, as it has been so far acted; that the judge, after finishing his career, go off in peace, without experiencing the slightest insult from any one; and that this will be the case I have no doubt." [*Madison's Note*]

coparties to and creators of the Constitution it might either so explain the Constitution or so amend it as to provide a more satisfactory mode within the Constitution itself for guarding it against constructive or other violations.

It remains however for the nullifying expositors to specify the right & mode of interposition which the resolution meant to assign to the States *individually*. They cannot say it was a natural right to resist intolerable oppression; for that was a right not less admitted by all than the collective right of the States as parties to the Constitution, the nondenial of which was urged as a proof that it could not be meant by the Resolution.

They cannot say that the right meant was Constitutional right to resist the constitutional authority for that is a construction in terms, as much as a legal right to resist a law.

They can find no middle ground, between a natural and a constitutional right, on which a right of nullifying interposition can be placed; and it is curious to observe the awkwardness of the attempt, by the most ingenious advocates [Upshur and Berrian].

They will not rest the claim as modified by South Carolina for that has scarce an advocate out of the State, and owes the remnant of its popularity there to the disguise under which it is now kept alive; some of the leaders of the party admitting its indefensibility, in its naked shape.

The result is that the nullifiers, instead of proving that the Resolution meant nullification, would prove that it was altogether without meaning.

It appears from this Comment, that the right asserted and exercised by the Legislature, to *declare* an act of Congress unconstitutional had been denied by the Defenders of the alien & sedition acts as an interference with the Judicial authority; and, consequently, that the reasonings employed by the Legislature, were called for by the doctrines and inferences drawn from that authority, and were not an idle display of what no one denied.

It appears still farther, that the efficacious interposition contemplated by the Legislature; was a concurring and co-operating interposition of the States, not that of a single State.

It appears that the Legislature expressly disclaimed the idea that a declaration of a State, that a law of the U. S. was unconstitutional, had the effect of *annulling* the law.

It appears that the object to be attained by the invited co-operation with Virginia was, as expressed in the 3rd & 7th Resolutions to maintain within the several States their respective authorities, rights, & liberties, which could not be constitutionally different in different States, nor inconsistent with a sameness in the authority & laws of the U. S. in all & in each.

It appears that the means contemplated by the Legislature for attaining the object, were measures recognised & designated by the Constitution itself.[5]

Lastly, it may be remarked that the concurring measures of the states, without any nullifying interposition whatever did attain the contemplated object; a triumph over the obnoxious acts, and an apparent abandonment of them for ever.

It has been said or insinuated that the proceedings of Virginia in 98–99, had not the influence ascribed to them in bringing about that result. Whether the influence was or was not such as has been claimed for them, is a question that does not affect the meaning & intention of the proceedings. But as a question of fact, the decision may be safely left to the recol-

---

[5] "The predominant feelings & views of Virginia, in her Resolutions of 98 & the comment on them in the Report of 99 may be seen in the instructions to her members in Congress passed at the same session with the Report. These instructions, instead of squinting at any such doctrine as that of nullification, are limited to efforts, on the part of the members 1. to procure a reduction of the army 2. to prevent or stop the premature augmentation of the navy, 3. to oppose the principle lately advanced, that the common law of England is in force under the Government of the U.S., excepting the particular parts &c [as excepted in the Report] 4th Repeal of the alien & sedition acts. . . ." [Madison's note]

lection of those who were co-temporary with the crisis, and to
the researchers of those who were not, taking for their guides
the reception given to the proceedings by the Republican party
every where, and the pains taken by it, in multiplying repub-
lications of them in newspapers and in other forms.

What the effect might have been if Virginia had remained
patient & silent, and still more if she had sided with South
Carolina, in favoring the alien & sedition acts, can be but a
matter of conjecture.

What would have been thought of her if she had recommended the nullifying project of South Carolina may be estimated by the reception given to it under all the factitious gloss,
and in the midst of the peculiar excitement of which advantage
has been taken by the partizans of that anomalous conceit.

It has been sufficiently shown, from the language of the
Report, as has been seen, that the right in the States to interpose declarations & protests, against unconstitutional acts of
Congress, had been denied; and that the reasoning in the
Resolutions was called for by that denial. But the triumphant
tone, with which it is affirmed & reiterated that the resolutions,
must have been directed against what no one denied, unless
they were meant to assert the right of a single State to arrest
and annul acts of the federal Legislature, makes it proper to
adduce a proof of the fact that the declaratory right was
denied, which, if it does not silence the advocate of nullification, must render every candid ear indignant at the repetition
of the untruth.

The proof is found in the recorded votes of a large and
respectable portion of the House of Delegates, at the time
of passing the report.

A motion [see the Journal] offered at the closing scene
affirms "that protests made by the Legislature of this or any
other State against particular acts of Congress as unconstitutional accompanied with invitations to other States, to join in
such protests, are improper & unauthorized assumptions of

power not permitted, nor intended to be permitted to the State Legislatures. And inasmuch as *correspondent sentiments with the present*, have been expressed by those of our sister States who have acted on the Resolutions [of 1798], Resolved therefore that the present General Assembly convinced of the impropriety of the Resolutions of the last Assembly, deem it inexpedient farther to act on the said Resolutions."

On this Resolution, the votes, according to the yeas & nays were 57, of the former, 98 of the latter.

Here then within the House of Delegates itself more than 1/3 of the whole number *denied* the right of the State Legislature to proceed by acts merely declaratory against the constitutionality of acts of Congress and affirmed moreover that the states who had acted on the Resolutions of Virginia entertained the same sentiments. It is remarkable that the minority, who denied the right of the legislatures even to protest, admitted the right of the *states* in the capacity of *parties*, without claiming it for a single state.

With this testimony under the eye it may surely be expected that it will never again be said that such a right had never been denied, nor the pretext again resorted to that without such a denial, the nullifying doctrine alone could satisfy the true meaning of the Legislature. [See the instructions to the members of Congress passed at the same session, which do not squint at the nullifying idea; see also the protest of the minority in the Virginia Legislature and the Report of the Committee of Congress on the proceedings of Virginia.]

It has been asked whether every right has not its remedy, and what other remedy exists under the Government of the U. S. against usurpations of power, but a right in the States individually to annul and resist them.

The plain answer is, that the remedy is the same under the government of the United States as under all other Governments established & organized on free principles. The first remedy is in the checks provided among the constituted authorities; that failing the next is in the influence of the Ballot-boxes & Hustings; that again failing, the appeal lies to the power that made the Constitution, and can explain, amend, or remake it. Should this resort also fail, and the power usurped be sustained in its oppressive exercise on a minority by a majority, the final course to be pursued by the minority, must be a subject of calculation, in which the degree of oppression, the means of resistance, the consequences of its failure, and consequences of its success must be the elements.

Does not this view of the case, equally belong to every one of the States, Virginia for example.

Should the constituted authorities of the State unite in usurping oppressive powers; should the constituent Body fail to arrest the progress of the evil thro' the elective process according to the forms of the Constitution; and should the authority which is above that of the Constitution, the majority of the people, inflexibly support the oppression inflicted on the minority, nothing would remain for the minority, but to rally to its reserved rights (for every citizen has his reserved rights, as exemplified in Declarations prefixed to most of the State constitutions), and to decide between acquiescence & resistance, according to the calculation above stated.

Those who question the analogy in this respect between the two cases, however different they may be in some other respects, must say, as some of them, with a boldness truly astonishing do say, that the Constitution of the U. S. which as such, and under that name, was presented to & accepted by those who ratified it; which has been so deemed & so called by those living under it for nearly half a century; and, as such sworn to by every officer, state as well as federal, is yet no Constitution, but a treaty, a league, or at most a confederacy among nations, as independent and sovereign, in relation to each other, as before the charter which calls itself a Constitution was formed.

The same zealots must again say, as they do, with a like

boldness & incongruity that the Government of the U. S. which has been so deemed & so called from its birth to the present time; which is organized in the regular forms of Representative Governments and like them operates directly on the individuals represented; and whose laws are declared to be the supreme law of the land, with a physical force in the government for executing them, is yet no government but a mere agency, a power of attorney, revocable at the will of any of the parties granting it.

Strange as it must appear, there are some who maintain these doctrines, and hold this language: and what is stranger still, denounce those as heretics and apostates who adhere to the language & tenets of their fathers, and this is done with an exulting question whether every right has not its remedy; and what remedy can be found against federal usurpations, other than that of a right in every State to nullify & resist the federal acts at its pleasure?

Yes, it may be safely admitted that every right has its remedy; as it must be admitted that the remedy under the Constitution lies where it has been marked out by the Constitution; and that no appeal can be consistently made from that remedy by those who were and still profess to be parties to it, but the appeal to the parties themselves having an authority above the Constitution or to the law of nature & of nature's God.

It is painful to be obliged to notice such a sophism as that by which this inference is assailed. Because an unconstitutional law is no law, it is alledged that it may be constitutionally disobeyed by all who think it unconstitutional. The fallacy is so obvious, that it can impose on none but the most biassed or heedless observers. It makes no distinction where the distinction is obvious, and *essential,* between the case of a law *confessedly* unconstitutional, and a case turning on a *doubt* & a *divided opinion* as to the meaning of the Constitution; on a question, not whether the Constitution ought or ought not to be obeyed; but on the question, what is the Constitution. And can it be seriously & deliberately maintained, that every individual or every subordinate authority or every party to a compact, has a right to take for granted, that its construction is the infallible one, and to act upon it against the construction of all others, having an equal right to expound the instrument, nay against the regular exposition of the constituted authorities, with the tacit sanction of the community. Such a doctrine must be seen at once to be subversive of all constitutions, all laws, and all compacts. The provision made by a Constitution for its own exposition, thro' its own authorities & forms, must prevail whilst the Constitution is left to itself by those who made it; or until cases arise which justify a resort to ultra-constitutional interpositions.

The main pillar of nullification is the assumption that sovereignty is a unit, at once indivisible and unalienable; that the states therefore individually retain it entire as they originally held it, and, consequently that no portion of it can belong to the U. S.

But is not the Constitution itself necessarily the offspring of a sovereign authority? What but the highest political authority, a sovereign authority, could make such a Constitution? a constitution which makes a Government, a Government which makes laws; laws which operate like the laws of all other governments by a penal & physical force, on the individuals subject to the laws; and finally laws declared to be the Supreme law of the land; anything in the Constitution or laws of the individual State notwithstanding.

And where does the sovereignty which makes such a Constitution reside. It resides not in a single state but in the people of each of the several states, uniting with those of the others in the express & solemn compact which forms the Constitution. To the *extent* of that compact or Constitution therefore, the people of the several States must be a sovereign as they are a united people.

In like manner, the constitutions of the States, made by the people as separated into States, were made by a sovereign authority by a sovereignty residing in each of the States, to the extent of the objects embraced by their respective constitutions. And if the states be thus sovereign, though shorn of so many of the essential attributes of sovereignty, the United States by virtue of the sovereign attributes with which they are endowed, may, to that extent, be sovereign, tho' destitute of the attributes of which the States are not shorn.

Such is the political system of the U. S. de jure & de facto; and however it may be obscured by the ingenuity and technicalities of controversial commentators, its true character will be sustained by an appeal to the law and the testimony of the fundamental charter.

The more the political system of the U. S. is fairly examined, the more necessary it will be found, to abandon the abstract and technical modes of expounding & designating its character; and to view it as laid down in the charter which constitutes it, as a system, hitherto without a model; as neither a simple or a consolidated Government nor a Government altogether confederate; and therefore not to be explained so as to make it either, but to be explained and designated, according to the actual division and distribution of political power on the face of the instrument.

A just inference from a survey of this political system is that it is a division and distribution of political power, nowhere else to be found; a nondescript, to be tested and explained by itself alone; and that it happily illustrates the diversified modifications of which the representative principle of republicanism is susceptible with a view to the conditions, opinions, and habits of particular communities.

That a sovereignty should have even been denied to the States in their united character, may well excite wonder, when it is recollected that the Constitution which now unites them, was announced by the convention which formed it, as dividing sovereignty between the Union & the States; [see letter of the President of the Convention (Washington) to the old Congress] that it was presented under that view, by contemporary expositions recommending it to the ratifying authorities [see Federalist and other proofs]; that it is proved to have been so understood by the language which has been applied to it constantly & notoriously; that this has been the doctrine & language, until a very late date, even by those who now take the lead in making a denial of it the basis of the novel notion of nullification. [See the Report to the Legislature of South Carolina in 1828.] So familiar is sovereignty in the U. S. to the thoughts, views & opinions even of its polemic adversaries, that Mr. Rowan, in his elaborate speech in support of the indivisibility of sovereignty, relapsed before the conclusion of his argument into the idea that sovereignty was partly in the Union, partly in the States. [See his speech in the Richmond Enquirer of the—.] Other champions of the Rights of the States among them Mr. Jefferson might be appealed to, as bearing testimony to the sovereignty of the U. S. If Burr had been convicted of acts defined to be treason, which it is allowed can be committed only against a sovereign authority who would then have pleaded the want of sovereignty in the U. S. Quere. if there be no sovereignty in the U. S. whether the crime denominated treason might not be committed, without falling within the jurisdiction of the States, and consequently, with impunity?

What seems to be an obvious & indefeasible proof that the people of the individual States, as composing the United States must possess a sovereignty, at least in relation to foreign sovereigns is that in that supposition only, foreign Governments would be willing or expected to maintain international relations with the U. S. Let it be understood that the Government at Washington was not a national Government representing a sovereign authority; and that the sovereignty resided absolutely & exclusively in the several States, as the only sovereigns

& nations in our political system, and the diplomatic functionaries at the seat of the Federal Government would be obliged to close their communications with the Secretary of State, and with new commissions repair to Columbia, in South Carolina and other seats of the State Governments. They could no longer, as the Representatives of a sovereign authority hold intercourse with a functionary who was but an agent of a self-called Government which was itself but an agent, representing no sovereign authority; not of the States as separate sovereignties, nor a sovereignty in the U. S. which had no existence. For a like reason, the Plenipotentiaries of the U. S. at foreign courts, would be obliged to return home unless commissioned by the individual States. With respect to foreign nations, the confederacy of the States was held de facto to be a nation, or other nations would not have held national relations with it.

There is one view of the subject which ought to have its influence on those who espouse doctrines which strike at the authoritative origin and efficacious operation of the Government of the United States. The Government of the U. S. like all Governments free in their principles, rests on compact; a compact, not between the Government & the parties who formed & live under it; but among the parties themselves, and the strongest of Governments are those in which the compacts were most fairly formed and most faithfully executed.

Now all must agree that the compact in the case of the U. S. was duly formed, and by a competent authority. It was formed, in fact by the people of the several States in their highest sovereign authority; an authority which could have made the compact a mere league, or a consolidation of all entirely into one community. Such was their authority if such had been their will. It was their will to prefer to either the constitutional Government now existing; and this being undeniably established by a competent and even the highest human authority, it follows that the obligation to give it all the effect to which any Government could be entitled; whatever the mode of its formation, is equally undeniable. Had it been formed by the people of the U. S. as one society, the authority could not have been more competent, than that which did form it; nor would a consolidation of the people of the States into one people, be different in validity or operation, if made by the aggregate authority of the people of the States, than if made by the plenary sanction given concurrently as it was in their highest sovereign capacity. The Government whatever it be resulting from either of these processes would rest on an authority equally competent; and be equally obligatory & operative on those over whom it was established. Nor would it be in any respect less responsible, theoretically and practically, to the constituent body, in the one hypothesis than in the other; or less subject in extreme cases to be resisted and overthrown. The faith pledged in the compact, being the vital principle of all free Government, that is the true test by which political right & wrong are to be decided, and the resort to physical force justified, whether applied to the enforcement or the subversion of political power.

Whatever be the *mode* in which the *essential* authority established the Constitution, the structure of this, the power of this, the rules of exposition, the means of execution, must be the same; the tendency to consolidation or dissolution the same. The question, whether we the people means the people in their aggregate capacity, acting by a numerical majority of the whole, or by a majority in each of all the States, the authority being equally valid and binding, the question is interesting, but as an historical fact of merely speculative curiosity.

Whether the centripetal or centrifugal tendency be greatest, is a problem which experience is to decide; but it depends not on the mode of the grant, but the extent and effect of the powers granted. The only distinctive circumstances is in the effect of a dissolution of the system on the resultum of the parties, which, in the case of a system formed by the people, as that of the United States was, would replace the states in the character of separate communities, whereas a system founded by the people, as one community, would, on its dissolution, throw the people into a state of nature.

In conclusion, those who deny the possibility of a political system, with a divided sovereignty like that of the U. S. must chuse between a government purely consolidated, & an association of Governments purely federal. All republics of the former character, ancient or modern, have been found ineffectual for order and justice within, and for security without. They have been either a prey to internal convulsions or to foreign invasions. In like manner, all confederacies, ancient or modern, have been either dissolved by the inadequacy of their cohesion, or, as in the modern examples, continue to be monuments of the frailties of such forms. Instructed by these monitory lessons, and by the failure of an experiment of their own (an experiment which, while it proved the frailty of mere federalism, proved also the frailties of republicanism without the control of a Federal organization),[6] the U. S. have adopted a modification of political power, which aims at such a distribution of it as might avoid as well the evils of consolidation as the defects of federation, and obtain the advantages of both. Thus far, throughout a period of nearly half a century, the new and compound system has been successful beyond any of the forms of Government, ancient or modern, with which it may be compared; having as yet discovered no defects which do not admit remedies compatible with its vital principles and characteristic features. It becomes all therefore who

---

[6] The known existence of this controul has a silent influence, which is not sufficiently adverted to in our political discussions, and which has doubtless prevented collisions, in cases which might otherwise have threatened the fabric of the Union. Another preventive resource is in the fact noted by Montesquieu, that if one member of a union become diseased, it is cured by the examples and the frowns of the others, before the contagion can spread. [*Madison's Note*]

are friends of a Government based on free principles to reflect, that by denying the possibility of a system partly federal and partly consolidated, and who would convert ours into one either wholly federal or wholly consolidated, in neither of which forms have individual rights, public order, and external safety, been all duly maintained, they aim a deadly blow at the last hope of true liberty on the face of the Earth. Its enlightened votaries must perceive the necessity of such a modification of power as will not only divide it between the whole & the parts, but provide for occurring questions as well between the whole & the parts as between the parts themselves. A political system which does not contain an effective provision for a peaceable decision of all controversies arising within itself, would be a Government in name only. Such a provision is obviously essential; and it is equally obvious that it cannot be either peaceable or effective by making every part an authoritative umpire. The final appeal in such cases must be to the authority of the whole, not to that of the parts separately and independently. This was the view taken of the subject, whilst the Constitution was under the consideration of the people. [See Federalist No. 39.] It was this view of it which dictated the clause declaring that the Constitution & laws of the U. S. should be the supreme law of the Land, anything in the constitution or laws of any of the States to the contrary notwithstanding. [See Art. VI.] It was the same view which specially prohibited certain powers and acts to the States, among them any laws violating the obligation of contracts, and which dictated the appellate provision in the Judicial act passed by the first Congress under the Constitution. [See Art. I.] And it may be confidently foretold, that notwithstanding the clouds which a patriotic jealousy or other causes have at times thrown over the subject, it is the view which will be permanently taken of it, with a surprise hereafter, that any other should ever have been contended for.

43. Political Testament

Madison's dying words, according to the published reminiscences of his slave-valet, must have disappointed equally the pious and the patriotic: "What is the matter, Uncle James?," his niece reportedly asked. " 'Nothing more than a change of mind, my dear.' His head instantly dropped and he ceased breathing as quietly as the snuff of a candle goes out." More than a year before (probably in October 1834) he had composed a more fitting message "from the tomb." Claiming the respect due to one who had served his country and the cause of liberty for half a century, Madison made a simple, soulful plea: for the Union. This last political testament reached the public in 1850 through the pages of the *National Intelligencer*. Once more a troubled nation, torn by slavery and sectional rivalries, quarreled over the legacy of James Madison. Cal-

---

·"Advice to My Country" [October [1834?], facsimile of Madison's manuscript draft, in Irving Brant, *James Madison: Commander-in-Chief, 1812-1836* (Bobbs-Merrill: Indianapolis, 1961), following p. 530.

houn's fire-eating progeny suspected forgery until Edward Coles, an intimate friend of Madison's, announced that he held a copy of the "Advice to My Country" (mislabelled by the press "The Dying Injunction of Mr. Madison") from the hands and in the writing of Mrs. Madison. Long afterward, the original manuscript turned up among the Madison papers in the Library of Congress.

Madison's legal will left to his wife his lands and slaves with other properties, subject to special bequests to nieces and nephews, to Princeton and the University of Virginia, and to the American Colonization Society.

ADVICE TO MY COUNTRY

As this advice, if it ever see the light will not do it till I am no more, it may be considered as issuing from the tomb, where truth alone can be respected, and the happiness of man alone consulted. It will be entitled therefore to whatever weight can be derived from good intentions, and from the experience of one who has served his country in various stations through a period of forty years, who espoused in his youth and adhered through his life to the cause of its liberty, and who has borne a part in most of the great transactions which will constitute epochs of its destiny.

The advice nearest to my heart and deepest in my convictions is that the Union of the States be cherished and perpetuated. Let the open enemy to it be regarded as a Pandora with her box opened; and the disguised one, as the Serpent creeping with his deadly wiles into Paradise.

Index